American Tricksters

AMERICAN TRICKSTERS

THOUGHTS ON THE SHADOW SIDE OF A CULTURE'S PSYCHE

William J. Jackson

Foreword by
Peter Thuesen

 CASCADE *Books* • Eugene, Oregon

AMERICAN TRICKSTERS
Thoughts on the Shadow Side of a Culture's Psyche

Copyright © 2014 William J. Jackson. All rights reserved. Except for brief quotations in critical publications or reviews, no part of this book may be reproduced in any manner without prior written permission from the publisher. Write: Permissions. Wipf and Stock Publishers, 199 W. 8th Ave., Suite 3, Eugene, OR 97401.

Cascade Books
An Imprint of Wipf and Stock Publishers
199 W. 8th Ave., Suite 3
Eugene, OR 97401

www.wipfandstock.com

ISBN 13: 978-1-62564-790-0

Cataloguing-in-Publication Data

Jackson, William J., 1943–

    American tricksters : thoughts on the shadow side of a culture's psyche / William J. Jackson.

    xxvi + 266 p. ; 23 cm. Includes bibliographical references.

    ISBN 13: 978-1-62564-790-0

    1. Tricksters. 2. Tricksters in American history. 3. Tricksters in motion pictures. 4. Tricksters in television. 5. Tricksters in fiction. I. Title.

GR524 J10 2014

Manufactured in the U.S.A.   12/15/2014

Dedicated to those
who claim they don't have the foggiest idea
what I'm talking about.

All boys are rascals, and so are all men.
—HERMAN MELVILLE, *THE CONFIDENCE MAN*

CONTENTS

List of Illustrations | ix
Foreword (by Peter Thuesen) | xi
Preface | xv
Acknowledgments | xvii
Introduction | xix

1. Yesterday: Tricksters in America's Past | 1
2. Today: Fifteen Kinds of Tricksters in America | 48
3. Tomorrow: Lessons We Need to Learn from Trickster | 138

Notes | 218

Appendix 1: On Archetypes | 249
Appendix 2: Some American Stories about Con Men | 250
Appendix 3: On Masks and Head Coverings | 253
Appendix 4: On the Clown in America | 255
Appendix 5: On Mortgage Fraud and other Cons | 257
Appendix 6: George W. Bush as Painter | 258
Appendix 7: On Torture | 260

Select Bibliography | 263

ILLUSTRATIONS

Figure 1. Coyote. Source: Wikipedia Commons | 13

Figure 2. Kokopelli. Drawing by author based on traditional depictions | 18

Figure 3. Davy Crockett. Illustration from *The Crockett Almanack*, 1841 | 23

Figure 4. "The Illusionist." Ink painting by the artist Thomas C. Jackson | 50

Figure 5. Photo of Bert Williams. Source: Wikipedia Commons | 77

Figure 6. Oil painting of clown, Chicago 1961, artist unknown | 78

Figure 7. Snapshot from the collection of Robert E. Jackson, National Gallery | 169

Figure 8. "If I Only Had a Brain." Painting by artist Rhea Ormond | 191

Figure 9. Photo of John Henry sculpture, Talcott, West Virginia. Source: Wikipedia Commons | 212

FOREWORD

When I moved to Indiana a decade ago, having no experience with the local culture, I was fascinated to learn that one of the state's genuine folk heroes is the gangster and reputed cop killer John Dillinger. His grave in Crown Hill Cemetery in Indianapolis is something of a pilgrimage destination, more popular than the grave of a US president (Benjamin Harrison) and countless other Hoosier notables. Over the years, so many souvenir-seeking visitors chipped away at Dillinger's tombstone that the original had to be replaced.

What accounts for Dillinger's popularity? In part, it's his reputation as a latter-day Robin Hood who deprived the rich of (some of) their allegedly ill-gotten wealth. But as William Jackson points out, Dillinger also partakes of a much deeper archetype: the trickster. At once benevolent and harmful, a trickster is at turns playful, unpredictable, rude, and uncontrollable. A glance at the most famous photograph of Dillinger seems to confirm all of these qualities. With his boyish good looks, cleft chin, sly moustache, and narrowed eyes, he stares back at us with a mischievous, slightly menacing smile.

The archetype of the trickster is well known to scholars of religion. I first encountered it in studying the African antecedents to religion among the American slaves. As the historian Albert Raboteau has shown, many African American religious conversion accounts include mention of a mysterious "little man" who is thought by some scholars to be derived from the West African god Legba, the trickster who opens the gate to the world of the spirits.[1] In the religious cultures of the African diaspora, tricksters also occur in female form, as my colleague Kelly Hayes has shown of Pomba Gira, the female counterpart to the Yoruba deity Esu. In Brazil, shops sell Pomba Gira statues depicting her as a femme fatale, sometimes clad in open cape with bared breasts. As Professor Hayes writes, "Pomba Gira is a trickster figure known for ignoring limits and exceeding boundaries, whether of social comportment or moral action."[2]

xi

William Jackson is no stranger to the study of world cultures and their archetypes. An internationally recognized scholar of South Indian religion, he has applied his training in the history of religions to contexts far beyond the Indian subcontinent. Indeed, in his 2004 book *Heaven's Fractal Net*, he quotes an ancient Chinese proverb that might well serve as the animating principle of his scholarship: "Though heaven's net has wide meshes, nothing escapes it." Like a net, the web of knowledge is flexible and interconnected. Its strands of mutual give-and-take unite the cosmos, encompassing all beings in a mysterious whole and banishing any sense that we live in what Professor Jackson calls "nightmarish apartness" from others.[3] The wide net of his scholarship has captured many lost treasures, including Americana, his earliest scholarly love (his first book was a history of a Vermont town). His 2008 anthology, *The Wisdom of Generosity: A Reader in American Philanthropy*, compiles myths, proverbs, poems, folktales, sermons, and other writings that collectively constitute the American wisdom tradition on giving. Now, in *American Tricksters*, Professor Jackson combines his prodigious talents as a scholarly hunter-gatherer with his keen insights as an interpreter. The result is a study of the American trickster archetype that is unparalleled in both breadth and depth.

In the pages to follow, we encounter a cast of characters ranging from the Native American trickster Coyote to Warner Brothers' "wascally wabbit" Bugs Bunny. We find "Big Bertha" Heyman (the "Confidence Queen"), who swindled wealthy men out of thousands and gave their money to the poor, and pop star Lady Gaga, whose taboo-breaking flamboyance masks a more philanthropic agenda focused on youth uplift and self-esteem. We also meet more sinister tricksters such as the king of the Ponzi scheme, Bernie Madoff, and the lesser known Ponzi swindlers Hassan Nemazee and Tim Durham, who bankrolled the Democratic and Republican parties, respectively, with part of the proceeds from their scams. Professor Jackson even ruminates on the trickster aspects of US presidents Richard ("Tricky Dick") Nixon and George W. Bush. The latter comes in for sustained analysis, with Professor Jackson finding the trope of the trickster woven throughout Bush's biography and presidency. Here Professor Jackson invokes a related archetype from Jungian depth psychology: the *puer aeternus*, or perpetual adolescent. Like other archetypes, its meaning is complex, both positive and negative.

Indeed, one of the inescapable conclusions of Professor Jackson's book is that tricksters can be either beneficial or baleful—just like the rest of us. "The human psyche's dynamics are intrinsically part trickster," Professor Jackson writes. "This vital aspect of clever impulses can get the better of us in self-destructive acts, or it can offer a vivifying awareness of how the soul relates to existence." We are, Professor Jackson concludes, our own worst enemies or our own wise friends. The trickster, in fooling us and exposing our illusions, helps teach us the essential art of staying alive. Professor Jackson quotes the late Professor Johnny Flynn on the lesson that Coyote teaches people: "Coyote knows that shape-shifting is not about changing the fundamentals of who they are. It is about changing how people perceive who they are." That is exactly what Professor Jackson, like Coyote, does in this book. He holds up a mirror to ourselves, showing the trickster in all of us.

Peter J. Thuesen

Notes

1. Albert J. Raboteau, *A Fire in the Bones: Reflections on African-American Religious History* (Boston: Beacon, 1995), 154–55.

2. Kelly E. Hayes, *Holy Harlots: Femininity, Sexuality, and Black Magic in Brazil* (Berkeley, CA: University of California Press, 2011), 4–5, 65.

3. William J. Jackson, *Heaven's Fractal Net: Retrieving Lost Visions in the Humanities* (Bloomington, IN: Indiana University Press, 2004), 11.

PREFACE

The process of working with information, ideas, knowledge, and wisdom is a tricky business. I've had teaching experiences in India, in Vermont (at Lyndon State College), at Harvard (as a teaching assistant and teacher of tutorials), and at Indiana University-Purdue University in Indianapolis (where I taught in the Religious Studies Department for twenty-five years, and served as Lake Scholar for three years). I've also been a guest speaker at various colleges, festive celebrations, and public events. I have been fascinated by tricky Loki in Norse mythology since I was twenty, and I discovered Lewis Hyde's *Trickster Makes the World* when I was a research fellow at the Rockefeller Research Center at Bellagio, Italy, in the spring of 2000. In the years since then I have gathered examples and ideas from media, books, friends, and from observing my own impulses. When I was the first Lake Scholar at the Lake Family Institute for Faith and Giving, a part of the Philanthropic Studies Center at Indiana University-Purdue University at Indianapolis, I studied historical examples of generosity in the American experience. But in considering the many stories of giving I often noticed the shadow side of human nature as well, and alongside the many bright examples of benevolence I was collecting, I began to notice in the news and in history many examples of trickery.

When I look back I see now that each phase of my life has taught me some things about the trickster archetype. Writing this book came out of all those phases, and, more than any other book I've ever written, this one seemed to write itself.

We can never follow all the tracks of all the tricks in any given culture, but without some knowledge of the trickster's presence, we are truly foolishly clueless. C. G. Jung wrote that a person who wants to understand the problem of evil needs self-knowledge, meaning the fullest possible awareness of his own wholeness. This means he has to thoroughly know his capacity to do good, and also the crimes he is capable of doing, and he must beware of thinking the good is the only reality, and that the crimes are an impossible fantasy. Both sides exist in a person and both inevitably emerge in his or her experience and require us to take them seriously, if we want to keep ourselves honest and live without self-delusion. The trickster leapfrogs over and slithers under us, especially if we are strangers to ourselves, and the trickster delights in shredding our self-regard and our vanities; hopefully he puts us in a position to trick ourselves a little less when we look in the mirror. (Otherwise we'll have to kick ourselves more, some day.)

ACKNOWLEDGMENTS

As a university professor I often felt as if I shambled onstage or into the classroom or to a conference podium looking like I'd just barely escaped from the trickster. I would glance over my shoulder, just to make sure he was not breathing down my neck. Arriving there I would look around nervously, only to face forward and find myself gazing at a room full of tricksters! This is no joke—how do I acquit myself to all these expectant ones? What can I deliver, what can I give birth to here in the dryness and quiet of the spotlight? I think: I'd better follow my own path and impulses, trusting to the trickster of life's momentum, hoping something good will come out of all this pulsing life and quirky quick-as-a-winkery. But who knows—some days you just can't win, and some days you just can't lose. Nothing is written in water, and nothing is carved in stone: everything is timelessly there in the air around us.

I thank the ones I face—in the classroom, in my family, and in all my relationships, and the part they play in my attempts to say something. This book came out of those performances, trials, and conversations, and it is like them: it is a process of explaining what seems like a pervasive thread in life. Yet it was written in solitude, taking down what came to me quickly, so the incidents of life would not distract me from my ideas, noting examples of tricksters, and concepts to understand them, arranging them to sketch the trickster's face. It seemed as if time, being a trickster, composed a self-portrait. This is a study with informal reflections, yet with many well-referenced sources. It is a series of observations about the history and psychology of tricks in America.

I am thankful especially to the friends and colleagues who read parts of this work and gave me feedback along the way. These include members of the Department of Religious Studies at Indiana University-Purdue University at Indianapolis—Professor Peter Thuesen and David Craig. And thanks to my friends Bruce Frazer, Terry Marks-Tarlow, William Morice, who are deeply versed in psychotherapy. Thanks also to Amy Frazer, who has befriended dogs, foxes, and wolves, and knows their tricks. And to my brother, artist, and photographer Thomas C. Jackson, and to my old friend Paul Meagher. I am also grateful for the keen-eyed editorial work of Rodney Clapp, and the help of Laura Poncy and Ian Creeger at Cascade Books. Thank you one and all for your reflections and encouragement on various parts of this book.

INTRODUCTION

Googling a "minor" 300 million dollar Ponzi scheme I had recently heard about—a scheme that was considered minor because Bernard Madoff's Ponzi scheme had bilked investors to the tune of 50 billion dollars—I came across a list of thirty-eight significant Ponzi schemes reported in the year 2009 alone.[1] Each scheme was a multimillion-dollar venture conducted in one or another region of America. Was this just the tip of an iceberg?

Every day the news includes stories of frauds and deceptive hijinks in the fields of sports, entertainment, politics, and business. There is a constant cavalcade of chicanery, cheating, and dishonest practices among the young, middle-aged, and old. So much so that I have to conclude the trickster spirit is alive and well in America today.

As someone who has compared wisdom and piety in Eastern and Western cultures, and studied archetypal examples of compassion and giving (most recently in my book *The Wisdom of Generosity*), I cannot help but be fascinated by stories of people in the public eye (and people trying to remain anonymous beyond the public eye) who become involved in intricate swindles and lies, or in skillful and talented trickiness, and sometimes in outright attempts at criminal deception. I can only conclude that the trickster archetype represents a deep dynamic in the individual human psyche and in modern society. Perhaps as some claim, "Mercury is rising."[2] (Mercury was the trickster god of ancient Rome, as Hermes was a trickster god in ancient Greece.) Signs of a trickster impulse are visible in just about every field, once one begins to notice them.

Some forms of tricksterism are very obvious. A sting operation catches swindlers, and they are arrested, found guilty, and put in jail. Others are difficult to sort out and understand; they are controversial and debated for years. Did George W. Bush lie and involve America in a war of choice based on trumped up evidence? Are dirty tricks in politics unethical or just realistic necessities in a world where nice guys finish last? What kinds of trickery are involved in government-sponsored torture and the attempts to hide it, and to justify it? What can we learn from the great range of tricks in human behavior, from little white lies to maneuvers leading to the massive 2008 financial meltdown in world banking? How many of us were suspicious when we heard that five trillion dollars of wealth had been lost in the financial meltdown? Isn't it the fear of betrayal and trickiness, lack of trust and wariness of con jobs, which has made many people uncertain about their government? Is America skillful and tricky enough to outsmart terrorists, or do some of the tricks America undertakes destroy its credibility as protector of human rights?

Such examples of tricks on our radar screens offer just a few object lessons selected out of many that suggest themes to reflect upon. Many more, some of them examples of innocent fun and necessary creative playfulness, can be gleaned from the full panoply of contemporary tricksters. A sustained consideration of examples, and a series of reflections about the patterns and meanings of trickster activities can be useful, and richly interesting.

I think that more analyses and ideas about trickster activities are needed today, both for our own well-being and for discovering more about human nature. How do people get so deeply involved in tricks that they lose the sense of who they really are? Both the criminal impostor and the undercover cop may lose their moral compasses and become confused about their identities. I believe that knowledge of some qualities of trickster dynamics is essential to self-understanding. We all need cleverness, a mentality with fluid possibilities, and an energetic ability to play and imagine alternative scenarios, for example. And regarding others' cleverness, such as scam artists, well, "forewarned is forearmed," as the proverb says. If we know more about the *modus operandi* of tricksters we are less likely to be hurt by them.

Looking through the American experiences during the last four centuries, we can find vivid examples of tricksters playing their games in the earlier days, too. The enduring nature of the trickster in American history is rather astounding. The examples are lively and learning about them refreshes our perspective. We can better understand some of our own contemporary American propensities and patterns by considering what our ancestors experienced, and some of the swindles they fell for. America offered a dreamlike ideal of free or inexpensive land to homesteaders, and sometimes salesmen sold the possibilities of a new life to immigrants in elaborate scams. It is not by coincidence that people in distant lands imagine the streets of America as lined with gold. There is something archetypal about sales pitches, with their dramatic symbols, all the better to appeal to the imagination.

The archetype of the trickster is so thoroughly embedded in human nature, and in some of the promises of the American Dream, that I feel the trickster's contemporary appearance is best understood in the context of looking back to the Native Americans ("first nations") and their perennial stories of tricksters, and to the examples of early con men who tried to pull the wool over the eyes of the first generations of Americans. And we need to remember folk heroes like Davy Crockett, who contributed aspects to the American character and psyche. And to reconsider the hazings of earlier times, which resemble some of today's hazings. If we first journey back to consider tricks of earlier times, we can better appreciate the payoffs we get in the colorful contemporary examples of tricksters in our midst, and better grasp the lessons they engender.

Thus, the structure of the book is threefold:

The first part is an extensive reflection on American tricksters. It is about the wiliness needed to survive, as well as the cynicism that exploits idealism. The Native American stories of Raven, and Coyote, Hare and Kokopelli offer interesting reflections of life's traits, and can stimulate our awareness of human resources for living with difficult threats, developing fearlessness and finding soulful courage.

The second part enumerates fifteen kinds of recent and contemporary tricksters. It is a rogues' gallery suggesting cultural figures with tricky behavior, from Americans' biographies and American pop culture and news, including political tricksters, rock stars, womanly tricksters, male comic tricksters, charismatic tricksters, sports tricksters, social commentator tricksters, scatological tricksters, outside-the-box tricksters, minority tricksters, ominous treacherous tricksters, business tricksters, Internet tricksters, large financial meltdown tricksters, and scientific fraud tricksters.

My aim in this part is to suggest the scope and variety of tricksters, not to go into depth in great detail with many of these examples. These examples represent some of the varieties of tricksters that turned up on the radar screen of daily news and media in the last few years. It was an experiment I conducted, seeing what kinds of tricks would pop up each day, and it proved to me how plentiful the signs of trickery are when one is attuned to them. Our American culture exists wherever we find it. I think culture reflects aspects of the worldview of the society in which it is found. Fictional TV series can offer examples of how America thinks and feels, and can reveal what the audience will accept as realistic, and what the audience finds entertaining and meaningful.

Some examples are sketchy notes caught in the midst of busy days—in the moment of "now or never." They capture a fragment of trickery that would otherwise have escaped. I congratulate them in surviving the competitive situation in which they came to light—whether heard on the car radio, on TV, in dark movie theatres, on the Internet, or in conversation. There was barely time to hear, appreciate, and record them, but they are bite-size nuggets to contemplate. Even fast-moving moments offer exquisite gems if one can jot them down before they become part of the vague past.

The third part is about life lessons we learn from the play of the trickster in our lives. Trickster wisdom is integral to knowing well our bodies, ourselves, our communities, and our nation. There are some tricksters who are pranksters helping us live with uncomfortable truths; others are risk-takers of ruin from whom we need protection. The personal learning about the trickster side of life is a part of growing up. The trickster archetype plays important roles in our psyches. We can deepen our appreciation by considering how trickster qualities of human intelligence help us learn, be resilient, and survive. In this section I explore the individual's life cycle, and the American psyche. I explore the example of war president George W. Bush, inquiring into his life and policies, considering them in light of insights garnered from exploring the trickster archetype. Reflecting on American culture I discuss ideas of thinkers in the field of archetypal psychology: C. G. Jung and James Hillman. I also examine the trickster legacy in folklore.

The Language and Thematic Order of the Book

Most of the book is written in the ordinary language of prose literature, but in keeping with the tone and nuances of the subject matter, some parts of the book express ideas in more colloquial vocabularies of the kinds of tricksters being discussed, to convey the flavor of their expressions and attitudes. In choosing this approach I have been influenced by Nelson Algren, James Hillman, Ralph Waldo Emerson, and Mark Twain—and really by all who have known how the force of spoken language adds depth and vividness to the written word. These linguistic quirks are there by design and give the book an American tone.

Because I use the terms "consciousness" and "conscience," and "unconscious" and "subconscious" in a number of places in the text, it may be helpful if I say at the outset what I mean by them.

Of course there is no universally agreed-upon understanding of "consciousness," but it is generally used to mean awareness—sentience and more—the whole spectrum of awareness witnessing existence that a conscious being experiences: perception, thought, feeling, and volition. There are levels of being inwardly aware, and they depend upon ignorance, learning, refinement, maturation through experience, etc.

"Conscience" indicates a self-reflective aspect of consciousness that wrestles with questions of good and evil. Conscience has been described as "inmost thought," the still small voice within, the "agenbite of inwit" (meaning the thought-source of the sting of remorse), and the internal moral navigator that recognizes the aspect of sorting right from wrong in one's motives and behavior.

I usually use the term "unconscious" in the way it is used by C. G. Jung. The depths of the psyche's activities are not fully accessible or fathomable by the conscious calculative mind. The unconscious is active in dreams, fantasies, ideas, and inspirations, and in dark impulses and instincts, manias and compulsions. The "collective unconscious" is the accumulated archetypal images of humanity's experiences. Below the level of conscious awareness, this depth determines a lot. (I explore the concept of archetypes in the text, and also in endnotes, and in an appendix.)[3] I share the accepted meaning of the commonly used term "subconscious" as indicating the part of the mental field the processes of which are outside the range of usual attention. These unconscious depths can include anxieties of which we are not fully conscious, manifesting in nervous tics and neurotic habits, inexplicable yearnings and animosities, etc. This term may be preferred by those who take the word "unconscious" literally ("without consciousness,") instead of thinking of it as meaning levels of awareness of which we are usually unconscious. The hidden aspects of existence, the unconscious depths, have been intuited by thinkers over the centuries. As Herman Melville wrote, "every . . . form of life has its secret mines and dubious side, the side popularly disclaimed."[4] We explore but do not fathom the depths.

Because this book is a thematic study, I am not attempting to keep every example in perfect chronological order. The point, in fact, is the timeless quality of a kind of human behavior, because tricksters' playfulness, cunning, and swindling happen in all centuries.

How to Relate to Trickster Vitality?

The trickster is ultimately about the mystery of life—vitality's urge to thrive and advance, and the indomitable non-linear imagination's ways. I use examples from "real life" and examples from cultural expressions such as literature, novels, poems, TV series, and blockbuster movies to illustrate American tricksters, because the imagination is integral to the topic—indivisibly found both in the psyches of con men in the headlines and in stories of tricksters told by fiction writers.

My main concern in all three parts of this book is to note examples in American history and culture, and to consider these examples as aspects of the trickster archetype. I do not offer moral evaluations for each case discussed, though the most egregious tricksters I do note as seriously destructive, and the more usefully creative ones I respect as beneficial. Naturally, anti-social acts are reprehensible, but I leave a further discussion of ethical questions to others, focusing here primarily on vivid examples in American life. Can anyone who saw Heath Ledger's portrayal of the Joker in *The Dark Knight* forget it? That wild role, which took the modern dramatization of a literary trickster to a new high point, is among the examples discussed in this exploration.

We always seem to forget that we and our world are in flux, as if being unconscious is the default. It comes as a rude awakening to remember: Our universe and mindset form a mixture of actuality and ideas and social constructions of our time and place on earth. We build up a world and lifeway out of conditioning and accepted customs, desires, fears, and symbols. The social fiction we arrive at and call reality is in large part hopeful pretending, a chronic subterfuge of trickster play, acting nice because decorum calls for it, becoming angry because our role and situation calls for it sometimes for good. Deception runs very deep in nature, and wishful thinking is a powerful human behavior. "Seeing is believing," and sometimes we see and hear what we want to. Building up this set of thought forms and illusions can be for good, but sometimes it is not. There is a subjective state in our experience, which is not objective reality, but also not pure imagination, fantasy, and daydream.

In various fields this viewpoint is explored. Anthropologist Michael Taussig, for example, asks us to consider that, oddly enough, most of us spend a lot of our lifetimes in "this silly if not desperate place between the real and the really made-up"; in fact most of our time is spent there "as epistemically correct, socially created, and occasionally creative beings."[5] That is quite a statement to make about where we're usually at for most of our lives. It means we are doing our best to make it up as we go along in a conscientious way, while pretending it's all solid and stable and foreordained and according to norms. Going along with our happenstance conditioning and doing our own socially conditioned things and rationalizing what we do, we act like our way is the only reality. We fake it, acting as if there were no mischief in reality, as Taussig puts it, as if "all around the ground lay firm. That is what the public secret, the facticity of the social fact, being a social being, is all about."[6] Social life is pretending the convenient norms we try to share are actual reality.

The relatively real is made up of the conventions and accepted behavior of the day in the culture we are immersed in. But reality is unfixed. Our cells are constantly worn out and renewed, our blood is forever being transformed. Our life on earth is fluid. It's music, on a changing planet with continental collisions, earthquakes, eruptions, a vast nonlinear system of processes with nonhuman principles. Our amphibious psyche knits together, in waking hours and in dreams, the totality. It's a double city—one above, and one below, or maybe it's more dynamic than that. When we shuffle the deck and get out of our settled fixedness by travel, or experiments that unleash our perceptions, we get to know the fluidity of living experience. We see it takes a trickster to play in an aware way in the midst of this ever-changing mixture of material, biological, mental, and spiritual realms. It requires a skillful, graceful trickster to look up to for our inspiration and guidance. Hence, our attraction to quirky heroes and quick-change artists such as Ulysses, Sherlock Holmes, Shakespeare, Gandhi, Bob Dylan, Julie Taymor, Whoopi Goldberg, and Lady Gaga.

Damon Runyon tried his best to give Americans a healthy dose of trickster awareness. He warned us that someday as we go through life we are bound to encounter a man with a crisp new deck of cards who wants to bet you that he can cause a specific card—the jack of spades—to leap from the deck and squirt some apple cider into your ear. Runyon emphatically warned us: Do not take this bet, because you will get squirted with cider.

Good advice. But the trickster is found in many situations and realms, not just in the scams of con men. This book may prove that to you. The times we end up laughing at ourselves are those times when we try to fool ourselves and then find that the joke is on us. Or when we try to trick the world, and then find that we're the ones who have been fooled. We are all grist for the trickster's mills.

What does looking at the world through the lens of trickster dynamics get us? This book is all about answering that question.

William J. Jackson, Indianapolis, April 1, 2014

Notes

1. "The Madoff Fraud: Scam of the Century. Ponzi Schemes Reported in 2009." http://madofffraud.boomja.com/Ponzi-Schemes-Reported-in-2009-22206.html.

2. See, for example, Deldon Anne McNeely, *Mercury Rising: Women, Evil and the Trickster Gods* (Woodstock, CT: Spring, 1996).

3. See, for example, the appendices.

4. Herman Melville, *Billy Budd, Foretopman* (New York: Bantam, 1965), 52.

5. Michael Taussig, "The Report to the Academy," in *Mimesis and Alterity* (New York: Routledge, 1993), xvii.

6. Ibid.

1

YESTERDAY

Tricksters in America's Past

Preliminary Reflections: Visionary Nation and Land of Coyote

> What constitutes the essence... the principle of diddling is, in fact, peculiar to the class of creatures that wear coats and pantaloons. A crow thieves; a fox cheats; a weasel outwits; a man diddles. To diddle is his destiny... he was made to diddle. This is his aim—his object—his end. And for this reason when a man's diddled we say he's "done."
>
> —Edgar Allan Poe[1]

In childhood we learn of the heroism involved in America's founding. We hear of the ideals of freedom and democracy from school teachers, political candidates, and dramatic presentations. We celebrate our nation's greatness on July 4th, Presidents' Day, Memorial Day, and Thanksgiving. We teach our children noble sentiments like Washington's "I cannot tell a lie." The glories of America are there for all to see in museums and historical re-enactments, on sunny baseball fields, and in our heroic attempts to solve the world's problems. But does America have a shadow? Could it be that the "land of the brave and the home of the free," some of whose founders were wise visionaries, is also a land of wolves and thieves[2]—coyotes and tricksters?

If tricksters are known by their deeds, it is undeniable that in America the actions of tricksters can be seen in great variety. They appear in a profusion of stories old and new, and in many degrees, from mild to intense, in many lives today. I believe there is a pressing need today to explore this topic anew, to call to mind some examples of tricksters we may have come to take for granted. Otherwise the figure of the trickster, who is so talented at blending in, remains hidden in the background. The trick[3] at hand is to tease this exploration of trickery into existence with examples and reflections that do not just entertain us, but reveal its significance with unflinching clarity. Otherwise trickery accompanies us like an unacknowledged shadow.

What does history tell us about how America might be different from other cultures? The poet Robert Bly once suggested in a talk about betrayal[4] that American Indians put trickster power in the ground. This is a symbolic way of connecting a previous era of America with traits of America today, a way of saying the First Nations, already on this soil for thousands of years before Europeans arrived, left a legacy of wisdom and lore about the trickster, and more—a trickster vibe in the earth and very air of America. Besides the traditional trickster figure in old Indian myths, there is another famous form of the trickster—the American con man. Though we acknowledge there are tricksters all around the world, we nevertheless need to ask why America might be an especially fertile breeding ground for tricky con men.

We could begin with the very name of "America." It derives from the tag-along traveler Amerigo Vespucci, a contemporary of the voyager Columbus. Vespucci claimed to be a seasoned navigator but the report, *Mundus Novus*, written before his first voyage and published under his name, was a forgery. Nevertheless, it led a German mapmaker to label a vast area of land "America" in his geographical representation of the New World. Vespucci seems to have been an opportunist, a dreamer and schemer who had a gift for moving on in life each time he tried something and fell on his face, boldly reinventing himself in different phases of his career—another American trait. So "America" was an appropriate name, even if it came to be used by happenstance.[5]

America and Land Fraud

One form of scheming and swindling that is especially associated with America concerns land fraud. Gary Lindberg, in his classic study *The Confidence Man in American Literature*, suggested that America has long been a Promised Land in people's imagination, a place where the sky is the limit for fulfilling dreams. And because hopes were so high in the New World there were many homegrown land scams intended to bilk the plentiful naive dreamers. In the nineteenth century hundreds of "land-sharks" engaged in town-site frauds between St. Paul, Minnesota, and Dunleith, Illinois. Maps and brochures showed beautiful buildings in bogus towns like "Nininger" and "Rolling Stone."[6] Victims bought land, sight unseen, packed their belongings and traveled, only to arrive at a point characterized by confusion, or find themselves seeking non-existent locations, or arriving at a parcel of land legally belonging to Native Americans. Other states, such as Tennessee and Georgia, also had their share of land fraud.

Beginning in the 1830s "Claims Clubs" were established—settlers' associations formed mostly west of the Mississippi. Ostensibly they were designed to make farmland available to settlers in need of land. Some of these were squatters' clubs, good old boy associations formed for mutual benefit implementing coercive and deceitful methods to accomplish their goals. During this time when Jefferson's land grant program offered acreage for establishing new homesteads, some families would squat on land that they had not legally purchased. Then, when the rightful new owner with a legitimate title arrived, the members of the Claims Clubs would vouch for the previous tenant as a longtime resident and rightful owner. Sometimes the Claims Club even had a portable dwelling, a sort of cabin on wheels, which could be moved around from lot to lot and set up temporarily, providing "hard evidence" that the "tenant" (who was actually a claim jumper) being vouched for had invested his time and efforts and had "improved the land."[7]

The Omaha Club, founded in 1854, was known for imposing violent frontier justice on those who could not be persuaded by words, enforcing their opinions on ownership by force, including dunking those with claims to land but not belonging to the club in the Missouri River while it was frozen. Another Nebraska club was known for beating claim jumpers and attempting to tar and feather squatters.[8]

Land sellers in the western plains used clever phrases like "Rain follows the plow" (meaning: if you plow dry land, rain will fall), promising a bright future in Oklahoma and other nearby states that received too little rainfall per year to support successful farming. Using such ploys, they tricked buyers into acquiring land that in time would turn to dust. In the early twentieth century, developers sold 3,000 lots in Boise City, Oklahoma. Boise City was at the center of the ecologically devastated "Dust Bowl" area with few attractive features. The developers claimed Boise was a bustling city replete with conveniences, services, streets, buildings, businesses, and a railroad station. Authorities eventually took the developers to court and jailed them for their fraudulent claims.[9]

Later, salesmen devised real estate pitches involving Florida swamp lands, using alluring images to misrepresent the properties as being full of rich soil, never in need of fertilizer, with great possibilities for development. Thus they presented the land as prime real estate opportunities for rewarding investments. They described tropical paradise land needing only wonderful homes to be built in order to become perfect settings for a happy life. These scams, which fooled many gullible buyers, became so famous that phrases like "I have some swampland in Florida I'd like to sell you" became part of American slang. In the 1960s another wave of con artists exploited nationwide advertising media to attract investors in Florida land. Midwesterners excited about an exotic region of America would invest their savings and find their land was a soggy swamp.[10] Some states, as a result, legislated laws against false advertising. With such an abundance of land and so many newcomers desirous of a plot, America has been especially prone to land fraud.

Americans' Soft Spot for Charming Con Artists

All along, there have been shrewd schemers in the American saga—some died as paupers, some amassed great wealth. The frontier, which moved westward during the formative period in American history, was often a lawless territory, with fewer authority figures, and many rootless mobile people. Lindberg observed that all the moving around Americans have done tended to make them "restless, unstable, thirsty for novelty."[11] One consequence of mobility may be an uncertainty that the unscrupulous can victimize. When change is constant and identity is up for grabs, a shifty con man can more readily exploit vulnerable people's hopes and needs. On the westward-moving frontier, where new settlements were being established and new social identities were being formed, there were necessarily many leaps of faith required, and wishful embraces of hopeful promise.

The first generations of Puritans had hoped that the New World would be a kind of Promised Land, a divine city on a hill, and the era of land speculation in eighteenth- and nineteenth-century America still carried with it a mood of optimistic belief. The New World was a land of promise, and a fertile ground as well for the "land sharks" who would prey on idealistic hope, exploiting settlers' dreams of betterment and temptations of greed. Rolling Stone City, for example, was a fictitious picturesque territory said to be ideally located on the Mississippi River. It existed only on paper, in glorious descriptions written by real estate swindlers who invented the place out of fantasies to entice gullible buyers. America in those formative times presented a novel situation. When identity is based on beliefs and hopes (rather than on an established ethnic community, or on class, as was the case in a feudal system) there is a larger scope for the unsuspecting person to be duped. Individuality means each person is on his own, independently exercising options. The confidence man gains people's trust by talking them into believing in him and in the future he portrays, in a variety of ways.[12] Lindberg noted two styles of American confidence men that overlap and bolster each other. One is the "gamesman-shapeshifter," which fuses with the "booster idealist." Summing up his characterization of America as a land embodying a tradition that is paradoxical, one producing inventors, and dreamers and schemers, such as "Franklin and Emerson, Jefferson and Augie March, Whitman and Gatsby and Huck Finn," he sees it as "the tradition of confidence men busily renewing the New World."[13]

In O'Henry's humorous short story "The Chair of Philanthromathematics," the narrator, who among other things was a wildcat prospector out West, says, "When a man swindles the public out of a certain amount he begins to get scared and wants to return part of it. And if you watch close and notice the way his charity runs you'll see that he tries to restore it to the same people he got it from." He further observes that the owning of a large amount of money causes the condition of "Philanthropitis"—one symptom of which is feeling an urge to do something *for* humanity, instead of just *to* humanity. Having gouged the public with petty schemes, he and his friend want to turn an empty building into an educational institution. They do, but it soon runs low on money. "Philanthropy, when run on a good business basis, is one of the best grafts going," the narrator observes. He concludes that to work efficiently the school needs a chair of mathematics. So the founders hire a mathematician who can work wonders as a Faro dealer, fleecing the rich young students to make the school flourish financially. Perhaps the moral is this: it takes a trickster with skill and savvy to make a go of things and turn them around—a kind of Prometheus figure.[14]

Ideas about trickster con men are prominent in the seminal nineteenth-century novel *The Confidence-Man*, where, employing multiple scenarios, Herman Melville explores topics of trust and tricks from shifting perspectives. The story is set on a steamer ironically named the *Fidele*, and all the action occurs on an April 1st—April Fool's Day. Melville gamely keeps shifting the deck, showing how the various passengers have their different cons and issues with trust. Multifariously, the trickster impulse does a brisk trade in the currency of confidence; as long as the con artist can draw upon the "trust fund" of the gullible sucker—the reservoir of confidence in human nature—he can tap those assets to his cynical heart's satisfaction. Reading *The Confidence-Man* scenarios about trust sensitizes the reader to develop sensible questions about even sincere people's appeals.[15] There is much evidence in newspapers, literature and the lives of heroes that Americans do love their straightshooters, but also have a soft spot for chameleon charlatans and sweet-talking Robin Hoods. Americans admire inventors who out-trick nature, and honor and sometimes even idolize self-made tycoons, smooth operators, and celebrities who are self-improvisers getting away with endless underhanded antics to further their own prospects in the seemingly boundless horizons of the New World.[16]

Why do people admire and enjoy con artists, and applaud successful cons? Is it because industrious and plodding drones show less gumption and imagination, less performers' verve, and therefore people naturally delight in skillful displays of those who put on an act and get away with it? The trickster con man pulls off a funny drama, bluffing and fluffing, fudging and faking. There's a colorful pop of cleverness in the performance, but then in the results of the trickery, people can get hurt, wrecked, and ruined. But before that happens, there is glamor and fun. Fascination with bravado and celebrity and notoriety may have to do with attraction to charisma. Women send convicted murderers coy and passionate letters, and even marry them, for the same reason—excitement spices up a life of boring routines lacking imagination. The epic tricks of Nuckie, an illicit liquor kingpin in the TV series *Boardwalk Empire* (2010–2014), for example, show a survivor's skills and attract a wide audience.

Americans often seem to look up to the skillful players of improvised self-invention and confidence games, despite the sleaziness of their actual crimes and their punishments. Americans unconsciously often seem to honor tricksters, applauding skillful tricks such as those portrayed in films like *Ocean's Eleven* (1960 and 2001) and *Ocean's Twelve* (2004),[17] the TV series *Leverage* (2008–2012), and the film *The Thomas Crowne Affair* (1968 and 1999). The two TV series *House* and *The Mentalist* both feature brilliant detective work by figures who are rogues, eccentrics who think outside the box. Dr. House is a genius at diagnosing rare diseases, and Mr. Jane is an intuitive super-sleuth finding clues to solve crimes. The *Mentalist* character played by Simon Baker is a daring trickster figure for whom boundaries are seldom taken seriously. His freedom, fearlessness, acuity, and playfulness allow him to find deeply hidden solutions to baffling mysteries. House, despite dysfunctional faults and antisocial eccentricities, uncannily knows or discovers facts to successfully diagnose confusing illnesses. Both are also unpredictable tricksters with a devil-may-care attitude, full of surprises and fascinating insights, always fun to observe in action. The 2014 FX television series *Fargo* is a dark comedy featuring a mysterious hit man, Lorne Malvo, played by Billy Bob Thornton. In the storyline, Malvo takes a hapless apprentice under his wing, the incompetent trickster Lester Nygaard, played by Martin Freeman. The bumbling Lester makes a perfect foil for the cool, slick, and ever-inventive Malvo, until the final episode in which both die. Another oddball genius is featured in the TV series *Fringe* (2008–2013). In that series the mentally disturbed scientist Walter Bishop's brilliant powers are sharpened by his troubled background. (There is a psychological truth to this: a wound can heighten awareness and sensitivity, as psychologist James Hillman has suggested.) Americans also admire trickster-like celebrity figures—rockers, rappers, and other stars who break taboos and play the bad boy or wild girl in their private lives, as well as in the spotlight.

There are now and have been in the past many confidence men who set up shop all over America, because it is such a celebrated place of opportunities. There were huge areas of unspoiled nature, not built up with cities as Europe and other parts of the inhabited world were. Even before there was an agreed-upon currency, there were trading posts, and Europeans and Indians making trades with such items as furs and wampum. Wampum represents an ingenious cultural symbolism and means of social bonding. A tribe could pledge a solemn promise with good wampum, and also remember and commemorate important events with wampum belts. One could pay a debt with wampum, and honor achievements by way of gift wampum. Using the language of the eighteenth century, wampum served to "grease the chain" of societal harmony and agreement; it worked as an emollient keeping neighborly connections smooth and shiny. Because wampum became valuable as a medium of exchange for a time, some trickster Indians and some Englishmen too tried to palm off counterfeit wampum belts and poor quality dyed beads as the real thing. The gullible were at the mercy of the shrewd. Laws were soon passed threatening harsh punishments to discourage such deceptions, which were so tempting to early American con men seeking to game the system.[18]

"In the beginning all the world was America," John Locke famously wrote.[19] Beginning as a geography of resources and a wilderness of seemingly infinite possibilities, America later becomes a grid of streets, a map of counties and states, zip codes and area codes; a set of demographics and a network of laws and regulations and authorities; a charted Google map and GPS maze of starting points, routes, and destinations. At first, the possibilities were more open here, expanding the ways people might satisfy their hopes, and also the multiplication of those who promise to supply fulfillment of dreams was more prolific. If "anything's possible" in a visionary nation, there will always be some who think that means "anything goes," and take advantage of those pursuing happiness. There are various factors that give the light-stepping American trickster a sure footing in this land. The snake-oil peddling Medicine Shows of old ("Buy Red Thunder Cloud's Accabonic Indian Princess Tea!") have given way to weight loss gimmicks posted on telephone poles and E.D. (Erectile Dysfunction) panaceas that bombard us on TV commercials, as well as email spam messages promising "male enhancement."

This study is meant to be a playful exploration, employing the topic of the trickster to think about some pertinent issues in America that are often visible only partially and fleetingly in the margins. Con artist tricksters are unofficial presences in our midst, black sheep of the commonwealth. Tricksters fly under the radar and thrive in a wide range of camouflaged forms. This study is not meant to be dogmatic. The point is not necessarily that America has more tricksters per capita than any other nation on earth; for all I know there are many places with far more tricksters. I am simply pointing to the presence of tricksters in America as a focusing gambit to explore their variety and deeds. This is a thematic framework that seems to offer opportunities for exploration, discovery, and reflection. The realm of the trickster is a tricky realm to fathom. We have to use our own trickiness to tease out the meanings and importance of the elusive dynamics of the trickster archetype. We have to gather evidence about the trickster's wily ways by following his tracks and observing him wherever we find him. First, we need to examine examples of trickster stories from long ago to establish a baseline for some qualities of the archetypal tricksters of myths. This will help us develop a perspective on tricksters in our own times.

What is the Trickster? Ancient Timeless Archetype

The trickster archetype is one of the great enduring figures representing a style of consciousness, a way of being aware and behaving in the drama of life.

Tricksters are known by their deeds. All over the world this is the case. It is an old story. Tricksters are ubiquitous. West African myths feature Anansi the spider.[20] The Dogon people of Nigeria tell tales about the Jackal, a loner trickster who breaks taboos,[21] and is also a deity of divination. In Japan, Susa-no-o is a chaotic trickster, fickle as the unruly wind. The Norse prankster god Loki, willful, stubborn, and fickle, is the cause of a great catastrophe. Raven and Coyote of the Native American traditions are well known stirrers of transformation.[22] Hermes is a well-known Greek mythic trickster.[23] All of these figures are associated with quirky behavior, both brave and cowardly, now benevolent and now harmful, sometimes rude and shocking in their blatant breaking of taboos.[24] All are wild and playful catalysts of transformation.

As an archetypal image, the trickster aspect of existence expresses itself in a spectrum of appearances in myths, legends, biographies, and fictions. He can be a hero of fairy tales and myths, and also a human villain in some real-life events—as newspaper headlines remind us each day. The trickster Raven of the Northwest Native American tales does good, but can also go astray and make mistakes. The trickster—Coyote, for example—can be a flouter of conventions, exercising the dangerous power of crossing social boundaries that others must respect. He is the bringer of significant transformations, an agent of the creator in some stories, a necessary catalyst. In others he's the bringer of ruin, deceitful and conniving, a turncoat, or devil in disguise. He shifts shapes, illustrates survival through clever adaptation, sometimes exhibiting extreme foolishness. He is the cause of chaos where things go wrong, and also can be the source of benevolence, helping humanity.

The old traditional trickster myths often involve cosmological powers, the elemental forces of nature. The trickster in these tales often has a quality of being unpredictable, fickle like inclement weather—wind-like, whimsically destructive, he represents the aspect of the universe that erupts periodically in chaotic turbulence, shaking things up. We know the earth is dynamic with monsoons, forest fires, floods, lightning, earthquakes, volcanoes, hailstorms. The Jackal (or other trickster figures), futzing around in the theater of dynamic change, personifies the chaotic eruptions, and illustrates this fact of life. He is an unreliable rat, sure to be obstreperous. That the sequences of life are not just linear logic, that there is fortune, the luck of the draw, the quirky chance, and that larger revolutions than are imagined by calculative thinking's logic, are basic facts of our experience. What is the universe saying in the trickster image? I think it is dramatizing some of life's surprising dynamics.

The mythical trickster's function often seems to be that of an agent of change, needed to overturn rigid structures periodically, to refresh a social system. This is a principle similar to annual rites of refreshment. Some societies have celebrations of cycles, feast and famine, self-denial and self-indulgence. For example, there are annual Carnivale celebrations before Lent in places like Italy, Brazil, and New Orleans, colorful displays that express this punctuation in cycles of time with masks and lavish costumes. Like Halloween and New Year's Eve, these celebrations point to submersion of smaller temporary purposive identities in larger wholes—growing seasons, generations of the ancestors, the cycles of time refreshed by periodic formless chaos dissolving rigidities, offering sensual enjoyments before a time of buckling down to discipline. The trickster archetype is also extremely important in the transformations of the psyche's inner life—metanoia, spiritual rebirth, change of heart, inner death and resurrection. The images of Judas, and Loki, and other tricksters, are archetypal figures[25] of this catalyst quality, playing a part in rebirth. As the necessary troublemaker who spices up life with needed complications, the trickster embodies the topsy-turvy unconscious play of desires, impulses of vitality turning into funny maneuvers. The cunning elfin spirit of life flits and darts, confides, eludes, deludes and hides, with skillful grace and playful quirks. (The word "cunning" comes from a Middle English word *can*, meaning "know.") The soul itself is a knowing and unknowing trickster, as Jung pointed out: "with cunning and playful deception the soul lures into life the inertia of matter that does not want to live." The soul draws us to have faith in unbelievable things, spurs us to life. The soul trips us up with allurements, "snares and traps," so that we fall into existence. Thus we become entangled, caught up in life, enmeshed in the complications of living.[26] The trickster promises lure lives into participation, flinging them into the dance, so they will become interrelated, actively taking part, not mere wallflowers.

An archetypal image holds together a deep complex of principles and issues, and can be seen in examples from culture, dreams, and everyday life, embodied in local habitations and various names. Of course many archetypes besides the trickster and Anima (soul as feminine muse) exist in the collective unconscious, and are also reflected in our fantasies, in literature, and in history. The Hero (not only adventurous, but also respectable, stable, accomplished, industrious), the Savior, the Mother, the Wise Man, the Child, the Warrior, and the Lovers, are examples of archetypes in the great enduring stories.[27] Archetypes are "strange attractors" of the psyche, imbuing our lives with moods, attitudes, visions, and programs to fulfill, tuning our temperaments, giving us focal points for devoted actions and inspirations in our strivings. The works of Carl G. Jung[28] and James Hillman[29] are helpful in deepening our sense of the ways archetypes function in our everyday experiences. The dynamic of the archetype is that it grabs you and moves you; the archetype concept helps us think about the imaginal processes in our own personal lives, and in the life of our culture. In Hillman's compelling approach, we get in touch with archetypes by paying attention to them. We may grasp the character of an archetype by spending time imaginatively dwelling on it, carefully describing the image, focusing on the image while considering its meanings, fathoming how the image is uniquely necessary, experiencing the rich depths of the image. It is an exercise in reflection and understanding.[30] In this study of largely American examples we will follow this path to delve into the various workings of the trickster image.

What are some quintessential qualities of America related to the trickster theme? Rebelliousness, unruly independence, playfulness, and individualistic liberty might be a good way to start. The trickster is the spirit of life's trickiness personified. What qualities are involved in acts of the trickster, what qualities are associated with the ones being tricked? Can we observe the trickster in our own inner psyche experiences, and in public figures acting out dramas, too, in the daily news? What are some American examples of the imagination being caught up in the trickster archetype? Considering examples from American history, and sketching some stories in folk culture, gives us rich materials to begin answering these questions. First, on this continent of North America sometimes called Turtle Island, let's consider Native American stories.

First Nations Trickster Examples: Coyote, Raven, Twins, Kokopelli

Tricksters are known by their deeds. Native American traditions are subtly attuned to the ways of nature and the traits of animals. All the creatures living on earth have characteristic activities. The young of all species play. Birds sing, cows chew their cuds, panthers pounce, whales hum ragas. Hyenas, loons, and jackals laugh. If we observe animals closely we recognize that animals often have some qualities associated with tricksters. Being alive, they are quirky. Kittens and puppies are fascinating, as so many videos and huge audiences can attest. They do spontaneously funny, unpredictable things, such as backflips and fake-outs. They entertain us because they are playful, and they entertain the impulses of life itself residing within them. Living creatures have their fateful inclinations: squiggly tadpoles become sleek frogs; caterpillars become butterflies. Jackdaws steal shiny ribbons to line their nests. Cats tease dogs; dogs train us to take good care of them. Laughing loons echo maniacally, flying over lakes in the night. Raccoons wear bandit masks and wash their food (stolen from your garden) before eating it. Mother partridge limps, faking a broken wing to distract attention from her vulnerable chicks. Some creatures come with structurally built-in tricks—squids and octopi squirt obfuscating ink and change their colors, hedgehogs extend needles, skunks spray smell, puffer fish and cats swell up to appear larger than they actually are. A fox can attract a cat by rolling on its back, feet in the air, like a playful kitten, and then kill and eat the cat. Orchids deceptively lure male pollinators (wasps and bees) with forms and odors like females insects. There is deceit and seduction in the ways fireflies blink their lights to signal mates—these are tricks of allurement and procreation. There are male squids and fish who are female impersonators. There are many manipulative sidesteps employed in the struggle for survival. Like nature's camouflage using misleading displays of optical illusions to get an advantage while expending little energy, human tricksters sometimes use costumes too—such as Ku Klux Klan robes or other impressive or weird garb—to spread fear and awe. They may also use awe-inspiring props and vehicles as signs of prestige, or they exploit photo-op scenery, or employ the best makeup artists of the day to their advantage. In all events, the closer we look the more we can see nature as a drama of tricky creatures. California ground squirrels chew sloughed snakeskins and lick themselves to keep rattlesnakes from detecting their presence by means of odor. This behavior has been confirmed by recent research. Creatures can't always run for cover, so nature evolves ways for them to hide inside an illusion. Toads and frogs can resemble leaves and bark, and katydids can look like lichen. Certain orchids bloom like dead animal flesh to use scavenger flies for pollination. Caterpillars with striking symmetrical markings can resemble fierce eyes. The tiger moth clicks like a poisonous type of moth that bats avoid. Fungus can grow in the shape of termite eggs, to fool termites and escape removal.[31]

In nature, and in the performances of tricksters, bold and sly behavior appears in response to threats and opportunities, and in displays of colorful plumage and noisy strutting. Coyotes exploit circumstances, adapt and survive. They possess a mystique of escape, of life in the margins, howling laughter beyond machinations that would trap or reduce them. They have come to stand for freedom, and freedom's potential foolishness and wisdom. Native American stories feature animals, such as Coyote, as beings full of irrepressible trickster spirit. Crazy, klutzy, ingenious, lucky and funny, Coyote, and Raven, and Hare, are full of life. In Native American stories they are vital with quirks of inevitability and uncanny genius.

The trickster plays tricks. In all play, from making faces and engaging in shadow play to writing poetry and waging wars, the fake-out, where one thing gets an advantage by looking like another, is a basic ploy. Playing possum, feigning left and going right, using camouflage, and exploiting confusion of all kinds, winners can laugh at losers, and say, "I fooled you," as Lead Belly sings in his song "Rock Island Line."[32] The trickster epitomizes wiliness, wildness, the wilderness in us, and the bewilderedness of being alive. The trickster embodies the mystery of instinct, the dailiness of hunger, the base quirkiness of libido, the self-centeredness of aggression, the foxiness of bargaining, the poignant craziness of audacious hopes and dreams. Coyote's jaunty trot is brisk, not lingering too long in any one place, but hotfooting it out of there as quickly as he came. Coyote has good eyes, a knowing tongue, sharp-pointed ears, an alert and curious sharp-pointed nose with a sixth sense for food. He's always moving on. Hip Coyote cases the joint; as he enters the scene he plans his escape route, as he makes his smart moves he acts dumb; he is aggressive-submissive, as if to say: "I don't want any trouble, I'm just passing through; chase me and I'll have to bite you. Don't mess with me."

Coyote may give an impression of being unruly, but paradoxically, there were traditionally exact and exacting rules of storytelling that had to be strictly followed in some tribes that kept the Coyote stories alive for centuries. Coyote myths were to be told only between the first frost and the first thunderstorm each year. This rule would confine the activity to a time of the year when attention was not needed for agriculture. Two other people who knew the story were required to be present. This rule would tend to keep the tradition true to the inherited ways of the past, because the people present could correct each other in retelling the story from memory. A Coyote story could be told by a person only once during any given storytelling season. This provision would give added focus and cause each tale to be specially prized. Coyote may seem to act on whim, but the traditional North American depictions of his acts are anything but random. He's crazy like a fox.[33]

In the Pacific Northwest there is an Indian story of how Coyote became cunning. It begins with life's origins. At the beginning of time, the Puget Sound Salish tribes say, Old Man Above created fishes and other creatures; then he created man. He gave this first man the job of deciding the respective statuses of the various creatures. The man responded with the plan of giving each animal a bow at the dawn of the next day, and decided that the length of the bow would indicate each one's rank. Coyote heard of this plan and thought to himself: "If I stay awake all night I'll get the advantage; I'll be first in line and get the longest bow." Listening in the dark to hoots of owl, howls of wolf, and flapping wings of bats, Coyote struggled to stay awake. But a little before sunrise, just when the robin and thrush were beginning to sing, Coyote dozed off and soon was sound asleep. He awoke to find he'd overslept—he was now last in line instead of first as he'd planned, and he received from the man the shortest bow of all, signifying the least status. Coyote grew bitter at being reduced to the meanest of all creatures, and he howled miserably, lamenting his unjust fate. The man heard the howls and turned to Old Man Above and appealed for a blessing for Coyote to ameliorate his misery. So Old Man Above decided that Coyote should be the most cunning of all the creatures on earth.[34] Thus Coyote, thinking so highly of himself, went to one extreme to win importance, but then through a failure of willpower arrived at the other extreme, as least important. But by receiving the boon of being most cunning, he at least becomes most of something—the most tricky, most unpredictable, most quirky with a cleverness that baffles and sometimes backfires. The story explains his trait of slyness with a kind of justice that comes from outside the rules of the contest—as is fitting for a trickster. We can't always get what we want—we get what we need.

As the most cunning creature, Coyote had a part to play in the unfolding of life on earth.

Coyote was a friend of the first people, and he wished the comforts of warmth and happiness for them. But in the beginning of time the sole fire on earth was up on a mountaintop where horrible Skookums—monster spirits—were keeping it from general use. Coyote therefore went around from place to place and met with various animals and garnered promises of help from them, and then he skulked up the mountainside, took a chance, and stole the fire. A horrible Skookum ran after Coyote and grabbed his tail, which has always been white ever since that fateful moment. Then Wolf took over the carrying of the fire from Coyote, and so the Skookum ran after him, but Wolf transferred the fire to Squirrel. Fire burned the back of Squirrel's neck and curled up his tail. Then Frog took the fire from Squirrel. The Skookum grabbed for Frog and kept his tail, which was never seen again. Frog spit the fire deep into wood, and it went far inside the wood and stayed there. Coyote taught the Indians the great trick—how to get fire back out of wood by rubbing two dry sticks together.[35] Rebellious god Prometheus, a trickster in Greek myth, also stole fire from the gods, gave it to man, and was punished. Coyote thus dramatizes life's necessary qualities of responsiveness, clever adaptiveness, and resilience.

In some stories about the origins, when there was only water everywhere, Coyote asked ducks to dive deep and see what could be found. After three tries one came up with some mud. Then Coyote had something he could work with. He blew on the bit of dirt and it grew. But the ducks said plain dirt was too barren, and so Coyote created plants, and also valleys and mountains, men and women, and creatures like elk and bear, and he named them. Then Coyote killed a monster who was devouring all the animals. He out-tricked the monster by getting inside his stomach and setting it on fire, thereby liberating his friends from peril.[36] Sometimes in playing tricks, Coyote would find that the joke was on him and he would get killed, and then Fox and the birds would have to bring him back to the world of the living. A trickster may seem finished, but then come back, ready for more. Coyote brings a breath of irreverence to rituals. After a serious ritual gathering of the Chumash tribe of California, including the traditional Kakunupamawa (rabbit) dance, when the last dancers are finishing, a dancer comes out dressed as Coyote, mimicking and mocking the other dancers. Then he lifts his loincloth and produces excrement, and he points to it and says, "Everything just done in these dances is there." Thus, Coyote with his irrepressible laughter brings everything back down to earth. Coyote appears at the sacred rituals to remind people not to take themselves too seriously.[37] Coyote by turns is a bully and a nuisance, a greedy dupe, yet also a heroic helper who bestows wisdom, provides food and gives man fire. The trickster in many traditions is a fluid tripster, moving through various circumstances, by turns cautious and sly, daring and crazy, blending in and sneaking out, making the scene and then going unseen. In modern times Wily Coyote cartoons play out tricky scenarios, and real-life coyotes still survive near suburbia and urban corridors, by being survivalists, clever predators, and cunning scavengers. They do whatever it takes to stay alive.

Raven is another trickster character, very important in the stories of the First Nations of the Pacific Northwest. Raven has an odd grandeur and uncanny powers, but is also sketchy, shady, shifty, dodgy; he is quirky with vitality, moved by impulses and appetites, wandering aimlessly in hopes of satisfying his hungers. In origin stories there is often a certain wildness, with shifting shapes and transformations, a vision of cosmic extravagance. In the story told by the Haida people of what is now British Columbia, Raven, in order to trick the old man who is hoarding the light at the beginning of creation and depriving the universe of illumination, first becomes a cedar needle. Swallowed by the old man's daughter, cedar needle-Raven grows inside her, becoming a male fetus. When the boy is born he steals the hidden light of the universe from inside the boxes where the girl's father has it enclosed. Then he becomes a raven again, flying and releasing the light to fill the world—the sun, moon, and stars.[38] Raven is ambiguous, the necessary agent of change in the cosmos, yet subject to suffering and disasters, stumbling and delusions.

Raven's character presents a funny combination of aspects, like the soul. Like the soul, he is always getting into troubling predicaments, then through necessity finding a way out.

Raven embodies the mysterious life-force, the quirky spirit of life with its appetites, transformations, mistakes, and successes. His cleverness is quirky as life itself, which always breaks out of galling limitations and overcomes obstacles. Suffering setbacks, driven by hungers, funny and clever, yet grotesque and awkward, Raven prevails. Raven is able to get out of dead-end corners and cramped quarters, and he is at home in the wide sky. He is daring and brave, a lonely wanderer, skulking on a beach in a blue funk, entangled in lives and destinies, busy, goofy, and shrewd. He is resilient and makes improvisational moves by taking non-linear leaps into the unknown. In the Northwest great new artworks and storytellers keep Raven in people's minds, and so do the skills and impulsive acts of the sleek black ravens seen in the sky. Native American trickster Crazy Hare became Warner Brothers cartoon character Bugs Bunny (or in the dialect of Elmer Fudd, "that wacky wascally wabbit!"). Chippewas say their culture hero Nanabohzo changed himself into Crazy Hare in primordial times, before the people had fire. Crazy Hare allowed himself to be caught by the sole woman who possessed fire, and she pitied him because he looked so bedraggled, drenched with the waters of Lake Superior. She let Hare get dry by standing near her fire, and when sparks landed on his skin he ran to the Chippewas and gave them fire. Ever since then rabbits have turned brown in the summer, they say, in memory of Nanabohzo being burnt in his act of sharing fire, and become white again each winter.

In Disney cartoons Bugs Bunny's smart-aleck smirk, his teasing and bullying, his ability to morph and his defiance of authority make him fascinating to children and adults alike. He seems like a bozo willing to do anything for a laugh—wisecracking, cross-dressing, and double-crossing. One of his famous lines is, "Ain't I a stinker?" He became a symbol of American pluck in the face of Hitler's Nazism during World War II. Because Bugs showed an impudent, indomitable gumption in going against all odds he was chosen as mascot by four Air Force bombardment squadrons. His trickster's flippant insouciance was the spirit men flying into danger needed.

We note in passing that Turtle and other Native American tricksters are important in some tribes' traditions, though due to space constraints we are unable to discuss them here.[39]

The twin trickster brothers in Winnebago stories are also important. All across the Americas there are Indian stories of this duo. We will focus on one story told by the Winnebago tribes as an example. In the early times, Father-in-law Ogre committed murder, taking the life of his pregnant daughter-in-law. His acts are gruesome. He opens her belly and takes out two infants—the twin brothers. One he tosses into a dark corner of the lodge, the other he places out in the hollow of an old tree stump. When the father of the twins comes back he discovers the child, known as Fleshy, in the corner of the lodge, and he raises him. The other one, Stumpy, comes out of his hollow tree and then the two reunited brothers play around together. When the father sees there are two of them he grabs Stumpy. He warns both his sons that there are certain places of danger where they need to be wary. The twins are mischievous rascals, and they have extraordinary powers. They kill various snakes, leeches, thunderbirds, and the ogre who killed their mother. They visit Earthmaker, the Creator, and, as tricksters always do, they wander around; they destroy a beaver, who is one of the foundation posts of the earth. Earthmaker is disturbed by the twins' mischief and dispatches a runner who delivers the message that they should stop their incessant roaming around.[40] Note how the brothers of precarious origins wander around and have powers to kill monsters and disturb cosmic order. They raise questions, shake things up, and give rise to new arrangements and situations. These are typical attributes of mythical tricksters around the world—they disrupt the order of things, bring change and new perspectives.

We can see the brothers archetype in many American stories, both literary and historical, once we are on the lookout for it. Huck and Jim become blood brothers. Consider also Cal and Aron in *East of Eden*, Rocky and Tayo in *Ceremony*, Terry and Charley Malloy in *On the Waterfront*, Happy and Biff Loman in *Death of a Salesman*, J. R. and Bobby in *Dallas*. Examples of brother-like pairs in popular fiction include Joe Buck and Ratso Rizzo in the film *Midnight Cowboy*, the title characters in the TV show *Starsky and Hutch*, the comic book and movie characters Batman and Robin, and Nick Carroway and Jay Gatsby in *The Great Gatsby*. Real life brothers who are dynamic duos include the Coen brothers and the Farrelly brothers (filmmakers), the Koch brothers and Hunt brothers (financiers), and the Smothers brothers (comics). Perhaps famous friend pairs like Emerson and Thoreau, and Kerouac and Ginsberg, should also be considered in this area—they instigate and help each other, debate and complete each other, like trickster brothers.[41]

Glooskap, (or Guskab), who is a trickster high God—the gigantic hero deity of the Abanaki, Algonquin, Penobscot, and Wabanaki—also killed monsters. (As we shall see, American frontier folk hero Davy Crockett was also a trickster who slew monsters.[42]) Glooskap enjoys smoking and is said to be able to hold his smoke more than anyone else. Mt. Katahdin, the highest mountain in what is now Maine, is sacred—to travel to the crest is taboo.

Pamola, an angry trickster, was sent by Glooskap to guard Mt. Katahdin, and to prevent intruders from encroaching upon that sacred space. Trickster stories like these alerted Indians to be respectful of sacred powers and watchful of life's unexpected twists and turns.

One more example is useful to consider here: Kokopelli, the ancient flute-playing life-spirit or fertility god and trickster of the Southwest Native American tribes. Images of his crescent-moon shaped body inscribed on pottery and stone have survived for at least 3,000 years. His profile seems to show him with a humpback, but this may be a bag of seeds he carried (a sort of proto-Johnny Appleseed) to plant useful vegetation on barren ground. Symbolic of the mystery of sex, life, and fertility, Kokopelli is often shown sporting a large male sexual organ. Ho-Chunk stories say his penis is detachable; he can magically leave it in a river and have sex with girls when they wade in to swim and bathe. The Hopis say Kokopelli, god of fertility and music, bears on his back the children who have not yet been born, giving them to the women who become pregnant.[43] (Perhaps this story has some roots in the memories of Aztec traders who in ancient times announced their arrival and advertised their presence in villages with flute music.) Kokopelli's quirky figure may also represent a primordial insect who in ancient stories was shot with an arrow and demonstrated the ability to survive, self-heal, and make music.[44]

The enigmatic Kokopelli is memorable—his zigzaggy full-body dancer silhouette says it all—his image is a favorite in Southwestern designs. Even without definite stories his popularity grows and grows. Kokopelli shares some traits with Hermes the Greek trickster god of music, seduction, commerce, and intercultural activities like translation/interpretation.

Raven, Coyote, Twin Brothers, Kokopelli, all are vibrant with the instinctive life spirit. Their actions are dynamic like lightning, with creative quirky energy and ribald humor. Like tricksters in myths worldwide, they have an aura of poignant vitality, and are timeless players in the dramas of the psyche.

With intelligence, plus instinct, plus mysterious vitality, plus a twist of quirkiness, the trickster in stories old and new is often too smart for his own good. Now brilliant, now addlepated, he's got wit and he moves the plot along, but the joke is often on him. Teasing, making mischief, fast-talking and mercurial, the trickster thickens life's plots and plays his part by embodying free play.

Yankee Doodle: The Resilient Yankee Dude'll Do

Yankee Doodle is an old American trickster figure related to quirks of life in the New World. Yankee Doodle originated in phases; first there was a British army band playing a song with the words "Yankee Doodle" in it at a harvest festival in the Hudson valley in 1768. The lyrics had an anti-American slant meaning something like "The stupid American, Yankee Doodle, foolishly stuck a feather in his cap and called it 'macaroni.'" One meaning of "macaroni" is that it was slang for the latest fashions from foppishly stylish Italy. Later, the song was adopted and adapted by the rebels themselves; it was played back tauntingly to mock the British while they were laying down their arms in battles at Yorktown and Saratoga, surrendering to "Yankee" forces. At that point when the American upstarts were rubbing it in, the king's men began to realize that Yankee Doodle wasn't just some goofy kid trying to yank their noodles, but someone they had better take more seriously. The song thus was a bit of cultural matter that migrated from the enemy side and was inventively transformed for new uses by revolutionary Americans to rub British noses in their own arrogant foolishness.[45] The picked-on kid was getting revenge on the bullies.

In presenting some traditions of the Yankee here I am drawing on the foundational work of the great scholar of American humor and folklore, Constance Rourke. Rourke noted that the Yankee figure emerged from the Puritan ethos—a moral mood and atmosphere of belief and outlook specific to New England, and that the character of the Yankee was shaped in a society governed by Puritanism. The Yankee grew out of that regional scene, but developed beyond it and became something more than a rural New Englander. The Yankee personality matured to become a representative American. Royall Tyler (1757–1826) wrote a play entitled "The Contrast," which was the first American comedy performed in a public venue by a company of professional actors. Opening in 1787, it was also the first original literary work to present a typical lanky Yankee, featuring an American character named Brother Jonathan, who contrasted in the folk mind with the stocky and stodgy conservative Britisher caricature known as "John

Bull." Jonathan was the trim New Englander, an early representative American, a figure eventually taken over by the folk symbol of Uncle Sam, who is also a gangly Yankee. Abroad, eventually all Americans became known as Yankees, as demonstrated by the yelled or scrawled anti-American protest slogan "Yankee go home."[46]

Rourke observed that like the song "Yankee Doodle" and its many verses, the caricature of the Yankee emerged from American folk experiences. (In *The Contrast*, Brother Jonathan sings some verses of "Yankee Doodle," and says he knows 190 verses of the song.) It was as if the people experiencing life in northeastern colonies and states felt the need to express what it was like to be them and gave birth to this new figure in the folk imagination. As if waiting in the wings for his cue, the Yankee figure leapt out into full-blown expression in the figure of Yankee Doodle, and in portrayal in Tyler's play. From a regional expression of American personality the figure was launched into higher standing as a national folk symbol.[47] A kind of hero of the imagination, impudent and individualistic, youthful, free, fun loving, stalwart, and high-spirited, the Yankee has an attractive jauntiness. Rourke noted that this new American folk character, the Yankee, resembled in some ways the English prototype of the "Yorkshireman," who was known for his warmth and friendliness but also for being stubborn and argumentative. The American figure was more lively, sharper, and shrewder than the stuffier English folk figure. He had a knowing wit and a New World personality, a dry drawl, a manner all his own, as he became more and more distinct and prominent in the imagination a little before the beginning of the Revolutionary War. In *The Contrast* the Yankee's trick is to refuse to conform to European-dictated fashions, and to use smart-aleck language. He's fluent in clever colloquial American speech, with a knack for using the latest lingo of the day. He is rough, too natural to have the artificial graces of city folk, and is likeable and not phony. He is not a manipulator, but is light-hearted and colorfully honest. He asserts his independence: "a true blue son of liberty . . . No man shall master me,"[48] showing the early sense of anti-authoritarian independence, a heritage which perhaps some Americans today have forgotten in the quest for safety and security.

The catchy song that soon became a great revolutionary rallying cry, "Yankee Doodle" celebrated the obstreperous freedom-vowed Yankee youth. Rourke noted that this song's "jigging tune" itself suggests "some of the complexity of the Yankee character," and its lively beat is a reminder that ought to dispel the falsehood "that Puritans suppressed all music and dance."[49] Lively nonsense lyrics ("Stuck a feather in his cap and called it macaroni") of the Yankee Doodle song immortalize the funny trickster's impudence and rebel spirit at the origins of American independence. The word "macaroni" was rich with suggestions at this time.[50]

The folk figure "Jonathan[51] the Yankee," seen in newspaper caricatures and other visual forms, came out of a Puritan background, hailing from somewhere in old New England. He had a reputation for being versatile, a clever peddler, a clockmaker, and a whittler. He is adept as a tinker, a mechanic, a lively character on the rural scene. He was of the generation that generally grew up outside the confines of strict Calvinism.[52] Rourke notes that the portrayal of Jonathan in cartoons and writings would not have been a public success if it had not been a feature of life recognizable by audiences—a familiar and likable personality with likenesses in many a neighborhood. The character represented the liveliest American personality publicly presentable at the time.[53] This New England folk character was the dominant and winning American image among a few other stereotypical American folk figures portrayed on stages and in cartoons of the time, such as the Backwoodsman, the Negro, the Irishman, the Pennsylvania Dutch, the Shaker, the Quaker, and the Western hunter. Jonathan the Yankee went beyond them all in his vitality, likeability, and winning ways. His surefooted stance and quick-stepping versatility in the New World won him a place in people's hearts. He belonged to an American people less straitlaced than the Pilgrim Fathers, more footloose and irreverent. The Yankee in cartoons and caricatures is associated with use of satire.[54] Satire, a medium that is lively and entertaining, is a trickster style, mocking others and one's own foibles. It tickles and nudges us with the startling remarks of someone fun to be with. Satire glances around lightly and quickly to give mercurial perspectives, not a stodgy old repetition of one way, over and over. That certain Yankee jauntiness with take-charge confidence, seeming brash, fun and capable, has long marked Americans at their best. "Brother Jonathan" came to mean "Yankee" for another reason as well. Jonathan Trumbull was governor of Connecticut during the Revolutionary War, and being a capable and cagey leader, he was entrusted by General George Washington with tricky responsibilities. Washington's referring of problems to "Brother Jonathan" caused the New England region to identify with the Jonathan nickname for Yankee ingenuity. The association suggested that a Yankee was more of a clever rogue than a fool, a witty man with common sense. The early idea of a Yankee was also that of a pack-peddler selling his wares as he traveled, smart in business and using wit in his talk.[55] The folk mind usually thinks of peddlers, pitchmen, drummers, and hucksters as tricksters—because they often are. Emerson admired New England Yankee adaptability. "A sturdy lad from New Hampshire or Vermont, who in turn tries all the professions, who teams it, farms it, peddles, keeps a school, preaches, edits a newspaper, goes to Congress, buys a township . . . and always like a cat falls on his feet, is worth a hundred of those city dolls," Emerson wrote. Why? "He has not one chance, but a hundred chances."[56]

Early American Yankee peddlers were known as a tricky lot. They traveled ceaselessly, selling "notions" and tin plates, and cheating customers (for example, selling wooden nutmeg). Some of them wore out their welcome, and so could not return to the same neighborhoods. In time peddlers opted for more reliable relationships based on bonds of trust and good reputation, rather than reaping one-time profits. The Yankee peddler, after a few entrepreneurial detours and gigs as showman and shifty businessman, ended up as a robber baron around 1900. In fact, some would say that the sixty tycoon families who soon ruled the American roost,[57] in many important financial, political and cultural matters, largely came from peddler and tricky tradesman origins. But before turning to examples of American tricksters in the form of robber barons, hustlers and con men, let's consider the great American folk hero Davy Crockett.

Davy Crockett: Local Yokel Comic and Cosmic Trickster God

The Davy Crockett of some American legends resembles an old mythical trickster found in traditional cultures much more than he resembles a historical human being. Of course, before becoming the stuff of imagination and literature, a settler named Davy Crockett lived as an actual person; he became a Tennessee congressman who opposed president Andrew Jackson's Indian policy of pushing tribes westward, a policy that led to the tragedy known as "the Trail of Tears." Crockett was born in Tennessee in 1786. He was known to his neighbors as an excellent marksman and a capable frontiersman, and he successfully promoted his colorful backwoods image to win political campaigns and attain status as a regional leader. His name and legends became well known in American storytelling, embodying the outlandish comic spirit and exuberant exaggeration of backwoods settlers in the 1800s. The real Davy Crockett's heroic death at the battle of the Alamo in 1835 fastened an anchor of historic fact to the wild and stormy tales of bravado and impossibly mighty deeds spun by storytellers' imaginations.

The legendary Davy Crockett provided also image that could be exploited handily in merchandizing—for example, in the 1800s there were Davy Crockett almanacs with information on weather, sunrise times, recipes, and home remedies. These popular products featured tall tales that capitalized on his towering celebrity and added fanciful episodes to his life, perpetuating his larger-than-life image in the folk memory. Throughout the twentieth century there were motion pictures about Crockett. In the 1950s Walt Disney's TV series featuring a somewhat tamer Davy Crockett than the subject of the wild folktales brought the hero's image back to life in the public consciousness, and made coonskin caps and buckskin jackets with fringe popular among children. The show's theme song, celebrating Crockett's birth in Tennessee on a mountaintop, was known to children all over America in the mid-twentieth century. Moreover, Fess Parker, who played the Disney Crockett with masculine charisma, presented a convincing image of how to be a man on the rugged frontier and influenced a generation of males.[58]

Davy Crockett, the mythological pioneer hero of cosmic-comic exploits with supernatural powers, could perform feats far beyond normal men's ability and live to swagger and boast about them. For example, he drove a full-grown pet alligator right up Niagra Falls; and when thirsty, he drank down the whole Gulf of Mexico until it was dry. He saved the United States from certain destruction at an opportune moment by ripping the tail from Halley's Comet and hurling it back out into space. He saved the solar system by using hot bear oil to unfreeze the earth and sun when they were frozen solid and stuck in their axes. Then he walked back home and showed the folks there the fresh daylight he'd grabbed—pulling a glowing hunk of sunrise from his pocket for all to see. These are reckless prodigious feats on a gigantic scale, like the Haida Indian stories of Raven freeing the light, or like Winnebago stories of Coyote stealing fire.[59] It is as if the settlers were European tricksters who not only stole the land from the Native Americans, but also pilfered their stories. Crockett in tall tales is also associated with images of gargantuan proportions, like the mythic American logger Paul Bunyan.[60] As a newborn, Crockett was said to have been the largest and smartest baby around in his day; he was fed on whisky and rattlesnake eggs as a growing

child. He slept with his head on an alligator-hide pillow stuffed with Indian scalps. He sometimes sounds like a one-man National Wrestling Federation athlete from back in the day. At age six he slew three wolves, and by age eight he weighed in at a staggering 200 pounds. Davy treed a ghost, fought Indians, and exhibited talents that matched the attributes of animals and natural forces: he could walk like an ox, run like a fox, swim like an eel, yell like an Indian, fight like the devil, spout like an earthquake, and make love like a wild bull. Just as King Arthur owned a sword named "Excalibur," Davy had a knife named "the Butcher." He owned a rifle named "Killdevil," and his dogs were named "Tiger," "Grizzle," and "Rough." He wrestled and beat a bear named "Death Hug." Crockett had affinities with Coyote, and other tricksters, as well—he killed monsters with ease, but was sometimes cowardly as well as heroic. Sometimes, like many other Americans in the 1800s, he was brutally racist. He represents rowdy feats that the era's folktale imagination delighted in dreaming up, portraying an American who could play roughly with the wild world around him. It was as if recognizing there are great fluid possibilities in life, and believing that wild desires can come true, Americans dreamed up a natural hero easily capable of overcoming dangers, and joking about the wonders he performed.[61] In the folk mind here was a man to match America's mountains.

Davy Crockett, according to an often-told tale, was short on money once while on the campaign trail, and needed rum badly to satisfy his voters' thirsts while he was "speechifying" before them. So, first he went into a saloon and traded his coonskin cap for a jug of liquor. But that wasn't enough to quench the voters' thirsts, so he had to get more rum. In all, this man with a mission went back ten times, retrieving his coonskin cap from behind the bar each time and selling it again to the dim-witted bartenders.

The mythic Crockett devoutly despised the Yankee peddler, almost as if he was a natural enemy contending for supremacy in the folk imagination. In one story a sly Yankee sold Davy a horse he already owned, and sold Davy's wife a clock that would neither stand up nor tick. Crockett saw Yankees as roaring hypocrites in their views on slavery. To Davy, the Yankee was a big pain in the neck, an untrustworthy nemesis. He said the Yankee was the kind of person who would put delicious-looking painted wooden bacon strips on his own dinner plate to learn the virtues of self-denial, instead of satisfying his natural appetites like a real he-man, as Davy did.[62] If we were to think in a cartoon-like fashion, today Crockett might be thought of as granddaddy of folks in the red states, and the Yankee might be ancestor of latte-drinking, sushi-eating blue state liberals with their Priuses and arugula. But those caricatures are too simple to be very useful.

The historical person named Davy Crockett was skillful at the trick of reinventing himself as a personage American-style. Self-promotion is an old American tradition in some parts, necessary to survival. Just as Whitman wrote reviews of his own book of poems, and Mailer wrote *Advertisements for Myself*, Crockett publicized his exploits in books, using outlandish homespun language to tell tall tales associating his own name with superhuman tricks and good old boy jokes. He developed and promoted a salable image of himself. As country singers might joke, he became a legend in his own mind.

So, if any had doubts, Davy Crockett shows us that the figure of the backwoods white man pioneer could also become a major league imaginal trickster. As such, he was revered with delight in the mainstream American imagination, and apotheosized into a figure of larger-than-life celebrity glory and cosmic power. Perhaps, overall, the unruly Davy Crockett tales were an outlet for wild hooligan spirits of the rough-and-ready wilderness days when the maverick-style frontier joker was running wild and was widely admired. There were silent movies made about Crockett in 1909, 1916, and 1926. In 1937, 1939, 1950, and 1953 there were feature-length "talkies" about him, and since then there have been several Alamo movies in which he was portrayed. "The Ballad of Davy Crockett," a song that was popular in the 1950s, features lines about Crockett fighting single-handedly in several wars, until the foe was defeated and peace established, and then, improving the government, as well as the laws, taking over the nation's capital and fixing the Liberty Bell. It is almost as if the song depicts the mighty Crockett as an omnipotent savior figure. Americans love their democracy, but also love the "king of the wild frontier." His motto was "Always be sure you're right, then go ahead." Davy Crockett gloried in being not just a boisterous rowdy, but in the ability to be the quintessential can-do frontiersman, up to any challenge, as tricky as any man could be.

In the modern age he was honored with the namesake of the M-388 Davy Crockett, the smallest nuclear weapon in the American arsenal, a recoil-less rifle projectile that was produced starting in 1956, and was deployed with Army forces from 1961 to 1971. The M-388 Davy Crockett brought the magical power of pioneer fantasies into the nuclear age with a bang, representing a force not to be underestimated. His story is still sung.[63]

The Naked Lady Scam and Others: The Trickster Does the Hustle

As I discussed earlier, in the beginning the white Puritans landed at Plymouth Rock and grimly set about building their sober civilization, which they hoped would be a city on a hill blessed by God. It is a common view that "the Puritan stands in thin-lipped contrast to the American confidence man."[64] Yet there were some tricksters in early America, and there were some Puritans who loved their earthy pleasures, too. Naturally there were scams regarding money in its various forms, including wampum, as I said. While wampum had a number of important uses for the Indians, it had only a monetary one for the colonial settlers in the seventeenth century. For the Europeans it was a valuable medium of exchange, as were gold, furs, and tobacco. (Cured tobacco became a medium of exchange especially in colonial Virginia.) Dutch traders in the New World began accepting wampum as a money substitute in 1627. One New York Dutch trader took some wampum to Plymouth, Massachusetts, and by 1640 wampum was an accepted medium of exchange for the Massachusetts colony. Four white beads were worth a penny.

Wampum continued to serve as tender for transactions among Indians and New England colonists almost until the end of the seventeenth century.[65] By around 1750 the exchange of wampum was in decline, and many Indians preferred to receive silver when they traded their furs. After the Indian stopped valuing wampum highly the colonists phased it out. But in its heyday Wampum was, in the words of New England economic historian William Babcock Weeden, "the magnet which drew the beaver out of the interior forests." Greed for wampum tempted trickster Indians and whites to make fake beads.[66]

Other scams were also part of life in early America. Old newspapers and pamphlets sometimes featured outraged complaints about cunning impostors. For example, a long piece was published in 1788 in New Jersey, "An account of the beginning, transactions and discovery of Ransford Rogers who seduced many by pretended Hobgoblins and Apparitions, and thereby extorted Money from their pockets in the County of Morris and State of New Jersey 1788."[67] The narrator describes how the "Judas-like" trickster pretended to communicate with spirits who said they were sent to give great riches, if only given the money requested first.[68]

A piece in an 1801 Massachusetts newspaper describes a charity scam in Salem, Massachusetts. "A fellow has been about this town and vicinity for some time past, with a paper, asking charity, and representing that he has been a prisoner in Algiers, and has had his tongue cut out there. He has the art of managing his tongue in such a manner as to have the appearance of having been cut; but it has been found that good liquor will restore it to its proper form, and set it to running glibly. On Saturday he was taken up and committed to gaol [jail] for an examination."[69]

Another scam of the 1800s was the naked damsel scam, in which a poor innocent girl turns up naked and needs help from the strangers who find her. Who could withhold sympathy from a clothesless girl found bound and gagged, defenseless and in such desperate need? One example of this scam was the discovery of a girl found outside the cabin of an old German couple in the town of Jersey Shore, Pennsylvania. Claiming to have been beaten and robbed, the girl attracted much sympathy, and a compassionate minister took her in and informed the local populace of her misfortune. She was clothed and fed, received many gifts; then she skipped town, never to be heard from again.

In 1918 there was another scam reported in a New York paper, involving "a man of uncommon large body stretched at full length on the street." There, he attracted the attention of an elderly woman and other passersby, speaking "in the high Dutch language." The man said he had been in the navy and had fallen from the yardarm of a man-of-war ship. The injured man seemed to be at death's door, and the woman asked him questions and the gathering crowd became sympathetic. Money was raised from the crowd to have the man carried to a hospital, and seeming to be almost dead he was carried away by four volunteers. But before he arrived at the hospital, the man removed from his clothes the stuffing that had made him look so large, and then jumped down from the conveyance with agility and speedily "made his way off with the fruits of the public charity in his pocket."[70]

In this and in other nineteenth-century records we see that the white Anglo-Saxon con artist practicing chicanery was at least a memorable small part of rugged frontier life. Or maybe it was a larger part than we recognize. Nelson Algren called early Chicago "a drafty hustlers' junction," and wrote that

> Yankee and voyager, the Irish and Dutch, Indian traders and Indian agents, halfbreed and quarterbreed and no breed at all, in the final counting they were all of a single breed. They all had hustler's blood. They hustled the land, they hustled the Indian, they hustled by night and they hustled by day. They hustled guns and furs and peltries, grog and the blood-red whiskey-dye; they hustled with dice or a deck or a derringer. And decided the Indians were wasting every good hustler's time.... They'd do anything under the sun except work for a living, and we remember them reverently... as "Founding Fathers," "Dauntless Pioneers,"

or "Far-Visioned Conquerors." Meaning merely they were out to make a fast buck off whoever was standing nearest."[71]

Was Algren being honest or jaundiced? If life in the growing urban areas seemed a hustle in the nineteenth century, it was even more unregulated beyond the settled centers. The lure of lighting out for "the territory" was attractive to some adventurers especially because it meant a chance to go outside the law, to break from the past, to not honor older customary norms and staid regulations. Instead, it was an opportunity to hustle. The restless West still attracts boomtown fortune hunters with both vague and detailed promises of paradise, or at least some prospect of a better life.

Each state has its own legendary tricksters. In Pennsylvania there were "log pirates" who snagged some of the logs sent floating down the Susquehanna river by upstream loggers. The log pirates removed all signs of ownership, sedulously sawing off the brands burnt into the wood. They were nicknamed "Algerines," for the famous Barbary pirates of Algiers. In Michigan, sly White Pine Tom sold fish by the pound to lumber camps. He filled some fish with sand to add weight. When caught, Tom denied any guilt, saying the fish ate the sand to use as ballast, so they could swim around on the bottom of the lake more easily. In the Ozarks, hunters had a trick they used when they went bear hunting. They injured the bear to make him angry enough to chase them home, saving them the trouble of hauling the carcass through the wilderness. Then after the bear had limped after them in wounded pursuit, nearing their home destination, they would kill the bear. Timothy Dexter was an eccentric Massachusetts tanner who liked to put on airs and made an ostentatious show of his wealth, earning him ridicule and resentment. To play a prank on him once, some trickster merchant's clerks talked him into sending a large number of oddly shaped warming pans with long handles to the West Indies. When they arrived and looked unusable to storekeepers there, Dexter, using his Yankee ingenuity, called them "skimmers." He told the storekeepers the pans were made especially for sugar-makers' needs, and they soon became all the rage in the West Indies.

Abolitionist John Brown, before leading his famous rebellion in the year 1859, collected money by saying it would be used for the welfare of slaves, but he spent it buying guns—definitely not what his Quaker donors had in mind. Wealthy abolitionists agreed to offer Brown financial support for his surreptitious antislavery activities. In December 1858, Brown undertook a raid to liberate eleven slaves, and at that time he stole horses and wagons. In October 1859, Brown made a daring surprise attack on the Harper's Ferry Armory, West Virginia, a storehouse of 100,000 muskets and rifles, which was guarded by one watchman. Brown sought to arm slaves, begin an insurrection that would free the slaves of Virginia and cause a collapse of the system of slavery. Historians consider his daring tactics a catalyst for the Civil War, tricks to pull the rug out from under the culture of slave labor in America. Local militia men pinned Brown and his accomplices down in the armory. He was tried for treason and convicted. Brown said he was following the teachings of the Bible. Without fortitude and conscience from religion, he would not have tried his underhanded tricks. Emerson, Thoreau, and Whitman praised him.

Ben Delimus fought on the side of the North during the Civil War. After the war he went to Alabama and specialized in tricking gullible freed slaves. Telling them that baptisms performed during the time of slavery were now invalid, he charged one dollar to rebaptize them. Then he worked the same scam with remarriage. He also sold hair-straightener for one dollar a bottle. Running for political office, he used his quick tongue to get elected. Once, at a speech, when an opponent said that Delimus was the kind of man who crucified Christ, he replied that he was not around in those ancient days, and if he had been he certainly would have stopped the crucifixion posthaste. This speedy brave reply won the ex-slaves' sympathy and votes.[72]

The trickery of some southern businessmen in the antebellum South is astounding. They found a way around the law that prohibited slavery after the Civil War. They did this by using cheap convict labor to work in coal mines, to make bricks, man sawmills, lay railroad tracks, etc. For decades state officials and businessmen colluded in profiting from the forced labor of legally convicted prisoners. It was as if they were addicted to a system of slavery, and were unwilling to give up the right to treat the vulnerable inhumanely merely because it had been outlawed. They forced convicts to work under inhumane conditions, and enforced cruel punishments like flogging, torture, and murder.[73] The shameful history of the brutal use of convict labor for commercial enterprises is well documented in many southern states, including Georgia, Alabama, Mississippi, Tennessee, the Carolinas, Arkansas, Louisiana, and Texas. The convict leasing system that circumvented the laws prohibiting peonage, involuntary servitude, and slavery, went on in some states into the early twentieth century, and was practiced by some prominent men, political leaders, and illustrious families.[74] Tennessee halted profiting from the forced labor of convicts in coal mines in 1893. The convict leasing system was abolished in Georgia in 1909. Other states quit the practice in that same decade—Louisiana in 1901, Mississippi in 1907. Sometimes convicted men were put to work from sunup to sundown, but it was not unusual for them to work later into the night and to be severely punished for doing less work than the owners demanded. Most of the leased convicts who were treated worse than slaves were African Americans. The tricks played by ruthless powerful men upon powerless ones leave a scandalous stain that's hard for people of the twenty-first century to face.

Perhaps we can say that the hustler was on the scene as America was settled and has multiplied ever since. The Puritan way of straitlaced life did not prevail as America grew more populous and secular, though puritanical attitudes remained under the surface. In the 1800s, earthy Americans like Abraham Lincoln laughed at Puritan priggishness. Various ethnic backgrounds diversified the population. The diversity made an impression on American life. African slaves were brought to this new world, and Native Americans were bought off cheaply and then were pushed westward onto reservations. Both ethnicities entered deeply into the collective memory of American culture, influencing styles and attitudes. Sometimes fear of the minorities was passed along as prejudice to later generations. They tattooed the American psyche with different rhythms, rhymes, and reasons than the European ones. Diversity thickened the cultural stew, adding vital elements to the establishment. Sometimes folk elements entered mainstream literature, like the tales of tricky Br'er Rabbit, or the Wily Coyote.

Along with the honest citizens of American society came rapscallions and scallywags. Like subtle pirates, these tricksters robbed people with their pens or tongues, instead of with sharp swords. A salty old-timer might put it this way: "Before there were men called 'hustlers' there were rustlers. To be on the receiving end of rustlers' deeds meant theft of your horses, getting left with nothing but the dung. On the other hand, con man hustlers are specialists in thieving by means of trickery, diddling, dealing in loads of dung." In time the anti-Puritan, the styles of the non-square con man or hustler morphed into traits of the hipster trickster, the smooth city slicker, cool and vain, full of bright ideas, sometimes too smart for his own good. The gregarious salesman, the verbose drummer, is not so different from the fast-talking con man. Both gather fascinated people with their compelling spiels, selling things of dubious necessity. It was a matter of differences of degree, not of kind. The street peddler opens his "tripe and keister" (folding display case set up on a portable tripod) and proceeds to hawk his goods with fascinating descriptions and extravagant promises. "Step right up..." (In the age of TV, Billy Mays, with his beard and passionate loud voice, was an example of this kind of salesman.)

For a nation whose most popular folk saint is arguably none other than Elvis, it should come as no surprise that a major culture hero is the confidence man. Colonel Tom Parker, Elvis's manager, was for much of his life not too distinct from the con man hustling gullible customers, according to those familiar with his life.[75] The confidence man is a living historical variation on the theme of one aspect of the mythological trickster archetype. The shadow of the confidence man falls across the American Dream, often obscuring, distorting, and dishonoring what actually transpires in the town square, on Wall Street, and in Washington. Nothing succeeds like success in America. Perhaps the trickster con man is victim to the compulsion of succeeding at any cost. He worships at the altar of the deity sometimes called the "bitch-goddess success."[76] Such a deity promises all happiness up there around the bend when success is finally attained.

In any case, con games, like the magic tricks of stage magicians, are exercises in misdirection, ensnaring our attention with wit or other verbal flourishes, leading our focus of clarity away from the real deal, fascinating the mind with a skillful illusion, a glittering distraction.[77] Glad handing you, taking you into his confidence, the con man befriends you with a closeness you would feel like a fool not to believe in. Confiding as much as any man is humanly able, he plays upon your need to play the social parts you learned while drinking mama's milk and getting burped. He opens up with backslapping and candid sharing, which only the crusty recalcitrant and hyper-defensive can resist. He butters you up with his confidences, he babies you and mothers you, milks your gullibility, flatters and suckers you into his real deal of a world, painting what you want to see, what you just might be able to believe in. He's the real McCoy—his earnestness affirms it's all the others who are too good to be true. He's the one true one you can trust, even if it's against all odds. He won't let you down, you can trust him, have no doubts. You can confide in each other, sure. He takes you in with warmth and charm, bullying your suspicions away as they rise. "Deception requires complicity, no matter how subconscious; we want to be deceived."[78] We go along like sheep when a master persuader plies his trade.

Every scam and publicity stunt, like most advertisements, tries to cash in on the trickster arts of grabbing attention, making promises, selling a viewpoint, getting one's way by any means necessary, and making a quick buck on the sly. Think of P. T. Barnum's ingenuity. When the popular Jumbo the Elephant died while on tour, Barnum had his skin stuffed, and toured with that dummy elephant while simultaneously exhibiting the elephant's huge bones also, for four years. Two for the price of one—Jumbo was more valuable dead than alive. In 1825, when Stub Newell "discovered" and sensationalized the supposed fossilized "Cardiff Giant," a stone body weighing 2990 pounds, Barnum called it a scam and offered the public an authentic petrified giant instead. The word "Barnumizing" was coined to denote the use of hype. According to Barnumizers, some people like to be humbugged—tricked and bilked. How else can we explain their eagerness to trust the surreptitiously persuasive, syrup-titious voice of a motor-mouth spieler? Why else would their pockets be so ready to be emptied by the smiling hustler? How else could they swallow the scam of an oily-tongued tout whose propositions go down so suspiciously smoothly? Advertising is the skillful art of trickily selling dreams of satisfaction, sometimes promising treacly sweet fulfillment. There is a fine line between smart business practices and taking advantage of others by floating little white lies and bending the rules,[79] a line so fine that it often cannot be found.

Some American Con Men of Yesteryear

The trickster as clever conniver duping the gullible has been sighted often in America in recent centuries. Some of his names are still well known, while others are well forgotten. William Thompson, whose career was at its height from 1840 to 1849, was the crook whose activities first inspired the term "confidence man." His modus operandi was to engage in conversations with a passerby on the street in New York, and then ask the stranger, after gaining his confidence, if he would trust him enough to let him borrow the man's watch until the next day. Those who fell under Thompson's spell never saw their watches again. Other nineteenth-century con men include Soapy Smith (1860–1898), a famous nineteenth-century bunko artist of the Old West. One of his scams involved selling bars of soap, some of which he claimed had paper money placed inside the wrappers. Two Kentucky grifters, Philip Arnold and Jack Slack, perpetrated the great Diamond Hoax of 1872 in San Francisco. Claiming they'd found rough diamonds in Indian Territory they interested investors, roping in gullible persons of wealth, big bankers, businessmen, and VIPs, involving them all in a huge fraud.[80]

James Fisk, Jr., nicknamed "Big Jim," "Diamond Jim," "Jubilee Jim," and "the Colonel," was another well-known con man of the nineteenth century. As a child Fisk ran away from school and joined the circus, then worked as a peddler and as a salesman, and later became a stockbroker and corporate executive. In his prime during the time of Boss Tweed's reign, Fisk was known for his "financial buccaneering," and for bribing judges and lawmakers. He was called a con man by high society but was a hero loved by working class and poor people. He was involved in shady business dealings, but he acted quickly to help victims of the Chicago fire, and was celebrated for that show of kindness.

Around the turn of the twentieth century there were many disreputable sellers of cures and panaceas. Among American charlatans, John R. Brinkley (1885–1942), who implanted goat glands in human males, claiming this operation could cure impotence, was one of the most famous. He became well known as the "goat-gland doctor," and was also a pioneer of radio broadcasting in America and Mexico. He owned and operated the million watt "border blaster" station KFKB, broadcasting rock and roll when the genre was just being born, and evangelical preaching for religious audiences, and he developed sales pitches for medical treatments. With diploma-mill credentials he confidently prescribed medical treatments on the basis of descriptions of symptoms in letters that had been mailed to him.[81]

Albert Abrams (1863–1924) was the advocate of "radionics" and various other kinds of quackery, selling devices using electricity as a panacea, in the early 1900s.[82] Charles Ponzi (1882–1949) developed and perpetrated the pyramid scheme, which still bears his name.[83] Victor Lustig (1890–1947) was a smooth operator—he sold the Eiffel Tower to two different customers who were in the market for scrap metal. He scammed many victims, and tricked even powerful Mafia boss Al Capone (1899–1947), who himself was known for bold acts of duplicity. George Parker in the 1870s became famous for selling New York monuments to unsuspecting buyers. Lou Blonger organized and ran a massive ring of con artists in Denver in the early 1900s.

The term "Johnson Family," coined around 1900, meant drifting bums, itinerant thieves, and other shady characters who were suspicious but not vicious. For every famous con man and crook with a big scheme, there are hundreds of small-time hoods and petty criminals plying their small-scale deceptions and tricks, pilfering, and embezzling. Small-time con artists used to be called "heel grifters" because they had to walk wherever they went. Swindlers[84] are called weasels, vultures, sharks, predators, sleazebags, and parasites. In American literature and film there are innumerable stories of con men's tricks, showing us again and again how the beguiling in many ways can relieve the guileless of their gilt-edged securities and cash.[85] A large part of a con man's brain is dedicated to some other agenda than the obvious one at hand in everyday life—so much so that his face and demeanor must become just the mask of a shill, a convenient manikin standing around for public display. Investors badly want to believe the "chance of a lifetime" is real, partly because America is known as the land of opportunity and success, and so they give their trust, reading goodness into the con man's phony face. They turn over their money without a qualm, when in retrospect some sense of misgivings may have been called for. But Americans often look up to con artists; some, like Will Ferguson, assert that the "true all-American hero is the confidence man: breezy, self-invented, ambitious, protean."[86]

The Name of the Game—the Vocabulary of Shady Deals

A culture's vocabulary grows out of necessity. There are few perfectly exact synonyms for trickery in the proliferation of English words, but a multiplicity of words for related activities grows to convey shades of difference and the inventive cleverness of different neighborhoods. I would like to spread out before you on these next few pages some of the extensive vocabulary of tricksters involved in fraud, past and present here in America. It is a deliberate attempt to lay it all out in its rich inventiveness and colorful sounds, the labels of con men and con jobs.

The names for devious activities of hucksters are myriad and vibrant: Fibbery, fakery, humbug, mountebankery, knavery, quackery, charlatanry, chicanery, coney catching, machination, subterfuge, and peculation; bad faith, sham, flim flam, scam, ruse, dodge, feint, jog, hollow mockery, fraud, bog, hokum, bushwa, bluff, bull, fluff, smoke and mirrors, moonshine, canard, cajolery, double-dealing, underhanded dealing, jiggery-pokery, tomfoolery, roguery, vagary. Deliberately misleading fabrications involve two-facedness, gazump, shenanigans, flummery, and bunk. There are so many ways to say "getting what's not yours": to hook, clip, cop, crook, swipe, punk, skag, lift, gank, kip, nip, kipe, cloy, jack, boost, heist (from "hoist"); to dip, siphon, skim, extort, extract, and to cabbage. So many ways to say "concoct a trick": to cook up, doctor up, trump up; to spawn hijinks, spoofery, puffery, to use weasel words, peacock words, taradiddle, and bring to bear backstairs influence. Con artists wheedle, put on, take in, fleece, shear, stiff, gaff, chisel, bite, gouge, glom, pluck, shave, screw, chouse, ramp, rip off, pull the wool, jimmy, bag, gild the pill, sell gold bricks, cog the dice, bamboozle, cozen, take for a ride, nick, euchre, nibble, plum, snare, waylay, tunnel or tunnel out, maraud, and forage, relieving the rich man of his gold. To hit a lick means taking action to acquire some easy money, whether by jacking, hustling, or bartering for it, or otherwise getting it without work. Throwing dust in trusting eyes, snatching purses from under unsuspecting noses, bending someone over, giving a Judas Kiss, engaging in skullduggery, diddling, finagling, pettifoggery; palming off counterfeit, sleight of hand legerdemain, shortchange, ape-ware, hanky panky, hokey pokey, juggler's trick (this can include the financial juggling of fly-by-night tin horn outfits), thimble-rigging and card-sharping,[87] artful dodge, fast shuffle; gyp, bilk, mulct, wring, badger, goldbrick, foist off, fob off; to colt, to bam, to pull bunk, four flush, sniggle, nobble, gaffle, gank, embezzle, hornswoggle; crimp, push hoopty, flap the jays, move the minches, put the bends, play the humps, burn, stiff, scrump, work the gaff, and diddle-doodle the dudeldopp.

Skeezy con man weasels slip and slide outside the law, they railroad us and buffalo us and bigfoot us, then, chameleon-like, blend into the crowd. They may use a cat's-paw or innocent tool to dupe us. The victim of fraudster trickery is called a dupe, fall guy, gull, patsy, a pigeon. ("In every card game there's a pigeon. If you can't figure out who it is, it's you.") The vic (victim) is a fish, sitting duck, hammer-squash, a mug, sucker, cat's paw, simkin, simp, a simpleton, simple soul, soft touch, a live one, easy mark,[88] hoaxee ("hoax" is probably a contraction of "hocus-pocus"), pushover, apple, cheecheeko, rube, tenderfoot, greenhorn; a jasper, bait-swallower, chump, dimwit, sap. In W. C. Fields's words, the sucker is a "naïve luddy-duddy, moon-calf, jabbernowl." Mr. Moneybags gets scooped in, rooked and snookered, he gets played. He's confused by the crossfire (the fast-talking grifter's slang and verbal pyrotechnics), he gets played, he sucks the mop—the victim gets punked.[89] Seductive Casanovas scam the "squirrels" who give in to them. Con artist means sociopath, manipulation man, a no-account knave, a heartless snake, cool operator, smooth dealer, coldblooded master bluffer. The fast talker is an inveigler, a coaxer, a wheedler, a cajoler, a palaverer, a swindleshanks. He is able "to flow" people, with charm and allure, and sell his schemes with smooth talk, highly skilled at talking strangers into risky or even preposterous deals. The nefarious swindler is a gun, conneroo, chiseller, gouger, schemer, scammer, concocter, grifter, shafter, fronter, dingboy, sharper, sharpie (the "sharpest trade" means the dirtiest tricks in transactions), a sly boots (seemingly a simpleton but actually subtle), a sly dog, sly old fish, crafty rascal, smooth citizen, pipe layer, ferret, cheat, charmer, diddler, crackerjack, trickster, beguiler, perp, fonfer, snickfadger, clank-knapper, gonif, gazlen, cosener, racketeer, rotter, snollygoster, scofflaw, scoundrel, scamp, skell, faker, smoothy, conniver, kombinator, piker, kite, slicker, hustler, hawker, poser, blackleg, jockey, whippersnapper, reprobate, rake, rip, roper, welcher, filcher, finger-smith, looter, jive artist, clip artist, douchebag, quack, gutter-prowler, and crook. He is a masquerader, a fakeloo artist, a bloodsucking leech, a jackdaw in peacock's feathers, an unprincipled cutpurse, a fancy-man, a charlatan, a shark, a sleazeball, a skeezicks, a vampire, a snake oil salesman, a confidence man gaining the trust of, and then betraying, the "true believers." He's a smooth operator, a cold-hearted bastard, a bloodthirsty leech, a nefarious ne'er-do-well, a crooked fly-by-night creep. He's the influence peddler or fixer who predetermines the outcomes of prizefights, ballgames, elections, and jury deliberations. He may use a shill or plant, a ringer to drive up bids at an auction or to exploit games of chance, and to do somebody brown or do him dirt. A grease man smooths the way for thieves or con men to get inside a business. Names for get-rich-quick con games include jerrymander, badger, salting the mine, the pig-in-a-poke, pigeon-drop, wire game, missionary conspiracy scam, melon-drop, glim-dropper, fiddle game, rigging bids, kickbacks, kiting checks, passing orphan paper, pyramid scheme, bait-and-switch, shell game, snow job, fastie, Murphy, gaff, shuck, thimble-rig, snake-oil scam, and the blessing scam.[90] There is plenty of paltering, fudging, juking (as in "juke the stats"), skating, wool-pulling, stone-walling, white-washing, boondoggling, two-timing, double-dipping, double-dealing, self-dealing (supporting private expenses from public funds), working both sides of the street. You can say a sucker got hustled using old single-syllable words: "The con man flimped a yack," or "pinched a swell." There are also four-syllable words like equivocate, prevaricate, and tergiversate. There are scams of pin-hooking (auctioneers selling their own shoddy goods along with others' high quality goods), short-betting (selling what you don't own), bribing, kumshaw artistry, double-crossing, phishing, predatory lending, the juice game or juice racket (loansharking), liar loans"—also known as NINJA ("No income, job or assets") loans, protection racket shakedowns; the fiddle game, the white van speaker scam, lonely hearts scam, romance scam, nanny scam, Chinese company/US toystore promissory scam. There is also the eyeglasses scam—the con man pretends a passerby has jostled him and caused his eyeglasses to break, and therefore insists the passerby must pay for the repair. There is lottery fraud, carousel fraud, welfare fraud, Medicare fraud, feather-bedding, ghost payrolling, sakawa, credit card fraud, identity theft, Jamaican switch, Spanish prisoner, bomb threat extortion, and log-rolling (tit for tat exchange of professional favors: "You scratch my back and I'll scratch yours"). To pull a Betsy means using feminine charm to act seductively and dupe a mark. To catfish someone means to assume a false identity online, to deceive gullible people using social media. There are lone wolf scams and there are team gags. There are trickster mentors who pass on their skills to disciples. (Pickpockets train by taking money from the pocket of a jacket on a manikin without ringing the bells attached near it.) There are scams in which homeless people are used as pawns in health insurance rip-off schemes. There are capers like lemon laundering, gaming the system, Mickey Mouse bookkeeping, whipsaw tricks (that cheat two ways at once), jury duty scams[91] and affinity group fraud.[92] In sweepstakes scams the victims receive the joyous news that they have won the sweepstakes—all they need to do is wire some money to pay the taxes in order to claim the big prize. There are car theft scams in which the con artist calls a towing service and asks them to tow a parked car, saying the keys are locked inside. The sovereign citizens fraud is an anarchist tax evasion scheme. Hassayampers (liars) spout all kinds of sells, swizzles, spiels, skeezing, blowing smoke, and spinning windies, stretching the blanket, and putting over rum fun, creating a house of cards. A two-way joint is a crooked business easily made to look legit when need be by posing with a respectable front. The paranoia scheme exploits a victim who is caused to become so worried about losing money that he entrusts his cash to the protection of the con man. The wash confidence trick is also called the black money scam. In this scheme the victim is shown what seem to be stacks of paper money, the surface of which has been dyed to bypass customs inspectors. Then the proposition is made: "If you will invest some money in the chemicals needed to wash off the dye, then we can share all the cash we have here." It is like the advance fee fraud, promising profits for laying out money up front with a promise of great gain in the near future. A rip deal is like a pigeon drop confidence trick—the victim's confidence is first built up with a profitable exchange; the second time around, as his greed makes him all the more eager, he suffers a great loss. Contrepreneurs are scam artists involved in schemes to get money for start-up businesses, or swindlers on eBay, Amazon.com, etc. A long con is a scheme that involves weeks, months, or longer to set the stage for the grab. Someone's always being caught up in a tangle of hoodwinkers, and someone's always robbing Peter to pay Paul. Anyone too trusting or distracted, powerless and not autonomous, becomes vulnerable as an automaton, and is bound to be a victim. The con man is always getting over on you, pulling a fast one. He's a samfi man, a buzzard who brazenly pulls a fast one, he shines you on, and you get juiced, and he gets away with murder. He makes out like a bandit, acting like a fox in the hen house. He takes you to the cleaners, you're left hung out to dry. You take a big haircut when you deal with him, and you lose your shirt. You're left high and dry, and he deep sixes the evidence, making it impossible to find, leaving no clues or trail to pursue. Only inept con men get caught with their hand in the cookie jar or pork barrel. The slick card-sharp or mechanic gives you Hobson's Choice, lets you pick any card you want—as long as it's the one he intends you to select. The sweet-talking con artist's honeyfuggling promises are bogus, baloney; he's a phony leading suckers down the primrose path, and eventually the Bunko Squad may be alerted. ("Bunko" is from a Spanish word for confidence trick: "bunco." It can be used as a verb, too: "You bunkoed me!") But by that time it's too late, the "wide boy" has already skipped out, absconded, flown the coop, and left the bilked fool holding the bag. He bounced, he skated, got away scot free. Victims of Ponzi schemes and other swindles may file "clawback" lawsuits trying to recover investments, but by then, once everything's gone sideways, you get zip. The caught con man complains that cops are pinning a bad rap on him. Cops and detectives who deal with rascal henchmen in cahoots with other perps often become hard-boiled. They've seen it all, and then some, poking around in the shadowy underworld of aliases and alibis, disguises and tall-tale excuses, counterfeit and contraband, piracy and conspiracy. The jaded Bunko Squad detective explains: "They don't miss a trick, do they? They know how to inveigle, to wangle, to allure, and to entangle. *They get you comin' and goin'*—extract your cash with a whiplash effect, this way, then that. They game every system that was ever devised, and keep a straight face while they laugh up their sleeves. There is no end to the razzle-dazzle contrivances, charades, and conceits of con men; every day they dream up new ones. Once you shake their hands you can kiss your money goodbye, because you've already been had. Con men rob you of self-respect, dignity, and your faith in humankind. They serve the purpose of disillusioning the naive, by breaking laws and hearts."[93]

The swindler can create not just confidence, but ardently abiding faith in his lies. Often the conned fervently want the promise to be true, and are in denial even after the truth emerges. Tim Hardin's 1965 song "Reason to Believe" sums up the feelings of the victim's captured imagination well, saying if he listened long enough to the one who lies to him he would find a way to believe that it was all true, knowing that he'd been lied to straight-faced while he cried, but still he'd look to find a reason to believe.[94] We all know there are none so blind as those who will not see. Whenever there's something important at stake the trickster strategist starts to kick in. To help beef up his persuasiveness the swindler may use shills—people planted in the audience to help cultivate enthusiasm for the spiel. That way the speaker is "preaching to the choir," and hooking new customers into the selling of his product. Theatres sometimes "paper the house," give away free tickets to fill seats, to give the impression that a play is very popular. Similarly, supporters may buy up many copies of a book so it will appear to be high on best-seller lists. There are various ways to stack a deck. Sometimes the trickery is revealed—like the "Payola" radio music scandal of the 1950s, and the *$64,000 Question* TV scandal of the 1960s, disturbing the veneer of fair play. Success, and access to success, is sought so intensely that the line of illegality is often danced around. Nothing succeeds like success except the appearance of success.

Among the people of any society, all confidence, trust and credibility, and all the sharing and cooperation we take for granted, require fidelity built up with hope and based on a tissue of mutuality. The con involves inward "bad faith," an act keeping up surface appearances of mutuality, while really there is a betrayal going on, a breaking of bonds with the other. To put it in a way that may sound naïve or like an understatement, in the ultimate outcome of his activities, the con artist evinces lack of commitment to the social bond. The con man's wounding offense is betrayal, and the damning complaint against him in many stories is something like, "You come among us, a fake, and ruthlessly trick us, taking what's ours, breaking our hearts." He presents a smiling front, with heartless, soulless emptiness inside.

What conclusions might we draw from the examples of scams and reflections on being taken in? What do such experiences teach us about tricksters?

Some part of the trickster mystique involves expectations. Tricks always do something other than what we expect. They catch us off guard. They find us looking the other way, "with our pants down." The trickster watches closely to read us, to see what we let out, to detect what we give away of our hidden feelings. Because we are not perfect at being tricksters, he finds it easy to outfox us. He treats us in a way that makes us say with embarrassment: "I should have known." The trickster can wear us down, wear us out, run us ragged, diddling around with our minds until we're dizzy.

Flattery, for example, can work wonders to distract us and seduce us. The trickster can use our vanity to get us in the right mood. Tricksters can reflect back the ideal self of their victims, puffing them up when they are deflated, buttering them up, so they can take a better bite. They can soothe insecurities, present ideas to make victims feel happy, self-affirmed. Posing as a poor helpless victim of an unfortunate mishap is another way to win victims over. The criminal trickster living by his wits makes a career out of skating around in public on thin ice. The trickster impulse deep in the psyche performs its greatest tricks out of sight. We stand amazed afterwards: "How'd he do that?" The trickster's sleight of hand, and the trickster himself, play hide and seek with our ordinary lives and fundamental assumptions. I guess you're in the trickster's realm whenever you're saying one thing and doing or thinking something else. The trickster archetype rules over splitting things into fakery, deception, conflict of interests, excuses, rationalizations; but is also involved in joining different aspects of personality.

The trickster and his play take many forms, including withholding information and juggling facts, as well as teasing. This includes playful kidding, needling and mimicking, mocking and hassling: "Psych! Just messin' with ya!" When teasing crosses the line into harassment it can become abusive and criminal.

All faking, hiding, denial, rationalization, and duplicity express aspects of the trickster archetype. To deny you have any trickster dynamics in your psyche is another example of trickster doing his thing. "Will it do the trick?" is a phrase meaning "to accomplish the goal," whether struggling hard to win a sports game or earn an A+, to save a life in peril, to administer lethal drugs for assisted suicide, to attempt a trillion dollar bailout plan or start a stalled car. Anomalous trickster spirit finds a way, or dies trying.

The American Robin Hood Trickster Figure, and Other Outlaws

Sometimes the outlaw is more sympathetic than the heartless corrupt establishment.

"Robin Hood" figures share a motto, "steal from the rich and give to the poor," which sounds like it could be a trickster fantasy, a salable cover story useful to help a robbing hood get public sympathy. A reputation for being a champion of the disadvantaged provides a cloak of attractive heroism. In American criminal history various jokers play cat and mouse games with the police, outsmarting the FBI for a time, then they get out-tricked and killed, their stories and crime scene shots splattered all over the tabloids.[95] Prohibition era beer barons were known for funding soup kitchens. New York crime boss Joey Gallo and others in his family had a Robin Hood reputation, because he gave people in the area near where he lived a neighborhood park.[96]

Former Illinois governor Rod Blagojevich tried to appeal to the American love of Robin Hood figures when he was being impeached in 2009, defending himself as a kind of outsider persecuted for helping the poor and championing the unfortunate. Blagojevich put on quite a show at press conferences, with minority beneficiaries standing nearby, but failed to cash in on the Robin Hood archetype, being impeached and then tried for acts of corruption. No doubt his book *The Governor*, about "the dark side of politics," for which he received a six-figure advance, uses some self-depictions that draw on the Robin Hood image and mystique. Sometimes even anti-American terrorists are seen as Robin Hood in other cultures.[97]

Popular American entertainment often features romantic outlaw heroes who pull off dramatic capers. The long running TV series *The Dukes of Hazzard* theme song, for example, celebrates "good ol' boys" who are happy just as they are and feel no need to change, picturing them as busy fighting against the system policed by Boss Hawg. And in a more recent series on HBO, *The Wire* (2002–2008), the character Omar Little is a very vivid example of a Robin Hood figure in contemporary culture. Omar is a likable and fascinating outlaw who boldly robs the richest drug dealers in the Baltimore ghetto, and gets away with it for some time. (Omar Little is said to be President Barack Obama's favorite *Wire* character.) An ad for the TNT TV series *Leverage* (2008–2012) described the characters as "like modern Robin Hoods—or Robin Hoodlums." They are five con persons (two women and three men) on the side of good, using their tricky brains and scam-running skills to beat the crooks at their own game. As the televised blurb says, "The rich and powerful take what they want; we get it back for you.

Sometimes bad guys make the best good guys. We provide leverage." The series presents the Robin Hood ideal in modern dress and high tech gloss.[98]

Perhaps America's culture creators have more of a penchant for the romantic "taking" hero, Robin Hood style, than for the selfless "giving" hero Johnny Appleseed, considered a folk saint by some. Maybe that's why some like to denigrate anyone who is held up as a hero. Glamorous outlaw figures who claim to steal from the rich to give to the poor fascinate the American imagination. These tricksters include Zorro, Joaquin Murrieta, Jesse James, and El Tejano. In the twentieth century Billy the Kid, John Wesley Hardin, Sam Bass, John Dillinger, Pretty Boy Floyd, Huey Long, and others, have been called Robin Hood-like. It is a recurrent theme in American folklore about outlaws. Legend has it that Jesse James after a robbery took refuge in a remote farmhouse where a widow said a debt collector seeking $1400 was expected at any time. James gave her the needed cash and then went out to the road and watched from behind a tree. The debt collector arrived, got his money, and was on his way back to town when James emerged and robbed him, then made his escape. Without actually losing any money, James had nevertheless saved the widow's farm, and that is the stuff of legends.

John Dillinger, a bank robber in the early thirties, when the Depression was causing woes and bankers were more and more despised, gained a folk hero status as a Robin Hood. When he was killed by FBI the nearby Chicago streets were filled with thousands of people. It is said that people dipped their handkerchiefs in his blood, as if to keep a relic of the famous man. Newpapers printed letters of readers cheering on the charming robber, saying he robbed the rich who had gained wealth from the poor, and saying he was better than crooked politicians. Poor people remembered him as someone who gave much of his ill-gotten gain to the needy. The tombstone marking his Indianapolis grave had so many chips cracked off it and taken by visitors wanting a keepsake that it had to be replaced. He was known for being polite to women during robberies, and for outsmarting the police who were often pursuing him. Bystanders cheered and that gave him more bravado. Those qualities endowed him with an aura of celebrity charisma in the folk mind.[99]

The Robin Hood reputation and style has bestowed an attractive aura on a number of feared and despised outlaws. Al Capone, getting out of prison in 1930, set up soup kitchens in Chicago, feeding the poor and giving money to those in need of charity, to rehabilitate and burnish his image. Instead of thinking of him as a convicted criminal, some began to consider him a generous philanthropist.

The original Robin Hood legend was about a dashing folk hero trickster in old England's Sherwood Forest. He was an anti-authoritarian, a kind of shadow hero of the noble knight image. It takes skill and prowess to live outside the law and thrive. Romantic fantasy or wishful thinking and ignorant rumors sometimes made mere Depression-era criminals into folk heroes. Some outlaws, even though they were murderers and drug dealers, were more admired by the common man than the law enforcers risking their lives in pursuing them, and their fans made them into celebrities. The outlaws' generosity may have been short-lived and small scale, but people on the margins of society wanted to believe in them and lionized them, giving the impression that Americans have a growing soft spot for (or at least a love-hate relationship with) grifters and violent takers with an attractive veneer of giving-back. The implications of this kind of big he-man hero-worship for the market culture sometimes seem guaranteed to shortchange nice-guy types and generous souls like the civic-minded mystic John Chapman, known as Johnny Appleseed, who is often portrayed as a small idealistic nerd.[100]

Nelson Algren suggested that "Like the city that bred him, [the modern Robin Hood type like the generous Mafioso kingpin] had a heavenly harpist on his bedpost as well as a hustler's imp stoking the furnace; when hard times came he fed and sheltered more hungry and homeless men than all the Gold Coast archangels put together.... For always our villains have hearts of gold and all our heroes are slightly tainted."[101] Thus, the trickster twist gives the American story the torsion of truth. Americans spurn the pompous ass, and find the bald-faced phony disgusting—they have a built-in lie-detector, if they're fortunate. "Wise up, sister," means *be ever on the alert for the crooked hustler*. Still, there are many Americans like Johnny Appleseed, a giver who must have had his own crafty wariness, a whole bag of wily tricks that helped him survive his long-range travels in the wilderness and on the frontier.

Another example of the Robin Hood-type trickster might be seen in the counterfeiter David "Robber" Lewis, of Pennsylvania, who lived from 1790–1820. In folklore Lewis would cheat poor people, taking their money, but then after conning a sufficient amount of money from the wealthy, he would refund some of his take to the poor.[102] There are many degrees of the Robin Hood type, and Americans like the idea. The New World Robin Hood has a daring admirable identity, providing a "noble" purpose for crime or wrongdoing—evening things out, taking from those with too much, to give to those below.[103] The saving grace, if there is one, of the outlaw, is the ability to be a Robin Hood. In Christianity to be "the good thief" is to be the one who ends up "this day" with the innocent executed Savior in paradise because he has good heart. To be kindhearted, not self-centered, to care for others with heroic skill and daring, makes it possible to become a rock star in the folk imagination for generations.

Because the Robin Hood figure has enduring panache in our imaginations it can also sometimes be used to symbolize a completely noble activity—helping people lift themselves from poverty. In New York, the Robin Hood Foundation[104] in the last couple of decades has distributed over one billion dollars to programs that show they are effective in raising people from low-income lives, especially through education, employment, and disaster relief. Celebrities such as the Rolling Stones, Lady Gaga, John Legend, and the Black-Eyed Peas have helped raise money, and philanthropists like George Soros have donated funds to the Robin Hood Foundation. Paul Tudor Jones began this project of venture philanthropy inspired by the work of another philanthropist, George Weiss, who initiated a program to help poor children in Harlem get a good education. He promised 500 children he would pay for their college costs if they graduated from high school. It takes a vision to succeed in helping disadvantaged kids overcome odds and escape from crushing circumstances. These of course are philanthropists using the panache of the Robin Hood mystique to do good.

Robin Hood types in the folk memory are sometimes "social bandits," to use a term popularized by Eric Hobsbawm. They are peasant outlaws, criminal heroes, rebellious figures who become beacons of popular resistance, anti-authority figures considered examples of defiance and leaders of insurgencies in the imagination of the collective consciousness.[105] They inspire others to try to outsmart "fate." Just knowing they exist can encourage others to undertake acts of daring, and remind them in darker moments that David-like underdogs sometimes find a way to do things others assume are impossible.

Needless to say, there are not only vicious sinister tricksters but also innocent-hearted, healthy-soul tricksters of playfulness, and a whole spectrum in between. Trickery is a multifarious quiver of activities. In fact, it's like the term "tricking," which designates a popular performance style in dancing, a fast-changing ready series of moves—rhythmic, gymnastic, martial arts bits, techno-robot miming, etc.[106] Trickster possibilities are legion; this means the archetype must be very deep in the human being and intrinsic to the psyche's vitality, a tireless inventiveness to be played out in so many ways.

Hustler as Pool Shark, Magician, Exploiter of Resources

The hustler is an important American type of trickster. The word "hustle" is related to the word "jostle"—to be pushy, to push and pester and pump others with impatient energy. Con artists bump and grind the soul; they jostle your faith, rustle your spirits, and hustle up confidence, the better to profit from your hopes. They seduce and diddle your trust, all to betray your charity. To "hustle" means to hurry,[107] and to rook, to outskill others in a game, to sell oneself, and to be a pool shark. Sometimes the pool shark's hustle involves initially pretending to lack skill, and then gradually, as the bets rise and a lot of money is at stake, to go in for the kill. The American hustler mystique is one of detached cool, the intense cool style of a bad dude. The antihero hustler hero has cut a striking figure in the male imagination for many years in America.[108] Now the pool hustler is becoming a dying breed. The author L. Jon Wertheim argues that the dwindling number of pool sharks signals the ending of a uniquely American pursuit. He sees the pool shark as a figure reminiscent of a frontier hero, rolling into town with just a stick (pool cue) and playing so well he earns his living from wagering. Such a means of livelihood requires skillful dexterity, sharp eyes, knowledge of human nature, self-sufficiency.[109] Hustling spawned an ethos, a magazine (*Hustler*), and a dance ("the Hustle"). It also gave young men all across America an attitude, a fantasy of traveling and living by one's wits. As a subculture, hustling has its pantheon of heroes, its outlaw patois, and its mystique.

Ordinarily, the professional magician does not reveal the tricks of his trade. Nor does the shaman-healer, nor does the skillful artist, nor does the political authority, the executive officer of a corporation, or any successful hustler. Of course Donald Trump and other CEOs write books on how to become wealthy, but some tricks of the trade are always kept secret. If people know the tricks they might lose respect, devalue the talents of the performer and his mystique. It's a trick as old as Aesop's fable of the cat and fox: cat does not teach fox how to climb a tree.

The fast-talking con man/salesman has a kind of cynical hip knowingness. His spiel is akin to the fast-talking wiseacre jazz lyric riff, with its in-the-know coolness, and its own vocabulary, like hipster patter. And it's like fast-talking comics' spiels, too, and even the hurry up of hip-hop. Some hustlers confess they love the thrill of the hustle, the adrenaline of the walk on the wild side to make a deal; the daring it takes to score, or to settle an old score. They find the toil of nine-to-five office work in "Dilbert cubicles" boring. They say they'll never quit the shadowy world of off-the-books transactions hidden from authorities. While Horatio Alger's American heroes[110] rose from poverty by their honest industry and square upright living, con men hotshots gained wealth and clout by deception, and sometimes they fell due to their own flaws. It is significant that Hermes is the Greek god who is patron to both merchants and also the tutelary deity of swindlers. The trickster Hermes, with his winged feet of nimbleness, stands for the dual aspect of skill involved in tricks, knowing two sides of a border in commerce transactions and intercultural translations and "hermeneutic" understanding. Hermes, the messenger god, is the intermediary between gods and mortals, and he guides souls from earth to the underworld; his caduceus with its interwining serpents is the symbol of his power to unite opposites and link two realms. Everyone, good or bad, is intrigued by the quickness of wit, skill, and unfolding fortune involved in playing a game well. What will we make of the chance each moment brings to us? What will fate allow us to win or lose?

Is it jaundiced to suggest that man bilks the maple trees and sugar cane of their sweetness, and tricks the salt and fishes from the sea? That he tricks the milk from the cow, and cons the earth of a multitude of resources—oil, gold, silver, uranium, iron, copper, tin, stone, and wood, to name but a few? That unless there is some thought of reciprocity and sustainablility the planet's exploitation by man is nothing less than a heartless trickster's scam? Or is that just being honest?

Isn't it a truism that to play a successful trick stimulates the appetite for more? As Neal Caffrey, the chief con man in the TV series *White Collar* says in the episode entitled "Scott Free": "The con is a rush. It's an addiction."

Sometimes it seems we live in a time of *Mercury Rising*[111]—an era of tricksterism abounding.[112] How do con men gain the confidence of their victims? They look for clues, follow paths of least resistance, mimicking, echoing, finding ways to seem similar to the sucker. They seek to seem in sync because social bonding happens fastest when there is mimicry, shared interactions on the same wavelength. Imitation, fitting in, friendliness charmingly exhibiting commonality, reflecting the other person's attitude—these self-similar displays allow the con man to beguile the unsuspecting by seeming familiar and trustworthy. Although they blend in externally, they guard within themselves against feeling too much sympathy for victims. The con man's motto is: "Never give a sucker an even break." That it's permissible to bilk a fat cat, a sucker or an opponent, is an unspoken rule even among amateur petty scam artists. To soak the rich is, in fact, a feather in their caps. (Of course there are con artists who specialize in serving and protecting the rich too. Anyone who follows politics notices this. "Steal a little, you land in jail; steal a lot, you become king," as the ancient Taoist philosopher Chuang Tzu wrote, and as Bob Dylan sang in "Sweetheart Like You.")

The most skillful hucksters have a ready rationale to alleviate all the mark's uncertainties with a beguiling guise of satisfying assurances. We get conned because we want to believe. We are conditioned as children and consumers to fall into line. The simpleton never suspects the ceaseless, incorrigible con man, so he gets laughed at, taken in by his own ignorance. To be aware of the trickster in the world outside one must be more aware of one's own trickiness.

We are not born knowing about this wrinkle in life. Damon Runyon, with his hard-boiled wit, tried to warn us that inevitably we will encounter a charming character offering to bet us that he can make a Jack of Spades jump out of his card deck and squirt some cider in our ears. His basic advice is, "Never make a bet with this man." The ambidextrousness and cuteness of the fool trickster helps him get away with all sorts of shenanigans, and when all that bald-faced lying fails, the ambidextrousness and cuteness helps him get away. Tricksters seem to have a sixth sense, to know every quicksilver trick in the book—quick-witted and quick stepping, fast-talking and rapidly adjusting. Yet for all their subtlety, they still sometimes let down their guard and end up sinking in their own quicksand.

The film *American Hustle* (2013) explores the theme of self-deception—the layers and tangles of self-delusion on the part of swindlers and law enforcement officials alike. The self-conning that goes into scheming, hoping, planning, and groping for success, wishing for a better life, is elusive. "Everyone is conning themselves," a character says, "just to get through life." We all tell ourselves what we want to hear at times, to boost our confidence and to try to better our situations. Near the end of the film this statement is made: "The art of survival is a story that never ends." When our hope is dashed, when a scheme or scam folds, another venture always seems to begin. *The Wolf of Wall Street*, a Martin Scorsese film released in the same year, is based on Jordan Belford's memoir and tells a story of Wall Street corruption and security fraud. It portrays the "irrational exuberance" of over-the-top profiteering practiced by investment industry daredevils in the land of opportunism. In our age there is admiration and gnashing of teeth upon seeing people make fast bucks then spending millions with great gusto.

In the larger perspective, it is good to remember that the trickster dynamic is like cholesterol—its different forms can be good or bad. Children playing hide and seek (or friends telling jokes) are not in the same category as a crook running off with others' money, though both are involved in the trickster impulse. Obviously, playfulness should not be criminalized and thievery should not be condoned. Antisocial tricks are harmful and cross the line of legality, while the free play of fun and games and creativity also requires trickster energy and inspiration, the dart of quirks and flit of fake-outs. The tricks of charm make life interesting, but antisocial tricksters who are harmful (such as violently destructive terrorists) require apprehension. To see through the tricks of civilization has been part of the human quest for millennia, from yoga to Plato, from prophets to reformers and modern culture critics. These and other aspects of the topic suggest how rich and important it is. As Edgar Allan Poe said, diddling is something which makes humans human.[113] They fiddle around with each other. Humans are loopy and light-footed. Maybe Neanderthals were too lumbering and ham-handed. Today's humans are more sprightly and tricky. They are capable of great nimbleness, with amazing grace in their sticky-fingered hands.

2

TODAY

Fifteen Kinds of Tricksters in America

> The tales at first seem strange. They should seem strange. Odd things happen.... It is a world of man-eating suns, of giants and talking excrements, of women with teeth between their legs, and of a race of cannibals with no anuses.
>
> —Zeese Papanikolas[114]

Prelude to Tales of Lootery and the Ludicrous

Relying on generalizations alone may cause us to underestimate the scope and depth of trickster activities. Therefore I have collected an inventory of many short discrete examples to help indicate the field, and to reflect on specific examples that call to mind some of the dynamics of this elusive archetype. Please keep in mind that this is by no means intended to be an exhaustive inventory. It is the result of a few years of gathering examples from the media and literature, so it does not pretend to be in-depth. The fifteen categories include a multitude of specifics, many of which should be familiar to readers, and in a few cases of major importance I explore the dynamics in more depth and detail. My main concern is to suggest vivid examples of a wide array of trickster activities in various fields in American culture and history. I do not offer ethical/moral evaluations in each case. The most egregiously antisocial ones I do note as seriously destructive. Those examples involve a misuse of cleverness and vitality in tricks that victimize. Other examples are obviously more playful and positive in their impacts. Generally, I leave the discussion of morality to others. My basic goal here is not to make ethical judgments, but to suggest a fractal tip of a much larger iceberg, a shadow world we often take for granted. I'm sure each reader could add other items he or she has encountered to this loosely organized list of items I found on my path in daily life.

Tricksters are known by their deeds. Obviously I am not saying that all the examples given in the discussion below are full-blown mythological tricksters like Coyote, Raven, or the Two Brothers found in Native American stories, or superhuman figures like the larger-than-life Davy Crockett in nineteenth-century tales. Newer expressions of trickiness that I discuss in this section do, however, share some qualities with the trickster archetype seen in myths. Rock stars who break taboos and get away with it, heroes who overcome monstrous circumstances, crafty folk who find a way to survive and thrive when the odds are against them, men making spectacles of themselves by feeding their astounding appetites in public—all have some trickster qualities, obviously. Each person, every living creature who ever faced an obstacle and needed to get around it has found the built-in trickster impulse within. Our instincts ask what clever ploy might work in dire circumstances and thereby save the day. Impasses turn the trickster gene on, or stimulate the trick-performing imagination—that's life.

1. Political Gazump

There are corruption tricksters among public servants, such as politicians who take bribes. "Pay to play" is a phrase known all too well today. There is also the influence-peddling chicanery of lobbyists catering to special interest groups—in 2013 there were 12,279 registered lobbyists busy in Washington, spending 3.216 billion dollars, according to the Center for Responsive Politics at OpenSecrets.org. Investigative reporting delves into the hidden side of decision-making, and the personal life of politicians, while the officials use the delete button, the shredder, and selective memory to cherry-pick and airbrush what they hope to present as a public image. Politics, like seduction, involves the art of getting what one wants.

Naturally, tricks of various sorts are often implicated in the art of getting one's way in the political systems of national, state, or local government. To gain support, smooth operators put on a game face and go forth to face the public. They shift their shapes, follow polls, smilingly accommodate different donors, and try to stay in the public eye through photo ops and press releases. They feign unawareness and inability to answer inconvenient questions. The political arena is a tricky theater of public spectacle amplified by media, a Kabuki drama in which people play roles, and say things formally that are far from their inner experience. One fraud of modern communications is that nothing really is as it seems. Words are prerecorded, with rehearsed spontaneity, ghostwritten speeches, and contrived slants catering to focus groups. Spin can explain, distract from or explain away, reality's rough edges.

Speechwriters know the expedient phrases to reach the sentiments they need to evoke. Candidates and officials pretend to feelings of friendship while really feeling enmity, and smile agreeably with opponents when debating them fiercely in public to make points for consumption by their base. Political strategists and advisers devise cynical battle plans to raise needed money for campaigns. Operatives and pollsters devise strategies and carry out plays in the sport of political contests using time-tested tricks. The funny-sounding term *snollygoster* denotes a shrewd, principle-less politician who, chameleon-like, changes with conditions, going any way the wind blows. *The Great McGinty* (1940) is an outstanding American film satire about tricks of dishonesty and honesty in politics, written by actor-director Burgess Meredith.

The fictionalized life of Huey Long as a Louisiana populist politician-trickster was the subject of a novel by Robert Penn Warren, entitled *All the King's Men*, and it was dramatized in two major films (1949 and 2006) using the same basic story and title. This work by Warren is a classic American story of political trickery exploiting populism and abusing power. The character Willy Stark, based on Huey Long, starts out as a naïve outsider and loser who advocates for the poor. He gets used by those in power before he wises up and learns political tricks. He changes when he learns how to win, and becomes a corrupt, manipulative power-broker, though he still tries to work for the anonymous poor. In the end he gets caught in snares of his own making. According to most accounts, Huey Long tricked his way to power by figuring out the cynical ploys that would work to get elected by the common man, and then played tricks with high finances and influence-peddling while in power. He learned how to make deals, and "soak the fat boy and spread it out thin." Finally, an angry critic sick of the big man's tricks assassinated him. During the Cold War era the former Soviet Union printed editions of Warren's book and sold them in Third World countries like India to publicize the mean tricks found in the crooked world of capitalist democracy, suggesting that communism could avoid such problems and deliver a better government to a poor nation.

The life of politician Marion Berry demonstrates the enduring popularity possible for a man beloved of the people. Caught on videotape smoking crack cocaine in 1990 while Mayor of Washington DC, Berry was elected mayor again in 1994 after serving time in jail. He recited "Amazing Grace" verses in public—to great applause and cheers—and found forgiveness and redemption. More recently, by popular demand, Berry was chosen for representation in Madame Tussaud's Wax Museum in Washington DC, getting more votes than the other candidates.[115] Politicians sometimes seem chronically prone to obfuscation, denial, bait-and-switch tricks, playing possum ("I forget") and relaxing on the good ship "Monkey Business." Sometimes they get away with these hijinks and sometimes not. Devious political operatives create a "tar baby" issue to get opponents stuck on, so their own candidate can play the victim, demanding apologies, putting foes on the defensive. They cause an uproar to obfuscate reality, in hopes that most people will be too busy or distracted to discern the truth, or too lazy to care what is really going on. To scam one's way into office through the distortion of facts or breaking of rules ensures that one will need to continue to rely on tricks to stay in power, and so the game goes on, cycle after cycle.

When a public servant is caught in unseemly behavior, there is a religious and political ritual—the trickster grovels for forgiveness, publicly confesses to atone, vociferously seeking redemption. A sense of equality got him into the mess—anyone can become a leader in a democracy, and regular guys are often elected, so even someone unfit may gain responsibilities he cannot handle. And a sense of equality is what gets him off the hook—he must publicly humble himself, disown his arrogant trickery in apologies to show he is accountable to the people who put him in office. He must dramatically demonstrate that he does not think himself above them. This situation demands that the trickster grovel in the spotlight, dramatically begging forgiveness for his sins.[116]

Politics is a tricky business. Many today bemoan the loss of civility in politics, the gulf between Democratic and Republican congressmen and senators, the loss of the ability to reach across the aisle in magnanimous friendship. Friendship makes it harder to play dirty tricks on opponents. If you keep opponents distant, you can more easily project your demonic shadows on them, and treat them like despicable rats. If you eat and drink with them you treat them more like fellow humans.

Cuban immigrant Antonio Prohias abstracted Cold War tricks in *Spy vs. Spy* cartoons, published in *Mad Magazine* beginning in 1961. These vivid graphics in black and white show silent tricksters desperately and giddily trying to out-trick fellow tricksters. Backroom government protectorates—KGB, CIA, SAVAK, ISI, Mossad, and all secret police and counter-intelligence teams, with endless intrigues in the interstices between nations, wiretapping, eavesdropping, etc.—these are trickster realms par excellence. They provide the fodder for countless trickster scenarios. There are sometimes mavericks, rogue agents who go off the regulation books to play tricks of their own, including counter-espionage. The trickster likes the moonlight of clandestine operations much more than the glare of the noonday sun. Sometimes covert Keystone Cop-style CIA activities come to light. Like the time CIA agents tried to assassinate Castro with an exploding cigar, just like in a Looney Tunes cartoon, or the time they put chemicals in Castro's shoes to make his beard fall out. Another time they tried to dispatch someone to put a poison pen in his hand, and they also rigged a conch shell to explode near him, and sought to put poison pills in his drinks.[117]

The film *Breach* (2007) tells the true story of Robert Hanssen, an FBI agent who sold secrets to the Russians. His life offers a case study in themes of lying and loyalty, truth and deception, public profession and compartmentalized interior life. What makes someone this deceitful? The "why" is unclear. Maybe he does it "for the game, not the gain." Or the ego thrill—everyone in the agency is looking for a mole and all the while it's agent Hanssen himself, outfoxing them all. Passing a polygraph test while lying is part of the espionage expert's "tradecraft." In the film there are terms like "ghosting school" for spy training, "dead drop" for leaving secrets in a place where face-to-face meetings are not possible, and "going to ground" for disappearing from the scene. "Sheep Dipping" is an American intelligence term for disguising the true identity of equipment, intelligence officers, or agents, blurring their links to the CIA by camouflaging them as belonging to a legit organization. Espionage and counter-espionage are stressful realms of paranoia and illusion, tricks the mind can play and get lost in. The world of espionage is a shadowy underworld of moles and sleepers, "eyes" and "rabbits," "bugs" and "chickenfeed," "cut-outs" and "blowback," "honeypots," "black-baggers," "tangoes" and "wet jobs." Steganography is writing hidden in messages; a "one time pad" is an encryption logarithm. Espionage involves "one-way voice links," "black bag operations," "false flag operations" (designed to look like another nation was responsible), "honey traps" (in which sex is used to lure enemy agents) and an assortment of tricks using unseen electronic communications devices. It's a realm of cagey, crafty spooks and slick high-tech surveillance tricks, a world of foes vying for secret knowledge and control, where things may end up "FUBAR" and when explored by conspiracy theorists they blare: "NOYFB!"[118]

When we consider the covert operations of America and other nations spiriting away captured suspects to unidentified interrogation facilities in foreign countries, it seems sometimes like an extensive trickster contest. As a variation on the Golden Rule ("do unto others. . .") in the TV series *Hill Street Blues* went, "Let's do it to them before they do it to us." (Another trickster joke about the golden rule is: "He who has the gold makes the rules.") Tricksters like to "get the drop" on others (a phrase originating in the 1800s to describe pointing a gun at someone before he points one at you). The stealth bomber expresses a deep trickster wish: to move invisibly, invulnerably, crossing boundaries as one wishes, seeing and acting without being seen or detected, making an impact without becoming vulnerable. Hiding is trickster's first trick.

When the first atom bomb was detonated at Los Alamos, New Mexico, July 16, 1945, officials tried to cover it up. They told area citizens that an ammunition dump had exploded, in an effort to reassure them. Seen in this light, the government might be seen as a series of exercises in crowd control tricks, and ways to keep voters complacent. The test director, Ken Bainbridge, said "We're all sons of bitches now"—that is, we are untrustworthy tricksters, gingerly taking our chances beyond the traditional norms. Those in power seek to reduce panic among the populace, unless they can exploit it. If they need to employ duplicity, they often seem to say (in the name of national security) "so be it."

One of our presidents (the thirty-seventh) came to be known widely as "Tricky Dick" because of his political tricks, and hidden antics that came to light against his will. In the Oliver Stone biopic *Nixon* (1995), Haldeman lists some of the tricks that put Nixon beyond previous recent presidents in the category of dirty tricks: The break-in at the Watergate Hotel; the attempted firebombing of the Brookings Institute; planting McGovern materials on the man who shot Wallace; trying to slip LSD to journalist Jack Anderson; asking Hunt to forge a cable implicating Kennedy in the assassination of the president of Vietnam. Whether Nixon was behind these shenanigans or not, they are part of his legend. Nixon, though seemingly a true sneak, did not have enough subtle trickiness when he said "I am not a crook," so he became the butt of jokes for more skillful clowns and witty critics.

Nixon's chief strategist in the realm of dirty tricks was Donald Segretti, who later testified about his nefarious 1972 campaign activities under oath. The shadow campaigns run by such tricksters included character attacks, disruptions, political stunts for public consumption: the manipulation of images, and creating embarrassments for the opponent by hiring a naked woman to run through a hotel where the opponent was staying, yelling his name. On June 17, 1972, dirty tricksters in the employ of Nixon's administration broke into the Democratic National Committee offices at the Watergate Hotel in Washington. When the "plumbers" (so called because they were tasked with plugging the leaks of secret White House policies), including G. Gordon Liddy,[119] were caught red-handed, this necessitated a cover-up within the administration. Because the cover-up was badly bungled, the incident is still remembered today.

In politics there are many underhanded ways of turning the tables, getting an advantage, and using political sleight of hand to divide and conquer, from special interest pandering to district gerrymandering. Segretti and others in his crew called voters in the middle of the night, pretending to be seeking support for Nixon's opponent, intentionally angering the opponent's supporters. Nixon's White House popularized the term "stonewalling," putting on a mask of cold stone when suspicions arise, paralyzing the conscience, vehemently denying any wrongdoing. Nixon was often caricatured by cartoonists with an ever-growing Pinocchio nose.

Campaign tricks may seem to have reached new lows in recent times, but actually they have been part of American politics for centuries. For example, in 1876 opponents of Rutherford B. Hayes falsely accused him of shooting his own mother, and of committing various frauds. The electronic age has made new devices available, making some kinds of tricks far easier to employ. There are now automated robot-dialing tricks used for telephone harassment in political campaigns—a candidate's backers arrange to have repeated phone messages sent seemingly on behalf of their opponent. This is the automated version of the trick used by Segretti and his crew. Campaigners have also used the trick of jamming phone lines, shutting down the other party's phone banks, disrupting their lines of communication, and vandalizing their voter transportation vehicles. There are direct mailing campaigns, sending out printed "hit pieces" of inflammatory political accusations and caricatures to rile up or disgust voters. The practice of "sandbagging" elections involves coercion or intimidation, frightening voters on sensitive issues to sway their votes. Such unfair tactics can backfire, bringing disgrace to those who stoop so low. Or, they can confuse and spoil things, giving a temporary advantage to spoilsports. They certainly play a part in destroying the higher ideals of democracy.[120]

On the national scale tricks of some of those who carried on where Segretti left off—Lee Atwater and Karl Rove, to name but two—are legends of manipulative legerdemain. The documentary *Boogie Man: The Lee Atwater Story* (2008)[121] is a character study examining the life of the political operative nicknamed "Darth Vader" and known as the GOP's "happy hatchet man." The title is well-chosen—"boogie man" means both someone known for scaring people, especially impressionable children, and a musician who can play wild boogie-woogie dance songs (Atwater played guitar). The film presents Atwater as a behind-the-scenes player known for not leaving his fingerprints on the dirty campaign tricks he devised and pulled on opponents. He came from a humble southern background, and may have been psychologically scarred by seeing his younger brother fatally scalded in an accident involving boiling grease. Some who knew him said he was not interested in political policy, only in seeing his side win. He served the country-club-like Republican party, joining the Young Republicans college club while a student at Newberry College in South Carolina, and getting involved in a series of elections. Over the years he worked for Strom Thurmond, Ronald Reagan, and George H. W. Bush. He became known as an agent of "ruthless, win-at-any-cost Republicanism." In one of the early elections Atwater was involved in spreading the grotesque image of his candidate's opponent as once having had his head "hooked up to jumper-cables" for electric shock therapy—an image sure to shock listeners, smear the candidate, and get a big laugh. He specialized in developing wedge issues, tricks to fool the electorate, swaying the vote to win. He became known as "Bush's pit bull," turning a presidential campaign into a series of "tabloid moments." For example, he vowed to "strip the bark off Dukakis, and make Willy Horton his running mate." Atwater was said to have always been fascinated by how a career could be suddenly ruined, and he used lies, innuendo, and the method of stirring up racial, sexual, and religious fear to win. His hope was to "stick it to the other guy first," playing to the cheap seats in sensationalistic skewing of opinions. One ploy he used while doing devious things was to "play dumb and keep movin'"—"slow-playin' it," putting on a slow-talking act, not seeming smart enough to be manipulative, while deviously outfoxing the unsuspecting press and the public.

Later in life, after he was being treated for a brain tumor, Atwater is said to have recognized the harm some of his tricks did to America. One commentator noted "life gets even with you in the end." Atwater himself had a sense of irony about this, saying he'd used the idea of getting "inside the head of your enemy" in the race against Bob Dole, noting that now cancer was doing the same to him. Some sympathetic observers painted him as an insecure kid who got to play in the big leagues, showing the world what he could do. Some say the hurt he did to dishonor others in his quest for success caused him to fear his own fate in the afterlife, and to feel that he had wasted his life for money, power, and fame. He apologized before he died, and said his life had lacked "a little heart, a lot of brotherhood." He also diagnosed the country as suffering from a "spiritual vacuum at the heart of American society, this tumor of the soul."[122] Political commentator Mary Matalin denied the value in the film's characterization of Atwater in terms of his last months of self-reflective regret, insisting he was "a brilliant strategist, not a dirty trickster." But the film uses Atwater's own conclusions. Matalin's denial that Atwater had anything to regret may hinge on a defensiveness necessary to buttress a public role and a way of life. Things look different when the "jumper cables" are on the deathbed trickster's head instead of on his victim.

No doubt Atwater was very skillful at manipulating impressions for his own purposes, coining the phrase "perception is reality" (insofar as the electorate will act upon a slant it has been fed).[123] Republican political campaign consultant Ed Rollins observed in the film that Atwater was a con man to the very end. Though Atwater told some friends he was reading the Bible, to make them like him, in fact Atwater's Bible was still wrapped in its original cellophane packaging after he died, never having been opened.[124] Some might see Lee Atwater ("Darth Vader of the Republican party"), Karl Rove (whose nickname "Turd Blossom," given by George W. Bush, suggests stink and a display of niceness, malicious trickery masked by pleasant smiles), and "dirty trickster" Roger Stone ("the dapper don of dirty deeds"), etc. as reverse Robin Hoods. Why? Because acting behind the scenes they worked against the interests of the common man, protecting the rich and powerful, obfuscating the truth with smokescreens of disinformation for all they were worth. But others would say they simply did the dirty work that was asked of them, in a world of competitive forces. The philosophical question "What would the world be like if everyone acted like this kind of trickster?" is a useful one to consider. Not all competitive trickery is "business as usual."

Ted Cruz, junior Republican senator from Texas, joined the ranks of prominent American political tricksters when he used a ploy to try and get rid of Obamacare—shut down the government by getting fellow members of his party to refuse to pass a budget. This not about substance, presenting a workable plan, but about spin, publicity, grabbing the spotlight and stunning with the appearance of something striking. Cause a crisis, then verbally repeat that it is the opponents' fault, use talking points on programs broadcast by right-wing media—this gamble can work if enough people are prejudiced and closed to other views. The bold use of outrageous ideas cleverly going outside the system to get away with something over the top steals the show regularly now in novels, movies, TV, and video games, so why not in politics? High concept outside-the-box tricks have been de riguer ever since 9/11, when the trick of hijacking airplanes and smashing them into buildings succeeded big-time, terrorizing many Americans. Surprise! They do it because they can do it! Surprise! "It's all a stacked deck, there's no one to check."

Strategists, spinners, and partisan operatives abound in Washington. The list of tricks used by both parties in election campaigns is long, changing gradually decade by decade. The list includes mean-spirited smears, "swift-boating," whispering campaigns using rumors to malign reputations, disinformation rumors spread by email, and hidden agendas determined by backroom deciders. It also includes tricks of stealing the opponent's thunder by co-opting his or her strengths, various kinds of voter fraud, and Internet and TV messages with code words to spread fear and revulsion. Candidates with weak positives may go after opponents' negatives; for example, a candidate who had never served in the armed forces unfairly smeared Max Cleland, a Vietnam veteran who lost limbs in battle, making him look weak. Those who spread lies today can point back to others in history who did it long ago. In 1836 Davy Crockett called the candidate Martin Van Buren a secret cross-dresser, claiming he was "laced up in corsets."

National political campaigns today include trickster tactics of publicly trivializing legitimate concerns, mocking and belittling serious gestures. Much brainpower is focused on ad hominem attacks, and concentrated efforts carefully orchestrated so that many spokesmen repeat the same catch-phrase or buzzword to smear and twist public perception.[125] Bullying can be found not only in playgrounds but in ads, on TV talk shows, in columns, on radio programs and blogs. Instead of discussing issues, a small statement or impression is seized upon, taken out of context and burlesqued, to tear down an opponent. This trick of taking a statement out of context, and pretending it was said point-blank, has been used extensively in recent years. The GOP built a good deal of its 2012 convention on such an out-of-context statement by Barak Obama that made the point that even important businessmen were indebted to the infrastructure and support systems around them, the roads, learning from the past, etc. He was pointing out the interconnected nature of reality. The GOP tried to use it as a slight, an insult taking away the accomplishments of the titans of industry. Seizing such an opening as an opportunity to get advantage is a trick that seems useful when one's own vision is weak; exploiting pride and fear have often proved successful in getting votes.

There are clever tricksters who profit from emphasizing divisive extremes, pushing polarization as far as they can. Those who do not have faith that the "truth will out" (as Shakespeare puts it in *The Merchant of Venice*), and to the contrary have a strong faith that the truth can and must be manipulated—spun, denied, finessed, reshaped, and subverted—in order for them to succeed, eagerly engage in character assassination and self-aggrandizement. The depressing result of negative ads makes us ask campaigners: How low can you go? Despite distaste, instead of raising the bar, elections involve an ever-lowered limbo pole.

Behind-the-scenes political tricksters prey upon dupes, sowing distrust and nurturing fears, stirring up reactions to emotional issues, spreading disinformation, and inciting noisy distractions. They produce political issue talking points for others in their party to memorize and chime in with when interviewed. Newt Gingrich is remembered for inventing ways like this for officials in his party to present a united front.[126] They generate lists of buzzwords and slogans for placards, they reproduce pamphlets and screeds to be distributed by others. They use obfuscation, cover-ups,[127] and diversionary tactics when they are caught. Desperate to be in power, they destabilize opponents with dirty tricks. Some have a knack for tapping into a great unconscious rage in people who don't know who to blame for their problems. Untrained in analyzing, unsophisticated in studying complicated information, unable to look within for quiet reflective thought, the dupes rely on guidance by trusted leaders and TV and radio commentators, tricksters in nice clothing. Clever political spokesmen set up scapegoats, and feed their followers over-simplified answers to complex questions. They formulate statements for signs and T-shirts that on the surface sound noble, like "Now is the time for all good men to water the imperiled Liberty Tree." But, as devised and distributed by these tricksters, the signs' subtext, which at first sounds so noble, is more likely "it's time to urinate on the opponents" or "drown out any new ideas." Sometimes, as in the 2009 healthcare reform controversies, the signs are carried by protestors wearing guns. While it's true that Jefferson wrote "The tree of liberty must be refreshed from time to time, with the blood of patriots and tyrants,"[128] that was written in the context of heroic idealism. It's also the case that this quote has other associations, including its use by right-wing sociopaths. For example, when Timothy McVeigh was arrested after he blew up a federal building in Oklahoma City in 1995, killing 168 and injuring over 680 innocent Americans, he was wearing a "Water the tree of liberty" t-shirt.

The inborn trickster in the psyche is tempted when seeing a double standard—a distinct public arena in which to perform and an offstage rehearsal space. On the one hand there is a private realm of deals, deceptions, and conniving tricks—back door, back alley, back room, and backstabbing; on the other hand there are sales presentations in store fronts, front-row seats at politicians' speeches, false fronts presented for the klieg lights and cameras. The tempting trickster's psyche adapts to a two-track reality: righteous mask on the face, cloak and dagger in the heart. Draped in a flag and made up like a doll of piety, camouflaged in noble patriotism, using others as manipulable dupes, some candidates seem so hungry to win they'll do anything. Then, once in power, they still seem to be starving to stay in power as long as possible, insatiable and never finding satisfaction. Mudslingers and "crap-weasels" of all stripes are members of the trickster tribe. Is the problem that the trickster won't play fair, or that we don't know how to level that playing field and outsmart him at his own game? Can we be equally tricky, and outfox him, or at least tie him up and stop him in his tracks? Or is trickster just drawing us into his arena where he has honed his skills?

Some political strategists, such as Henry Kissinger, have the reputation of being brilliant manipulators of politicians, and some, such as Michael Deaver, are known as shapers of public opinion through media images. To "spin" is to distort so that the interpretation of an event seems to favor and exonerate oneself, to prove the correctness of one's political stance, to weave an effective political cover, to disguise catastrophe as an inevitable event for which one shares no blame. To spin is to refocus everything from a different perspective, a bias determined by self-interest, self-justification, self-importance. Spinning is a clever trick at odds with the truth; it forfeits a view of whole reality, blocks honest assessments. The trickster as spin doctor sizes up situations, notes weak spots, finds lines of least resistance, and asks: "What can I get away with?" Some political commentators have an amazingly long shelf life, even though their analyses usually prove wrong; some remain in the public eye even when their sole concern for service is self-service.

One man's excuse is another man's ruin. There are tricks of moral persuasion as well as tricks of statistics in the art of governing. A leader with a faith-based style of ego and self-importance, instead of a fact-based style of statecraft, requires immense amounts of hoping and pretending, cover-ups strenuously going against all evidence. What kinds of tricks must a ruler play with his own perceptions to keep up pretenses to greatness and intentions of building for the future, when so many signs contradict such assertions? Leaders play their bumbling tricks and then fade into history; Nero fiddles (or rides a bike) while Rome burns. Administrations come and go, the rivers and mountains abide, as an old Chinese poem says.

American history shows that scandals involving trickster scoundrels have erupted in every century. The eighteenth century saw the Yazoo Land Scandal of the 1790s and the XYZ Affair. The nineteenth century is remembered for the Petticoat Affair, a sex scandal leading to a number of Andrew Jackson's cabinet members resigning, and the Black Friday Scandal, and Tammany Hall machinations, with boss-controlled politics. In the twentieth century the Teapot Dome scandal was in the limelight. It involved oil—the leasing of government oil rights to Mammoth Oil Company without bidding in the early 1920s. There were San Francisco graft problems, and in other regions too, bribes, corruption, "revolving door" conflicts of interest, influence peddling, indiscreet words and deeds—all involving tricksters who eventually got tripped up by their own shenanigans.[129]

The ploys of Ralph Abramoff, Tom DeLay, Ralph Reed, and Grover Norquist, deceiving their clients, the government, and each other in influence-peddling operations, are part of the historical record.[130] They offer vivid examples of lobbying tricks. This group perpetrated the Mariana sweatshop scam to preserve inhumane conditions of immigrant workers, and the Indian casino interests scam, and they were involved in transactions taking money from powerful Russians to get the American government to help bail out the Russian economy in the 1990s and later. The trickery of this group of former Young Republicans involved constructing shell operations to wield influence, spending money illegally under the cover of causes supposedly concerned with moral righteousness, and building a money machine in the state house, with access to the White House.

The abuse of non-profits to funnel money to lawmakers has not abated, but Abramoff was sentenced to five years in prison for illegal activities, Tom DeLay was indicted and sentenced to three years in prison, and Ralph Reed's reputation was tainted when his association with the influence-peddling money was revealed. One explanation for these illegal acts was that the conservatives felt that the liberals had no morals, and were nothing but thieves, therefore the Republicans would be justified in pulling the necessary tricks to rob robbers.[131] (Later, DeLay tried so hard to redeem or rebrand himself in the public eye by dancing on TV that he broke both his feet, literally—he dropped out of *Dancing with the Stars* because of stress fractures. Sometimes the trickster loses control and is tricked by his own tricks. If one projects evil onto one's opponents, one becomes numb to it in oneself.)

This is not to say that the trickster spirit is all negative in politics. There are also good-natured tricksters in politics. Abraham Lincoln was known for gentle humor, playfulness, and a taste for odd amusements. (A very tall man, he would sometimes invite a dwarf to the White House, causing laughter with the contrast.) His trickster gift for joking around was a boon to lighten his somber spirit and enjoy human soulfulness. He joked that one man was mistaking fleas in his own eyelashes for lost cattle in the brambles. He rhymed "Barefoot boy with cheeks of clay, here tomorrow, gone today." Life played many tricks on Lincoln, with physical ailments stretching his psyche and body, perhaps giving him more of a sense of irony and humility than other presidents. As Jacques Barzun wrote, the career of Lincoln seemed rather improbable. Because of his career's unexpected twists Lincoln must have felt he alone was not the only directing force in shaping his destiny. Once he had done everything he could, Lincoln let the uncontrollable stream of events that acts upon lives shape the results without feeling regrets. Barzun saw signs that Lincoln delighted "in the fact that this world always defied figuring out by rule and system."[132] Therefore, we can say that Lincoln appreciated the quirks of unpredictable trickster fate, and got a kick out of jokes, harmless pranks, and surprises. But he famously trusted some basic trickster-proof wisdom of the people in a democracy over the long haul of time: "You can fool all of the people some of the time and some of the people all of the time, but you can't fool all of the people all of the time." Or, perhaps, it was a trickster who put those words in Lincoln's mouth—they are contested.[133]

Some politicians are remembered for their abilities to play the game skillfully. In Steven Spielberg's *Lincoln* (2012), we see Lincoln's maneuvers to get a the Thirteenth Amendment to the Constitution through the House of Representatives. It took all of his persuasiveness. Franklin Roosevelt (like John Kennedy) performed in the office while hiding the physical disabilities they endured. Dwight Eisenhower had an intuitive talent for getting a roomful of divergent temperaments to reach an agreement upon an issue. Lyndon Johnson was good at horse trading, deals, compromise, tit for tat politics. Ronald Reagan covered his weaknesses, and made good use of his gifts as "the great communicator."

We might also say that the resilience that lives in democracies is the built-in order of checks and balances that allows the play of the timely positive trickster impulse that pushes things along, turns things around, articulating a fresh response, getting beyond one-sidedness and monopolies on power. One-sidedness is the source of problems of unbalanced outlooks. The nimble dance of the imagination solving problems is vitality itself, spirited play in work. This vital impulse is not mean-spirited, nor does it delight in smearing others, cheating in the games of life and hoping to get away with it. It has grace that comes from respect of the whole and joy in coexistence.

Nevertheless, during every election season one might easily get the impression that politics is a wanna-be show biz, a theatre in which the would-be actors who are running for office say the lines they hope will get applause and turn the trick of winning votes that will put them in power. The trickiness of it all is denied with stonewalling faces by conniving inveterate liars who can't admit the truth. New TV series set in the world of politics, such as Netflix's *House of Cards* and ABC's *Scandal*, enjoy great popularity because we want to imagine kinds of backstage conniving and plotting in the political world. For decades we have been fed sound bites of political figures answering questions, and they have whetted our appetite for the cunning "poly-tricks" we intuit are there.

2. Taboo-Buster Rock Star Tricksters and Hollywood Heroes

Little Richard (Richard Wayne Penneman, b. 1932) was an early rocker with musical genius and charisma who stirred controversy and gained teen admirers by crossing stereotypical lines of race and sex. Little Richard stole thunder from the black spiritual style, and made exciting rock and roll, wearing makeup and fancy clothes. According to his own story, after engaging in wild orgiastic behavior, he went back to religion, becoming a minister.[134] Controversial rock star taboo-breakers in the headlines over the decades include Jerry Lee Lewis (who caused a scandal by marrying his thirteen-year-old year old cousin), Rick James, James Brown, and more recently Michael Jackson, R. Kelly, Britney Spears, and Courtney Love,

Prince, Kanye West, Katy Perry, Miley Cyrus, Justin Bieber, etc. Now a veteran flashpoint of the rock scene, Madonna is another example of a star with the ability to provoke excitement and reinvent herself anew repeatedly over the decades—a trickster feat.

In some artists' lives and works the trickster plays a big part, reappearing in a new guise every time we begin to forget about them. Consider Bob Dylan and his songs. In one, the innocent drifter escapes from the unjust trial when lightning strikes and wrecks the courthouse. The authorities are shocked; like the judge who holds a grudge, maybe they need a new perspective. Maybe we all need to turn around and glimpse the frowning jugglers and clowns who have been busy doing their tricks for us and getting our kicks for us. And the singer himself gets a comeuppance sometimes too. Wearing a raincoat and a hoodie in an Hispanic working-class neighborhood on a rainy evening in Long Branch, New Jersey in 2009, Dylan was stopped after looking for some time at a house with a "For Sale" sign in front. "For nearly five decades, Bob Dylan has chronicled the adventures of scruffy wanderers and tricksters nearly laid low by the cleverness of a waitress here or a girl with calico eyes there" but the woman who actually questioned the songwriter in 2009 was a Long Branch police officer named Ms. Buble, and she "may have been the first to ask for ID, [and] she's very much part of a tradition of women and authority figures easily perplexed by him."[135] Put upon by a quizzical suspicious waitress in a Boston restaurant on a holiday (in his song "My Heart's in the Highlands"), "deceived by 'the clown inside'" in the song "Abandoned Love," and amused by the ironic Joker in "All Along the Watchtower," Dylan shares much trickster play with listeners in his mercurial lyrics. In his song "What Was It You Wanted?" he seems to be turning the tables on a schemer. With simple questions he deeply inquires into unclear motives and relationships that may be deceptive. In the eerie atmosphere of "Man in the the Long Black Coat," the narrator suggests his love disappeared without a word with a mysterious stranger—maybe the ultimate trickster, death. The tour de force "Visions of Johanna" opens with an observation about the night playing tricks just when the singer's trying to be very quiet. In "Man of Peace" evil personified can be a trickster, appearing in the guise of a man of peace, a great humanitarian, and a philanthropist. He is snakelike, shedding layers of skin and keeping ahead of conscience, "the persecutor within." Dylan is a skillful manipulator of crowds, and a twister of dreams. Dylan's song "Trust Yourself" is the ultimate answer to the issue of tricksters. Shifty Dylan (note that the name "Dylan" in Welsh means "son of the sea") sometimes seems like an offspring of the ever-changing restless ocean, mercurially fluid.

Celebrity tricksters of rock and rap are often known to break taboos and amass further power from their notoriety. The antics of rock stars with drugs and groupies, trashing hotel rooms, etc., are legion. Kurt Cobain, Jim Morrison, and many punk, glam rock, big hair, and heavy metal bands are known for their wild antics outside the norms.[136] Rappers gain "street cred" with gunplay, violence, and the refusal to snitch. The public may admire the slick way a songster trickster gets away with it all—riding high in limos above the fray beyond serious consequences, enjoying immunity. On the other hand, we scratch our heads, asking, "Where did he get the clout to flout the rules with such impunity?" So the public also likes to see celebrities fall, and some paparazzi earn big money for catching stars like Paris Hilton and Lindsay Lohan off guard, in the midnight act of being themselves in disarray. It certainly takes tricky ingenuity to outrun and dodge the demonically resourceful paparazzi, as many celebrities, including Justin Bieber, would testify.

Show biz may have more than its share of tricksters. Hollywood is in the business of selling dreams and shadows of dreams, and stars are the focus of many American fantasies. Publicity agents can help actors and actresses project the images they want to promote. Agents have their tricks, and so do directors and producers. The tricks of Hollywood include high technology's special effects, computerized touch-ups making actors on invisible wires look like they're flying through the air. Movie heroes seem braver and stronger and more skillful than any human could ever be, more wonder-inspiring. In *True Lies* (1994) Arnold Schwarzenagger portrays a character bravely and skillfully defeating terrorists in ways no human could, and so does the Jack Bauer character in the TV series *24*. Hollywood can use fantastic artistic tricks in the service of storytelling, becoming increasingly astounding, sophisticated, and slick. The more incredible the depiction, the more real it is made to appear, with dozens or hundreds of specialists creating the special effects, using the most advanced technology. Sometimes less than great films make millions thanks to hype and wild trailers. Whole volumes and encyclopedias have been compiled to document Hollywood trickery regarding stars, starlets, executives, agents, and publicists.[137] Conventional Hollywood's tricks and treats are skewered to a turn in Ben

Stiller's Hollywood movie *Tropic Thunder* (2008). Such critiques can have a tonic effect, stimulating greater self-awareness among the audience and the people in the movie industry. The Hollywood establishment itself is plagued by parasitic tricks of criminal gangs selling counterfeit DVDs.

Philosopher and historian Eric Hoffer observed that there is a certain timelessness in controversial people, noting that today's rebel "is twin brother of rebels in all ages and climes."[138] Manifestations of the trickster archetype exhibit family resemblances, whether as zoot suit dude or flapper girl, rebel without a cause or hipster beatnik, hippie or punk. Consider the example of Lux Interior, who was the lead singer of a punk-rock band, the Cramps, which began performing in 1976. He took elements from horror films, rockabilly music, and dark psychedelic atmospherics, as well as rude, rough punk rock sounds, and wove a style that became known as "psychobilly." Lux Interior wore tight black rubber clothes, discarding them while performing until he had on only leopard-skin swimming trunks. For her part the Cramps' female guitarist, wittily named Poison Ivy, wore bondage costumes. Together their sensational appearances, primal sounds, and raucous artistry grabbed attention forcefully, expressing strong emotions and stirring the imaginations of their cult-followers in the audience. This example is one of many—each successful rebel entertainer, large or small, can grow a fan base and develop a uniquely devoted cult following.

Through the power of sound and showmanship, trickster musicians can get people to do what they want—raise arms, weep, get goosebumps, start riots, dance, or sing along. The beats of the drum affect the nervous system, making different parts of the body move, almost involuntarily. Music can bond, can stir patriotism, can calm or excite the pulse. We are subject to the music the Pied Piper trickster plays. We forget ourselves as the music reaches our deeper feelings and satisfies our nameless cravings.

3. Womanly Tricksters

Many traditional myths of tricksters concern male figures, and folklore scholars have discussed the issue of why there are not so many female tricksters.[139] But in some old tales there have been trickster women, and in American history and popular culture, there are plenty of women known to have been scam artists.[140] I have mentioned the naked lady scam of the 1800s in which a helpless nude woman mysteriously turns up and needs the help of others. Another example of an American woman con artist of the nineteenth century was "Big Bertha" Heyman, a woman of German ancestry born in 1851. She was known as the Confidence Queen, the most bold and expert of the women con artists of her time. She swindled a number of men out of many thousands of dollars by pretending to be wealthy but temporarily unable to access her riches. She was known for her generosity toward the poor, and said she especially liked to swindle proud men who thought they could not be "skinned." Her tricks included using forged securities to con a Wall Street broker.[141]

There are also women attracted to male tricksters, women who seek to tame and save the straying and rebellious, or simply to keep him company. Some women like to ride the trickster's high or his winning streak for all it's worth, as if married to or having a love affair with Coyote. In earlier times there were maidens of moonshiners outfoxing federal agents, mistresses of bad boy bootleggers, and molls of mob wise guys. In more recent times we might note the lady friends of tax swindlers and drug dealers. There are perennial examples of women tricksters seducing, turning tricks,[142] operating smoothly, using all their wiles to get their way, sometimes even getting away with murder. There are also the women who betray their husbands. Blues songs call the man who sleeps with the wives and girlfriends of servicemen and prisoners "Joe the Grinder." Cuckolding and other "bed tricks" are played out with new twists in every generation, and often the young players assume they are doing something original.[143]

Some would have us believe that when women, trained in patriarchal societies for centuries to be compliant, begin to be more independent and defy convention, it's not a pretty picture. Others would say there's nothing prettier. Mae West, Theda Bara, Jean Harlow, Marilyn Monroe, and Jayne Mansfield were American sex goddess tricksteresses who specialized in using all the ancient wily tricks of flirting to accomplish mass media seduction. They dramatized with glee the naughty powers of the sex kitten, flaunting a beautiful body, arousing desire, seducing and dominating the red-blooded American male imagination. The presence of such a woman could, and still does, cause a stampede. "Painted Women" have a long historical past and no doubt a promising future in the American psyche. In American burlesque alluring striptease tricksters dance slowly, undressing to the music, entertaining at the edge of men's desires. Sally Rand, Gypsy Rose Lee, Sherry Britton, Zorita, and Lois de Fee were stars in the legendary galaxy of twentieth-century American trickster strippers. But already in 1896 a vaudeville artist named Charmion was performing a spicy trapeze act, disrobing in midair. Today there is no shortage of exotic dancers earning a living from displaying their wiles at "gentleman's clubs"—at least a third of a million exotic dancers work in America the last time I checked. This art of charming takes a potent savvy, the ability to portray and incite lusty desires, a craftiness of wiggle and slink, teasing with ease, yet remaining just beyond the grasp of customers.

In the archives of America's folklore there are many "Farmer's Daughter Jokes," telling the tales of a ripe rural girl, protected by her father. She is often attractive and/or seductive. These are red-blooded libido stories of desires flustered, and frustrated, and of desires fulfilled, and also desires laughed at. In this simple family farm setting with a small cast of characters, dramas of American sexual fantasies, fears and foibles are played out extravagantly. A shotgun, corncobs, a storm, sheets, vegetables, and other everyday items play their parts. There are tricks to get around prohibitions, wordplay, and sometimes a surprise ending. Like a game of "scissors, rock, paper," sometimes the farmer or his daughter trick the salesman, and sometimes the salesman tricks them. There's something peculiarly American about these raunchy and silly scenarios, and their longtime popularity in folk humor is a testament to an abiding fascination with life's sexual trickiness, seductiveness, and surprise endings.

Joyce Carol Oates, in her novel *The Gravedigger's Daughter*,[144] narrates the story of an immigrant couple's daughter who transforms herself to survive in the American environment. She takes the American identity of Hazel Jones instead of using her given name, Rebecca Schwarts. She learns about American ways while working as an usher in a theatre where she watches Hollywood movie scenarios, and shifts shape to become more like a Rita Hayworth kind of woman. Then, as a clerk in a music store, she sees that the composite female persona she has taken on is "distinct as a comic strip character: Olive Oyl, Jiggs-and-Maggie, Dick Tracy, Brenda Starr Girl Reporter."[145] She lives a life of pretense, out of necessity. Or, should we say that like many others, she learns what is fashionable and most approved and enviable from celebrities, cartoons, entertainment media, and ads?

Such learning shapes her life—the culture takes her in, provides her with attitudes, opinions, a way of life.

James Baldwin's character Ida, in his novel, *Another Country*, says: "You think women tell the truth. They don't. They can't. . . . Men wouldn't love them if they did."[146] Smart, wily women can pretend, hide feelings, use subterfuge, and employ men's imaginations as weapons against them, when they need to. As in the famous scene in *When Harry Met Sally* (1989), they can convincingly fake orgasms and any other kind of delight.

Over the decades there have been a good number of infamous American women con artists who preyed on unsuspecting men. Susanna Mildred Hill is remembered for conning men in the 1960s. When she was at least in her sixties she became the pen pal of a number of young men, and charmingly convinced them she was twenty-something. She successfully enticed them to send gifts to her for years. Some "feminine" tricksters are even less what they seem. Charles Daughterty assumed the false identity of "Storme Aerison" in Colorado Springs in the 1990s, engaging in credit card fraud. Daugherty was a black man posing also as a seventeen-year-old white blond female high school cheerleader and model named Cheyen Weatherly. In this amazing case, Daugherty fooled many people with his girlish charms.

Some women are world famous for coquetry, the ability to flirt in a lighthearted playful manner, playing tricks of coyness, and to tease and trifle. French philosopher La Rochefoucauld wrote, "All women are coquets, tho' all women do not practice coquetry; some are restrained by fear, others by reason. . . . Women are not aware of the extent of their coquetry. . . . It is a sort of coquetry, to boast we never coquet. . . . Coquets take a pride in appearing to be jealous of their lovers, in order to conceal their being envious of other women."[147] Because these observations were made by a man, we should take them with a grain of salt. But the unconscious tricks of flirting and funny banter nevertheless seem to be an integral part of human relations.

The history of American comediennes includes stars like "Jackie" Moms Mabley. Raped as a child, Moms grew up to develop a boldly comic stage persona. Frumpily dressed and topped with a floppy hat, she spoke her mind with outrageous frankness and hilarity, joking about sex on the chitlin circuit. Moms Mabley's edgy comedy treaded on dangerous ground, candidly broaching the subjects of racism and an older woman's attraction to younger men. ("Ain't nothin' an old man can bring to me, exceptin' a message from a young man!" and "A woman will always be a woman, but a man's a man only as long as he can.") The history of women comics also features Imogene Coca, Lucille Ball, Gracie Allen, Rusty Warren (of "Knockers Up!" fame), Jean Carroll, Carol Burnett, Joan Rivers, Lily Tomlin, and Whoopi Goldberg; sometimes they acted dumb when they were really "the brains of the outfit." Cloris Leachman in TV sitcoms and comic movies made audiences laugh for decades. Phyllis Diller poked fun at American social relations, including family life, performing in outrageous clothes and gloves like those worn by clowns. ("All clowns wear gloves, including Mickey Mouse," Diller said.) Roseanne Barr upset the status quo with her persona of "domestic goddess." Rosie O'Donnell, Ellen Degeneres, Margaret Cho, Tracey Ullman, Wanda Sykes, and Chelsea Handler all spring new tricks for subversive laughs, featuring new takes on women's lives, and postmodern observations on what it is to be an American. Sarah Silverman acts dumb, the better to get the goat of unsuspecting targets—including those who assume norms of good taste will always be respected. Silverman speaks with a deadpan delivery and pretends to have a deficit of understanding, so the audience members feel smart, until they are rudely shocked by point-blank outrageousness. Like Coyote, she's a trickster of sly stupidity, breaking rules of taste with glee. These comics are American amusers, loved for being so tricky, always one step ahead of the game. They seem full of truth's quirky surprises, giving fresh angles on actualities that turn the tables on the unsuspecting. In my book, their names form an honor roll of those who slyly reveal the way things are.

Perhaps the greatest lady trickster performing in recent years is the ever-changing activist rock star Lady Gaga. Always imaginative and controversial, outrageous in costume and makeup, arriving at the 2011 Grammys in a large egg carried by six palanquin bearers, for example. Her 2011 televised Thanksgiving special seemed strange in its attempt to convey her ordinariness. Gaga celebrated traditional values of family and Catholic school childhood, when usually her trickiness trades on defiantly and flamboyantly playing around with taboos. It is hard to submit and defy at the same time. Tradition requires submission, following the familiar. Initiating the new and flaunting boundary-crossing actions requires a breakthrough of the unfamiliar, a refusal to carry on in the old way. It was interesting to see her challenge herself. Instead of the sex goddess championing individuality, she sang for her grandfather. Her songs about defending one's unique self against bullies and conformity stir many people to have courage in standing up for themselves.

America, in advertising and entertainment, and styles of fashion and beauty, often projects the image of a hypersexual culture. Using sexually titillating tools and tricks of salesmanship, designers construct atmospheres and influences, promoting fads, products, and attitudes. They trick out a world of self-image for fashionable women to inhabit. But women look at trickery in their own way. *Lie to Me* (2009–2011) was a Fox-TV series about investigators specializing in seeing through lies and tricking the truth out of suspects devoted to hiding it. By observing unconscious gestures, like "mouth shrugs," "hand shrugs," and facial expressions of "asymmetrical sadness," the discerning eye can see through the lies. As the humorous dialogue in one episode goes:

Man: "Have you ever had any deception training?"
Woman: "I've dated a lot of men."

Men do a lot of deceiving, and skillful women have to endure and outsmart their unfair contrivances.[148] There is a familiar ring to the famous complaint of Annie Oakley: "When a man hits the target they call him an expert marksman; when I make the mark they call it a trick . . ." But the Native American Sitting Bull knew Oakley was more than a trick shooter—he wanted to adopt her because she was such a good shot. Perhaps it takes an underdog to to recognize great values being underprized.

Women are not all saints, needless to say. They are not strangers to the temptations of flimflam. A hoax in Colorado came to light in November 2012 in which a twenty-two-year-old woman, Briana Augustenborg, collected money for a nonexistent boy said to be suffering from cancer. At that same time the former comptroller of Dixon, Illinois, Rita Crundwell, pleaded guilty to embezzling 53 million dollars from the city. She had become a big fish in a small pond. How she was able to purchase hundreds of horses, a number of impressive houses, and a 2.1 million dollar mobile home on a comptroller's salary became a great puzzle to the people of Dixon, who were so familiar with this neighbor woman's face. Women are known as great nurturers, but they can also be great obfuscators and swindlers.

4. Male Comic Tricksters

The comic trickster spirit gets people to laugh—this amounts to a temporary seizure of control. But for what purpose? There is more than one purpose, no doubt: release of tension in enjoyable outbursts, ridicule of opponents, building oneself up at the expense of another, etc. Comedians are tricksters who often use wit to accomplish a collapse of pretension. The unruliness of Jerry Lewis contrasted perfectly with the suave nonchalance of Dean Martin. The darting subversive intelligence of comedic geniuses like Mark Twain, Will Rogers, and Charlie Chaplin was well known and loved by the world, and they continue to cause fans to marvel. Twain famously said of humorists, "ours is a useful trade, a worthy calling; that with all its lightness and frivolity it has one serious purpose, one aim, one specialty, and it is constant to it—the deriding of shams, the exposure of pretentious falsities, the laughing of stupid superstitions out of existence; and that whoso is by instinct engaged in this sort of warfare is the natural enemy of royalties, nobilities, privileges, and all kindred swindles, and the natural friend of human rights and human liberties."[149] Chaplin was a counterforce, a trickster mime for the "po' folks" of America; a beloved comic tramp of humble hopes, paltry prospects, and soulful mishaps; an innocent clown of zany screwups and yet a champion for the cause of justice. Running from the Keystone Cops, tripping over his distended flapping sole, Chaplin sympathized with the weak. He was a humanitarian genius rib-tickler of refreshing laughter and wellbeing, somehow always escaping the messes of life with a wink, and cheerfully walking on, spinning his cane.

Phil Silvers was a comic known especially in the 1950s and '60s for playing "Sergeant Bilko" on TV, and playing carnies, con men, and anti-authoritarians in stage productions. Bob and Ray spoofed incompetent authorities, and the inventive Stan Freberg made novelty records parodying American songs and stories, while Jonathan Winters portrayed zany characters like Maude Frickert from Merlyville, Ohio, and Lord Buckley retold Bible stories in hipster idiom ("Here come da Naz, walkin' on da water!").

I am astounded to look back and think of all the vibrant comic voices active in my lifetime. Lenny Bruce, Mel Brooks, Richard Pryor, Rodney Dangerfield, Bill Hicks, and Sam Kinison all skewered mainstream hypocrisy with frank, hip, colloquial revelations, and daring explorations of usually suppressed realities. Richard Pryor, trying to keep it real on TV and on stage, and in movies, was the kid from cathouse pool-hall Peoria, telling the funny truth about whites and blacks. He lived out his life in the spotlight for paying customers. He burned himself out again and again, and lived to tell jokes about it. "They can kill you, but they can't eat you," his grandmother used to say. He made us laugh, and made "reality TV" look like scripted lies. Lenny Bruce was a martyr for frank talk, and all daring comics today have to thank him for dying for their sins, as one comic put it. Mel Brooks' over the top outrageousness, as in the *Producers'* song and dance number "Springtime for Hitler and Germany" is extraordinary. He said that comedy is "spotting the insane and bizarre in the commonplace." Like Richard Pryor, Sam Kinison was a daring comic from the smalltown American dreamland (he was also from Peoria). He is remembered for his primal screaming onstage, getting laughs with his hysterical outrage. His evangelist roots could be heard in some of his intense in-your-face tirades. Offbeat comic Andy Kaufman had a knack for hitting the funny bone with his strangely serious deadpan eyes and outlandish bits. Black comic Redd Foxx used blue humor to poke the truth home. Bill Cosby often used spontaneity to tickle us with wry observations on childhood, and Bernie Mac, like the Wayons Brothers, probed American life with style and verve. The raw truth hurts but it also relieves us, like a psychic escape valve. The trick of telling the zany truth in a world of repression and denial takes precise skill and bright intelligence.

New rib-tickler tricksters continually appear—R. Crum finds his voice, depicts his obsessions and keeps on truckin'. Al Hirschfeld perfects his lines portraying celebrities with a stylish flair. Matt Groening through *The Simpsons* barbs the contemporary American family. Art Spiegleman brings wry surrealism to horrific events, and many other American cartoon comics, including Al Capp, Gary Trudeau, the artists at *Mad* magazine, have been bringing the insightful and delightful tricks of imagination that enable audiences to see life anew, or at least from fresh perspectives.

Willfully to blur the concealed and get it past all the censors, deniers, liars, control freaks, establishment guardians, and status quo institution worshippers—and to do so with impunity—is no easy feat. Sly innuendo can go a long way. The jester tickles us for laughs, to express the underside, and to lighten the heaviness of self-righteousness and guilt. His humor is contrary, doing the opposite of what convention dictates. W. C. Fields went against the grain, knocking children and playing the alcoholic curmudgeon, but he found an audience that wanted to see someone stepping over those lines. The goofy Marx Brothers ensemble, playful and anarchic as an oodle of rambunctious Labradoodles (a cross between Labrador Retrievers and poodles), formed an important influence on the Beat Generation writers, according to Jack Kerouac. Bob Newhart's "button-down mind" brought leavening to the '60s and later decades. Mort Sahl's disarming stealth in cardigan sweater with newspaper in hand ("Liberals are guilty about what they've earned; conservatives love everything they've stolen, they're proud of it!") thoughtfully observed the absurdities of twentieth-century American experiences. Steven Wright jokes on his own wavelength; with a face as deadpan as Buster Keaton, this cosmically laconic, balding longhair stand-up comic specializes in spaced-out absurdities and bizarre coincidences of consciousness. His brain's warped double takes seem more surreal and postmodern than earlier American comics like Red Skelton, Jackie Gleason, Milton Berle, or Johnny Carson.

The Emmy award-winning TV program *The Daily Show* is remarkably skillful in poking fun at hypocrisy, mocking spin doctors, and bringing the obvious foolishness out of the shadows and into the laughable forefront. Such a treatment of the serious events of the day is cathartic and hope-giving—relieving the emotional atmosphere like a steam valve releasing pent-up pressure. *The Daily Show* excels at retrieving clips of politicians' statements and comparing them. These clips serve to help keep people honest, performing a great public service that other TV news shows often neglect. (Note also that the ringleader bag-of-tricks-man Jon Stewart can bring together archrivals Bill O'Reilly and Chris Matthews to do a skit together in a benefit show raising money to help autistic children.) Like Timothy Leary (1920–1996), who said he sometimes wrote exaggerated views in newspaper letters to the editor under assumed names, Stephen Colbert on *The Colbert Report* presents views so archly conservative that people may be led to draw their own conclusions about arch-conservative credibility. His disarming persona of the right-wing dumbbell allows him to say things and get laughs instead of negative responses. He plays between the areas of liberal and conservative with great freedom, wit, and fun—the trickster as go-between who doesn't have to pander or over-explain, and the insight master who can play dumb to shine a bright light.

Woody Allen and Larry David are brilliant schlemiel schtick tricksters. Woody Allen's long career as a comedy writer, comedian, actor, screenwriter, and director has been very influential on other performers, and shows he is able to play the fool for laughs and to produce art over the decades as well. He's not a one-trick pony but a master trickster of many talents. From the archetypal nerd character to the author-director of *Blue Jasmine*, he has spanned many years and a spectrum of comic and serious art. Larry David makes humorous hay from the quirks of everyday life and our odd personalities. He builds wildly funny plots from squeamish subjects like race, ethnicity, disabilities, social mores, taboos, and embarrassing moments.

Eddie Murphy Raw (1987) presents tricks and games that men and women play with each other, keeping it real with uncensored language. Murphy, like Jamie Foxx, made the transition from clowning comic to serious actor with astonishing skill. Dave Chappelle's routines often feature him as a trickster spoofing racial stereotypes. Richard Pryor and others had pioneered in this topic. It's a rich theme. Listen to the unique humor of Tracy Morgan's *30 Rock* character joking about repressed memories of growing up in the ghetto:

> I slept on an old dog bed stuffed with wigs! I watched a prostitute stab a clown! Our basketball hoop was a rib cage! . . . Some guy with dreads electrocuted my fish! I saw a crackhead breastfeeding a rat. A homeless man cooking a Hot Pocket on a third rail of the G train! . . . I once saw a baby give another baby a tattoo! They were very drunk![150]

Cheech and Chong riffed on spliff humor. Carlos Mencia is a postmodern Hispanic comic and daredevil jerkster, flipping everybody off for a laugh. George Lopez is a soulful Hispanic wit telling it as he sees it, with his feet on the ground and an eye for irony. Bill Maher pokes fun at hypocrisy with blunt and sometimes courageous remarks that are politically incorrect, on a TV show of the same name. Steve Martin, Gary Shandling, Robin Williams, Billy Crystal, Will Farrell, Jerry Seinfeld,[151] Conan O'Brien, and Chris Rock, have all daringly exposed self-delusions and societal foolishness, getting us to laugh at ourselves and our culture. Publicity hounds grab attention any which way they can; but these slippery souls who glare out from the spotlight fearlessly do not seem happy unless they're making a sharp point, aiming it well, and making us laugh. In an appreciative light, these comics compose an honor roll of democracy's bright tricksters.

Some comics are tricksters probing the national spirit, taking the pulse of the zeitgeist; some are quite quirky, daring and over the top. Some are wise and last a long time, others burn out more quickly, but the best deserve our attention, respect, and thanks. It's not only the military that contributes to the well-being of a nation. Doctors, teachers, librarians, researchers, engineers, community activists are obvious contributors too—and so are fearless curmudgeons who have the courage to speak truth to power and cause an uproar. Consider George Carlin, master craftsman of comedy and language genius, who said the duty of the comedian is to ascertain where the line is drawn and then to deliberately cross it. (He also compared sports: the quintessential American sport of football is about the acquisition of ground, like the struggle the first settlers were involved in, while baseball is more pastoral, and is about "going home.") Tricksters of freedom play in serious areas; they are not just like drivers of Good Humor trucks offering sweet refreshments; they are also first responders, door openers, children pointing at the emperor's (missing) clothes. As Tommy Smothers reminds us, sometimes they represent the soulful American stance that yelled: "Don't tread on me!" They are jester-tricksters in the court of liberty. Their observations about language can help bring into focus our presuppositions about reality, and can question facades and explode false assumptions. But mostly not on prime time. As Bill Hicks, Texas outlaw-persona comic who died young, said, "They don't want you to talk about ideas on TV." Mainstream TV wants goofy jokers but not real mavericks.

Comics fling their daring ideas through the air with audacity, and the lucky and skillful ones find their audience. Louis C. K., whose work in some of his series episodes has a Kafkaesque quality, has a gift for looking with bewilderment at the strange situations he is caught up in. He breaks new ground in his stand-up act by broaching very personal matters, and in doing so he finds that many people are already there, welcoming openness about intimate experiences hidden too long.

This honor roll of male comics is far from complete, but it will have to do. Our great comedians tell truths with sly wit, so that with a slanted glance we too can view embarrassing realities, so life can be a bit more bearable. Critics may say they are a kind of circus, distracting audiences and draining off activist energies, but I see them as possessing a penetrating intelligence that fearlessly notes the emperors' lack of clothes. They are Jeremiahs, Diogeneses, Socrateses.

The trickster takes many shapes; he or she lives at the crossroads, dances along the borders, fooling around with limits, always goofing around and stepping over the line. What can he get away with? In 2006 Sasha Baron Cohen's character Borat, in the film *Borat: Cultural Learnings of America for Make Benefit Glorious Nation of Kazakhstan*, traveled across America, slyly hoodwinking gullible hosts and experts, putting on miscellaneous unsuspecting helpers and enablers, exposing a naive strain in too-trusting American personalities. In some instances he was incredibly obnoxious and repulsive.

Going overboard, stepping over the line is a trickster thing. The irksome trickster doesn't know when he's outstayed his welcome. We get tired of his excessive teasing and feel sorry for his victims. But then after a while we yearn again for the trickster, when there's not enough levity, wit, reality, meaning, or vision; we crave the trickster satyr's satire, stirring up the staid and stagnant, bringing chaotic energy to refresh the social order. The trickster makes us forget monotony, gives us something to thrill to, to laugh and cry about. The trickster respects no class as beyond ribbing, but tickles, twists nipples, and gives wedgies and charley horses to one and all.

Hip-hop performers are sometimes consummate clowning tricksters, from the parody-performing Ludacris to the bumptious Souljaboy. Self-parody is foreign to some rap artists, but others, like Lil Wayne of New Orleans, and Snoop Dogg of Long Beach, thrive on exaggerations and clowning in their videos. Snoop's persona is the sly trickster, smooth and calm beyond the fray. All successful rappers have to be both tricksters of imaginative language and tricky dancers. Lil Wayne is a good example of this, and despite his sagging pants and his holding a mike instead of a flute, the visual impression of his stomp-romp dance performance can be Kokopelli-like. In a serious vein, the hip-hop duo named Insane Clown Posse, which uses shocking horror, performs in the persona of two evil clowns. Tupac Shakur seemed to thrive in fans' minds all the more after he died—a trick Elvis and Michael Jackson also somehow pulled off. Eminem's hilarious caricatures of other performers, such as Axl Rose, and of himself, show both humor and technical tricks of rapping, such as the rapid spitting of rap lyrics sounding like a sped-up machine.

Comic tricksters in American media are signs of the vitality of democracy's freedom of speech. Daring comics tweak changes into existence, twisting the tail of the cosmos and making a difference by changing attitudes and opinions. How far can they cause a change of heart, bringing true transformation? If they were impotent, people in authority would not fear them, harass them and cause them to be removed from the public eye by locking them in jail?[152] Rulers often do not like to be laughed at. It's embarrassing for a VIP to be the serious butt of trickster's jokes. In the early 1960s America Lenny Bruce was harassed for speaking his mind; in recent years, in places like Burma and Yemen and Tunisia, Arabia and Egypt, comedians who make authorities uncomfortable have been arrested, jailed, and fined.

The compulsion to make people laugh sometimes comes from sadness and outrage. The tragic clown, the secretly crying buffoon, is often portrayed in schmaltzy popular art, as well as in respectable pop music and jazz—such as "The Clown," by Charles Mingus.[153] Henry Miller wrote, "A clown is a poet in action. He is the story which he enacts. It is the same story over and over—admiration, devotion, and crucifixion."[154] (This brings to mind French artist Georges Rouault's expressionist paintings of tragic clowns and bold-stroke images of the suffering Christ.) As Indiana-based Joe Lee, who trained and performed as a clown and wrote a book about the significance of the clown traditions entitled *The History of Clowns for Beginners*, told me, "There are some clown scenarios in which the clown dies and comes back to life."

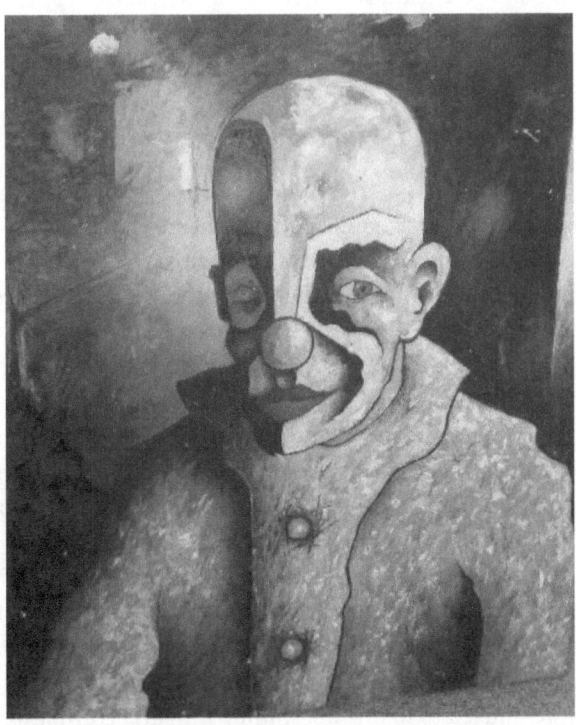

The clown figure in America has a wide potential for multiple kinds of manifestation. Both Patch Adams and John Wayne Gacy dressed as clowns, one for good, to heal, and the other to deceive and kill. Cindy Sherman, who has been called "the unchallenged cornerstone of postmodern photography," is a trickster of many identities and genres in many self-portraits, including a menacing clown. The archetype, like human souls, can appear saintly or sinister.

The trickster spirit is the deep-down soul of comedy shticks and is the pulse of superb timing. The trickster's wise guy punchlines, seeming so spontaneous, give the impression that he's already up there ahead of you, hip to what you need to realize, divulging it to clue you in and catch you up. The trickster is seen in the comic spirit, which points up absurdities, spins fantasy scenarios about things that don't make sense, piercing through tired habits to divulge the vivid truth. Sometimes the timing of the trickster is so superb it takes your breath away. Rip Torn played a consummate trickster at the end of Norman Mailer's 1970 film *Maidstone*, antagonistically wielding a hammer against the hero (played by Mailer) and surprising everyone with a demand for harsh reality, not satisfied with a phony veneer. It would seem to be almost a law of the universe: shallow pretensions and pompous hypocrisy's false proclamations call out for a trickster to appear and reveal what's real, or at least to mock obvious obfuscations.

5. Charismatic Tricksters, Actors, and Others

Tricksters, both in ancient stories and in real life, plan performances, and they stage surprises. With dynamic personalities and talents they can charm wide audiences. They spring tricks, cute or smart, dumb or crazy, catching people off guard. Such jack-in-the-box stunts teach us that life is dicey, prone to disaster, yet they also show that opportunities lurk in disguises and unsuspected hiding places. In America near the end of popular minstrel shows in the 1840s, there was often a skit about southern plantation life, with entertaining songs, dances, and slapstick comedy routines. Some of these stories featured trickster slaves who outwitted their masters.

The African American minstrel-clown-singer Bert Williams has been called the first black star. He appeared in blackface makeup and sang songs like "Nobody," which tugged on hearer's sympathetic heartstrings in the early twentieth century. One must be an extraordinary trickster to play within the conventions of one's own day, and yet transcend them. Louis Armstrong also did this, later. Bebop and jazz artists like Miles Davis and Dizzy Gillespie refused to follow the smiling minstrel conventions and won a grudging admiration for the neat trick of their aloof new style.

American history also includes the example of John Wilkes Booth, an actor with a sociopathic trickster streak, who in the most dramatic manner imaginable assassinated Abraham Lincoln. After firing upon him at close range, Booth leaped onto the stage yelling the Latin motto *"Sic Semper Tyrannis!,"* breaking his ankle before making his escape. All assassins seem to have one or another kind of trickster scenario up their sleeves, often mixed with delusions of their own grandeur. Booth, a self-centered actor born in a prominent Maryland family, seems to have labored under the strange delusion that he was heroically rescuing a nation that would thank him. He saw himself in the role of liberator of a nation suffering under a tyrant. While hiding in a swamp and a forest after assassinating Lincoln, Booth wrote thoughts in a notebook that show he felt betrayed when he saw himself denounced in newspapers. He had expected to be hailed as a patriot. He was unrepentant, writing, "God simply made me the instrument of his punishment." It seems Booth's passionate conviction gave him the tunnel vision that made him become a destructive trickster. He complained of being taken for "a common cutthroat" when he felt he did what Brutus, in killing the tyrant Caesar, was honored for. Booth's mummified corpse, shriveled and far less handsome than in his heyday, was later displayed in a carnival.[155]

On the positive side, there are voices that have been strong over the decades and will have a chance to endure for centuries. The prophetic voices of James Baldwin, Allen Ginsberg, Bob Dylan,[156] Alice Walker, and Maxine Hong Kingston display trickster aspects—now playful, now taunting, now crossing the line and shaking up the status quo. Iconoclastic Elvis was a trickster breaking through the conformist confines that had kept styles of white and black cultures separate in America. Marlon Brando always seemed in his performances to bring forth seldom-seen, daring truths about spontaneous behavior, the quirks of being in the moment. In *Missouri Breaks* (1976) his anarchic spirit played with a tricky, changing mix of multiple personalities in the chameleon character David Braxton, a bizarrely eccentric bounty hunter in the Wild West. Trickster method actor James Dean turned his feelings inside out, exposing the private moody truth in public with irresistible charisma. Jim Carrey in *The Mask* (1994) brought his shape-shifting talents of "making faces" to a story about archetypal Norse trickster Loki's mask. Revelatory collective-unconscious-inspired actors with trickster talents also include Jack Nicholson, Robert De Niro, Al Pacino, Johnny Depp, Will Smith, Leo DiCaprio, Sean Penn, Forrest Whittaker, Robert Downey, and Jeff Bridges.[157] These mercurial tricksters don't play fair. They explore boundaries, roam outside the box, and break rules; they take risks, experiment and transform themselves—they transcend conventions in the spotlight and sometimes in their private lives.

Other entertainers' styles of tricksterism distinguish them from their contemporaries. Mel Gibson and George Clooney are known as incorrigible practical jokers on movie sets. Johnny Cash dressed in black to show sympathy for the poor and victimized. He cultivated an outlaw persona and sang in prisons to reach out to society's outcasts. Sean Penn went to Iraq before the US invasion in 2003, and spent time on the road in Venezuela with Hugo Chavez in 2007. These rebel examples of transgressing boundaries and doing the unexpected have a tricksterlike dynamism and resonance. They fly with wings of daring spontaneity. In film versions of the fictional story *Batman* (1989) and the animated TV series *The Justice League* (season 2, 2004), the character known as the Joker plays out archetypal villainous trickster fantasies, whether portrayed by wide-smiling Jack Nicholson or evoked by the mercurial voice of Mark Hamill. But these incarnations of the Joker are pale forerunners of what was to come.

The Batman film *The Dark Knight* (2008) featured the late Heath Ledger as the ultimate Joker, a sociopath who promotes chaos and terrorizes both good and bad guys, ruthlessly. Ledger tapped into the trickster archetype as an agent of havoc, gleeful to jeopardize his own life for the chaotic hell of it, and even happier to kill others for his cause. The first philosophical line the Joker says is a paraphrase of Nietschze: "I believe whatever doesn't kill you makes you stranger." A vicious psychopath who has no rules, Ledger's Joker says of the establishment, "Their morals are a bad joke," and observes that, "The only morality in a cruel world is chance." Therefore, he reasons, "The only sensible way to live in the world is without rules." He characterizes his acts by saying, "I try to show schemers how pathetic their attempts to control things really are," and says "The thing about chaos is it's fair," that is, it doesn't play favorites—anyone can be harmed, whoever they are. The message when he lights a huge stack of paper money on fire is "everything burns," sounding much like the Buddha's diagnosis of the world's ills. A crime fighter comments, "Some men just want to watch the world burn," and they can't be reasoned with. The Joker's memories (unless he is playing a trick and lying about his past) include a brutal father hurting the Joker's abused mother, and asking his son, "Why so serious?" The levity of Joker's irresponsible pathological actions—murder, arson, etc.—are tragically ridiculous, like the smeared makeup of the mock clown face on his shoulders. If paranoia is a disorder of meaning, Joker's meanings, thoroughly disordered, are a virulently aggressive paranoia, boldly acted out beyond even the most bloodthirsty terrorist's wildest dreams. Some terrorist tricksters, like certain stages of hopelessness and pain, are beyond normal limits. They can't be reasoned with as if they're civilized and rational, because they are not. They're outside the box.

The actor who plays a part well has to find the role in his own personal being; to experience a rageful don't-care-if-I-live-or-die part of the personality is to cut open a gaping vulnerability in one's own life. Critic David Denby commented that when Ledger wields a knife in this role, the viewer wonders "how badly he messed himself up in order to play the role" and he observes that "this young actor looked into the abyss."[158] This reminds us that the trickster archetype is rife with mysteriously powerful energies that can be dangerous to the psyche. It is like playing with fire. When Jack Nicholson, who also played the Joker, heard of Leger's death, he said, "I warned him." Acquainting oneself with the depths of the psyche opens the way to discovery, but also to the potential for damage. To dare to go beyond usual boundaries and test limits is always a risky endeavor. The line between "real life" and the mind's imagination of life becomes unclear in the experiences of the collective unconscious. Playing with the fire of good and evil, the soul can end up tricking itself—you laugh uncontrollably only to find the abysmal joke was on you. Who can be the joker instigating catastrophic free-for-alls, playing around with others' destinies and courting death in a giddy free fall, and be sure of surviving with impunity? Why are some drawn destructively to dramatic scenes depicting thrilling anarchy, like the twenty-four-year-old gunman who attended the midnight premiere of the film *The Dark Knight Rises* in Aurora, Colorado on July 20, 2012, murdering a dozen people and wounding fifty-nine?

It takes trickster testosterone to go out on a limb and be a rodeo broncobuster, a bungee jumper, a hang-glider, big-wave surfer, a skydiver, or high-speed race-track driver. Death-defying stunts are trickster territory. Evel Knievel was the twentieth-century American daredevil stunt-driver trickster par excellence. His trickster shadow doppelganger was "Super Dave" Osborne, "Teflon man," a dimwitted comic character dressed up like a daredevil driver, appearing regularly on late-night TV shows. Super Dave's laconic speech and moronic unconcern about performing dangerous stunts that all ended up in catastrophic accidents won him fame. All the action heroes making hairbreadth escapes in scenarios of daring doodoo and derring-do are playing the trickster role, showing what it looks like to dodge death and survive in a world of dangers. Characters played by Bruce Willis, Mel Gibson, Vin Diesel, Harrison Ford (especially as Indiana Jones)

are examples. It is savvy trickster advice to say "Grab the bull by the tail, not by the horns, *so you can let go when you need to.*" Wise trickster strategy likes to stay a step or two ahead of the game.

Austria-born Arnold Schwarzenegger arrived in America having already won the Mr. Universe contest at age twenty. A pumped-up bodybuilder with greasy stuff in his hair, Arnold spoke almost no English. Soon he showed up in action films—as Conan the Barbarian, then as a cyborg from the future in *The Terminator*. When he married Maria Shriver he added other aspects to his aura. Every year after the age of twenty-six most men lose 14 percent of their body's natural production of the human growth hormone, but Arnold continued to grow. He also grew from a silver screen hero into a politician, becoming California's governor (nicknamed the "governator"). At the 2004 Republican convention he presented himself as a great immigrant success story hero, embodying the American Dream. When Arnold was introduced there the music and visuals were a takeoff on a *Saturday Night Live* opening, as if to say, "See how the GOP is young, vital, hip and countercultural too! Join us in the fun and the country will be well-run by fine young Republicans!" Years later it was revealed that Schwarzenegger had fathered a son with an employee who worked in his home, a housekeeper, a revelation that wrecked his marriage.

In every twenty-four hour news cycle, many of the stories are about tricksters and/or victims of trickery, about people with fame and charisma, about politicians who deliver "red meat" to the base, and about people you love to hate. Sometimes we feel we are being manipulated by their sympathy-seeking tricks. Other times we encounter American tricksters who are heartwarming. Consider Wavy Gravy, a hippie clown and bodhisattva storyteller working for a better world. Ram Dass said of him: "This wise clown of compassion is a genuine Mahatma of the Cosmic Giggle." Paul Krassner said of him: "Wavy Gravy is the illegitimate son of Harpo Marx and Mother Teresa." Or consider the work of the Bread and Puppet Theatre, with protest parade puppets, and circus plays.[159] Abbie Hoffman and the Yippies, Tim Leary and Richard Alpert, Hunter Thompson—all are known as charismatic counter-cultural tricksters of the '60s. Thompson was a wild trickster figure.

A gonzo journalist druggy jester, he said that without drugs his thoughts would be those of a second-rate accountant. Johnny Depp played the part of the hallucinating Thompson in the 1998 film *Fear and Loathing in Las Vegas*.

Different cultural heroes resonate with different audiences. With their various tricks and mesmerizing gimmicks they galvanize different personalities, inspiring them in different ways. But every performer has tricks up his sleeve; and if not, won't the audience get up and leave?

We could also enumerate a list of charismatic Elmer Gantry-like religious leaders who have gained the confidence of gullible believers—men of the cloth who have seduced parishioners, run off with the money donated, etc. Women of the cloth might be included too. Aimee Semple McPherson (1890–1944) was an evangelist preacher and media celebrity of the 1920s and 1930s. She disappeared in 1926 in a dubious "abduction" that was never fully explained. Their congregations do not suspect their shepherd could be a wolf in sheep's clothing.

The relationship of the performer to the audience is constantly being experienced on both sides of the footlights, but it is seldom discussed. The great actor Marlon Brando made an enigmatic statement that reveals an insight into it. "If you want something from the audience you give blood to their fantasies—it's the ultimate hustle."[160] I take this to mean that the actor becomes a live embodiment of someone else's daydreams, fleshing out their wishes and whims for a livelihood. It can be more than a hustle, a generous art, with the right material.

6. Sports Hero Tricks

Fans today would do well to remember that the first Americans were hunters who arrived in North America 12,000 to 15,000 years ago or earlier. They came here via the Siberian-Alaskan land link, which remained above water until 8000 BC. Therefore, sports on this continent have ancient roots. American ball games can be traced back to Mayan ball games, which had cosmic symbolism. These games, which were sport and ritual at once, served as a metaphor for the cycle of life and death. Teams of the conquered and vanquished played out the game with a predetermined destiny in the arena, ritually enacting central beliefs of the Mayans. The archetypal two trickster brothers, found in stories of North American Indian tribes all across the continent, were ball players. In a sense, today's sports heroes go all the way back to those ancient stories and games, that spirit of competition, and that ethos of tricky skills. The ritual importance of the games is more on a shadowy subconscious level now, but is still very powerful.

Macho fun and sports hero hype together form a large arena for tricks. According to stereotypes, the great athlete is supposed to be a trickster, a fun-loving joker with a crooked smile, snapping his towel in the locker room. Grinning like Tim Robbins in *Bull Durham* (1988), skillful on the field and clowning around in bars and bedrooms, he is often thought of as prodigious at partying. The public persona of young Cassius Clay (later Muhammad Ali), born in 1942, was that of a trickster upstart who rhymed to tease opponents. He floated and stung with imagination and with his boxing gloves and boots. The play *Fetch Clay, Make Man*, by Will Power, investigates the unlikely bond between two very different and powerful cultural icons—the youthful Cassius Clay and the older black Hollywood stereotype actor Stepin Fetchit. Both embraced the trickster sensibility of mercurial adaptation and surprise to accomplish great success in a world of prejudice and daunting odds. Their wise trickiness gave a vibrant shape to the legacies they created during the struggle of the civil rights movement in America in the mid-1960s.

Other athletes trick more underhandedly—"Say it ain't so, Joe," is a well-remembered line from a disappointed young fan about a hero, Shoeless Joe Jackson (d. 1951), who was tried for involvement in a conspiracy to fix the World Series and was banned from playing baseball for the rest of his life. The growing controversies about cheating in sports by using steroids constitute another trickster scenario—involving, for example, Mike McGuire, Barry Bonds, and Alex Rodriguez. Other baseball players in trouble for doping include Jose Canseco, Manny Ramirez, and Andy Pettitte. Football player Bill Romanowski and athletes in other sports, such as boxers and wrestlers, were also fined for using drugs to enhance their abilities. It was revealed in October 2012 that cyclist Lance Armstrong for years ran sophisticated juicing and blood transfusion operations to gain advantages for himself and his teams in international biking competitions, including the twenty-one-day, two-thousand-miles-long Tour de France. He denied the charges for years. But in January of 2013 Armstrong admitted his guilt. The annual Tour de France race began in 1903. In the early years contestants used ether, cocaine, and strychnine, or chugged wine in bars along the route to fortify themselves. In the 1940s amphetamines were popular among the racers. When Armstrong became a professional racer the performance-enhancing Erythropoietin (EPO) was the drug of choice used by many racers.[161]

Basketball player Dennis Rodman earned notoriety as a trickster surprising fans and fascinating viewers with ever-changing hair and clothing styles, including a blond wig and white wedding gown, which in 1996 he wore in New York when autographing copies of his book *Bad as I Wanna Be*.

Don King, known as a legendary fight promoter, and known for his fancy verbal footwork, said he made the time he served in prison (for non-negligent manslaughter) serve him. Emerging from the personal crisis by finding religious faith, King said he moved "to higher ground." (Asked later about brain damage in prizefighters, King pointed to risk inherent in all opportunities, and the courage needed to succeed: "They break your leg and then ask you why you're limping.") King's ability to survive and thrive seems partly due to skills and tricks of wariness and daring. King served as promoter for a number of boxers, most of whom later sued King. (One of them was champion Mike Tyson. Tyson, like a street fighter, once chewed off an opponent's ear in the ring, and sometimes taunted opponents' with crude threats of crushing their testicles while in the same breath thanking Allah.) Don King also promoted George W. Bush during the 2004 election campaign.

Wrestlers, with their caricaturish scenarios, dramatic costumes, and macho gimmicks, their outlandish moves, and choreographed demonstrations of sadomasochism, replete with amplified sounds of slamming into the mat, etc., create a cartoon-like sports world all their own. The flamboyant display makes the matches more entertaining, firing up imaginations and suspense. Without the opera-like histrionics of tricky wrestlers like Gorgeous George, Haystack Calhoon, Beautiful Beauregarde, Gorilla Monsoon, Andy Kaufman, Jerry "the King" Lawler, "Daisy Mae" Morgan, Road Warrior Hawk, etc., wrestling would have far fewer fans. Charismatic tricksters play prodigiously outside usual boundaries and borders, and some of their fame, acclaim, and magnetic power derive from that outlawism. Such outlandishness is not confined to wrestlers. In his 1991 book, *A View from Above*, Wilt "the Stilt" Chamberlain boasted of 20,000 sexual conquests. His feats on the court were impressive, and his stats off the court were even more amazing. Another sports trickster, O. J. Simpson, has been a polarizing media fixture for decades. Skater Tonya Harding's story can never be told without reference to a dirty trick played on rival skater Nancy Kerrigan.

Harding's ex-husband was involved in clubbing Kerrigan's knees before an important Olympic competition. The assailant's name, Jeff Gillooly, is now used as a verb to denote a violent sneak attack, as in "they Gilloolied him."

Every sport has tricks and devices designed by players and coaches to get an edge on opponents. Baseball great Johnny Sain said, "The point of pitching is to fool the batter." It is best if baseball pitchers have a poker face or some other mask over their true emotions and thoughts. The legendary pitcher Satchel Paige (1906–1982) had a trick in which he acted like he was going to pitch, then did not pitch. Then all of a sudden he did pitch, just when the batter's stride had been thrown off. An injured pitcher has to hide all the signs of pain he's feeling so that the batter won't know how to take advantage of the situation. Foxy opponents master the element of surprise. Other kinds of tricks may be associated with the sport as well. Great baseball players like Babe Ruth and Pete Rose have been known as gambling tricksters, placing illegal bets on baseball games secretly.

Customarily, every team has a mascot, a kind of resident trickster rooting for the home team, whose personality is both tamed and unleashed by wearing an outlandish costume. A trickster spirit ignoring rules in the seeking of victory may be just as ubiquitous. In an article about recent and past spying incidents in sports, with coaches using tricks to get an advantage over rivals, Mark Bowden wrote that "cheating in football is as traditional as the coin toss."[162] Bowden asserts that the 2007 case of spying and videotaping involving Boston Patriots coach Bill Belichick "one of the most acclaimed and successful coaches in NFL history, may be indefensible, but it is also commonplace."[163] Shadowy tricks of the thinker working overtime to win on a never perfectly level playing field will always seek to know the plans and plays of rival teams, because, as the saying goes, "forewarned is forearmed." As Bowden notes, amateur sports also involves intense desire to achieve victory. "If cheating is part of the game when victory means only bragging rights it will always be part of the game when victory comes with substantial rewards."[164] The attitude today for a significant number of people is that playing by the rules is for chumps and losers in sports, and also in politics, business, war, and other endeavors. Instead, winning at all costs, by any means necessary, is a value which necessarily brings out the unscrupulous trickster in the psyche.

Some kinds of sports tricks are not about winning. They seem cruel and senseless. A little teasing or joking is one thing, but loading up a fellow player with a constant stream of insults is abusive. An example is the "hazing" incident reported in November 2013 in which Miami Dolphins lineman Richie Incognito sent thousands of text message threats and insults denigrating Jonathan Martin. Locker room horseplay became bullying and psychological torture in this case, like the teasings of a psychopathic hater and race-baiter on steroids.

"Titanic Thompson," the alias of Arkansas-born Alvin Clarence Thomas (1892–1974), was a golfing hustler who bet on the golf games he played in country clubs all across America. One hustle was to play a round right-handed, which he could do fairly well, and then bet he could beat his opponent playing left-handed. Born left-handed, Titanic was an even better athlete playing left-handed, and won big stakes.

Playing "dirty pool" means using devious tricks that do not offend against official rules of billiards, such as "snookering" rivals by pretending to be unskilled and clumsy at first. After higher stakes are agreed upon, the player then begins to display his true prowess. Such fake outs and feignings are deployed in various competitions. In official drag racing competitions, if the "dial-in time" is registered as slower than the actual performance time it's known as "sandbagging." A baseball player sliding into home base and aiming himself at the catcher cleats-first was once considered dirty pool. In basketball, jabbing with elbows was once dirty pool. Also, "snowing the goalie," spraying ice in his face with your skates during a hockey game by skidding to a stop near him, is a form of dirty pool. In poker, slow-betting and bluffing are thought of as dirty pool by naive people. In the sport of politics there are times when a candidate first acts in a way that lowers expectations, so that he can successfully shine brighter later.

Each sport has its charades and gambits of fakery used by team members to get an advantage over opponents. NBA basketball players commonly yell and shriek at the moment of trying to make a basket. The loud sounds are made to fool referees into thinking there was a foul.[165] A hilarious bit by comedy team Key and Peele demonstrates "flopping," which in basketball, soccer, or football, means suddenly falling down as if fouled by a player on the opposing team, even when little or no contact was made.[166]

Idols of all sorts become what their fans want and expect (except when stars refuse to follow those conventions, courting boos instead of cheers). They often find eventually that following their own public images they have gone to excess, and then they must change and out-trick their own fate to survive. Fate is always throwing us curve balls, and we have blindspots that cause us to be easily outfoxed. Therefore, we all have to be learning new tricks all the time just to survive and thrive.

7. Social Comment Gadfly Tricksters

Humor enables people to play around with serious issues, and make controversial social comments, and get away with it. There are sly trickster impulses in Michael Moore documentaries, in *Saturday Night Live* sketches, in *Prairie Home Companion* skit dialogues, treating known personalities lightly with satire. Garrison Keillor has tricks that get around the staid Minnesota Lutheran conformity, bursting out with irrepressible larger-than-life-like scenarios. Weird Al Yankovic seems able to make a humorous mockery out of any kind of pop song, from rap to punk, placing a fun house mirror before them all. *The Simpsons, South Park, King of the Hill, Squidbillies,* and Robert Smigel's cartoons all satirically mirror contemporary issues, language, and celebrities of our day. Political cartoonists poke fun at leaders and see what they can get away with. There's a force that "comforts th' afflicted, afflicts th' comfortable," as journalist Finley Peter Dunn said of the press. Commentators like Rachel Maddow keep alive the American tradition of fearlessly shining a light on hypocrisy. Watchdogs cause trouble, and gadflies[167] shake up rigid and stagnant situations. Witty commentators stir things up so blocked energy begins circulating again; they help solve problems by stimulating conversations and new possibilities. They bring needed resolution—like Haida Indian stories of Raven releasing light that has been hoarded from the universe for far too long. Trickster can be a boon to systems that need a kick in the pants.

The custard pie-in-the-face trick is a well-known trickster prank. Among equals and friends—brothers and sisters, cousins and co-workers, fellow students and inmates, it is a joke. It is on a par with toilet-papering the front yard trees of someone singled out for the honor. But when a prominent person receives a custard pie in the face at a public event, flung by an anonymous attendee, the gesture is a more serious protest, an insult, a means of expressing disapproval; it is a humiliation, a leveling, a comeuppance, a comic way to cause a sudden loss of stature. In late 2008 near the end of the George W. Bush administration, when an irate Iraqi reporter threw his shoes at the president's head, commentators spent much time trying to explain the meaning of the gesture. Probably in America the gesture that comes closest to this would be spitting in the face. On trial the reporter explained that when he heard the president bragging about victories in Iraq, and not acknowledging the many innocent Iraqis killed in the process, "I was feeling the blood of innocent people flow under my feet as he was smiling. I felt that he is the killer of my people and I am one of those people. I became emotional because he's responsible for what is going on in Iraq, so I hit him with my shoe."[168] When he was released in September 2009, many Iraqis and others hailed him as a hero. It got him in trouble and earned him a punishment, but it was an understandable trick.

Pranks of protesters, street theater skits, topical songs, and many jokes circulating by email all have a trickster aroma. On the Right, Ann Coulter is known for outrageous statements impugning and insulting leaders of the Left. Rush Limbaugh and Bill O'Reilly point their fingers with righteous arrogance at faults they perceive in others, but these millionaire media-maven big boys of the Right with their sneering public personas have their own tricks that they have tried and failed to keep private—such as Limbaugh's abuse of painkillers, and O'Reilly making crank calls that constituted sexual harassment (he settled a lawsuit out of court to avoid public scrutiny of the details).[169] Such gadflies are like Coyote and other mythical tricksters; they challenge boundaries, throw dirt around, mix things up, unsettle sediment, and fool around with excrement, smearing it on others and themselves. They break eggs to make omelettes, and toy with feces for fun and profit. (In Harlem once I heard a wise woman warn, "If you mess with trash you'll get some in your eye.") Gleefully and often in bad taste, social critics raise dust and break up routine habits. They startle sleepwalkers and amaze dullards who've become too habituated to conventional routines. They sometimes poison the waters of public discourse and then laugh all the way to the bank. They live at crossroads and trade controversial accusations, dishing out lies, smears and hyperboles, taking cheap shots, playing dirty tricks at busy intersections where traffic is heavy. In the jungle, the jackal is known for exploiting opportunities in chaos, stealing parts of carcasses while other animals squawked over them. There are con artists who employ similar tactics. Obstreperous tricksters stubbornly speak their piece until everyone's honking their horns. Even if they are unpopular with some, with others who share their anger they may become big heroes. They may parlay chancy exploits into successful careers, becoming well-paid mouthpieces of men who gloat in the shadows.

A commentator like Glenn Beck, with Alice in Wonderland logic and crocodile tears, shows how a demagogue charisma plays tricks with conspiracy-oriented minds trying to understand what is going on in the complicated world around them. Beck makes a striking image on the screen: a huckster prophet, with crew-cut and plastic magic dime store peepstones to help him read the mysteries of the buzzing world around him, and to see with paranoid lenses lies of hated "progressives" like the villain Woodrow Wilson. The shoes he wears are not Bozo the clown's but also not what millionaires usually wear when appearing on TV. They are more like the kind worn by an eccentric middle-aged man wishing he was a college kid. He dramatizes the image of a bluff-master crying like a victim for sympathy, in rage and dismay, presenting half-grasped, half-baked, half-thought-out opinion points and semi-factoids, serving up a piecemeal hodgepodge of slapdash learning. Beck is a self-proclaimed former "scumbag" now claiming to be a conscientious cracker barrel philosopher, a blackboard chalker of revelations about conspiracies, exploiting distrust, wanting to pull back the Wizard of Oz curtain for the deluded audience, to enlighten it. He specialized in being a gadfly harasser of Obama, who studied hard, succeeded, became the leader of the free world. The trickster knows a moving target is hard to deal with, track, fact-check, and keep a focus on. The trickster creates disjunctions, uses lack of continuity, and employing a fascist symbol here, or a tragic emotion of America's supposed loss there, takes on veneers of dramatized sincerity to scoot around and stir up controversies. Disguising his shallowness in plain sight, exposing DaVinci Code-like symbols in obvious places—"fascism on a common dime, on the other side of the mercury head; someone wanted to plant a fascist symbol here! It's an outrage!"—he conjures up an atmosphere of weird horror. "I caught Diego Rivera, socialist artist, plastering his propaganda on Rockefeller Center! Look at this photo!" There are trumped up scandals: "This artifact was kept hidden in the basement of the Smithsonian! It's Hebrew writing on an old Native American slab—someone doesn't want you to know! Someone wanted to slide sneaky tricks right by you! But I found out and reveal it here on TV for you!" Huckster trickster's pure shuck is a Kabuki show dramatizing the gnawing and jawing activities of moths chewing through silks, creating doubts about character without evidence, accusing caricatures of dreaded enemies with crimes. He presents all this with a straight face, a put-on caricature of sincerity, like a puffy cherub stirring up hysteria and fear—"Look how much gold China is buying!"—between commercials trying to sell gold. What kind of a man would use his born-again experience to make money, get fame, manipulate others, cause confusion and pain? Someone willful, self-centered, unconscious, or a trickster seriously deluded by his desires, an opportunist with a public platform. Former politicians, radio talk-show hosts and political commentators with anger and bitter spite do strange things. Such people use deliberate confusion, like talk of "death panels." Or when money (some of it foreign) is donated anonymously to candidates by being funneled through "The United States Chamber of Commerce," they feign confusion: "My dad belonged to that!" They pretend it isn't the national organization of big business funneling money, but just the little local hometown clubs, being discussed and blamed for spending fortunes to sway elections. The jackal trickster exploits chaos to his own advantage, runs out, grabs some cadaver parts and runs back to safety in glee as other creatures fight over the bones of the carcass. He exploits selective focus, making a living from spin with John Birch-inspired paranoia. Playing dumb while calculatingly clever, playing clever while dull and dumb. Feeding anger by slanting, honey-voiced pitchman playing the spoiler, the moth, the chronic complainer, seeking the simple days of *Our Town*. In January 2014 Beck said he regretted some of his divisive rancor during his time on Fox News: "I remember it as an awful lot of fun and that I made an awful lot of mistakes, and I wish I could go back and be more uniting in my language because I think I played a role, unfortunately, in helping tear the country apart."[170] The trickster is known by what he does and how he tries to dodge his own handiwork.

Zen poet Lew Welch, in this brief poem entitled "The Basic Con,"[171] diagnoses psychological and political manipulations as the basic trick recurrently played on humanity. The poem basically says that people who have nothing for which to live are able to make up things for which they might die, and then go on to get everyone else to lose their lives for that cause also. It is an indictment of warmongers and their games. Welch disappeared in the Sierra Nevada mountains and was never heard from again, except in the dreams of his friends, like poet Gary Snyder.

Buddhist teacher Pema Chodron spoke of the guru's role of being a "troublemaker." Chodron is an American woman, a parent and a grandparent, humorous and mature, trained in Tibetan Buddhist analysis. She has developed an understanding able to address contemporary issues and resonate with a wide spectrum of humanity. It is sometimes the discomfort caused by trickster teachers that gets us out of our habitual attitudes and routine ruts. Some spiritual teachers on the mystical path goad seekers onward by criticizing, pointing out faults, joking in ways that can seem insulting. They are wise tricksters who irritate and bedevil seekers to urge them to work on themselves and grow.[172]

Smart tricksters force us to shift our perspectives. Truly proficient debating tricksters are good at the jousting and swordplay of wits, engaging in wrestling matches of conceptualizing and emphasizing certain perspectives. They are skillful in the chess and checkers tournaments of matching and outsmarting ideological opponents' strategies. They could probably persuade us, for a while, of just about anything. Then in the middle of the night we might wake up and say, "Wait a minute! How did I get hoodwinked? I bought into something and invested so much, unconsciously!"

8. Scatological and Off-Scene Jokers

Trickster Coyote plays with feces and other forbidden, taboo, or impure substances in many native American stories. There seems to be something funny about fooling around with filth and getting caught in a mess of one's own making. As someone who grew up in a river town—Rock Island, Illinois—I feel that a comic genius for scatological language seems indigenous to the American Midwest heartland, and the many jokes about prodigious bodily functions, fascination with excrement, gas expulsion, all show a trickster element. The trickster tells unprintable dirty jokes, anecdotes never filmed or recorded, events never officially recognized.[173] Even at formal gatherings, whether historical or contemporary, the obscene trickster may be on the scene just under the surface, tickling ribs with barnyard embarrassments, ready to shake the walls with rude outbursts. In one story, for example, Coyote goes hog wild in eating food that acts as a laxative, and then suffers from raging diarrhea. As Deldon McNeely pointed out, "Trickster's ribald enjoyment of his own oral, anal, phallic impulses is very reassuring for children ... Br'er Rabbit teaches us that the spiritual cannot be separated from the physical, that even flatulence is sacred and enough to slay enemies."[174] Obscene language, and crossing the line in wearing daring clothes—doing an "end run" around the archetypal censor Miss Grundy—these sometimes seem as American as apple pie. Janet Jackson exposes a breast at the Super Bowl in 2005, and this famous "wardrobe malfunction" is deemed so scandalous that it is replayed on TV shows again and again, and discussed for many days running. Paris Hilton, Britney Spears, Lindsay Lohan, and Miley Cyrus outrage commentators and attract paparazzi by getting out of cars awkwardly, exposing private matters, and breaking other conventions. Such stories often draw more gawkers than the news of distant wars, political deals, and social issues that appear at the same time. Some things have primal pulls on our attention.

Our impulses and moods may sometimes prove to be tricksterish and embarrassing. Old photos may surface showing a wild time in a somber official's life. We are all human. Everyone, at some time or other, might go astray and need to make a U-turn. Midnight party photos on Facebook, or YouTube video antics, for example, may interfere with the image presented by the recent graduate who is a job applicant wearing a new suit at a nine a.m. job interview. Just when you feel so polite and formal, the trickster produces from the past the times you were rude and boisterous—humbling you. The trickster is representative of the way a life is not just many little separate fragments, isolated bits, but everything inter-stitched with one long loopy line, a thread of soulful fate binding one's life-moments all together. The trickster plays in the boomerang, the ricochet, the backfire; the trickster brings the bad man sorrow, the good man comfort. The trickster rides around making the tires squeal as he does U-turns, arriving again and again at the inevitable. "That's the way it goes," he says, "so you better learn to roll with it." And the trickster flattens your tires, just when he's the last thing on your mind.

Whenever grown people are "soiling their pants" in dismay and anger, whenever "the shit hits the fan," and whenever someone is shouting "holy shit!" in horrified shock, you can be sure the trickster has been futzing and "farting around" and then watching his crazy plans solidify. There are secret pranksters who foul some public nest and then disappear. They turn up, leave their solid waste in department stores and elsewhere as a lark, and they leave, gloating with a sly trickster smile on their faces as they think about their surprise gift of feces, like a Cheshire cat who just used a kids' sandbox for a kitty litter.[175] People whose homes are foreclosed because they have failed to pay their mortgages may express their anger in tricks discovered after they are gone. Some break holes into walls, or rip off built-in cabinetry; others smear their excrement on banisters and doorknobs.[176] Yes, there's the trickster's weirdly pleased face, grinning wherever there's someone playing with feces, and wherever an unsuspecting party finds a system all gummed up. We usually look the other way and forget strange occurrences like these as fast as we can, but they are right there in the midst of "civilized" modern human behavior. Our shock at finding such drippings and droppings, like the homeowner on Halloween answering the door to find a burning paper bag full of excrement, is the surprise caused by almost seeing the trickster, always arriving too late to catch him red (or brown) handed.

9. Thinking Outside-the-Box Tricks

Perhaps it requires serious old-fashioned shamanic tricks to protect the wealthy from fears, worries, and ghosts. Sarah Winchester, the widow who inherited a family fortune from Winchester rifle manufacturing, built a labyrinthine home in Northern California. The Winchester mansion, constantly under construction for thirty-eight years, had 160 rooms arranged in a maze-like design to befuddle any vengeful spirits of dead victims who might still be angry from having been shot by Winchester rifles.[177] The widow supervised the construction daily, as the structure grew from 1884 until her death in September 1922. The cost in today's figures would have been 71 million dollars. The Queen Anne Style Victorian mansion is famous for being so large and so devoid of a coherent master building plan, that anyone alive or dead would become confused in it. The deliberately baffling maze-like structure was a trick to elude ghostly forces seeking to attack inhabitants. Rich or poor, nobody has it easy, it would seem; everybody at some time or other has to find ways to cope skillfully somehow with uncommon threats like dread, loss, and sorrow, uncanny forces, and bad luck.

Henry Lee Lucas (d. 2001) was once considered America's most prolific serial killer. Taken into custody in 1983, he began confessing to many crimes committed in Texas. In one count he confessed that he had been involved in 3,000 murders. In another count he confessed to committing 350 murders. As some would say, his claims were all over the place. It is likely that he did kill his mother and possibly some other people, but the longer list of murders he claimed he was responsible for turned out to be a hoax. Why did he lie? As long as he kept confessing he was fed well and given cigarettes. Lawmen from various parts of Texas arrived and questioned him, and he confessed to all the crimes they described, and thereby helped them "clear" many unsolved crimes from their records. They swallowed hundreds of his stories, often supplying details to help the process along when Lucas was "remembering" incorrectly. Eventually it became evident that Lucas was actually in places far from the locations of the crimes he had confessed to. He was the only prisoner whose sentence was ever commuted by governor George W. Bush—not a repentant person, or an innocent person, but a con man who had gamed the system in this case. A trickster was not executed; remorseful criminals were.

James Earl Ray was another man known for obfuscation. His acquaintances said, "You can tell he's lying—if you see his lips are moving." Someone who studied Ray's life and wrote a book about him compared his ability to spread confusion to that of a squid emitting ink.[178]

Some criminal tricksters who are prosecuted for their crimes plead insanity in court, assuming an insane asylum will be easier to live in and escape from than a prison, or that the defense of insanity will help them avoid the death penalty. But authorities who have seen this ploy over the years say it's not always that simple. To be locked up in a facility for the insane can be a very serious matter, hard to endure, harder to get released from, more impossible to escape from. The trickster caught in his own tricks may find that his fate is every bit as miserable as it would have been had he submitted to the processes of justice. The trickster's web of karma is no joke. How can the long-spun web be undone? Where can one hide if one's life has been constructed of tricks? Punitive attempts to correct habitual criminal tricksters in the past have had mixed results. British philosopher Jeremy Bentham in the early nineteenth century wrote that prison, ideally, would be "a machine for grinding rogues honest." But in actuality, "the imperfect machinery of deterrent and reformatory discipline" did not often result in the desired penitence, honesty, deterrence, and reform.[179] To give offenders a fresh start is an ideal most systems fail to provide in a realistic way.

Tricks used to gain advantage in an unconventional way can take many forms. Author Clifford Irving in 1971 tried to sell publishers an autobiography of eccentric reclusive billionaire Howard Hughes, based on bogus interviews. He received $750,000 in 1972 from publishers such as *Life* magazine and McGraw-Hill for the "exclusive story" that was soon discovered to be an audacious hoax. He was convicted of fraud and served fourteen months in a federal prison. (His story is told in *The Hoax* [2007], a film starring Richard Gere, directed by Lasse Hallstrom.) But tricks are nothing new in the literary world. Washington Irving was the first writer in America to earn his living from his pen, and he established himself by a hoax, attributing his book *A History of New York,* to a fictional author, Diedrich Knickerbocker. Walt Whitman publicized his *Leaves of Grass* by writing reviews of it and publishing them under pseudonyms.

Perhaps we could say that all literature is made up of tricks with language. In his youth John Updike was a prankster, and in maturity he brought great skill and magic to the tricks and finesse of his sentences. To determine which authors are most thought of as tricksters in their actual writing would require a vast voting process in which readers would fill out ballots. Gerald Howard could cast his vote this way: "I find Bret Ellis' scalding, cynical, brittle, savagely unillusioned worldview curiously refreshing. He is the Loki or Trickster of the literary world (or maybe the Lou Reed), poking sharp sticks in our eyes and daring us to figure out if he could possibly mean that. Deal with it."[180] Others would vote for Mark Twain, Gary Shteyngart, Toni

Morrison, Maxine Hong Kingston, Louise Erdrich, or a host of others who trick us with their narrative skills.[181]

Belgian-born Paul de Man came to America in 1948, and hid the part of his past in which he wrote for pro-Nazi publications, publishing some anti-Semitic writings, and some writings praising pro-Nazi writers. In America de Man became well known as an influential literary theorist. Many of his early writings for pro-Nazi papers carefully avoided dealing with political issues. His experiences of adapting to the milieus in which he found himself taught him how to be fluidly flexible with changing times, and to use literary criticism to develop philosophical concepts and earn respect in the competitive (but highly politically correct) world of literary theory while teaching at great universities—Cornell, Johns Hopkins, and Yale. He was a key figure in the deconstructionist school. He argued early in his career that morality systems were destructive and time-bound, becoming stagnant, so that the past must be rejected to affirm a new present.[182] After his death his writings for pro-Nazi publications came to light. So did problematic issues in his financial and domestic life, including a period of time when he was married to two women. A scandal ensued. Georges Goriely, who knew him well in his younger days said de Man was "completely, almost pathologically, dishonest." He said de Man was a crook who had caused his family to go bankrupt. "Swindling, forging, lying were, at least at the time, second nature to him."[183] Some concluded that if one believes in nothing it is easier to do things that are unconscionable. De Man has his defenders and his critics, and they are still debating his tricks.[184]

In February 2014 John Lefevre, who had become popular on twitter for his tweets about Goldman Sachs written as if he was overhearing comments in the elevator there, signed a six-figure contract with Simon and Schuster. When it was discovered that he did not actually work at Goldman Sachs and was not riding in the elevator to get his material, his book deal fell apart. Two weeks later, he signed a contract with Grove Atlantic for a six-figure advance, for his book titled *Straight to Hell: True Tales of Deviance and Excess in the World of Investment Banking*. Perhaps the word "true" in the title should be taken with a grain of trickster salt, since the book will be "an unusual memoir" employing "hyperbole exaggeration," not literal reportage.[185]

The veracity of memoirs and reportage is perennially questioned, and the line between fiction and non-fiction is often a blurry precinct. Few writers are comfortable saying much about the experiences of creating believable stories.[186] We all have our debts to the world around us when we compose works in verbal or visual forms. We follow inspiration from nature, from great works, from influences, and forgotten impressions. The sources of artworks can be a thorny issue, whether resolved in a lawsuit or discussed by critics and creative people. The last major project of Orson Welles, the film *F for Fake* (1974), is the story of Elmyr de Hory, a narrator remembering his experiences as a professional art forger. The film explores what it means to be an author, what "value" and "authenticity" mean, and looks into the dynamics of tricky illusions.

The dapper and prolific bank robber Willy Sutton (1901–1980), because of his disguises (telegram messenger, police officer, maintenance man) was called "Willy the Actor." It is said he never carried a loaded gun because he abhorred violence. The artful Sutton escaped once from Eastern State Penitentiary using a plaster model of his head made by a sculptor inmate to fool guards with a dummy in his bed. Meanwhile he was going through a tunnel, which he and others had dug in secrecy for two years. That escape was short-lived, but Sutton was a slippery prisoner who escaped from confinement two other times in his career as well. The imaginative tricks of escape are often highly fascinating.

The "Barefoot Bandit" is another example of a legendary eccentric American trickster, breaking the law, and doing outlandish things like stealing an airplane after a string of burglaries. Colton Harris-Moore evaded police in stolen planes, boats, and cars during a two-year crime spree. The judge who sentenced him to seven years in jail in December 2011 said, "this case is a tragedy in many ways, but it's a triumph of the human spirit in other ways." Harris-Moore told authorities he had studied manuals and videos on the Internet to learn how to fly a plane, and said that the thrills he experienced while piloting stolen planes renewed his passion for life (after the childhood abuse he had suffered at the hands of his alcoholic mother). He said his experiences of flying would help him have the motivation to rehabilitate himself while serving his prison sentence. "The euphoria of the countdown to takeoff and the realization of a dream was nearly blinding. . . .

My first thought after takeoff was 'Oh my God, I'm flying.' I had waited my entire life for that moment." He became a folk hero to many for the outrageous tricks he pulled.[187] In January of 2012 he was sentenced to six and a half years in prison.

Tricksters can be hip and highly respectable, too. Consider the great Catholic writer Thomas Merton. He was a Trappist monk who would sneak out of the monastery to go to jazz clubs some nights, and, though he was a vowed celibate, had an affair with a nurse.[188] He showed a poet's zest for life, which is hard to confine in conventional conformist boundaries. Tricksters can be hip, and wild, and crazy, like Ken Kesey and the Merry Pranksters, with their electric Kool-Aid acid test and their psychedelic-painted bus named "Further." Kesey, as a graduate student in California in 1960, took part in government testing of "psycho-mimetic drugs" and he brought some home for his friends, who soon became the Merry Pranksters. He called the incident "the revolt of the guinea pigs." In 1964 he and friends journeyed east to Millbrook, New York, to see Dr. Timothy Leary and the League of Spiritual Discovery. Kesey said the reason for taking psychedelics was "to learn the conditioned responses of people, and then to prank them." Both he and Leary were involved, each in their own ways, in tricks to awaken people, and make them more aware of their conditioning, playfully encouraging them to explore consciousness, to know the deeper recesses of their own minds and potentials.[189]

The artist known as "Poster Boy" uses a razor to cut and rearrange parts of the advertising posters on New York City subway platforms. Because this making of collages with private property in public is illegal, he works secretly at night to elude detection. Of course vandalism and defacing posters has been popular for a long time, but Poster Boy made it more an art form and act of social criticism with his use of witty juxtapositions. In February 2009 Henry Matyjewicz (b. 1983) of Brooklyn was arrested and accused of being Poster Boy. Poster Boy has been called the "Matisse of subway ad mash-ups" and an "anti-consumerist Zorro with a razor blade." His recombinant works, which are photographed so that even if they are removed from the subway stations they can be viewed elsewhere, often employ social commentary on topics such as the occupation of Iraq. Poster Boy compares his spontaneous alterations of visual images and words to hip-hop free-styling—making up rap verses on the spot with a mike and audience.[190] Graffiti writers, collagists using found objects and mixed media, street artists of all kinds are tricksters playing with public spaces. For example, Ellis Gallagher made chalk drawings of shadows on New York streets, playing with perspectives on light's changes. Shepard Fairey's street art is an example of a trickster playing around with public places and memorable images. The documentary

Exit Through the Gift Store illustrates the tricks of the LA art world. Banksy, a British graffiti artist, did a series of public wall art works in New York City in 2013. Another prankster artist who plays around with reality in public places, Banksy at Disneyland in 2006 put on display a mannequin dressed up like a prisoner being held at the Guantanamo Bay detention facility. You never know what will appear next with such artists lurking around.

Unprepared to expand one's mind outside the box of restricting conventions, one will encounter one's limits soon. Unprepared to think of evolution as a way the mysterious Source of being may work, fundamentalists suspect the theory of evolution is all a hoax by trickster atheist scientists, who enjoy nothing better than denying the divine. Meanwhile, some scientists see much of religion as tricks of a priestly class played on the gullible faithful. Some scientists, in fact, see all preachers, from Billy Graham to Joel Osteen, as disingenuous Elmer Gantrys.[191] Some religionists in turn see all scientists, including Albert Einstein, who respected religion as an integral part of human life, as heartless atheistic usurpers of the throne of Truth's authority.

On the positive side, the element of play, a sense of the ludic in the imagination, is essential in thinking outside the box and necessary for human adaptiveness and learning. If one loses the ability of free play, the world becomes a too serious place, a realm of horror and grotesque loss—and rigor mortis sets in. If one overdoes play, one loses meaning in fantasy, and insanity. To be the world's most rational man is a great trick, like being the world's fastest talker, or the best unicycle rider. The trickster has many ways to get out of tight spots and figure out needed answers. If he can't outsmart someone he might be able to out-dumb him. If he can't out-think someone in linear thought, maybe he can out-dream him. If all else fails, he can passively play possum. Where there's a trickster there's a way around every impasse.

10. Minority Tricksters

Native Americans have a great tradition of humor, teasing, and great trickster stories. Some trickster-related customs are built into the annual cycles of life. For example, there is a tradition of Hopi visionary Pueblo clowns whose function is to refreshen and re-energize life, using humor, doing everything backwards as a way to return to a primal level and relate to the depths of existence, and to release tensions. In Lakota tribal traditions the Heyoka is the sacred clown. Like comics at a "roast," the Heyoka satirizes and keeps people humble and smiling. He lightens things up, keeps people's feet on the ground. Humor can deflate arrogance. Chaotic nonsense can liberate crippling inhibitions, tensions, deadening habits, all with joyous laughter.

Gypsies are commonly thought of as tricksters in American folklore. The Dom originated in North Central India, migrating to Europe in the fourteenth and fifteenth centuries. They were deported from England in the late 1600s, and in the early 1800s Napoleon was responsible for transporting hundreds of them to Louisiana. Spain and Portugal also banished the Dom to the New World, and many came to America in a diaspora from Eastern Europe in the 1880s, 1890s, and 1900s. Thus, the gypsies came to America because they were unwanted in other lands, and because they needed new lands to wander, a new host country to explore. They became known as shrewd horse traders, buyers and sellers of trucks and cars, and wily traveling tricksters.

So, as gypsies kept coming to America in waves, beginning in the 1700s, settled citizens saw them as tricksters on the horizon, passing through settled towns, surviving by their wits. Appearing in horse-drawn wagons, selling baskets and beads, often out-bargaining the rooted householders, and with their women telling fortunes, the gypsies seemed colorful and curious. Many American folk memories tend to focus on gypsy tricks. For example, a settled bakery woman remembered a colorful gypsy girl coming and holding up cash in the air while pointing to bread. The baker woman put loaves in a bag and held it up and pointed to the cash. The gypsy girl ran off with the bread without paying, smiling. Gypsy men traded questionable horses, and later sold used cars that sometimes turned out to be lemons. They seemed to be an exotic minority liable to fleece gullible suckers like sitting ducks. Then they would move on, tricksters heading off toward the horizon. No doubt survival for a people always on the move sometimes depends on making a roadside chicken disappear, and not getting cheated in trading. Itinerants need a quick wit, making things up on the spot, and knowing also how to "get while the getting is good." Each person should be known by his own merits, though, not by stereotypes. Nevertheless, gypsies have a colorful legacy in America.[192]

There are many different kinds of duplicities. There are devious self-serving tricksters, and decent tricksters who realize "you gotta do what ya gotta do" for a noble cause. The powerless underdog is often in a difficult situation; he must say one thing and feel another, just to keep peace. He must bite his tongue and smile; this subterfuge is not the same as a powerful man's deliberate manipulation of facts, imposing his will on the external world in order to get an advantage. Minorities often must use tricks to outwit the powerful, merely to stay alive. "Shuckin' and jivin' " means putting on an act to fool an authority figure. Such an act was not for fun, but to avoid serious consequences of displeasing "The Man," incurring punishments.

James Baldwin wrote in the 1960s, "I have spent most of my life . . . watching white people and outwitting them so that I might survive." In Baldwin's experience the establishment was a power "to be outwitted in any way whatever."[193] The trickster in this case is the model of outfoxing the steamroller of social injustices and prevailing by surviving. The bottom line is staying alive. Not only the majority's establishment, but also threats from one's own kind, must be survived. Consider Malcolm X's description of his early life in the dog-eat-dog hustler world of the urban jungle in Harlem. "I was a true hustler, uneducated, unskilled at anything honorable, and I considered myself nervy and cunning enough to live by my wits, exploiting any prey. A hustler knows that if he ever relaxes, if he ever slows down, the other hungry, restless foxes, ferrets, wolves, and vultures out there with him won't hesitate to make him their prey."[194] Not a calming thought, is it? In that position one must take charge of his own fate, knowing he is known as an outlaw.

African American writer Albert Murray spoke of his own "horizon of aspiration" or source of incentive while growing up in Alabama in the 1920s and 1930s, in this way: "how I felt about the socioeconomic and political circumstances" caused him to think of himself "as having to be the ever nimble and ever resourceful mythological Alabama jackrabbit" who thrived in the Uncle Remus briar patch. Because of this he never considered himself a victim. Instead he was something much more, "the fairy tale hero who would marry the fairy tale princess."[195] Such a self-image is helpful in the struggle to survive when a minority person faces a hostile world. A story that cannot have a happy ending is unworthy of the good guy trickster hero.

In American society some women have had to dissemble about their identities for a variety of reasons. Some women of color have had to pass for white. For example, Belle da Costa Greene (1879–1950) was a learned woman of color who traveled in high society circles of New York City. She worked for tycoon J. Pierpont Morgan, helping him build a great library. She had to present herself as a white woman to do her work and play her role. There have been women who have convincingly passed for men (for example, as soldiers during the Civil War), and many other kinds of posers, impersonators, and imposters.[196]

The greatest challenges minorities face have to do with escaping the tricks of the majority that seek to marginalize or dehumanize. To let others define you is to be trapped and determined by those others; wise tricksters resist this. It is a trickster ploy to take a negative name[197] (like "nigger," "queer," "witch," "punk," "Jesus Freak," "bitch" [or "bee-atch"]), and to use it as a "power word," wearing it as a badge, flaunting it, using it like an electric shock buzzer in one's palm when reaching out to shake a hand. The term "Quaker" was first used derisively by outsiders to ridicule the "trembling and quaking" valued by George Fox and his followers as the ideal response to God's word. Fox and his followers accepted the name with pride, and adopted it, along with the term "Friends," as an honorable title of self-identification. Those bold enough use the electricity that charges the forbidden slur. In this trickster turning-of-the-tables they may even find power, fame and riches. The taboo allure of the two syllable "N word" in rap has helped sell many millions of CDs and furthered the careers of a number of stand-up comics. (Another way to think about this is in terms of scapegoating. Hiding one's own faults, one scapegoats another to take the pressure off. When the scapegoated person accepts the label with a sense of irony, reveling in awareness of the ignorance of the prejudiced, coming out stronger, he has stolen fire.) The dynamics of this inventiveness and originality show that creativity flourishes in unpredictable ways. Greatness performs cultural tricks that defy expectations, in marvelous ways almost like defying gravity—diving and soaring freely in the sky, playing in our imaginations. New greatness stubbornly crosses impasses like pilgrims fording rivers in ancient times, reaching the shrine of accomplishment by any means discernible.

The tricky jujitsu of nonviolent protest used in civil rights struggles led by Martin Luther King, Jr., and others, shows a compassionate trickster skill and patience in the face of injustice. These tricky tactics were learned from the successful stunts of Gandhi, who claimed to be "an artist of non-violence," and from the ironic teachings found in the Sermon on the Mount. It took a long journey to Mecca for Malcolm X to realize the possibilities of peace. The trickster archetype helps makes reversals possible, including changes of heart, but the trickster archetype is also involved in violent reactions—assassinations that surprise the victim and the whole world. A surgeon uses a sharp blade and a light to operate on a patient; a thief uses a sharp blade and a light to rob a victim. The trickster archetype can cut both ways.

Minorities often strive for equality, and in their status and struggles they often see the shadow of official society's surface. They see a proud and arrogant culture as through a glass darkly, unmoved by its glories that are enjoyed by the mainstream majority. They develop a wary skepticism, a critical clarity, seeing through the wool pulled by jingo artists and the bragging of hyperpatriotism. As Marcus Garvey somewhere said, "The whole world is run on bluff."

One of the greatest American masterpieces on trickster selves is the novel *Juneteenth*, by Ralph Ellison, which profoundly ruminates on race and democracy, ideals, and betrayals. In this novel, both the preacher Hickman, and the boy he raised, who became a movie-maker and flimflam man before becoming a US senator, are tricksters.

11. Ominous Treacherous Tricksters

Sometimes people from distant countries where they lack opportunities are tricked into coming to America with false promises. In mid-seventeenth century England there were many indentured servants, and some were tricked into coming to America with promises of opulence and ease. When they arrived, they found instead harsh conditions. Mail order brides, nannies, and *au pairs* were sometimes brought to America under false pretenses. South Korean women have sometimes been promised work as cleaning ladies, and arrive to find that they have been tricked by sex traffickers. Sometimes immigrants fool themselves, finding they have committed themselves to lives of overwork, isolation, and substandard wages. They realize it was too good to be true.

The trickery involved in border-watching, border-crossing, all the hide and seek of illegal immigration, these make up a massive conundrum that American lawmakers cannot seem to resolve. In the Southwest, those who lead illegal immigrants into America are called "coyotes." Consumers and businesses needing laborers for low-paying jobs, and corner-cutting workers without papers in constant conflict with federal laws, together set up nod-and-wink trickster scenarios that seem intractable. No one is satisfied with the situation of illegal immigrant labor, but no way out has emerged. Sober plans fall through; only the tricks of the moment remain.

Trickster games are often involved in the playing of precarious roles, such as the undercover cop in a sting operation; and the crook disguised as a cop to make a heist. There are law and order gangsters, and prim and proper tricksters under deep cover. There are wolves in sheep's clothing creating a false impression, bad shepherds pretending to care for a flock while secretly fleecing it to death. There are parasites disguised as hosts, and hosts disguised as parasites. The true story of a New York policeman who sought to expose corruption in the police force was dramatized in the film *Serpico* (1973), starring Al Pacino. Cops on the take, detectives fudging some kinds of evidence and burying other kinds, lawmen slanting truth as it suits their needs, soon become indistinguishable, morally, from the criminals they are hired to pursue. Trickster cops and other authority figures sometimes drift to "the dark side," making deals, taking bribes, dealing in contraband. With lots of freedom at their disposal they begin to feel above the law. Sometimes they cause innocent men to serve time or even be executed, in order to protect and reward their paid informants. They may file bogus arrest reports, steal from criminals, sell goods taken as evidence, and depend on the "blue wall of silence" to conceal their acts. In one particularly notorious case, undercover narcotics officer Tom Coleman locked up a series of innocent victims in Tulia, Texas, until his injustices were exposed to public knowledge.[198]

Denzel Washington in the film *Training Day* (2001) played an officer of the law involved in unsavory acts. Because he is the trusted authority a rookie gives him the benefit of the doubt, until his acts become so outrageous no one could ever explain them away. *The Shield*, an FX TV series (2002–2008), is another drama about police corruption. Vic and Shane are crooked cops, playing many illegal tricks under the cover of being law-abiding family men. In the end their serious crimes are uncovered and in different dramatic ways they have to pay the piper. In some ways *Recruit* (2003), in which Al Pacino plays a CIA undercover agent trainer who is a renegade turncoat, is like *Training Day*. It is tricky business to catch a slick trickster who is a powerful leader, and prove his guilt to those officials over whom he has authority. Authority figures who toy with power and betray their charges lacerate trust in the system.

The TV feature "To Catch a Predator" on *Dateline* (NBC) televises sting operations, tricking online trollers into thinking they are setting up a sexual encounter with an underage female. When the trickster web-troller shows up, the trickster-announcer confronts him, and police arrive to arrest him on camera.

Conservative activist James O'Keefe has a long history of pranks employed to prove the validity of conservative and libertarian perspectives. He has used disguises and secret cameras to catch people off-guard. The 2009 "Acorn Sting," in which O'Keefe and right-wing trickster friends filmed a man disguised as an outlandish pimp seeking advice from Acorn community organizers about circumventing the laws of prostitution, turned out to be not only a trick played upon Acorn with a hidden camera. It also was a trick of editing, making it look at the beginning of the tape as if the man in the pimp outfit was dressed that outrageously when asking questions in an Acorn office, and other tricks of manipulating footage. O'Keefe was charged in March 2011 with a felony, tampering with the phone of Senator Mary L. Landrieu in New Orleans. In March 2013 O'Keefe agreed to pay $100,000 to settle a lawsuit with an Acorn Employee who was smeared by the manipulated tapes. Thus he avoided going to court and facing public examination of his activities. The trick damaged Acorn, and the idea of community organizing in the minds of many, including those in Congress who make federal funding decisions. Acorn went bankrupt. One of O'Keefe's collaborators, Lila Rose, also filmed controversial advice given by an abortion clinic employee. A hidden-camera taping by O'Keefe of an NPR employee talking with men posing also as Arab donors is another example of an Ashton Kutcher *Punked*-type prank. With new technology, possibilities for "gotcha moments" expand, as tricksters use their imagination, hidden camera technology, and the ability to edit tapes to create false impressions. Conservative scandal-monger Andrew Breitbart was another practitioner of this kind of trick.

It often takes great pro-social efforts and subtle intelligence to unravel antisocial forbidden tricks, and convict the sneaky perpetrators. Neil H. Rodreich II, a sex offender in his late twenties shaved his body and wore makeup to pass himself off as a twelve-year-old seventh-grader named "Casey" in several Arizona schools. Three other men impersonated relatives of "Casey"—his uncle, grandfather, and cousin, and lived with him, helping him enroll in Arizona public schools. In September 2008 Rodreich pleaded guilty to six felony counts and was sentenced in 2009 to more than seventy years in prison. His enablers also faced charges for their parts in the elaborate charade.[199] As Malcolm Gladwell reminds us. "A pedophile . . . is someone adept not just at preying on children but at confusing, deceiving, and charming the adults responsible" for taking care of children who are victims. Gladwell notes that people who devote so much of their effort to deceiving others "usually succeed."[200] Using obfuscating tricks, misdirection, distractions, decoys, and runarounds, they create veils of confusion, uncertainty, and doubt, sometimes for long periods of time.

To out-trick the criminal trickster who is an abductor requires thinking outside the box, acting contrary to expectations. For example, a kidnapped person can act like he/she is attracted to the captor, convincing him that he is liked. Then, when the abductor's guard is down, the kidnapped person can get a message out to someone who can help him/her escape.

The child molesters among the ranks of the priests, minister, rabbis, and others in positions of community leadership are tricksters of a corrosive and self-destructive kind. Pedophile priests in recent decades have cost the churches billions of dollars in lawsuit payments and have damaged many people's trust in religious leaders. All sorts of vandals, firebugs, sociopaths, and mischief-makers exhibit trickster traits when they strike. While America sleeps, stealthy scrap-iron thieves strip the lead, copper, and aluminum from buildings, and craftily remove catalytic converters from vehicles. They rip off manhole covers and lamp posts and sell them by the pound. They break down air conditioners for copper and other metals. Antisocial tricksters act like moths and locusts, all across the land. Car-jackers, assassins, robbers, rapists, all strike with trickster shock and wreak havoc. You go on vacation and return unexpectedly to find the engine being removed from your car, the contents of your home being emptied.

Corporations can also play the trickster, stripping the land of trees, coal, oil, precious metals, and then abandoning it, moving on to greener pastures. The greedy, exploitative trickster sees earth as dead matter to pillage, nothing more. Sometimes trusted watchdogs are paid off to look the other way. Fortunately, there are also conscientious stewards and conservationists who work to see that ruthless tricksters do not succeed in pulling off all the tricks they would like.

No one sane admires these and the other darkest examples of antisocial criminal tricksters in America. These include infamous names, such as Charles Manson, Jeffrey Dahmer, Lee Harvey Oswald, Richard Speck, John Wayne Gacy (the serial killer who wore clown costumes), Dennis Rader (the "TBK killer"), and Ted Bundy. They include Dylan Klebold and Eric Heller (the Columbine killers), David Berkowitz ("Son of Sam"), Richard Ramirez (the "Nightstalker"), Gerald Stano (the "Hillside Strangler"), Wayne Williams (Atlanta child murderer), Theodore Kaczynski (the "Unabomber"), and various other rippers, slashers, bombers, bluebeards, kidnappers, and captive-holders. These psychopaths all made surprise attacks on unsuspecting victims. Predators in America's armed forces must be included in this category, committing seventy sex crimes a day, as reported in 2013. Pathological tricksters have a sickness that makes them seek to outwit society, wound deeply, get revenge, get away with sadistic attacks and deadly violence. They sneak around in the darkness, conniving to play a series of dirty tricks, like the Joker in Batman stories and other cartoon villains.

Perpetrators of the most serious offenses, such as serial killers who sacrifice the innocent, sometimes elude detection for years because they are such consummately cunning tricksters of destruction. One of the most wanted international terrorists, at large for years, was "Carlos the Jackal," a trickster of violent attacks in the 1970s in Paris and London. His birth name was Ilich Ramirez Sanchez, and he was an expert at disappearing and popping up unexpectedly for acts of bloodthirsty terrorism. Other terrorists-at-large continue to elude law enforcement's best efforts for years—for example, the post 9/11 anthrax powder mailer. Some of them inspire copycat tricksters.[201] In the news we also repeatedly see evidence of youthful psychopaths' despicable tricks, such as surprising homeless people while they sleep, beating them with baseball bats, setting them on fire, etc. These are ominous signs of inhumane heartlessness and ignorance, tricks of a numb psyche destined to learn lessons the hard way. There are more transients and homeless people in hard times, and more crimes against them.

The sick trick of killing defenseless homeless people has increased in the last decade. At least 880 unprovoked violent attacks, with 244 fatalities, were perpetrated, often by youths, in the last ten years. The police say many of these sick tricksters are "thrill offenders" who brutalize, beat, shoot, and burn homeless victims. When caught, these savage tricksters sometimes say they were drunk and do not know why they needed such a scapegoat or where their hatred came from. Sources in the culture for these cruel tricks include "bum fight" videos, a sense that drifters are worthless, and a heartless feeling of life being without meaning.[202]

"Fragging" is a military term used to describe the dirty trick of killing a disliked officer. It comes from the Vietnam War, in which fragmentation grenades were used. When tricksters play with fire, they often end up harming or destroying themselves. The tricksters of Columbine, and other teenage shooters who cause mayhem in schools, and the haywire postal workers, and others who snap, go to the office and kill supervisors, coworkers, and bystanders, are sociopath tricksters of rage fantasies. Every time they strike, and every time an armed gunman takes hostages, or a divorced man with a restraining order kills his ex-wife, those who hear the news relive horrified feelings of bewilderment and helplessness. Berzerk trickster strikes again.

12. Monkey Business Tricksters

The business world constitutes a large playing field for the trickster in a variety of guises. Bernard Mandeville, in his 1714 book *The Fable of the Bees*, wrote, "All Trades and Places knew some Cheat, / No Calling was without Deceit."[203] Many tradesmen are looking for angles.

The tricks of unscrupulous car salesmen are legend. They first flatter the buyer, saying in various ways, "You're so smart, hip, cool, and understanding," then they make their special offer. Lowballing, highballing, pulling "lap dog tricks" (making the customer feel obligated), becoming fast friends, guilt-tripping, slipping unmentioned "add ons" into the contract, pretending to make "special deals," using ruses to stall for more time to work on the customer, "bouncing the trade-in," "sucking back," leaving out details, "puppy dogging," not telling customers the actual drive-out price that includes extra charges and taxes, "spraying," turning back speedometers—there are many tricks of the trade. Low-price car ads in the paper are explained at the lot as undesirable bargains—"But let me show you a really nice one. My wife drives one just like it, and loves it." It's an old story: selling substitute products, palming off lemons, denying all wrongdoing. Real estate agents are also known for tricks like sprucing up a dump, "putting lipstick on a pig."

Trickster businessmen sometimes cash in by wrapping themselves in the American flag, grabbing the Statue of Liberty and the eagle, deploying the images of Washington and Lincoln to sell cheap schlock, strapping on any device that sells their products, probably without even thinking about it. Robert D. Hare, a psychology researcher who specializes in studying psychopathy, seems to say there are many tricksters in the business world (as well as in other professions) because it is a realm where psychopaths can fit in and do well.[204] So was Chicago writer Nelson Algren honest, or jaundiced, when he speculated: "the fraudulence essential to successful merchandising becomes pervasive so that the class which is economically empowered becomes emotionally hollowed"?[205] In Algren's view the successful seller tends to be concerned with appearances, presenting the public with a brand, motto, and image, and concerned with "staying on message," instead of caring about authenticity, integrity, conscience. White collar tricksters know that nothing succeeds like success—a foot in the door, a good first impression, dressing for respect, impressive CEO bonuses even when performances are dismal. Winners are winning people, with confident smiles and self-assured style, gracefully plumed with panache.

Some kinds of trickery seem approved, encouraged, winked at in our individualist go get 'em" culture, where unspoken mottoes include "Me first," "Numero uno," "Don't get caught," and "You can lie if no one knows." In such a world the rich have the advantages, and there is a kind of feudal ethos. Consider "dead peasant insurance," which denotes the practice in some businesses where the employer insures the employee and receives payment as beneficiary when the worker dies. Sometimes expectations really do seem different in the realm of commerce transactions in comparison with the realm of personal actions. For example, "It was a business lie, not a life lie," a character in the film *Sunshine Cleaning* (2008) explains approvingly, as if business is a cynical realm that makes everyone hard-boiled and jaded in their dealings. This also implies there are two sets of rules—public business and personal life, except if things get mixed up.

Some say modern people have been tricked out of a vital sense of place by products like cell phones, cars, and fast-food franchises. Consumers are tricked by ads into feeling they are not really living well and are not really successful unless they own and use certain products. Consumers may feel they are defined by the products they possess and the services they pay for. Tricksters of business include CEOs who reap huge bundles in their pay packages even if the corporation fails, while ordinary workers struggle to survive, even under the best of circumstances. When CEOs pay themselves many millions of dollars even while their corporations stumble, fail, and go bankrupt, it seems to ordinary folks like the biggest con in human history. The bosses of some companies require mid-level managers to sell their souls, as it were, for efficiency and shareholders' profits, enforcing drastic measures at the expense of the workers. Big businesses—oil, coal, and chemical industries, mills, and auto manufacturers responsible for environmental pollution—have routinely sought to deny the harm done by the unregulated release of toxic substances: exhaust smoke, chemical fumes, and waste fluids. Environmental research, reportage, and activism have often incurred wrath from the powerful offenders. Devra Davis, in *When Smoke Ran like Water: Tales of Environmental Deception and the Battle Against Pollution*, has portrayed these issues well.[206] Such accounts make us question if big businesses are able to be better citizens or not.

While workable democracy has leaders, laws, and regulations to protect customers, "cashocracies" have front men and unregulated commerce. When Ralph Nader came into prominence, representing consumer concerns and unmasking tricks by investigating questionable practices in the early 1960s, car manufacturers feared he was a communist. They hired private detectives to stalk him and uncover possible dirty tricks. They were surprised to find Nader was not funded by the capitalism-hating Soviet Union, but was driven by his own idealism and conscience.

For a food critic to have the maximum effect, there is a simple trick: don't reveal who you are—that makes all the difference. The anonymous critic, unknown, identity veiled, keeps everyone in the restaurant business on their toes. The waitresses and waiters, chefs and managers try to please all the customers, because anyone could be the critic—they are accountable to the trickster who is the real critic and does not reveal her identity. As an anonymous food critic for the *Washington Post*, Phyllis Richman inspired vigilance, value, efficiency, and promptness, as well as great taste, with her reviews. In New York, Ruth Reichl was also known for playing this trick. Perhaps other businesses could use a "mystery customer" too, to raise their standards of service.

War profiteers sell shoddy materials at exorbitant prices and make shady deals that cost lives—their numbers have not diminished. Use of contractors in just the first five years of the Iraq war cost over 100 billion dollars—a much larger amount than contractors cost in any previous war—with many allegations from investigators of over-billing, fraudulence, shortcuts, shabby work, and other tricks. As America faces budget problems, debt, and the danger of bankruptcy, it is necessary to contemplate how over 53 billion dollars were spent in "reconstruction" efforts in Iraq. So much cash was spread around carelessly there that the slang word "daftar," meaning a pile of hundred dollar bills, came into existence. Peter Van Buren's book *We Meant Well* would be a good starting point for those wishing to get a realistic grasp of the ethos and practices of Iraq reconstruction projects, the delusions and cynicism involved.[207]

British businessman Jim McCormick was found guilty of fraud in April 2013. He devised a trick that brought in 55 million pounds when he took a novelty golf ball finder and sold it to the Iraqi government as a bomb detector to be used at security checkpoints. The device had no ability to detect bombs, and hundreds of people have died from undetected bombs where it was in use. The Iraqi general who ordered the device is in jail on corruption charges. The dysfunctions of the Iraq war are myriad and show the tricks of those who have lost the ability to listen to their own consciences. The character Joey in Jonathan Franzen's novel *Freedom* is an example in contemporary fiction of a person who profits from useless and dangerous products sold as supplies for a distant war. He knows it's wrong, but goes ahead and takes the money with coldblooded greed.[208]

Arthur Miller's play *All My Sons* tells the story of a World War II profiteer who was caught taking fatal shortcuts. Miller's classic American play *Death of a Salesman* is another useful example of a story from the world of business. From one angle it could be called "Death of a Con Man," since selling requires getting the confidence of the buyer. But the salesman, when sales fall off, is the one who ends up feeling tricked—used and discarded by a heartless boss and business. In another American story, told in the film *Citizen Kane* (1941), a magnate is shown at the end of his life still seeking meaning and love. The film was based partly on the life of William Randolph Hearst, fabled millionaire businessman who owned newspapers known for running sensational trumped-up, fact-distorting news stories, and interviews which were spurious. *Citizen Kane* explores how the powerful may outsmart others for years but fail to attain or understand their own deepest needs in the end.

The company known as Blackwater, later renamed Xe, created more than thirty "shell companies" or subsidiaries and received millions of dollars in American Government contracts during the war with Iraq.[209] Blackwater paid no Social Security, Medicare or unemployment taxes. It evaded paying millions of dollars in federal taxes by classifying armed guards and other personnel not as employees, but as independent contractors. An encyclopedia of these tricks would comprise many volumes.

Is there inevitable trickster betrayal involved in journalists gathering information for their writings?[210] Was it a double-cross when Truman Capote befriended killers for his book *In Cold Blood*, coaxing stories from them? Journalists, researchers, and biographers use necessary tricks of the trade. Janet Malcolm wrote an essay about biographers, and their relationship to their subjects as one inevitably involving deceptions, and calling the journalist a "kind of confidence man," acting one way for the sake of getting information, making an impression to gain the trust of those with something they may or may not reveal.[211] Of course there are also reporters who have been caught inventing news stories—New York Times reporter Jayson Blair, for example. Memoirists have sometimes caused uproars by fabricating their stories. Why? Some say there is a heightened feeling of thrills associated with getting away with a false story. Perhaps the rush of "duper's delight" is like the risky excitement of kleptomania. Sometimes slave narratives passed off as authentic memories have been written by whites. The author of the controversial fictional memoir *The Education of Little Tree*, about the life of "Asa 'Little Tree' Carter," a Cherokee, was found to have once been a Ku Klux Klan member. Another book touted as a memoir, *Angel at the Fence: The True Story of a Love that Survived*, about a couple who met as children during the Holocaust, was later found to have been fabricated.

Competitive tricks of the fashion industry are depicted in *The Devil Wears Prada* (2006) and other films. A hyperactive interest in style and status often induces a kind of one-upmanship. As Deldon McNeely wrote, "The continual rise of commercialism, communication explosion, relativity of values, prominence of satirical comedy, high energy, fast pace, preoccupation with sexual imagery of our times characterize the Trickster rising."[212] There are seasons and eras—and considering the elements just mentioned, we might conclude that this must be the season of the tricksters. Racketeers are sometimes not much different from corporate profiteers selling mediocre quality luxury goods at inflated prices.

There are scads of trickster maneuvers in advertising. As the axiom goes, "You sell the sizzle and not the steak." One way to create a sizzling stir is to use promotional teasers. Teasers of all kinds are tricks, manipulative strategies. Gimmicks of attraction, teasers are meant to stir up interest, engagement, involvement, seductions, and sales. Teasers are gewgaw gimcrackery, come-ons, hooks, freebies, temptations: "Betcha can't eat just one!"

Among the most reprehensible tricks of advertisers and promoters is the marketing of harmful products to children, and misleading consumers into confidence. "Smoking is good for your health," and "Nothing gives you energy like sugar," are examples. The novelty of products that glowed with uranium, the reassurance that asbestos is just one more mineral to be mined, and the idea that alcohol does not addict one the way "hard" drugs do, are others.

And there is tricksterism in publicity stunts, in price fixing and gaining monopolies, as well as in the shadow businesses of pirating and bootlegging products. The much-vaunted competitive spirit of capitalism, supposedly spurring people on to do their best, is also often mixed with the feisty untrustworthy trickster spirit, one way or another. Criticisms of the negative side of the capitalist spirit are often portrayed in literature and films. In a fictional story of early twentieth-century capitalism, consider the oilman Daniel Plainview in the film *There Will Be Blood* (2007), based on Upton Sinclair's novel, *Oil*. To trick people into selling their land, he uses an orphan's sweet face to disarm them, and he forces a humiliated minister to confess, "I am a false prophet; God is a superstition," before killing him. That's cold. Plainview is industrious and plays ingenious tricks to succeed in a competitive world, and he ends up morally bankrupt. To bring out the best in others, probably more than the tensions of tricky competition are needed.

The American financier Robert Vesco (1935–2007), who gained international notoriety in the 1970s, is a good example of the businessman trickster. He was accused of swindling investors to the tune of 200 million dollars, and he was also accused of illegally donating funds to Richard Nixon's 1972 presidential campaign. He was investigated for his part in a bribery scheme to get Jimmy Carter's administration to allow Libya to purchase planes. Vesco was charged with illicit drug trafficking, and was jailed in Cuba for ten years for involvement in a miracle drug scam. He cut a dashing figure for years, a tall man with sideburns and a casual clothing style, flaunting luxuries like a private plane with a disco and a whirlpool bath. He kept a step ahead of the law for years, hopscotching in the tropics from one banana republic to another. He tried to buy a Caribbean island from Antigua so he could set up his own laws there, and in Costa Rica he tried to pay authorities to pass a law that would protect him from extradition. His allegiance was to power, wealth, and self-aggrandizement, it would seem, rather than to any nation state. A Slate.com article, in 2001, called Vesco "king of the fugitive financiers." Others have been known to stage their own deaths, making it seem they have jumped off a bridge, for example, and then go into hiding.[213]

Consider also the tricks desperate businessmen may employ when the chips are down. Trying to save his collapsing DeLorean Motor Company from bankruptcy, automobile engineer and industry executive John DeLorean was arrested on multi-million dollar cocaine-trafficking charges in 1984 in a FBI sting operation. The DeLorean design featured gull-wing doors, opening upward at the sides instead of swinging back like ordinary car doors. But the novel gull-wings could not lift the car into popularity, and the FBI could not be gulled by DeLorean's method of smuggling, and so high-flying success eluded him. Sometimes the rich and famous are caught in risky stock deals involving insider trading, or tax fraud, or shoplifting, smuggling illicit drugs, etc. Do they need the money, or is it the thrill they seek, the adrenaline-fueled experiences of living a risky life on the edge? There is a mischievous delight in acting like a defiant Dennis the Menace brat toward Mr. Wilson-type representatives of the grown-up world.

America, famous for thriving with venture capitalist values and known for con man tricks, has influenced the new ventures of Chinese, Russian, and Indian entrepreneurism. Sometimes players in these new capitalist systems take short cuts and cause catastrophes. Trickster ploys are seen in Chinese manufacturers substituting dangerous ingredients for real protein, and in the use lead-based paints. China is known to be partly police state and partly like the Wild West. China's economy, becoming so big, seems to be embodying at times some of the worst Marxist nightmares of capitalism. Are the Chinese learning from American con games how to be modern tricksters, or are American style structures opening opportunities for them to find basic human means of deceit? Is outsourcing a trick, which electronic communications makes more possible, sleight of hand to get the job done with cheap labor? American gangs sometimes say they model their drug dealing on the structures of successful corporations. Claims about the "greatness of capitalism" sometimes seem rather ironic, or like a kind of fundamentalist faith. The tricks of unrestrained capitalism are often problematic, not panaceas, in the world at large. Honest criticism of ills of the system are sometimes met with accusations as if it was heresy. The sacred status of capitalism is the result of public relations tricks. Capitalism is not so much a divine right or a perfect institution as much as it is a human invention, five hundred years old. It began in Venice, when groups of people invested in ships going to Asia to bring back spices to Europe, and it has gone through evolutionary phases. It's a series of human experiments, trying an economic structure that offers opportunities but also may include some potential pitfalls and injustices.

New Age scamsters have included exploiters of spirituality, whether ersatz Eastern style, Native American style, or other esoteric styles of religion for profit. Leonard Orr's "Rebirthing," Werner Erhard's "est" training, and the enchantments of "yuppie guru" Frederic P. Lenz (alias "Tantric Zen master Rama," known for his book, *Surfboarding the Himalayas*)—all led people to try new pathways to enlightenment. It is sometimes hard to know the difference between sincere wishful thinking and "gaslighting"—when someone plays mind games that make a person doubt his or her own sanity. Selling dreams of salvation and nirvana is an old enterprise. In this field, and in other fields, including eCommerce, suspicion and distrust burgeon when people sense they are being burnt, and in moments when they remember their feelings when facing previous tricksters and dangerous encounters. No consumer likes to have smoke blown up her skirt. "Cheaters' backlash" occurs when similar-seeming people are tarred with the same brush. When greed and corruption are exposed there is an undermining of confidence in systems based on trust.

The dot-com bubble riders soared high until the investment bubble burst; how many tricks were played at the height of hype and hope around new electronics and expanding Internet possibilities? Cyberspace made possible a new sort of investment scam. There was no end to the great electronic dream web in the sky. American "e-business" entrepreneurs were doing land office (like a virtual version of Rolling Stone real estate?) business until the bubble burst. WorldCom, like Enron, enjoyed an aura of prosperity and prestige until it became clear that the coffers had been cleaned out when no one was looking. "And all the kings horses and all the king's men" couldn't put the workers' retirement plans together again. The letdown left many as bankrupt as Motor City in the early two thousand and teens.

The legal profession is one of high prestige and social importance. Laws keep order in society, but some lawyers are not exactly on the side of order (they are on the side of the dollar), and others are conscientious tricksters—they hope to move society toward increased justice for the disadvantaged or for progressive ideals. High profile lawyer William Kunstler was "a silver-tongued trickster, a pied piper, an inciter of riots," for civil rights causes, according to his daughter. But crooked lawyers also exist, and are known as "sharks," "shysters," and "ambulance chasers." On the popular NPR show *Car Talk*, the fictitious law firm "Dewey, Cheatem, and Howe" is a humorous reference ("Do we cheat 'em? And how!") to this unscrupulous strand of the legal profession. "Lawyer talk" means speaking in a misleading way that is not literally false, but is a half-truth, a disingenuous equivocation. A "lawyerism" is slang for contradictory behavior, or for verbal nitpicking, such as Bill Clinton saying that "it all depends on what your definition of 'is' is." Successful lawyers are known as sharp strategists able to outsmart opponents while barely staying within the letter of the law, using courtroom tricks and loopholes in the fine print to get by. A famous example of a corrupt American law firm is Howe and Hummel, a New York active in the latter part of the nineteenth century. A brief account will suggest why.

William F. Howe dealt with most of the firm's criminal cases, handling over six hundred murder trials in his lifetime. He was known for his flashy clothes and jewelry, but when defending clients in murder cases he always dressed more soberly, and when the trial neared its end he wore a somber suit and black tie, the kind worn at solemn occasions like funerals. He spoke with great flourishes. In one case he knelt for two hours in front of the jury, giving his dramatic closing argument. Howe could shed tears on cue. In one case he convinced a jury that the accused murderer's finger accidentally slipped and fired four bullets from the revolver she held. His partner, Abraham Hummel, was no slouch either, in plying the tricks of the lawyer's trade. Hummel discovered a procedural error in the conviction of 2,490 criminals imprisoned on Blackwell's Island, and got them all released on the same day. They had other tricks up their sleeves too, gaming the system in various ways.[214] We will always have with us flamboyant trial lawyers, with their knowledge of legal loopholes, their flair for dramatic showmanship, and their relishing of a prominent public role.

Another kind of legal tricksterism involves "patent trolls" who emerge from their offices under the bridges of Shystertown, and sue companies, accusing them of stealing innovative technology ideas. Patent infringement suits cost millions to play out in court, even when the companies are innocent, so they are often settled out of court. Many inventors suffer the activities of "patent trolls" (also known as patent extortionists), forces which stifle innovation and kill creativity. The *This American Life* radio program on NPR aired a feature entitled "When Patents Attack,"[215] which explored this kind of trickery by interviewing people involved in various aspects of it. The threat of a lawsuit is like a mafia shakedown, where protection is offered if there is a payoff.

The talents of real estate tycoons and other high power salesmen involve the trickster ability to persuade. Donald Trump's great ability to present a bold and savvy face, to give a spiel to TV cameras, to spin his own accomplishments like a wonderful musical top, even at the moments when he was facing collapse and bankruptcy, is impressive. Trump keeps himself in the news with TV appearances of power ("You're fired!") and political attacks. A trickster's kit must include all the proofs of confidence, because appearance is all-important when selling a P.O.V. (point of view). To make a tinhorn outfit seem like solid gold is the carnival barker's stock in trade.

Perhaps such examples are all too obvious, like shooting fish in a barrel. In the American business world, even strict orthodox religious communities have their unethical tricksters. Consider the Amish dog factories, where fast breeding and hurried selling are the main concerns. Or the Kosher meat plant in Postville, Iowa, where the hard work was done by hundreds of undocumented immigrant laborers. In the latter case, the manager of Agriprocessors, Sholom Rubashkin, was sentenced to twenty-seven years in prison for financial fraud.

On the back roads and on Main Streets, among believers and disbelievers, one need not search far to find business tricks. In fact, some argue that not only business cheating, but also cheating by average Americans, is on the rise. In his book, *The Cheating Culture: Why More American Are Doing Wrong to get Ahead,* David Callahan investigated the doings of Enron, WorldCom, Global Crossing and shows that the same kinds of corner-cutting and deceptive practices could be found also in education, sports, the media, and in the dealings of average people, who often fudge on taxes and at the workplace, denying it all the while.[216]

Signs of increased awareness of underhanded policies are visible in some of the recent stories we watch on TV. In the 2013 season of the TV series *The Good Wife,* the title character remembers advice from a wily old client named Mr. Ashbow: "Always play the fox. They'll never know you're the smartest man in the room." After years of being caught off guard, Alicia (the "Good Wife") becomes tricky in her own right. Not naively taken advantage of in the rough and tumble games of commerce and romance, she learns to survive in free-for-all melees of the corporate world. The TV series *House of Lies* is an example of dramatizing the postmodern business world, the energies, excitements, hopes, and deflations of high rollers and fast changes.

Among the tricks of "Gotcha Capitalism" today are unexplained added fees, which, even when minimally explained, are obscure or confusing. Consumer-advocates are dedicated to exposing these tricks and leveling the trading ground. Karen Silkwood delved into the tricky cover-ups of the nuclear power industry with its dangerous pollution, but it took an Erin Brockovich using tricky powers and charms to uncover evidence on behalf of suffering victims. Moral: It takes a hero trickster to take on an unethical trickster and stand a chance of winning.

Obviously the tricks of big business are not all sinister and underhanded. To compete successfully in a crowded world requires enough smarts to out-trick the rivals in one's field. Bill Gates, a billionaire at thirty-one and a full-time philanthropist at fifty, is said to have been influenced by the tricks of Napoleon's strategic thinking. In *The Highwaymen*, Ken Auletta writes that Gates has sometimes seen himself in Napoleonic terms, as a planner of battle strategies victorious over opponents. In the 1990s Gates's tactics earned him the nickname "Black Billy." In *The Microsoft File*, Wendy Rohm writes of Gates's leveraging prowess, and his intellectual sticky-fingeredness. Gates skillfully retained patents and license rights that gave him sometimes monopolistic ownership of computer programs that nearly everyone needed to use, making him the richest man in the world. This also enabled him to become perhaps the greatest philanthropist of this age, making great contributions to the healthcare and uplift of some of the poorest people where the need is greatest.

Philanthropy is another kind of business to consider here. The scale of tricksters' activities in non-profit organizations is astounding when we see the statistics. In a *New York Times* article by Stephanie Strom, embezzlement and other fraudulent activities in the non-profit sector account for a loss of $40 billion a year, about 13 percent of the total of annual philanthropic giving. But all organizations, non-profit, governmental, and commercial lose 6 percent of their income annually to fraudulent activities.[217]

Much of what happens in the business world is a process beyond any single person's control—massive transactional energies, chaotic traffic, spur of the moment tricks, uncertainty and guesses, gamblers' decisions, and the wildness of fortune: Lady Luck. Briefly enumerating several kinds of tricks in the world of commerce can only provide a small sampling, but these examples are suggestive of the many appearances of the trickster spirit in American life. The con man, whatever his game, does not play fair. He is not committed to rules and to values, but to winning a jackpot by whatever means he can devise. He wants to extend the saying "All's fair in love and war" to include partisan politics, moneymaking businesses, sports, self-promotion, entertainment, and whatever other endeavor might make him a winner. But as an archetype in the processes of the psyche, the trickster can stimulate awareness that can help us realize insights concerning some profound dynamics and issues in our lives, both as individuals and as a society.

Casinos and other establishments of organized gambling are huge businesses where those with the time and money can enjoy games like roulette, slot machines, cards, and dice, spending their disposable income in hopes of winning. Considering the tricks gamblers use to beat the odds in games of chance, we find some clever and risky ploys. They include wearing disguises and counting cards dealt in blackjack games, and also elusively remaining nameless, off the casinos' lists of unwanted customers. A 2008 film titled *21*, starring Kevin Spacey, involves a professor and group of MIT math students who use their brains and trickster teamwork to win at blackjack in Las Vegas. Such tricks as signals in poker games and diversions created by sexually provocative partners are well known, but probably the best and brightest of the tricks are kept secret by those who use them.

America is a hustling, bustling nation. Advertising is often a hustle, politics is often a hustle, entertainment is often a hustle, and even activities masked as good old sincere trustworthy non-hustles often have elements of hustle in them. (The "Crying Indian ad" seemed the height of sincere feeling; but it featured a non-Indian, and was sponsored by Keep America Beautiful, a front group for bottlers and others who oppose reuse and recycling laws.)

We are all tricked by the modern food industry; products we buy are often not exactly what they seem.[218] The burbs and the ghettoes hustle, bag-ladies and squeegie-men come out of the shadows to hustle, salespeople hustle, and leaders hustle. Charming us to get our trust with sweet sounds like Mr. Softee's music-box tinkle, folks with mansions hustle us, and country bumpkins as well as slick city psychos hustle us. At home and abroad we're always getting yanked by some hustle or hustled by some Yank. In his song "Pretty Boy Floyd," Woody Guthrie sang, "Some will rob you with a six gun, and some with a fountain pen." And some with a fake website. Crafty players on Wall Street can do it with credit default swaps. Moral: Let the buyer beware, unless he wants to be known as "BooBoo the Fool." America has a lot of the trickster in its bloodstream, and it is good to stay aware of that fact to avoid getting skinned by cons.

13. Charlatan's Web: Cyberscammers

Like mail order diploma mills of yore, bogus virtual universities have proliferated in the boundless new territories of cyberspace, offering unrecognized degrees and sham credentials for a price. This is not to suggest that all online education programs are scams. There are great sources for knowledge. Just consider the MITOpenCourse programs and the millions of students from around the world it attracts. Wikipedia is also great collection of free knowledge. But we sometimes need to be reminded that not everything found on the Internet is on the up and up.

Criminals use online classified advertisements to sell stolen goods. Internet pranksters generate viruses and website vandalism, wasting much time and causing massive trouble to prove what they can do. Hiding out on the Internet, the trickster can easily wear the mask of anonymity, and strike from great distances, phish, spear-fish, peer into records, break into email systems, spread viruses, and play games with the minds of others.

For example, there is a scam that is carried out by email, in which con artists present themselves as "hit men" already hired by others to kill the recipient, and attempt to extort a payment to prevent them from carrying out the contract. Another scam, using the social network Facebook, involves con men who create fake Facebook profiles. Using stolen photos of soldiers they develop relationships with women on Facebook, sending messages of love and promises of caring. Then they ask for some financial help—a check for a much-needed cell phone, for example. One victim gave $25,000 to a fake soldier with a sob story. The Army announced in February 2011 that hundreds of cases of this kind of fraud have been reported.[219]

"Scareware" scams lure online computer users to click on a pop-up warning that gives the alarming message that their computer is infected with a virus. They warn the recipient that the computer's security has been breached, and that files are in danger of being damaged and corrupted, tricking the user to download costly software to correct the bogus "problem."

In other computer trickeries, during 2003–2004 Joker-like hackers spread software "worm" programs with names like "Blaster" and "Sasser," wreaking chaos in business and home PCs. Some hackers make a game of finding vulnerabilities in Microsoft programs especially. Some programs used by hackers to burrow into computers are called "Trojans," in honor of one of the most famous tricks in ancient literature, "the Trojan Horse" used to cause the downfall of Troy in Virgil's epic poem, the *Aeneid*.

A further cybertrick involves "malware," which hijacks online PCs, converting them into "botnets"—zombie networks of hijacked computers converted to robots performing functions programmed by the hijackers. "Conficker" or Downadup" beginning in January 2009 was able to connect infected computers together into an immense "botnet," a super computer run by hidden operators. These chains of electronically commandeered cyber-robots then automatically send out spam messages to a large number of email recipients, seeking financial data to be exploited by the promulgators, and spreading the installation of unwanted software, in yet other PCs. This trick of spreading illegal parasite-like computer infections involves millions of computers.[220] The Conficker worm was the worst infection since "SQL slammer" in 2003. The fact that there were 32,000 suspected cyberattacks each day caused Microsoft computer engineers to mount serious defenses against the "digital plague" spread by botnets. They launched counter-tricks by setting up decoy computers for the predators to exploit, and then they collected the necessary evidence to prosecute the criminal hacker-tricksters. But as with organic viruses, botnets are tweaked to evolve rapidly, adapting in order to elude previous means of detection and prevention. The runners of botnets lurking behind these malware tricks are called "bot-herders."[221] (It's an odd postmodern name, "bot-herder," conjuring up a pastoral shepherd and lashed together destructive, time-wasting robot computers.)

Cyber scammers can pick pockets with a click of the mouse. In May 2013 it was revealed that hackers stole 45 million dollars in an ATM scheme that involved people located in over 24 countries. In New York City 2,904 ATM machines were bilked for a total of 2.4 million dollars during a 10-hour period on February 19, 2013. The scheme required both hackers and criminals on the street to work in coordination. One wonders how many high-tech pilfering schemes have been perpetrated but never solved.[222]

In April 2014 a dangerous security flaw known as the Heartbleed bug attracted attention. This flaw in OpenSSL technology, the system most used on the Internet for encrypting consumer information, had been found a couple of years prior, but in 2014 became known to millions. The Heartbleed Internet breach enabled users' credentials to be stolen when they logged in at various sites. Hackers could then maliciously exploit that data. This widespread vulnerability meant users needed to alter their passwords, and vendors needed the development of further protections to safeguard consumers.

Cyber scammers can dangle bait and string the online gullible along with a digital fish hook. Downhome-style websites can give the appearance of speaking for ordinary folks, when in actuality they may be funded by the powerful wealthy elite. This fake "grassroots" aura has been called the "Astroturf of the Internet." The gullible are impressed by surface styles of webpages, and swallow propaganda as if it were objective information, the plain truth. In a nice font, with slick graphics, false information looks official. There are hacktivists who hack into systems to represent their causes, get attention, and revenge, and there are also cyber vigilantes who lurk and interact with others on social media under assumed identities. Hacksters and cyberclowns can play tricks that turn web worlds upside down. Cyber scammers can use cyber shills to help cyber-bamboozle cyber marks. They can use "sock puppets," phony-named commentators, creating "avatars" to influence opinions online. Some schemes in the world of books generate thousands of reviews for a mediocre book on Amazon.com. *Caveat emptor.*

Millions of computer-owners regularly receive Ponzi-like chain-letter email messages, with promises of reaping vast rewards if they send out more emails to others, who in turn, will send out more emails, and so on. In earlier times chain letters required postage; now one adds to cascading messages by simply clicking on "send." When the receiver sends the chain letter to others, it often includes the email address of the scammer who sent it, and so can generate a growing mailing list or requests for further information. The potential for cyber-scamming is great—enough to make anyone cautious, if not paranoid and reluctant to respond to even innocent messages. A forlorn email from a friend saying she urgently needs your help in the form of thousands of dollars is likely to be a fraud, especially if it doesn't sound like her. But such frauds perpetrated from Nigeria, China, or elsewhere fool smart people all too often.

Antisocial media meanness is another kind of web tricksterism. Mischievous tricks of cyberbullying can lead to tragic consequences. This abuse of the web is called "antisocial netiquette." A teenage girl in Missouri committed suicide in 2006 as a result of mean-spirited online insults from a grown-up using an assumed identity. In July 2009 a federal judge acquitted Lori Drew, the adult neighbor who was accused of perpetrating the MySpace hoax that led to the thirteen-year-old hanging herself. To "flame" online means to unload vitriolic verbal attacks. Heartless tricksters are sometimes guilty of causing torment and death by "flaming," publicly defaming defenseless victims, with messages like, "the world would be better off without you." There is a certain impishness or demonic impulse that can come into play when one feels one can strike at another with anonymity and impunity.

The rash of high school students involved in drunken rapes, sexting misadventures, and suicides in the recent years of the Digital Age is troubling. Laurie Halse, the author of *Speak*, a book about the effects of a high school rape on a victim published in 1999, said, "What really strikes me is that, when it comes to recording sexual assaults and wanting to show it off, the young men committing them are not seeing them as crimes, they see them as pranks."[223] Similarly violent acts by youths against homeless people and immigrants are often seen as pranks. The assailants record the acts and post videos on Facebook and other social media to get laughs and street cred. Treating the acts so lightly, they are then surprised when police discover and use the videos as evidence.

The tricks of championing transparency in government are fraught with uncertain effects. When Wikileaks released messages containing the "inner workings of American diplomacy," the hidden tricks and the "shadow self" of America, it caused a lot of distress among the politicians, who are the supposed "servants of the American public." Countering these massive information leaks from US government communications, which Julian Assange released in November 2010, a hacker (or "hacktivist") self-dubbed "th3j35t3r" ("the jester") took down the WikiLeaks website. "The jester" said he wants to attack the jihad recruiting websites next. Tricksters strike, and attract the attention of other tricksters, some to join in on the fun and games, and others to crash the party and stop tricks which endanger and offend. Chelsea Manning (formerly Bradley Manning) revealed classified diplomatic memos and information about the Iraq and Afghanistan wars, and Edward Snowden revealed secret information about the National Security Administration's snooping, and both have lived with the results of that revelation—a conviction of espionage charges for Manning and the threat of extradition and trial for Snowden. The messy and polarizing trick of divulging secrets makes some consider the revealer a hero, while others consider him/her a villain. "Whatever we think of Snowden—self-aggrandizing creep or self-sacrificing crusader against creepy government spying,"[224] his tricks were a response to what he felt was intolerable trend of trickiness in surveillance practices. He sought to bring clarity or transparency where he found deceit and obfuscation.

14. Colossal Cons—Financial Meltdown Tricksters

In American literature (such as the work of J. D. Salinger and Ernest Hemingway[225]) a "phony" was a term of condemnation for a number of decades, not just indicating a grating artificiality, but the duplicitous scam of falseness. The "phony" fraud was a despised trickster. But in recent decades, if the tricks succeed, the fraud might be widely admired. As the character played by Michael Douglas says in the film *Wall Street* (1987), "Greed is good." The disappointing results of this outlook are now being experienced as a disenchantment with the frauds who stole from the resources of the common good for their own personal gain. *Wall Street 2: Money Never Sleeps* (2010), set in 2008, expresses a more sobering assessment of greed.

One theory about periodic financial speculative bubbles in America is known as the "Greater Fool Theory." This view sees economic bubbles as caused by optimistic market participants' activities. Hopeful and sometimes greedy fools purchase overvalued assets, planning to sell them at a large profit to still other speculators—the "greater fools" for whom the theory is named. It is a kind of Ponzi scheme that expands by including more and more investors, reaching its climax when the utmost price is paid and no further buyers can be found to pay a higher price. The profiteers are tricksters who were lucky in their timing.

Distress investors are known as "vultures"—they prey on opportune situations in markets experiencing financial crises. Each decade has its shake-ups and what I like to call "opportuneurs." The 161-billion-dollar Savings and Loan debacle of the 1980s and 1990s, involving Charles Keating and other bankers and financiers, and the Subprime Mortgage crisis of 2008–2009, were also caused by such bubble-like economic structures fed by deceptive tricks that caused credit to expand precariously then collapse. This decentralized subprime crisis resulted in adverse economic reverberations across America and beyond, affecting Saudi, British, European, Australian, and New Zealand banks. The loss to banks is estimated to be about one trillion dollars.[226] What were some basic tricks involved in the Subprime Mortgage debacle? The US government set the stage by deregulation of the banking industry. On the side of the borrowers, there was deception regarding incomes (which they inflated), and debts (which were under-reported), and this affected their actual ability to make payments. The borrowers lied about their incomes, and the companies buying and selling mortgages to banks turned a blind eye, refusing to do basic checking to determine if the figures given by borrowers were genuine. Lenders went along with the charade willingly, so that the loans would be granted and there would be a short-term gain on paper. The borrowers and lenders were both tricksters—looking at each other through a two-way mirror, or shaking hands across the desk while winking. In Florida alone 10,000 of the people in the loan business had criminal records.[227] In the early years of the twenty-first-century gangs such as Chicago's Black Disciples, which had previously made money from selling drugs, turned to mortgage fraud for income. It was easy to buy low-value buildings, borrow a large amount of money for the mortgage, then disappear.[228] Deceptions on both sides made up the shaky shady deals that grew sky-high, then collapsed. In other cases, borrowers' greed buying more than was affordable, and lenders' greed pretending all was well—keeping quiet when suspicion was in order—led to the selling of the precarious mortgages to banks elsewhere in the world. Foreign banks realized too late that they had bought into an El Dorado type swindle. Instead of buying default rights to a mythic golden American kingdom on solid ground, they had bought a house of cards built by institutions similar to wildcat banks in Wild West boomtowns, where con men busily made transactions conning other con men, issuing currency and agreements that turned out to be worthless. The true costs of the housing mortgage crisis that began to paralyze America's economy in 2008 may amount to a trillion and a half dollars or more, with unfortunate ripple-effect consequences.[229]

To sum up the crisis, a large number of fraudulent mortgages had values that collapsed and caused widespread losses. The criminals knew what was going on, and the banks were complicit, like foxes guarding henhouses. Inevitably the scam so sweet to those who profited from it turned bitter for everyone else. If the reality is that Wall Street is rigged and the world (including the financial system) is unstable, then trickster dynamics are obviously at play on several levels. It is common knowledge that *things aren't what they seem; one hand doesn't know what the other is doing.* So why is it news that there is conniving and also unconscious depths, forgetfulness and wishful thinking, shrewd vulture con jobs and conscientious attempts to tell truth that may be rebuffed by those who don't want to hear it? An expert tells us that those who bet against the subprime mortgage derivatives scheme were not stereotypical short sellers. Their consciences eventually kicked in when they feared the whole world economy boat would be dangerously rocked, and that the boastful capitalist democratic America would go bankrupt. Some tried to tell the SEC about the huge problem with the massive subprime mortgage bonds, but nobody would listen, no one wanted to hear a warning, no one could buy talk of doom and gloom.[230]

According to New York University economist Nouriel Roubini, speaking in 2008, America had not just a subprime mortgage market problem, but a subprime *financial system,* which is problematic. The financial crisis inherited by Barak Obama, and the 787-billion-dollar stimulus plan designed to revive the economy, seem to prove Roubini was right. With the collapse of Bear Stearns (the fifth largest investment bank in America) and Lehman Brothers, and the government bailout of Fanny Mae, Freddy Mac, and AIG, investment bankers were no longer being called the "masters of the universe." As China, Russia, and the Gulf States loan money to America, there is a danger that America can lose her precarious independence. We can only preserve our childlike faith by shrinking our adult awareness of dishonest trickery and crookedness.[231]

"Opacity and complexity are the rogue's best friends," as Christopher Hayes said.[232] Some respected leaders have called the financial crisis that emerged and confronted the government in 2008 "a giant Ponzi scheme," and "banking fraud on a grand scale." Financial analysts say AIG, insuring bad loans and selling them, was running a legal scam. Justice may be symbolized with a blindfold, but consumers and citizens in a democracy need to see clearly and beware of scams pulled by con men dressed up like the most respected of men. A bailout of the deregulated financial industry, costing hundreds of billions of dollars may mean that—as often happens—we carefully close the barn door only after trickster has disappeared with the cows.

Fareed Zakaria, known as a sober analyst, wrote of the 2008 bank bailout, "The whole country has been complicit in a great fraud."[233] Part of the problem was that for some decades unregulated capitalism, "the free market," had become sacred, sacrosanct, unquestionable. Some call the decades of Reaganomics and Margaret Thatcher's policies "market fundamentalism" because there was unquestioned faith in the market to solve all problems. A generation began to assume that the cartoon of the market's workings that they had in their hopeful brains, was a reality corresponding with the dynamics of actual history. They assumed all non-capitalism—socialism, communism—was evil. This naïve faith, according to some economists, helped turn the world economy into a vast casino bubble. Only after a humbling collapse do commentators say things like "capitalism is a giant confidence game—it depends on trust, credit, fluidity of exchange loans, hoped-for futures, injections of confidence even when it's not warranted." To sell or buy a derivative of a derivative of a derivative sounds like a risky business, like selling guesses and buying secondhand promises, bets about bets, and third-hand projections of possibilities. Conservative investors prefer "a sure thing." A bet on a bundle of bets or a bundle of bet-upon bundles is a metameta-investment in debt, like believing in fool's gold, or gambling on a project built on sand.[234] To pragmatic Americans such megabanking sounds "curiouser and curiouser." In this scenario, time is the great trickster, undoing the seemingly carved-in-stone with the tumble of Dow Jones Averages, the decline showing month after month in the telegraphy of the undercrawl headlines on TV. It also looks like trickster play when bank executives, bailed out by the government to the tune of billions of dollars, spend some of the money on luxury items—an $87,000 carpet, a $50 million dollar corporate jet, $28,000 curtains, a $13,000 chandelier, a $35,000 commode, etc.[235] There is also the matter of millions of dollars of bailout money going to pay bonuses to bankers whose banks have failed. This seemingly inveterate high-on-the-hog style reminds me of what a childhood friend of mine said of a trickster pal: "He turned over a new leaf—but it's the same on the other side!"

According to a respected thinker in economic sociology, Ezra W. Zuckerman, the most likely suspect in causing the Wall Street and banking crisis is structural—"the lack of transparency in the derivatives markets and the (resulting) absence (until recently) of a straightforward way to bet on subprime and other overvalued real-estate derivatives. This means that the bearish sentiment was largely suppressed, thereby leaving the market to the bulls."[236] The bulls have their tricks, and the bears have theirs, and they both play in the market and in our psyches like action heroes. Charging and slashing, growling and stamping, each role has its gambits and each can forget all else in the game. Caught up in the moment at a prosperous point we lose track of longer-term cycles, merry-go-round booms, and busts.

American history tells us that in 1825 there was a banking panic, and in 1837 a depression in the Northeastern region that lasted until 1844. In 1907 there was another panic and banks froze their activities. In 1929 there was a stock market crash, and in 1932 a great depression. All these collapses follow euphoric speculative excesses, bubbles caused by our delusions.[237] As economist John Kenneth Gailbraith noted, boomtimes hide lots of crooked dealings that emerge in periods of bust. When the crash comes the total trust people have invested in each other and the system is undermined by total suspicion. The words used to refer to the subprime crisis are a little unstable too—"credit crunch," "meltdown," "downturn," "black hole," "recession," "panic," "depression," "the great unwinding," "collapse," "credit tsunami," "global aftershock," "the great mortgage implosion," "hundred year flood," etc.[238] Sometimes it is described like a natural catastrophe, rather than a man-made problem.

At times, it seems Americans are tricked into fear about threats from without, and don't notice dangers within. "America will never be destroyed from the outside," Abraham Lincoln wrote in the nineteenth century. "If we falter and lose our freedoms, it will be because we destroyed ourselves." In the twentieth century Indian poet Rabindranath Tagore wrote: "Power has to be made secure not only against [external forces of] power, but also against weakness [within]; for there lies the peril of its losing balance. The weak are as great a danger for the strong as quicksand for an elephant." Internal weakness in a nation includes addictions, corner-cutting, con-jobbing (deceptive practices), laziness, corruption, promises of easy money, temptations to vice, and excessive partisan politics. President Dwight Eisenhower perceptively warned that people can destroy from within what they are trying to protect from without.[239]

Consumer agencies report that there are more and more frauds aimed at people who are in financial difficulties—scams to refinance home debt, for example. Also, the vulnerable old and the inexperienced young, the distraught poor, and the disabled and feeble are among the most victimized by mortgage fraud, foreclosure scams, Internet fraud, high-interest payday loans, and shoddy repair and construction work scams. "Pump and dump" con men are scammers who use the World Wide Web to hype stocks with junk mail. They artificially inflate stock value to raise the profit margin on sales of shares that they own.

When more people busily hunt for a way to earn a living, feeling worried and desperate, the number of employment scams aimed at increases. PhishBucket.org is a non-profit web site that compiles information and news about online employment scams. PhishBucket estimates there is about

33 percent more fraud in 2009 than there was in 2008. Three examples of employment fraud will suggest some of the current types.

One. Invest in yourself to start up a job. Some fraudulent "employers" hire workers to do supposed "work-from-home jobs," with only one hitch—they require that participants first buy equipment. The hopeful worker uses his or her own money and some "earnest money" supplied by the employer to sweeten the deal. The ordered equipment never arrives, and the worker is conned out of hard-earned savings. *Two. The "money mule" scam.* A worker is recruited by fraudulent international companies in need of agents for "receiving payment." These agents or "money mules" are supposed to take money sent to them from "customers" (victims of identity fraud) and deposit it in their own bank accounts, and then send 90 percent of the money to the company. *Three. "Re-shippers wanted."* In this scam "re-shippers" are hired by international shipping companies who advertise for "logistics managers" to receive such merchandise as computers, cameras, iPods, tablets, etc., and then send them on to another country. In this scam the money invested by the re-shipper is never deposited into his account and he is left holding the empty bag. Craigslist screens out scams regularly, but a site that is accessed by so many people (about fifty million per month) is bound to include some fraudulent activity. Where there is opportunity there may be dirty tricks.[240]

New computer-age tricks have been evolved to "cook the books" in business enterprises, and then delete the evidence. Owners of small businesses sometimes use a software program known as "the zapper" to manipulate sales figures and evade tax payments. Such "automated sales suppression devices" alter the computerized cash register records. They allow owners to remove cash and then enter amounts that match desired final cash totals; the zapper erases the record so the tally will hide the actual amount of cash received. During a four-year period, one twelve-store chain of restaurants in Detroit is said to have used this device to skim over twenty million dollars from sales transactions.[241] I'm no expert, but I would guess that when a great city goes bankrupt, there has been mismanagement, cheating, and fraud on multiple levels.

To explore the vast scale of global tricksterism in illicit profiteering is beyond our scope, but we can note that it comprises as much as 20 percent of world economic transactions. Marijuana trafficking in British Columbia, drug cartels in Columbia, Russian organized crime, sex and labor trafficking from the former Soviet Union states (as well as Africa and Asia), Chinese and Japanese criminal gangs, Nigerian scams, Somalian pirate operations, and Middle Eastern weapons-trafficking, are examples of the immense shadow commerce. Outlaw moneymaking always going on in the margins of society. Trickily feeding voracious appetites, a global-mafiosa-type ethos takes many regional forms.[242] The examples of organized crime in the Russian Mafia of Brighton Beach in Brooklyn are vivid with many tricks. These criminal tricksters are active in extortion, diamond dealing, cigarette smuggling, and customs fraud. They engage in product fraud, such as making vodka, dying it blue, and bottling it as windshield cleaning fluid for export; then they remove the dye and rebottle it as vodka. They are active in credit card fraud, theft of signals to clone cell phones, and theft of excise taxes in the fuel industry. They are also involved in false insurance claims, rigged accidents, bogus billings, and other cons.

Sometimes legitimate businesses use questionable tricks. Burger King tried to infiltrate the Student/Farmworkers' Alliance to spy on their activities regarding tomato picking migrant workers in Florida.[243] This is just one example of corporate espionage. Walmart, Exxon-Mobil, and other huge corporations use former FBI, CIA, and Secret Service workers in their security and intelligence activities. Collusions between the sectors of the military-industrial complex, political and media domains, fuel and construction industries, and lawmakers, abound with tricks, some of which come to light and make headlines. Sometimes con men impersonate IRS agents, or law enforcers, to get credit card information and Social Security numbers by telephone or computer. Wily businessmen have many tricks up their sleeves, such as dummy corporations, offshore havens to evade taxes, and Cayman Island mailing addresses to exploit loopholes in laws. For example, at Ugland House, in George Town in the Cayman Islands, 19,000 companies are registered as residents, so they can claim that location as a legal address. They are not located there, but are able to evade US taxes that way. Barack Obama called this the biggest tax scam on record. The titles "biggest heist,"

"the biggest scam," "biggest tax scam," like the tallest skyscraper, are surpassed again and again by flourishes of greed reaching higher.

There are collusions among big businesses—for example road construction companies and fuel companies. If "rumors are the meat and drink of markets" you can imagine how the tricks of spreading rumors can cause both feasts and famines. Public relations experts and "talking heads" are paid to create an impression in public perception. On Sunday morning TV talk shows the con men from business and government are all tricked out in their Sunday best, skillfully hiding the guilt of shifty-eyed stealth. Price-fixing among competitors helps them avoid the need to compete. Crooked auctioneers plant shills among the bidders to drive up the bidding. On Wall Street there are crooked practices such as "short-selling."[244] Some tricksters' names become household words. Michael Milken is remembered for creating the "junk-bond" market in the 1970s and 1980s, and for milking fortunes by packaging debt in attractive packages. He pleaded guilty to six securities violations and served his time. In recent decades Milken has been active in philanthropic endeavors.

The practices of "creative bookkeeping" and fancy dancing around regulations, and many older and newer "sharp practices," dishonest and/or illegal, involve betrayal of trust. Actual creativity and strengthening of real trust are basic necessities of thriving governments and businesses. The revelations of immense frauds appear regularly in the news. In December 2008, a sixty-five billion dollar Ponzi scheme perpetrated by respected Wall Street Broker Bernard Madoff came to light. As of June 2010 about eighteen billion dollars were missing. The scheme fleeced some of the world's richest private and corporate investors who were Madoff's clients, as well as philanthropic institutions. The smile seen on Madoff's face in news photos, described as enigmatic and serene, like a Buddha statue or the Mona Lisa, is fascinating. Perhaps it is a key to understanding his success and failure—success at keeping his Ponzi scheme a secret, and failure at living up to ethical standards. It is a smile exuding confidence. To earn the trust of others one must show supreme confidence. The root meaning of "confidence" is "sharing faith," and that is also what the confidence man trades on. The con man smiles, unperturbed, presenting a great trustworthy façade that sends the confident message "steady as she goes, my friend, all is well, the fix is in, A-OK."[245] Or even better—"all your prayers are answered, trust me to be your personal protector." Meanwhile, that smile, which was Madoff's little joke on the world for years, was like the Claes Oldenberg sculpture of a three-foot-tall screw, entitled "Soft Screw," which was exhibited on Madoff's desk in his luxurious office—like a secret blurted blatantly, but only grasped in retrospect.

Trust in a money manager upon whom our future material welfare depends sometimes inspires emotions akin to faith in God. For example, Elie Wiesel said, after finding that Madoff had used up thirty-seven million dollars of his charitable foundation's fund and his own personal investments, "We thought he was God." Frank Rich commented, "It was this crook's ability to pass for a deity that allowed his fraud to escape scrutiny not just from his victims but from the S.E.C. and the 'money managers' who pimped his wares. This aura of godliness also shielded the 'legal' Madoffs at firms like Citibank and Goldman Sachs."[246] It is useful for tricksters who mount Ponzi schemes and other scams to have an aura of great prestige, and, if not Godlike qualities of mysterious knowledge and a pacifying protective appearance, then an aura of sagely wisdom, saintly compassion or angelic holiness. "In God We Trust," and in hands that seem providential and benevolent we place our fortunes, especially when promised extraordinarily high returns.

When Madoff was sentenced to 150 years in prison in June 2009, the people who were defrauded by him reportedly felt bitter anger mixed with vengeful gladness. Burt Ross, formerly mayor of Fort Lee, New Jersey, who lost five million dollars, said, "When Bernard Madoff leaves prison, which means after his death . . . he will then go down to the depths of hell where he'll join those other people who are in the mouth of Satan."[247] This is representative of the bitter feelings generated in investors who gave their money to Mr. Madoff. Perhaps Madoff represents a selfish Robin Hood type: stealing from the rich to give generously to his own aggrandizement. Others, like Raj Rajaratnam, convicted of insider trading in 2011, also belong in this category. Such people are examples of criminal tricksters cheating in a market system to make themselves and some others rich at the expense of victims in the game who play fair. Madoff smiled for years, administering the slow and costly turn of the screw.

We often look up to those who have a veneer or reputation of charismatic heroism, even when we do not know much about them. "In the bubble culture, money ennobled absolutely," Frank Rich observed. One of the ex-Wall Street executives who knew Walter Noel vouched for him in a dramatic way. (Noel headed an investment firm on Wall Street that funneled 7 billion dollars into Madoff's Ponzi scheme.) "He's a terribly good person, almost in the sense of Jimmy Stewart in *It's a Wonderful Life* combined with an overtone of Gregory Peck in *To Kill a Mockingbird*." What greater personas of reassuring trustworthiness could be found in popular culture than the handsome and lovable movie star heroes of our childhood?[248] Of course if you've lost nothing in such recent financial debacles, then you may not care—it's "no skin off your nose" because you had no "skin in the game." But to those who had money on the line and thought they were sitting pretty it was a rude awakening. To some it now means scrambling to find a way to survive in old age. Madoff's Ponzi scheme is famous because it was so large. Other big cases of investment fraud were uncovered, though not as well known. Reed Slatkin perpetrated and was convicted in 2003 of running one of the largest Ponzi schemes in America. And since Madoff's fall, more Ponzi schemes keep popping up. Mark Dreier was arrested for running a 400-million-dollar Ponzi scheme, for which he was sentenced to twenty years in a federal prison in July 2009. Dreier said he was trying to build a fortune, and his ambition tempted him to attain great success, by first stepping into quicksand and doing a few underhanded things. In February 2009, Texan billionaire Allen Stanford was charged in an over 7-billion-dollar investment fraud with 30,000 victims. The Securities and Exchange Commission charged the financier with orchestrating "a multi-billion dollar investment scheme," a fraud said to have been based on empty promises and false historical return data. Accusations against Stanford, three of his companies, and two executives of those companies, were lodged following a raid by US marshals on the Stanford Financial Group in Houston. Such cases are signs of the tricky times in which we live. The times are abundant with hopes and promises abloom, and illusory bubbles aburst, inflated numbers filled with the gases of hubris, naiveté, and greed. When the puffed-up rise like balloons and need to get their feet back on the ground, tricksters always turn up to oblige the trusting fools, wielding pricks to puncture with sharp betrayals.

There is a quite impressive list of multi-million dollar Ponzi schemes that were discovered in 2009–10, but many of them are not publicized much, because in comparison with the multi-billion dollar ones they seem like small potatoes. For example, in August 2009 Hassan Nemazee, a fundraiser for high profile Democratic candidates, was charged with bank fraud. He is accused of running a 292-million-dollar Ponzi scheme. Vijay K. Taneja of Fairfax, Virginia was sentenced to 7 years in jail for a 150-million-dollar mortgage fraud scheme. In May 2010 Kenneth I. Starr (not the Ken Starr of Monica Lewinsky fame) was charged with running a 30-million-dollar Ponzi scheme that preyed upon celebrities. Also in 2010 Tom Petters of Minnesota was sent to prison for operating a Ponzi scheme that bilked investors of 3.65 billion dollars. A former boss of Petters said that Petters "could talk your wallet right out of your pocket."

In 2011 Indianapolis businessman Tim Durham was prosecuted for running a Ponzi scheme that defrauded 5,000 investors of 200 million dollars. He was a GOP Robin Hood who generously donated at least 800,000 dollars to Indiana Republican office holders and candidates. In order to maintain their status and keep up appearances, high profile swindlers often have to fool themselves about what they're doing, fantasizing optimistically, daydreaming of ways it might all work out for the good. They imagine how investments and purchases they make might, with luck, in the long run reap huge profits and enable returns to be distributed to investors. The hopefulness makes them feel innocent and above-board, despite their deceit and guilt. Author Michael Zuckoff shows that Ponzi scheme men are able to convince themselves that they are clever and legitimately successful. They often make grandiose plans to take their ill-gained profit and make sound business deals with it, in order to right their crooked books in the future. In their pretending they sometimes forget they swindled, fabricated, and over-promised, and they convince themselves and others with repetitions of what they want to be true. "Acting is believing," theatre coach Charles McGaw entitled his classic book for would-be stage actors.[249] Similarly, the more shadowy and spidery trickster erects his stratagems of fooling others, and then reinforces these webs by fooling himself. "Everything that deceives can be said to enchant," Plato observed millenia ago.[250] This ancient insight about the coinciding of cunning and stunning describes well the contemporary con man's hypnotic charm.

Wall Street trading institutions now use high speed computers to engage in "high-frequency trading" to get the edge on investors by engaging in split-second transactions before other traders even realize that there is such a fast race going on. In micro-seconds a high-frequency trading computer program makes calculations and comparisons and suggests decisions based on statistical arbitrage. The high-tech early bird reaps the bonus. The language is intriguing: it includes phrases like "high-frequency trading," and "dark pools" (trading stock in the dark—in privacy, unseen by other buyers and sellers). "Front-running" is using foreknowledge concerning upcoming changes and making money by trading before the change-bringing trade happens. Front-running is illegal when done by a person, but legal when a computer does it. Microwaves conveying financial data bypass the obstacles of mountains between Chicago (for example) and New York by means of special computers giving trades magical wings, all the better to skim profits and scalp investors with. Such velocity employed by the high-frequency trading firms was partly to blame for the "Flash Crash" of 2010, when the stock market suddenly dropped drastically. Of course speed is an ancient trick in the trickster's tool kit. Tricksters get chased, and elude pursuers with speedy disappearances. While critics such as Michael Lewis, who wrote *Flash Boys*,[251] contend that high-speed traders are rigging the intricate system of financial trading to get unfair advantage over others, the high speed traders argue that they are merely using their brains to make money in the capitalist world we live in.

Among the tricksters on Wall Street are academics—physicists, math professors, and computer scientists, who may be disguised as economists, brokers, and financial strategists. They were recruited to devise methods to exploit the system. Some of them today admit that they took part in breaking the bank in the 2008 crisis. Are such tricksters ever humbled or apologetic? Maybe not, because rationalizers who cause cataclysms can always use their sharp rational brains to think up and believe in ways to blame others, or to see huge events as inevitable.

15. The Importance of Being First: Tricksters of Science and Discovery Fraud

Priority is paramount in scientific discoveries. The importance of being first can create tensions that distort the facts. It is as if there can only be one husband who deflowers the virgin accomplishment. Therefore the competition to be recorded as first to discover a fact is great. In reality there are usually several people or teams working on a similar research topic, and work is based on contributions of previous researchers, and credit may not always go the most deserving workers. Sometimes in the hurry to be first, corners are cut and tricks get played in the history of scientific research and in geographical exploration and discovery.

For example, frauds surrounding the claims of discovery of the North Pole in 1909 are still hotly contested. Both Robert E. Peary and Frederick A. Cook ventured (on separate expeditions) to the Arctic regions, and both explorers convinced people they had reached the North Pole, even though neither presented absolute proof they had done so. Each had followers who held strong beliefs about their heroes, and when contradictory evidence was presented to them they found ways to adjust their understanding to conform to opinions they already held instead of changing their minds. This ability to explain away inconsistent evidence to preserve a belief has been called "motivated reasoning." The *New York Times* championed Peary, and called Cook's claim of reaching the North Pole "the most astonishing imposture since the human race came on earth"—a wildly extravagant claim, if one stops to think about it. The North Pole is so remote from inhabited areas, and so difficult to pinpoint with the measuring equipment of the early twentieth century that healthy uncertainty would be a natural response to both claims. But the *Times* and *National Geographic* already knew what they wanted to be true, and that was that Cook was a fraud who was handing the public "a gold brick." Skepticism, uncertainty and doubt can be very inconvenient once one has decided what is true and gone on the record in asserting it. Some have said the controversy, which has lasted a century, concerns the most profitable and popular modern scientific fraud.[252]

Between 1912 and 1916 there was a famous case of fraud perpetrated in England by an amateur archeologist named Charles Dawson, who claimed to have found ancient bones of "the missing link"—the remains of a hominid bridging apes and humans. This hypothetical being came to be known as "Piltdown man," and was later proven by paleontologists to be a hoax.

Sometimes in competitors' suspicions or because of an appearance of massaging evidence, researchers are wrongly accused of being tricksters. Sometimes accusations and debates go on inconclusively a long time. In 1913 a physicist named Robert Millikan won the Nobel Prize. Sixty-five years later he was accused of manipulating data—in 1978 and 1981 researchers found proof in Millikan's notebooks that he had cherry-picked certain aspects of the data to finagle it in a way that made his findings more clear and elegant than an unfudged account would present.

From 1967 to 1974 dermatologist William Summerlin fabricated evidence in reporting his research concerning the transplant of skin from black mice to white ones. In 1974 he admitted he had used a black magic marker to color the skin of white mice, a trick so crude none suspected it.

Dr. John Long, working at Massachusetts General Hospital from 1973 to 1977, reported that he had been able to subculture permanent lines of tumor cells that were malignant, using specimens from patients with Hodgkins lymphoma. He confessed in 1980–81 that he was lying when he made such claims.

In 1975 David Baltimore won the Nobel Prize for his work as a virologist. Later he was tainted by fraud associated with his work on retroviruses and their reproductive processes, when certain of his experiments could not be duplicated with the same findings. Professional authorities and a government committee found Baltimore's lab assistant, Thereza Imanishi-Kari, guilty of making fraudulent claims, and so Baltimore resigned as president of Rockefeller University. Later the problematic work they had done was found to have been based on errors, rather than on fraud.

In 1981 Dr. John R. Darsee at Harvard Medical School claimed he had experimented with dogs, injecting them with drugs that caused myocardial infarction. In 1982 investigators found that Darsee had not conducted the experiments, he had made them up.[253] In 2010 Harvard researcher Marc Hauser's work was investigated. Hauser is a psychology professor who studies primate behavior and animal cognition. Michael D. Smith, dean of the Faculty of Arts and Sciences at Harvard, announced to the faculty in a letter that there were eight instances of scientific misconduct that Hauser had apparently committed. Whether the misconduct was done unknowingly or intentionally, the accusations show the scientific community is debating issues that some see as tricks and others see as bad judgment—which often means tricking ourselves, seeing and interpreting what we wish to be the case.

There are many other examples of scientific fraud, but these at least give an idea of some prominent recent ones in this area of tricksterism.[254]

As I indicated at the outset, the fifteen kinds of tricksters discussed above are intended to sketch a few examples of the topic, to offer a suggestive, not an exhaustive inventory, which would take an encyclopedia. Some tricks we just have to laugh at, because life's play is rife with tricks, and they tickle our sensibilities. In other cases we are fooled and blithely go on our way, even though we may be ignoring tricksters' capers at our own risk. Eventually, some become quite obvious as scams and have to be repudiated and terminated. The trickster impulse may stem from a variety of sources, but it never fails to fascinate us with its clever games and sheer vitality. In the next part of this book we will explore some of the important lessons that the trickster archetype can teach us, if we are tricky enough to learn things from this universal aspect of behavior.

3

TOMORROW
Lessons We Need to Learn from Trickster

We are made up of falsehood, duplicity, inconsistency; and we hide and disguise these things from ourselves.
—Blaise Pascal[255]

What Soul Lessons Might Trickster Teach Us?

At first blush it may not be clear what useful roles might be played by tuning in to the dynamics of the trickster archetype in the psyche's processes. Some may worry that paying attention to tricks might promote deception, fraud, instability, and disorderly conduct. I believe a wise awareness of the dynamics of the trickster archetype has a salutary effect and is useful for a variety of purposes. In traditional societies trickster stories have offered life-supportive functions. Sometimes trickster stories teach people about their limits, illustrating pitfalls to avoid, reminding them about the disastrous results of certain acts. With awareness of the mythic trickster there is an embrace of the psyche's non-linear depth reality. Without any sense of the trickster archetype, there is some degree of humorless rigidity—no matter how soberly and responsibly one comports oneself, there is a flat dullness out of tune with life. Without appreciating trickster's shrewdness and gumption, one is victim to irrationality or one-sidedness of one sort or another. Experiencing trickster lessons is often no picnic, especially when it involves learning things the hard way; but that experience is a needed corrective to excessive naiveté.

Trickster is as trickster does. But what does trickster know? What knowledge does he embody? And what does knowledge of tricksters allow us to know? When there is soulfulness in the trickster it involves knowing about life, knowing the score, being seasoned and not green, not naive about life's ways. James Baldwin observed in the 1960s that Europeans and African Americans often characterized Americans as children. Why? "Americans have so little experience—experience referring not to what happens, but to whom—that they have no key to the experiences of others."[256] I would add that we Americans often lack a sense of the interconnectedness of people, suffering from an illusory sense of isolated existences. Those who have a bent toward authoritarianism don't trust their own experiences; they aren't sure how to think for themselves. They crave the comforts of simplicity and would like to put up a "do not disturb sign" on their doors. To have a blank slate and to lack caring when thinking of others is to be numb, unable to resonate with other humans' lives. Experiences of living outside America and knowing the experiences of minorities inside America can add dimensions of understanding, as many former Peace Corp volunteers can attest. Lacking such dimensions makes one narrower, less able to know oneself and the rest of the world. The trickster traipses across borders, bridges gaps, wanders, and interacts; even his aimless acts end up linking realms together and revealing interconnections. The trickster teaches: "Don't take either trust *or* tricks for granted; appreciate the bonds of interrelations among us, and also know the play possible in the spaces between us."

Inspirations—delicate outbursts of ideas—are sparked in our experiences. What inspires us? A beautiful muse drawing us out of ourselves, or inventive trickster curiosity exploring playfully, following its own wagging tail like a puppy? Vitality finding connections and stitching patches of existence together? Sometimes the muse is a trickster, and vice versa. The trickster acts behind your back, off the scene, cooking up surprises of trouble and delight which you weren't really sure if you were capable of, as Anima (the muse-like soul of vitality) pulls you further into the unknown.

If you think the trickster doesn't make sense, consider the possibility that absurdity may be a sign indicating the presence of the human—the weirdly quirky, the nonsensical, the playful fun, and the grin behind the joker's poker face may reveal humanity. In size we're absurd creatures, somewhere between the stars and the atoms. The story that doesn't add up and the crazy idea that works—both reveal the trickster. If you want to be caught off guard by life, avoid learning about the trickster.

The trickster archetype alerts us to life's dynamism and helps us venture further into awareness of life's unrealized swirls and swerve-backs—life's dynamic dualities. Who is the real thief—the wise guy who acts like he thinks he knows, or the one who really knows and acts like he doesn't? (Both Lao Tzu in ancient China and Socrates in ancient Greece are known for stating this idea more than two millennia ago.)

Trickster introduces different parts of the brain to each other, different classes of society, different elements of existence, different drives, specialties, obsessions and concerns. Trickster stirs the mix, and then you do with it what you may. Formalities, official and strict, keep each thing in its own place, distinct from all else. Informal, spontaneous, brilliant inspiration strikes like a trickster bringing different things together with panache, stealing fire, laughing joyfully in the moment. All kinds of surprising connection-embracing humor and awakenings abide in the trickster's realm. The trickster is not just some silly little diversionary clown, but a major player, the archetypal ringleader who brings together dynamic forces, levels of awareness, characters otherwise spread out in time's far-flung drama; the trickster makes ends meet, introduces opposites, he surprises us by collapsing the inflations that have grown from illusion.

Violent force can make for much misery and plant thorny resentments that grow into the future. Nonviolent tricks of humor can overcome obstacles in their own way too. As Mark Twain observed, "Against the assault of laughter, nothing can stand." All you need is wit. The trickster's mockery can wither foolishness faster than might can. To survive and thrive among obstacles, people, and problems that are prickly, one must be wily—wisely tricky. The trickster ensures that life doesn't take things lying down. The trickster stands for the fact that the heart is fickle, and the ego hypocritical, and the soul is restless. Life exists on a sliding floor, not a static, stable base. The trickster is the dynamic factor in the soul that ensures that life doesn't just take things lying down, but dreams up options.

The trickster impulse is full of rich liveliness, not just deception. For example, along with the trickster presence appears the prospects of fun, tomfoolery, horsing around, teasing, laughing affection. The positive side of the trickster is inventive, and does not just accept things as they are, but is proactive—if he's lucky he's rewarded, if he meddles too much he gets blowback. Tricksterism is inherent in all aspects of human life—in the layers of conscious and unconscious awareness, in impulses and impishness, in seriousness and playfulness. The trickster is there in earnestness and jokery, in heaviness and lightness. In the immortal trickster aspect of humanity, the inner and the outer aspects of mortal life uncannily reflect each other. Ray Bradbury puts it this way, if we paraphrase his words: the trickster is like a clown, who within contains a Death's head; alternatively, the trickster is like a skull upon which is perched the crown of a fool.[257] This bothness is inherent in the ubiquitous and elusive topic we are considering.

The trickster genius is equivocal, as we see in stories of the classical Greek example of the messenger god Hermes; he is now a healer, now a jokester, now an inspirer, now a misleader. In the fabric of our lives, disastrous disruptions and fortuitous connections are both the work of the trickster. The human heart has both of the trickster's impulses: the selfish pig, and the self-giving saint. His extraordinary intuitive quickness, if used deviously for self-aggrandizement, cheating others, can cause great harm. If used wisely and skillfully to get through life's complex and tricky situations, when caught in dilemmas between rocks and hard places, trickster wisdom can liberate us from dead ends. If the trickster is the only archetype we're in touch with, we're in trouble; but if we're never aware of the trickster side of things, we're in trouble then too.

Are Americans trickster-savvy and tough? Or have we become numb and soft, thanks to high-tech luxuries? Are we foolhardy and fooling ourselves, or are we foolproof, with a knowledge of foolery which is unimprovable? What lessons might still be valuable for America to rediscover about the trickster?

The Trickster Gives Survival Power

The human psyche's dynamics are intrinsically part trickster. This vital aspect of clever impulses can get the better of us in self-destructive acts, or it can offer a vivifying awareness of how the soul relates to existence. We can be "our own worst enemies" or our own wise friends. In traditional societies stories about tricksters are used to teach subtle lessons. The trickster, like the other archetypes in our psyches, represents a style of consciousness, a mode of existence, a way of relating to conditions.

In Native American stories, Coyote knows how to go on living, ever able to adapt and survive. To know how to roll with punches, figure out advantages, and defeat monsters—these skills comprise the essential art of staying alive. Coyote is a master of disguise, a genius of shape-shifting to conform to the illusions in the mind of the ones he needs to elude. My late friend

Johnny Flynn, a Potawatomi Indian who was the best storyteller I knew, put the lesson people can learn this way: "See, Coyote knows that shape-shifting is not about changing the fundamentals of who they are. It is about changing how people perceive who they are."[258] The ability to adapt is the trick of resilience, getting out of the way of a steamroller, meeting the needs of opportunity, avoiding being crippled by slamming doors—mercurial trickster fine-tunes our inborn talent to survive.[259]

The trickster is the initiator into knowledge of life's twistiness, revealing that life is beyond any one person's control. "Nothing alive stands still," the trickster observes, and he suggests we live accordingly. The spirit of Coyote, Raven, and other tricksters is active in the imagination of nature writers able to bring humor and other subtle touches to their understanding and appreciation of the living environment.[260] Coyote is not numb or inert; Coyote responds, always ready to do his thing and reinvent himself and the world around him.

But in real life, how much of one's self can one legitimately invent? The world will decide. Controversial scholar Ward Churchill claims a Native American identity, but many Native Americans say he is a fraud. In the past there have been well-known cases of people taking on the identity of Native Americans for their own purposes and being denounced by those who question them and find their credentials to be lacking. An African American named Sylvester Long, for instance, said he was a Blackfeet Indian and called himself Buffalo Child Long Lance, and became a celebrity. An author claiming to be a Navaho named Yinishye Nasdijj wrote *Geronimo's Bones* and other books about being Native American, and was later found to be a fraud. Forrest Carter, a white segregationist, wrote a purported autobiography, *The Education of Little Tree*, portraying the life of a Cherokee. Archibald Belaney was an Englishman masquerading as an Ojibway, calling himself Grey Owl, and becoming a well-known spokesman for conservationism. The taking on of ethnic identities in autobiographical narratives still goes on today, and it is done for a number of reasons including admiration, profit and lack of ethnic identity of one's own. William Styron wrote in the voice of Nat Turner, enthralled by his voice and story.[261]

Bogus war heroes, ersatz "Vietnam vets" who never served in Vietnam, men claiming to have been Navy Seals who are not authenticated by the Navy—all are rejected or at least questioned in their attempts to claim to be someone they are not. The world does not give a blank check to all who try to pose as something they are not. Fakes often end up caught in their own tricks—"Oh what a tangled web we weave when first we practice to deceive," as Sir Walter Scott wrote in *Marmion*.[262]

Catching flies with flypaper is a good trick. The desires of the victim lead him to the adhesive surface where he sticks. Setting a trap involves the ancient art of rigging up reality in a way that can manipulate others, creating illusions to spring a surprise, overpowering and snaring the unsuspecting. Every trap is a trick; are all tricks traps to capture something, one way or another? Do all tricks seek to snare game, to catch someone off-guard, to capture attention, confidence, money, affection; or to grab someone's sympathy by playing a victim, or to snatch away someone's seriousness to get a laugh, or to take someone's sense of what's real and supplant it with illusions? Awareness of tricks can inoculate one against being victimized.

The trickster can be a reminder of caution, warning of danger. The suspicious shifty-eyed guy squints, on the lookout for the next wide-eyed, unsuspecting guy. The naive man doesn't see any danger approaching. Sometimes seasoned friends propose wise precautions against the devastations of would-be tricksters, just as they warn us of the capriciousness of threatening weather, hostile politics, economic misfortune. The worldly wise are those who know about life's trickiness. Knowing about tricksterism in the world gives one a "heads up," a warning to keep some skepticism in reserve for those extremely solicitous of one's trust, or overly interested in one's valuables. "You have to be careful, Ellen, everyone is looking to play an angle," Patty Hewes warns her protégé, in the TV show *Damages* (2009). The irony is that Patty herself is dangerously untrustworthy, having her own angle in presenting this sentiment of acting protective of Ellen. Great optimism seems like a false mask to somber realists who find the worst-case scenario as likely as the best case. Painting only rosy outcomes, the cheerful con man smooths the way to clinching the sale. Our awareness of tricksters and their scenarios helps us beware and protect our vulnerable interests. It sounds obvious: watch out for con men, embezzlers, and officials who abscond with peoples' life savings and retirement plans or spend their companies into bankruptcy. But many who lost their pension plans never saw it coming. Naiveté, with its concomitant unwarranted trust, leads one to get taken for a ride. Betrayal, which is a disillusioning, painful loss, can at least help us earn clarity. Knowing that there are tricksters, we can watch out for duplicity.

America is about a vision of a city on a hill, but it is also Coyote's America, a distorting shadow of that ideal vision. Natchez-Under-the-Hill, on the other side of the tracks, was an underworld of illegal activities, bawdy houses, gambling dens, saloons, and other clip joints. Its shadowy criminal nether-belly makes a mockery of respectable Knob Hill up above. In a sense, Natchez-Under-the-Hill still exists in all the alleys, seedy dives, clip joints and cat-houses still going strong in America. In its nineteenth-century heyday Natchez-Under-the-Hill, a port town in Mississippi, hosted a constant stream of transients who flowed from steamboats and flatboats. Today it is a historic town for tourists to visit, said to still be haunted by the ghosts of some of its legendary denizens.

Aware of tricksters, we may flush out untrustworthy heartbreakers seeking to harm us, and avoid scofflaws of duplicity who wish to do us dirt. If we are too simple and trusting some devious joker will pop up and bamboozle us; he will complicate life for us beyond our comfort zones. The trickster lens provides a useful focus, teaching us to be wary and watchful, not to trust too blindly. When we become too relaxed in a picnic atmosphere, the trickster reminds us there may be a snake in the grass, or a trail of ants stealing sweets.

From another angle there is a trickster quality in the ability to bring out the best in others. Eric Hoffer, for example, cautioned the overly suspicious: "Good judgment in our dealings with others consists not in seeing through deceptions and evil intentions, but in being able to waken the decency dormant in every person."[263] Hoffer believed that if we are able to see through ourselves, then only can we see through others. This positive ability is not to be the paranoid inquisitor seeing through the evil trickster, but to be the good-natured generous trickster whose free play is able to find their good and bring it to fruition. It is creative play, not poisonous demonizing.

The trickster can be seen as transformation genius incarnate. Could it be that the most successful Americans have some qualities of the con man? That they are loser and more open-ended in their range of gambits, more playful, and sure of self? But perhaps some losers are like that too—mercurial, prone to gamble, eagerly self-assertive? The winners in America use skillful tricks, apt schemes; they're savvy and resourceful, adaptive and entrepreneurial—"taking lemons and making lemonade." The losers in America transgress laws, get caught, self-destruct in a downward spiral. The winners know their limits; the losers don't know what is viable—they are childishly confused about what they can get away with.

To change during the life cycle and enjoy new experiences in different phases, to embrace the fluid realities of vital processes, is a powerful aspect of the trickster archetype. The term "joker's wild" means the value of the joker is changeable and can be substituted for any other card—like the trickster, the joker card is versatile, with multiple aptitudes, rife with mercurial possibilities. Like the mythological Chinese dragon known for dynamic energy and transformations, the trickster can't be pinned down or reduced to one label alone. When you think you've caught on to him, like a flash of lightning he's already gone on beyond your understanding. Ultimate trickster stealth is always beyond one's control, unpredictable like the sneak thief who comes in the night.[264] Like the Anima, the trickster archetype educes—*leads onward* the development of the psyche. He keeps you in the game, puts you in the jackpot, leaving you unsure what will happen next. The trickster puts us through our paces, and the trickster forever changes, and the trickster is there when we graduate from a level of existence and find ourselves at the next stage. The trickster is the opposite of blinkered, isolative, strict, formal, rigid, unyielding, and unimaginative ways. Cryptic and contrary, show-offy and getting into trouble, then unknotting oneself from trouble, the trickster fascinates us, playing on life's stage, a pretzel-like divine fool. Innovative architect Frank Gehry and other Houdinis escaping the straitjackets of conventions in various fields are polymorphous in their approaches to problem-solving. They embrace a host of possibilities to succeed and make their quantum leaps in answer to challenges. *The trickster's qualities—contrary vitality, playfulness, and sly quirkiness, for example—display unknown mysterious powers.* Even the most abstracted mechanical representations of the trickster's mercurial transformative quality fascinate millions of children, generating huge streams of revenue—for example in the form of the toy products known as "Transformers."[265] Ever-changing trickster spirit keeps us aware of options, many possibilities, so we don't get locked into one kneejerk reaction or repeated routine. In many predicaments, whether in struggles with others, or within ourselves, the trickster does best to outwit, instead of trying to out-hit. Brute force, struggling obstinately, only tightens the problem like a knot. It is more useful to trick the knot open, undoing it with indirection or subtle humor and intelligence that tentatively pulls here and there to try things out. "Resist ye not evil" is a venerable injunction for that very reason. Confronting conflicts head-on intensifies them; using tricks of intelligence, one can put out the rug from under the problem, releasing with subtle surprise other possibilities.

In trickster dynamics overreaching cleverness is humbled and quickness of foot is rewarded. Sometimes it seems the emphasis of the trickster archetype is about cleverness: the power of being sharp. To be not clever enough is a problem—the naive are conned, betrayed, robbed, left as victims in dire need of a good Samaritan. But to be too clever (as in "too clever by half," "too smart for his own good") is also a problem. In the thrall of this attitude one thinks one can get away with things one cannot, and commits crimes and misdemeanors. One overreaches, and takes chances, thinking one will never get caught. Tricksterism involves what we hide from others, what we veil, what we deny and suppress, and what we bury deep inside. It encompasses all the realms of subterfuge—wise modesty, feints and decoys, coy blinks, polite white lies and criminal deceptions; the way we forget some things in order to skillfully put our best foot forward. Every psyche has tricks to keep the game of life going, to play along the way. In Norse mythology Loki the trickster turns away, refusing to mourn, when the rest of nature mourns the innocent god of summer sunshine Baldur being struck down, and that holding back has a power. Tricks of diverting, perverting, subverting, and reverting make up the many twists of fate. Sometimes *not* doing something, like paying tribute due, can have a greater effect than doing something: tax dodgers get arrested. Cold aloofness when all others share deep feelings may never be forgiven or forgotten.

Sometimes we take for granted that the imposing forms and established order of the institutions of our era are eternal realities. The trickster reminds us that all organizations and names come from the human psyche, from human imagination, from needs, images, and fantasies. The formidable marble capitol buildings in Washington DC were designed by architects (based in part on designs from earlier ages) and in a million years will be gone. Governments and civilizations with their collective projects based on ideas, choices, models, and scenarios, rise into existence in the psyche. They change and fade, and return in new forms. All this proneness to change is the playground for the trickster. He delights in Emerson's "sliding floor" of reality.

The energetic trickster helps us prize our individual freedoms—showing that we can learn to be flexible and fluid, seizing opportunities. We can become more ready to go with the flow of necessity, shifting to find a different approach when need be, avoiding dead ends and stagnation. The brave and the free can play the trickster even in precarious situations and at death's door.[266] They kid around to lighten the load. This shows the intrinsic vitality of the trickster impulse in the psyche.

Without the trickster, what would life be? The integrative binding force of the principle that is at home in the different realms and levels of the conscious and the unconscious would be missing. The trickster is the force in the psyche fooling around with and embracing all the different parts of one's existence, the facets of one's personality. The trickster archetype is thus known as the guide of the journey of individuation—finding our genuine whole self. In depth psychology, Mercurius, the tricky Roman god of trading, similar to the Greek god Hermes, is a mediator—like humor—functioning between the outer and inner realms. The depths of the unseen unconscious may be "banished from awareness as too frightening, too unworthy, too challenging, or too confusing,"[267] and when this happens life takes on a kind of one-sidedness, a selective cherry-picking of focal points in reality. This obscures parts of our total view with blindspots. As a writer about the trickster archetype, Del McNeely, explains, "An individual psyche requires a mediating or integrative function to tolerate the pushes and pulls of conflicting energies." Both in the psyche's inner dynamics, and in its relation to outward figures such as a deity or ideal, the fluid go-between experience that mediates in projections is vitally necessary in its uniting function; "its absence results in disturbing feelings, such as emptiness, and self-contempt, and then in protective devices against such unpleasant feelings." Furthermore, McNeely insightfully names the defense mechanisms that are activated against this inner splintering: "narcissism, extreme arrogance, attempts at over-control of one's environment, and rationalizations of contradictions in behavior or beliefs."[268] If you think tricksters are troublemakers, you should see the trouble that grows where the trickster wisdom's depth, humor, and honesty are not allowed to work. In that case there is a flourishing of ignorant know-it-alls, narrow meanness, self-righteous, self-important personalities stuck in dysfunctional mode, acting important, accomplishing little, sucking the oxygen out of the air. Life needs trickster wisdom as lentils need salt, as earth needs water. The trickster in Haida stories is a necessary agent of change, an agent of the Creator active in the creation.

Observations on Trickster in the Life Cycle

1. Childhood and Initiations

Of course, to realize the significance of the archetype you have to see the trickster at play in your own biography—your whole life-cycle drama. The trickster plays his dynamic part in all of life's phases: the play of tricks in childhood; and naiveté betrayed in adulthood, by surviving deceptions, learning from them, finding new stages of growth, as well as in transformations, and the vantage of looking back on the whole unfolding in maturity.

We are conned to sleep as children by lullabies, conned into eating food we don't feel like eating by tricks, conned into going places and playing and learning when we resist. We are tricked into conforming by parents and grandparents, presents and promises, stories and tall tales.

It is said that the greatest achievement in life is magnanimous integrity, becoming one's own unique, authentic person. Individuation is realization of a life's living wholeness, the oneness of levels and contrarieties together, so we act as we speak, think as we feel, know and be who we are. At its best, life is not about being a splintered lost soul of many confused masks, simple false fronts, involved in con games at cross purposes, and in the end panicking and asking "who am I?" when it is too late to know. Instead, it's to have self-knowledge and integrity, to get it all together.

The experiential crisis regarding authenticity of identity is like a zen koan. Why should someone who has been socialized, and who has been so shepherded by authorities, feel so inauthentic, as if he is a big fraud? We are asked to conform and pretend, for example, that a high school diploma, or a college or graduate degree program, has made a profound impact, and has left a life-changing impression, when, in fact, our experience may not have felt very deep.

All our learning begins with mimicking. All learning is based on seeing, hearing, doing something in response to models we observe—like playing peekaboo, and echoing sounds. To make a skill one's own is to integrate it deeply. At first one functions like a mockingbird or parrot; one apes others. How long does it take before this magpie-like or tricksterish learning becomes second nature, the unconscious reality absorbed and integrated deep into one's bones as one's character, as natural wisdom? Having enough time to absorb learning, in an age of hurry, is an unacknowledged factor, and so we sometimes experience inadequate training leaving us with half-baked skills, and consequent uncertainties.

In Benedict Carey's "Feel Like a Fraud? At Times Maybe You Should,"[269] an article reporting on recent research regarding feelings of being inauthentic, the word "trickster" is not explicitly used. But if in the discussion the underlying strategies, the unconscious wisdom involved in respect for limits and facing uncertainty with an awareness that allows for some playfulness were personified, they might be seen as appearing like a kind of trickster spirit. As Carey notes, "Feelings of phoniness appear to alter people's goals in unexpected ways and may also protect them against subconscious self-delusions."[270] Sometimes it's wise—especially for a neophyte—to reduce expectations and embrace humility, through self-deprecation. Acknowledging ground yet to be gained is a beginner's wisdom.

We necessarily learn by mimicking. "See one, do one, teach one," as the jokey adage goes in Harvard Medical school, regarding surgical operations. We could mimic a lawyer, a truck driver, a bank teller, a professor, or anyone else, it seems, and so it may feel like we are playing superficial roles when we are journeymen. It takes an initiation into a way of life, a profession, a discipline, to make a deep impression, to shape identity. American folklore features abundant examples of newcomers being joshed and welcomed by means of a trick. "Hazing the greenhorn" is a way to make the naive kid grow up fast. The way it typically happens is that old timers acquaint the newcomer with the lay of the land by making him or her suffer the results of his/her ignorance. In this way the neophyte learns for him/herself the lessons that initiations are supposed to inculcate. It is something like throwing someone into deep water to teach him to swim. Initiation can also be seen as a kind of taming—the inexperienced newcomer is uncultured and needs to be tamed, taught, refined by joining the common membership and learning the shared knowledge. In this trickster betrayal of trust the purpose is to promote further learning and bonding.[271]

The Pennsylvania Dutch initiated greenhorns by having them take part in catching the *elbedritsch*—much like the snipe hunt found in other groups. In Mississippi, at Natchez-under-the-Hill in its heyday, a tenderfoot would be invited to a staged funeral in which all attendees were expected to go close to the corpse or even kiss it. When the greenhorn got close, the "corpse" would reach up and grab him, not letting him go as the other guests beat the greenhorn until he promised to treat them all to drinks. This was known as "the Spanish burial."[272] Out West, seasoned cowboys told "circular tales" to test the gullibility of greenhorns. In the Northern woods veteran loggers tricked "green 'uns" by telling them to ask the cook to fry up a "crosshaul," a name for paths jutting out at right angles from logging roads—obviously not something the cook could provide, but a request sure to arouse scorn and abuse. New sheep farm workers were hazed by old timers who told them, just before lambing time, to "Go get all the sheep together and bring them in—and be sure to get every single lamb too." The greenhorns would come back with sheep, but also with a few stray rabbits, because they were so careful and thorough, and because no new lambs had been born yet that season. For their earnest labors they were rewarded with mocking laughter. On western gold fields "salting the claims" sold to prospectors was a common fraud and initiation. Miners sprang "whizzers" or pranks on a tenderfoot, concealing a gold nugget under the bark of a jack pine. The tenderfoot would immediately declare he wanted to stake a claim on some jack pine trees, raising howls of laughter. Sometimes newly arrived would-be miners would be charged a fee to enter a public park, or billed for any number of foolish charges, just to see how naive they were.

Tricks played by "old hands" initiate the novice into knowledge, teaching him not to be fooled. The newbie is called "rookie" because he's the wet-behind-the-ears one who starts off by getting "rooked." The pranks played during the larking done by seasoned ones in the field are often the first tricks of the trade learned by the rookie in training. A toughening of the skin is needed so the "tenderfoot" can become properly calloused, and move about in the prickly and lacerating world with ease and skill. "Initiation is not a demythologizing into 'hard' reality, but an affirmation of the mythical meaning within all reality."[273] Every person has to face hardship sometimes, and learn how to be something of a hero. The rituals of initiation seem to say, "You're going to face a lot of crazy problems, because that's the nature of the beast, it's the way of the world, the basic human condition. In spite of it all, keep your head and deal with whatever comes up. Remember you're a member, and don't let crazy stress throw you. It may be outsize but it doesn't have to overwhelm you. You're not alone, you're one member of a band of brothers and sisters with a story going back in time." The ideal initiate facing hazing is the hero overcoming cosmic obstacles, prevailing against monstrous chaos and becoming capable. To be a confident hero one must be as wily as the trickster, not get caught off guard in youthful folly.

A shivaree, in the nineteenth century and the early part of the twentieth century in America, was a party held to haze or welcome to the community a newly married couple. The practice of shivarees was dramatized in the action of Rodgers and Hammerstein's musical *Oklahoma!* The word refers especially to a wild, noisy welcoming celebration thrown for newlyweds by a crowd of well-wishing family members, neighbors, acquaintances and friends. (This word *shivaree* originally was used to denote a performance of wild rough-and-tumble music, used in English folk tradition in the United States. It may be related to the word *jamboree*, a gathering of scouts, or a get-together of musicians.) The shivaree celebration had some features like obnoxious trick-or-treat practices of Halloween, and others like hazing pranks done in fraternities and sororities. The musical aspects involved group singing, like Christmas caroling performed by strolling singers. Let's look at an example of shivaree trickery.

First, the group of shivaree celebrants might gather at one of their homes to have drinks and "warm up" their vocal cords. After dark the friends would all go over to wherever the newlyweds were staying, attempting to arrive just after the couple had gotten into bed together. Then the party of drunken revelers would suddenly bang pots and pans, sing snatches of songs, and yell out for the man and wife stop whatever they were doing and come out. The leader of the group would then pound on the front door, demanding: "We want to come in and propose a toast to your health, to help celebrate your wedding." Sometimes the groom would come to the door and hand out some drinks, food, or cash, requesting the party go elsewhere to have their fun. Ignoring the clamor meant chancing that the rowdy crowd would break through the door and run off with the groom, leaving him alone far away without his usual clothes. A Kansas newspaper depicted a shivaree in terms of rough handling and vandalism: "They [the shivaree crowd] performed such tricks as shooting bullets through the windows, breaking down the door, dragging the couple out of bed and tumbling them about on the floor, and indulging in other equally innocent tricks."[274] These bullying tricks were meant as a good-natured kind of initiation into frontier community life for a new family. I suppose such a prank could quickly cause the newlyweds to deepen bonds and realize they were really a couple and that at times it would be "us against the world." Tying tin cans and streamers to groom's car and writing "Just Married" on the windows with soap or magic markers seems like a mild remnant of the rougher jokes pulled when America was younger. Today if a couple received that treatment, with bullets shot through windows, lawsuits, vengeful violence, or a lifetime of ill-feelings might ensue, rather than joyous feelings of belonging. Raucous fun was a kind of bond to express and celebrate the rowdy pioneering spirit of frontier community life. Recent shivarees have included putting cornflakes in the newlyweds' bed sheets, or removing the slats from their bed so the mattress falls through, or installing a video camera in their bedroom, or placing signs around town announcing a six a.m. moving sale at their address on the morning after their wedding.

Today, some high school groups and college sororities and fraternities still initiate freshmen secretly through illegal hazings that often involve tricks and tests like those played on greenhorns in various professions, sports teams, and fraternal groups. Sometimes the process of letting new members join a group by hazing is abusive, dangerous, and even fatal. Traditionally "hell week," or some other length of initiation time, meant a period when fledgling pledges endured ritualistic harassments. This involved submitting to experiences of daring and humiliation, and a leveling of individuality in a group experience, to enable a sense of membership via going through a shared ordeal to forge a bond among initiates, and to impress on the psyche's memory an identity. (For example: at Carleton College freshmen had to wear beanies, so everyone would know they were the newbies.) Going through a humbling and uproarious event that one will never forget is a way for newbies to feel a new identity and to form potentially lifelong bonds. The rude awakening of initiation has to hurt a bit, it would seem—otherwise it's just more of the same old same old. Recent examples in the news show that going to extremes in the attempt to haze can be horrifying and fatal.[275] "The wound that is so necessary to initiation ceremonies ends the state of innocence as it opens one in a new way and another place, making one suffer from openness, bringing to a close the world as wonder," as James Hillman puts it.[276] The soul uses the hurt that makes us wince to get beyond the child state, in order to grow in experience. The wound becomes a scar, a memory in the flesh.

If we do not learn by means of the welcome wagon of rude awakenings, a typical American way to learn something is to act like you already know, never admitting you're a neophyte, pretending you're already an old hand. As David Sedaris writes, "The thing about sports, at least for guys, is that nobody ever defines the rules, not even in gym class." I think if men look back and think of their own first experiences in sports they will find this is the case, as Sedaris says: "You're just supposed to know, and if you don't there's something seriously wrong with you."[277] You bluff, and fake it, and pick skills up as you go along. And often this trick works. You watch and try and improve, taking to the flow of the game like a duck to water. Or you fail, floundering without basic skills: "Sink or swim," as the saying goes, "Root, hog, or die." Learning the tricks by haze or failure, we are seasoned like timber; we mature like fine wine by way of the tricks of time that we weather. Like Adam and Eve tasting the apple, we are tricked into new awareness and wariness. "Won't fool me on that one again!" the wised-up neophyte exclaims. And he may look forward to fooling next year's batch of initiates himself. This pattern is evident in dialogue in Akira Kurosawa's film "Scandal" (1950), spoken by a sad lawyer:

> I'm no good. I'm a petty crook . . . a loser, not even a skunk. . . . I'm just a worm. What have I become? There was a time when people always tricked me. People tricked me then laughed at me, laughed at me then tricked me. Somewhere along the way I got fed up with it. To protect myself from being tricked I started tricking others. . . . Man is an extremely tragic creature. And so weak. Because he's weak he pretends to be strong. That's our trouble.[278]

We are educated, inspired, and made whole, or corrupted and ruined, by tricks. Therefore, one reason to focus attention on the dynamics of trickiness is to see ourselves and understand our situations more clearly.

Life cycle rituals, Christian sacraments (for example, confirmation), and initiations, bar and bat mitzvahs, weddings, and other ceremonies in all religious traditions are examples of the officially sanctioned character formation rites that shape the community's time-honored roles of social identity. In the modern age there are sometimes unlabeled professional rituals, but they are not always deeply effective, memorable, and meaningful ones. For example, welcoming orientations where policy seminars are conducted, retreats to discuss new programs and ventures, celebrations to acknowledge incoming employees, etc. We learn by mimicking, but it is also true that we individuate by turning against conformity, attuned to our individual conscience. We are all tricksters who chime in with others and mimic, learning the ropes by playing new roles, and sometimes exploiting opportunities by taking advantage of the vulnerability of others with our talents, wiles, and charms.[279] Even wisdom uses every trick it can think of—rhymes and stories, symbols, and passionate expressions—song and dance routines to convey deep understanding in a memorable way. Trickless, even the greatest wisdom is bland, ineffectual, soon forgotten, so much ho hum blah blah blah and yada yada yada.

The trickster toys around, plays the fool in childhood silliness, amusing himself with people and situations. The trickster spirit involves a style of play, a mode involving detachment to make moves in a game, not being caught in the throes of life, but taking them in stride with the distance of irony. Its opposite is hyper-sincerity, literalism, and rigidity, taking one's actions so seriously one forgets that the world is made up of cycles and symbols, and that religions are symbol systems, and that roles are all temporary. If one is too serious and one-sided, one may become a fanatic or a terrorist, ready to raise tensions to a crisis, even a bloodbath, because there seems no other way out. How detached does one become before one is dangerously numb, and how anxiously sincere, before being out of touch with imagination's possibilities? The trickster archetype sometimes helps us see and understand the good in the bad guy, the bad in the good guy, the tricky nuances in the seemingly monolithic. The trickster keeps us in touch with childlike playfulness and vitality.

2. Adolescence and Adrenaline

Coyote, American Trickster extraordinaire, is no respecter of boundaries. There's a Winnebago Coyote story about a trickster getting a girl pregnant. No, wait—actually in this one the person who gets pregnant is Coyote himself![280] The trickster comes to a village and sees good things there. Little Fox, son of the chief, heroically hunts, shooting many animals. He has never mated, and is thinking about marriage. The trickster thinks of becoming a woman and marrying him. His drag disguise is quite elaborate. He uses an elk's liver for a vulva, puts an elk's kidneys on his chest for breasts, and slips into a woman's dress to complete the disguise. Coyote looks very pretty as a woman, and in time becomes pregnant by mating with Little Fox. Furthermore, "she" also becomes pregnant by mating with Blue Jay; and, oops, does it again with Hetcgenîga, the chipmunk. Pregnant from mating with all three, "she" goes to an old woman go-between, who helps Coyote announce his/her intention to court the chief's son. The youth wants to marry "her," and sees to it that "she" is well fed on bear ribs and dried corn. (Some say

Coyote's hunger for this feast was the main reason he wanted to get involved with the proud youth to begin with.) They are married; "she" gives birth to three boys. In some tellings the chief's son's pride is humbled by Coyote in his wedded life.[281] There's nothing like an irrepressible trickster to put an arrogant ego in its place.

Unwed teenage pregnancies are a complex issue, and one not to be taken lightly. There's a lot of tricksterism involved in teenage pregnancies—the seduction, the boy getting his way, causing life-changing events, proving he is a man, all against the wishes of the girl's family. It often takes irresponsible duplicity, clever inventiveness, sneaky deception of the inflated ego, to impregnate someone on the verge of adulthood. The excitable and dramatic developing adolescent brain, plus raging hormones, fuel the reproductive imperative itself, forming a powerful drive. This urge, expressed in these ways, and stimulated by media and peer pressure, surmounts obstacles, and overcomes better judgment even among adolescents in good families. In the age of sexting and social media new minefields of tricks crop up to further complicate adolescents' paths.

Ladies' men, Casanovas, mack daddies, pimps, and fancy dudes who seduce, exploit, and abandon—all spend their talents and energies in suave tricksterism. In youth one has the potential, the surplus of energy and hormones needed to devote oneself to the exploits of eros. By succeeding, the impregnating trickster burdens teenage girls with early child-rearing duties, postponing or thwarting their own development. The exploitative trickster takes advantage of vulnerabilities, sensing undeveloped understanding as an opening.

The heartless seducer offers candy, valentines and roses, dinner and wine. Sometimes seducers play on emotions to get sympathy as victims. While the sad face depicts an achy-breaky heart, hiding inside is the trickster's fakey-snaky art. The female seductress is another story. To get what she wants the trickster gold digger professes undying love and/or promises lasting pleasures. Adulterous affairs are also betrayals, two-timing double-faced tricks that bring heartbreak. But when the trickster betrays a naive soul, he plays a part that can engender wariness. To take part in the dance of life means learning lessons, becoming inventive in sidestepping disasters, not just passively going along with hurtfulness as if it is fate. One learns to make use of one's wits, and to face life's challenges, sidestep dangerous temptations as a result of encountering others' tricks. Old timers who've seen it all warn us: as long as you are caught in denial of tricks, refusing to admit you've been taken, you can't quit being a sucker and wise up.

Adolescence, often a crisis time of vulnerability and feelings of self-doubt and fear of rejection, brings uncertainties: who are you, and whom can you trust? You have to put on an act, be fast, cool, tough, hard, sure, mean; you can cheat, steal, vandalize, to be like the other kids in the gang. If you grow up, learn lessons, and move on, becoming a successful, decent human being, rediscovering in the wisdom of maturity the child you were before becoming an adolescent, you may become almost unrecognizable to your old gang with its bullying ways.

Life is change, and so even the sly Lothario, when he grows up to be a father, feels protective toward his own innocent daughter. It is natural to feel sympathy for the poor unfortunate one who is in harm's way, in danger of being duped. We want to protect, rescue, and give refuge. And as we get older we may feel anger at devious, manipulative tricks. The excitement-craving moods of bored adolescents may lessen as our energies are devoted to difficult mundane tasks. Sometimes we have to be tricked into undertaking necessary disciplines. They seem boring compared to the excitement of risk, fast rides, fun gambles, the thrills of sticking your neck out.

We see tricksters's subterfuges in the pursuit of sex in films like *Wedding Crashers* (2005), in which a couple of would-be Casanovas go to strangers' weddings to pick up chicks, and *About a Boy* (2002), in which Hugh Grant plays a character who attends a meeting of a single-parents support group called SPAT (Single Parents Alone Together) specifically to meet women. In various stories like these the typical male strategy is to make the woman feel sorry for them. The logic is easy to grasp: sympathy is warmth; warmth wants to share love, console, make things better, cause smiles and pleasant feelings instead of sorrow. Pleasant feelings and mutual warmth are not far from caresses, intimate embraces, and fondling, which are not far from erotic stimulation and affection, which are close to sharing the mutual joys of sex. In these stories the trickster often ends up getting tricked by deeper feelings into a deeper relationship than he was initially looking for with a woman.

People who love the adrenaline rush—athletes, sportsmen, fighters, gamblers, daredevils, roughnecks, rowdies, and youthful tricksters attracted to risk—in maturity may harness these energies to help others. Dangerous professions—such as firefighting, law enforcement, emergency response work, and the military services—all require workers who can function when their adrenaline is flowing. Surviving risks, daredevil roughnecks may become stunt men for films. When they are more mature and dedicated to the common good, some youthful thrill-seekers may find society has given them a badge to make pre-dawn raids with their guns drawn, and the license to break down doors with an ax or battering ram. They may be Navy SEALs, DEA agents, pilots, parachutists, divers, or other rough and ready responders to emergencies, needed by the country whose early flags warned: "Don't Tread on Me."

3. Maturity, Rejuvenation, and Death

The tricks associated with surviving the long slog, enduring years of professional challenges and repetitive routines, the tricks of married life, and maturity, are devices that at their best offer resilience and stamina, and at their worst bring derailment and breakdown. The juggling of many responsibilities is no simple trick. Our middle life is rich and busy with many roles, relationships, responsibilities, moods, lessons, and ways to be industrious, while also trying to find enjoyment in life on the run. During this time, there are steady endeavors, industrious investing of time and energy in growing, "getting bigger boots," salting away the resources grain by grain that will give security in the future. The multiplicity of subtle interactions in middle life is like the wind blowing through the many leaves on the tree of life. There are gentle, joyous, and refreshing breezes and there are storms that harass and threaten to tear off leaves and branches too. The skill required to perform well in this phase is no joke. It requires a combination of tricky performance talents—like dancing with a variety of partners, and like responding to challenges with martial arts moves, defending against incoming harms, whether deliberate or accidental.

The autumn and winter of life stimulate us to develop new arrays of tricks. For as long as there has been culture there have probably been tricks to cover physical losses and to downplay one's decrepitude. Consider the old folk song from around 1900:

> After the ball was over
> Mary took out her glass eye,
> Put her false teeth in some water,
> Hung her false hair up to dry,
> Put her wooden leg in the corner,
> Hung her tin ear on the wall,
> And that was the end of Mary, after the ball![282]

Today, in a time far advanced from the old art of falsies made of goose-down padding, we have state-of-the-art plastic surgery and various regimens, treatments, and tricks to rejuvenate our innards and make our outsides appear younger. Injections of fetal sheep cells, chelation therapy, hyperbaric oxygen therapy, anti-oxidant pills, multiple vitamins, and other methods promise to provide a fountain of youth. Botox, liposuction, tummy tucks, face-lifts, and other procedures represent billion dollar industries in a culture that worships youth. Today there are more body modifications, to transform one's gender and bolster appearances, than ever before. From this angle I suppose all the cosmetics, perfumes, deodorants, etc., seem like tricks to cover, entice, enhance, or deceive. There are many aids to help us with the quirks with which we are born. Senator Everett Dirksen, nicknamed "the Wizard of Ooze" for his ornate oratorical style, gargled with a mixture of Ponds Cold Cream and water, to keep his voice smooth and mellifluous. Restylane is self-proclaimed as the "world's premier filler" used by men and women to improve facial features, filling out cheeks, lips, neck, etc. At present 60 percent of women dye their hair. (Some sources say the number is higher.) Men use hair dye, weaves, and hairpieces of various kinds. When all else fails cryogenic facilities offer us hopes of heroically outfoxing death's decay process by freezing our bodies until better methods of rejuvenation and medication are found by new research.

With realistic psychological understanding, Jung wrote insightfully of old age.[283] He observed that while "the young neurotic shrinks back in terror from the extension of his tasks in life, the old [does the same] from the dwindling and shrinking of the treasures he has attained."[284] Jung observed that hard-won accomplishments can eventually become burdens, and even vampire-like forces draining life from the person who accomplished them.[285] He also reflected on the importance of letting go when the time is ripe, noting that beginning sometime in the middle of life only those who are ready to die are able to remain alive.[286] Jung reminds us that only in the autumn of life do we see and experience the fruition of all the seeds we have sown in the springtime and summer of our lives.[287] That increased perspective on the whole of life may bring up awarenesses that are creative, but also regrets that can be depressing. We may be surprised in looking back at facts we repressed earlier, such as our own faults and failings, and the pain felt when those we feel attracted to spurn us. And Jung notes the very positive fact that later in life, when one has less physical energy, the diminishing abilities enable a person to better understand and contribute to culture.[288] He observes further that young people have less past and so are likely to have less of lasting value to contribute to culture. "It is the privilege and task of riper age, that has passed the meridian of life, to produce culture."[289] These are deep observations on the latter parts of the life cycle. At a time when many people live longer and continue to work longer, Jung's observations offer valuable insights to consider. We may hope that the youthful culture of modern life will continue to value cultural products from the mature. One thing about ageism is sure: those who practice that prejudice are someday bound to suffer from it—if they live that long.

Life's momentum, built up by pursuing desires, emotional entanglements, necessities and luxuries, and will o' the wisps that entrance us, seems unstoppable sometimes. But for all mortals, including the trickster of unconscionable activities, there comes a time when, like Wily Coyote in cartoons running off a cliff and treading thin air before realizing he is about to obey gravity, the momentum does end. One may hide losses of ability, aches and pains, and other signs of aging from the physician for years, but in time the reality of decline becomes evident to the world, no matter how much the trickster denies it. In time, the charade is over when the elderly man or woman is lowered into the grave, often after pretending he or she is still youthful far into advanced old age. Ads encourage gray-haired and bald, forgetful and chair-bound elders to buy new products that promise happiness. American culture does not include much of an initiation into the realities of old age and the arrival of death with dignity. In the end, when it is too late, one may suspect that one has been hoodwinked into buying distractions and hiding from reality.

These truths reflect the fact that the art of living is the great challenge, a genuinely tricky feat to pull off, and that the successful trickster of this art of growing old gracefully is much rarer than the tricksters of Botox, etc. It would not be in America's best interests to have a "spoiled brat" reputation, or a mean teen personality, in the world arena. America's culture needs to keep on maturing. She cannot betray coming generations of creative people by selling them short on their potential. What tricksters would wish such ill on their descendants? While great artists trickily fabricate honest work, reflecting life, liars fabricate dishonest schemes to get off the hook, and end up alone in jangling inauthenticity. The greatest of all tricks is getting magnificent order out of dismal chaos, the feat orchestrated by the mysterious power of consciousness. That is the secret of health and growth, beauty and wisdom, the fullness of vibrant life.

At the end of life, we may be very attached to possessions, habits, persons, and places. We may need to be lullabied on to the afterlife. We may need to be tricked into letting go, relaxing, and releasing ourselves into the hereafter or whatever. The interplay of will power's control of decisions, and the eventual surrender to inevitable processes, is a tricky realm to understand and articulate, as well as to navigate. Those who pride themselves on knowing and leading may find that death is an unfathomable trickster teaching them lessons of humility and submission. They may learn then that the art of listening and following is a process far deeper and subtler than they had imagined. And some may seem like sly tricksters themselves, when they pass away so silently in their sleep.

Is it cynical or realistic to say, as old con men have said to younger ones for generations, that everyone alive has an angle? It's realistic, although our conscious awareness of the angle at any given time can vary wildly.

Before closing these ruminations on the life cycle, let's consider what Jung had to say about the stages of life, and see if we find the trickster dynamic involved in the larger overall patterns he discerns in the problems each person faces in a lifetime. In our culture's symbols the first trick on a human is the devil's tempting Adam to eat the apple. "The biblical fall of man presents the dawn of consciousness as a curse."[290] The rude awakening, the hurt of a mistake that earns exile, the sin-stain of betrayal, the memory of a loss, is dramatized in the story. It reminds us that the paradisal child-state flows along with no problems. Ignorance is bliss, oceanic consciousness is not bothered by divisions, repressions, or defenses. All is well. The problem comes with verging off, being at variance with oneself. The mother is often the person first seen and imprinted in the child's mind, like a mother duck seen by a duckling. Then in adolescence comes trouble, as other role models appear—peers, rebellious kids. A second ego seems to grow that can wrest control from the first one, as the child sprouts an adolescent rebel self for an alter ego, a joker of rowdy foolery.[291] It's a trick the simple child could not have predicted. It complicates things. There is a problem in early life when we trick ourselves into false presuppositions. When we have exaggerated presuppositions there are inevitably letdowns. Unjustified optimism and underestimation of difficulties bring disappointments and disillusionments. Often our first conscious problems involve feelings of inadequacy, uncertainties in search of bolstering, incentives to achieve status, power, and possessions.[292] Serious problems are never fully solved. Jung pointed out that the whole point and purpose of chronic problems is that they cause us to work on them incessantly.[293] This situation is like a trick on the soul, a means to keep it busy in life. It takes creativity and constructive work to change a negative self-image, and by accomplishing the noteworthy we approximate feelings of more worth. As we get nearer to middle life, entrenched in social positions, established in the establishment, we feel self-satisfied, as if we are content that we have chosen the right course, and have found eternal verities. But this causes us to forget that the achieving of society's rewards comes at the cost of lessening our own personality. The sides of our life that we have not experienced because of conforming to societal expectations are lurking in the closet, because we achieve individuation not by conforming or submitting to society. We may feel we have been tricked by responsibilities into a boring dead end, unfulfilled.[294]

At around age fifty we are often tricked into a stance of defensive intolerance and fanaticism. The Glenn Becks, Rush Limbaughs, Bill O'Reillys, and other reactionaries may help stir feelings of self-righteousness, conservative outrage. We may grow angry at those who act like our own younger selves. There is also a "reversal at noon" in our genders. Women grow mustache hair and think more logically, men mellow and get sweeter dispositions. The joke is on us and our fixed ideas. Surprise! You look like the father you couldn't stand! We can't control our own destinies—no matter how fanatic we are. It's like a steroid user becoming so strong he starts to get weak and ill. No one can outfox the waxing and waning of a lifetime's moons.[295]

So Jung sees the first quarter of life as a childhood in which we are only problems for others. In the second and third quarters of our lives we are facing problems that make us ultimately more conscious. And in the last quarter of life, in old age, we are not so concerned with becoming more conscious by struggling with problems, but again we become someone else's problem. We depend on assisted living, caregivers, healthcare programs like never before. The "second childhood" is like the first, a submission to "unconscious psychic occurrences." It is a kind of welcome back home, as our unknown depths trickily invite us to bathe, swim, and sleep in their waves; we are immersed in the sea realm of dreams, fantasies, and archetypes, and nothing finally can hold them at bay. In middle life we had to be very conscious to take care of the tasks we undertook—here we have more time and scope to daydream and wonder. These brief reflections on life cycle progressions and predicaments remind us that none of us are strangers to the tricks we endure and play, even if we are not always conscious of them day by day.[296]

Trickster Wisdom in Life Lessons and Festivals

The trickster shows us ironically how shortcuts may lengthen the journey and how short circuits in cramped spaces may backfire. Today we realize there are different kinds of intelligence: intellectual, emotional, social, creative, etc. The trickster traits stand for the darting improvisational, experimental intelligence, resourceful and resilient. It takes a trickster mind to be ready for a trickster mind; you have to think like a thief to defend yourself from thieves. Otherwise, the hip city slicker rips off the square hick's cash. Something we don't understand about life, some mystery too deep for us to grasp, exists like the image of a trickster deep inside the human soul. Modern men may seek the connections of love, physical intimacy, shared friendship, a trusting mutual exploration with a soul mate, a bond with others in beauty and joy, and the relief of fun, but they may end up alone with porn—a romp with a virtual celebrity-like image, nothing more real than an inflatable bimbo. What trickster inside shortchanged them? This is the tricksterism of fooling one's own brain. The realistic image of a woman stimulates the brain's pleasure center. Or is it a trick that allows insatiable instinct to experience a simulation of what it otherwise could not have, a poor man's release through subliminal veneration of the goddess in images?

The 2014 film *Don Jon,* featuring Joseph Gordon Levitt, explores the dilemma of a young man who finds more pleasure in porn than in sexual relations with women. The Internet enables Don Jon's imagination to find ideal thrills in self-stimulation, pleasures untroubled by the dissatisfactions (I almost wrote "shortcomings") of actual coupling. His daily porn offers illusions of caricature beauties, smooth and simple erotic glamor, easy access, with no efforts or inconveniences, no strings. The only thing the free pleasure of "having one's will" with the desirable sex object lacks is the joy of intimate mutuality. Don Jon realizes he can "lose himself" in porn, but not in sex with women. He has no solution until he meets a woman more mature than he. She tells him, "You have to lose yourself in the other person, and she has to lose herself in you." He finally realizes how all the false and unsatisfying aspects of life fade away when he and a woman are "lost together" in mutual self-forgetfulness and self-fulfillment. Self-oblivion with the beloved, eclipsing the ego, is the happiness Don Jon has been seeking.

Drugs such as heroin and Oxycontin fool the brain's chemistry with a sensation of reward; in real life feeling good comes as a reward for our meaningful efforts. Shortcuts to short-term happiness on the cheap, which are plentiful, may cause us to underestimate the subtlety of consciousness and the nature of the psyche. As soon as you act naive and feel arrogant there's a good chance a figure will step out of the shadows and say, "If you believe that, there's a swell bridge in Brooklyn I'd like to sell you,"[297] or, "Welcome to Las Vegas, home of true happiness and prosperity for all!"

At every turn on the path of life the trickster impulse finds an excuse or a way out, a means to exonerate oneself and pat oneself on the back. When blame comes near we pull our disappearing act. Simple logic can be the charlatan's best friend. Our inner rationalizing trickster is the soul of self-serving argumentation. If you are dedicated to self-exoneration and self-justification, there are always tricky ways to convince others: "That wasn't my fault. I'm not guilty. All those other factors were to blame—not me." Such justification can end up devouring one's soul and credibility.

To ingratiate oneself with those who can further one's career is a handy trick. To go from rags to riches in America, from gutter to skylight, the legendary advice is to be nice to the right people on the way up, because you're sure to meet them again on the way down. The trickster is good at putting on a show, engaging in a self-serving masquerade. He is good at acting dumb, but concealing cleverness beneath the mask; or, acting smart and in the know, when being a fool; or, acting righteous when being ruthless. The trickster is always zigging when the world is zagging. He finds a way to gain sympathy votes (Reporter: "Favorite thinker?" Candidate: "Jesus." Voter: "You've got my vote!"). The trickster wins power—whether he knows what to do with it or not. As Deldon McNeely writes, "Acted out unreflectively, the Trickster is unpredictable and possibly destructive, even sociopathic. Under its influence we can destroy other species and self-destruct as a species."[298] But on the other hand, when we "invoke and integrate the Trickster" consciously into the psyche we "experience a creative and transformative archetype."[299] There is a dynamic richness in the trickster archetype, which should not be oversimplified. Trickster powers are mercurial, for good or for ill.

The trickster archetype is also about interrelatedness, the play of interconnectedness of the layers of existence and the organic parts of whole systems. The trickster's purpose, as McNeely puts it, is "to further awareness and communication between all possible factions."[300] *The Daily Show* with Jon Stewart, for example, holds up both Republicans and Democrats to ridicule, exposing silly human blindspots, denials, and hypocrisies. The comedic trickster lampoons the absurdities of arrogance and the foolishness of taking heroic delusions too seriously.[301] The trickster is involved in the funny business we engage in behind our own backs, when our right hand doesn't know what our left hand is doing. The trickster is also involved in exposing that unconscious activity, and freeing us from our old outgrown selves. The trickster dude needs wiggle room, the better to wriggle loose from handcuff and noose, locks and stocks, from tall walls, dead ends, and the long arm of the law. The trickster gets you into trouble and also extricates you, with the loopholes of changeability—repentance, reform, renewal, and rebirth. The trickster is involved in freedom.

The trickster can be as nettlesome as a raven, and as refreshing as rain. One function of trickster stories is to warn us about a trait of the universe—it can be capricious, quirky as the Raven in Haida stories. Lightning flashes, volcanoes erupt, storms cause floods, the earth quakes, plant life withers and blooms. The trickster wises us up with rude awakenings after we've ignored warnings and overslept. He breaks naive trust, initiates us to something deeper than our lazy habits, our scheming ego, and social conventions. He helps us recover primal inevitables, depth dynamics of existence, like daily and seasonal cycles of time. He expresses frankly the basic needs of flesh—food, warmth, water, the effort needed to overcome obstacles, resilience of the spirit of life to roll with punches. (Think of Coyote losing his eyes and having them replaced with odd substitutes, as in a story told by Indians of the Southwest.) The trickster displays freaky unlikelihoods, good-natured humor, irony, and gets his comeuppance. With the trickster we face the basic, undeniable facts of life, beginning with the bodily finctions. We got here due to sex. We stay here due to food. We move through time. The trickster tests, defies, and is taunted by natural limits. We leave here due to death. The trickster rides the rails and is sometimes driven out of town on a rail.

Festivals sometimes have qualities and features associated with trickster dynamics. Traditionally, calendars feature stretches of workaday weeks punctuated by cyclical holidays marked by refreshing topsy-turvy saturnalia. Halloween, the New Orleans Carnival, the Burning Man Festival, and Fringe Festivals worldwide are examples of refreshing celebrations that aim to stir energies anew in chaotic festivities. Another example is the old "First Turn" of the annual Indianapolis 500 Speedway races, where there was a "snake pit" of drunken people doing outlandish and orgiastic things, bravado feats and sexual escapades, with "Girls Gone Wild" type shenanigans and men with beer pongs behaving badly. Such scenes of excess may stir feelings of fear and anger in the sober-minded, but they are an old aspect of human behavior in many societies all over the world, an annual chaos to refresh the usual order.

Pranks sometimes stir up surprising self-awareness. Orson Welles and the Mercury Radio Theatre in 1938 presented *War of the Worlds* so realistically that many listeners believed earth was being invaded by Martians. The hoax caused many panicked listeners to call the police, to seek refuge and protection, and to report seeing invaders. Such events teach us something about our gullibility. TV shows like *Candid Camera*, *Punk'd*, and *Howie Do It!* feature people being put on by a trickster with a camera.

In recent years clown workshops have offered ways to explore reality and society by means of comedy. They employ exercises that help participants penetrate "the politics and politesse of life to reach the simple truths of our existence." One participant said, "It's a vehicle to freedom, it's a way to soften and to find truth." It may not occur to most people that exploring clowning can be a way to reflect on the nature of life, but a journalist researching the workshops wrote, "The instructors' approach is an unexpected lesson in soul searching and self-discovery."[302] This shows an approach to the archetype of the clowning trickster that can be both therapeutic and artful.

Customs sometimes express the kinds of wisdom that the trickster represents. America herself was born in the overturning of oppressive rule—with unruly, unsubmissive trickster strategies to get out from under the thumb of the British king. The trickster spirit sometimes gives hope that we can bypass old norms, and transcend stultifying systems. In the Gulla Islands off the coast of Georgia, descendants of escaped slaves follow their old customs. Every year between Christmas and New Years Day, islanders visit their neighbors, eat, drink, and celebrate life together by forgiving and forgetting any mistake of the previous year. This custom expresses the wisdom of keeping goodwill energies circulating, transcending bad blood, and inhibiting the growth of grudges.

On April Fool's Day (which in a way is the trickster's holiday) in 1996 Taco Bell put out a press release proclaiming the company had purchased the national treasure enshrined in Philadelphia known as the Liberty Bell, and that from now on it would be officially designated "the Taco Liberty Bell." Many Americans immediately called the National Historic Park where the bell is kept to vent outrage and register complaints. Soon thereafter Taco Bell announced it was a joke.[303] Another April Fool's day hoax was an article in the April 1998 *Newsletter of New Mexicans for Science and Reason*. Written by physicist Mark Boslough, and based on an idea in Robert Heinlein's 1961 novel *Stranger in a Strange Land*, the article reported that the Alabama Legislature had recently voted to revise the value of the mathematical constant pi so that it would conform to the "biblical value" of 3.0. Tricks like this are able to bring laughter, reminding us not to take ourselves too seriously, to relax and lighten up.

The Wild One, a 1953 film starring Marlon Brando, depicted a gang of youthful motorcycle punks like the fabled Hell's Angels taking over Main Street in small California town. It was based on a short story, which in turn was based on a 1947 July 4 weekend event in Hollister California—a biker's street party, which became known as the Hollister riot. Monopolizing the roads, goofing on squares, unruly carousers were drinking in public, etc. This kind of commandeering of public spaces is still happening—in New York it was in the news in 2013, when a congregating group of bikers began taking over some public roads and meeting at an announced time in Times Square. This practice of takeovers amounts to a group prank—a designated place becomes an unwitting host for a flood of people on a certain date. A flash mob shows up to have fun, and the joke is on the place that the crowds overrun. A wilding, a takeover of a bar, a park, a street or a neighborhood is a kind of trick, a massive group prank. An example is SantaCon in the Lower East Side of New York, and elsewhere, on the Saturday a week or more before Christmas. Hundreds, in fact thousands of people—30,000 according to the *New York Times*—wear Santa Claus costumes and show up beginning at ten a.m. to carouse from bar to bar, drinking and disturbing the peace.[304] Annual St. Patrick's Day celebrations in many towns across America are another example of longtime costumed revels that often go to excess. Obviously these kinds of takeovers can become an unacceptable nuisance, representing an inconsiderate aspect of human nature. Self-centeredness causing disturbances and self-forgetfulness in fun are both sides of a single coin.

We should not enjoy ourselves at the expense of others, but the trickster can teach us to laugh at ourselves, not just at others, helping us to become more tolerant. Unsolemn trickster fun reminds people not to take themselves too seriously, to relativize their absolutes a little. Trickster pranks help blow off steam and the stink of self-importance, to relieve the misery caused by excessive egoism, to humble arrogance. This is why a trickster such as Coyote has escapades that deal with excrement, comic grossness hidden and denied, repressed in polite conversation. The trickster can help us understand ourselves, heal our wounds, adapt, and recover energy. And the trickster also helps us question our assumptions and rigid views, and guides us to individuation—appreciating the quirks of one's own life, following one's own path, becoming one's own person, not slavishly in step with conformity.

How's Tricks (Including Our Own Balancing Acts)?

Tricksters of Native American myths, such as Coyote or Raven, are symbolic of bodily life with it's own necessities, quirks, conundrums, and built-in compulsions beyond the conscious mind. (As I wrote above, Lincoln is said to have appreciated the irony that life is not determined by rule; others suggest that it is not always wise to follow all rules, that the exception to the rule sometimes overrules.) The trickster spirit is also about a quick brightness in our embodied existence, about the awareness that life is a game we all play. The trickster is about quirkiness—having a "wild hair" up one's nose or other orifice. The trickster archetype presents life's crookedness and surprise twists. Going through time, life is gnarled, twisting back around like an old apple tree branch, then proceeding on again to burst into blossoms and droop low with fruit.

What can we say the trickster is, after all, besides what he does? The trickster represents the interplay of aspects of microcosms and macrocosms, a strange loop, the dynamics of a nonlinear system, a complex organic whole. The trickster is like the cursor that travels all over the screen, navigating, making precise clicks and open-ended searches. The trickster is the hidden freakiness of life, the down-to-earth, rough awkwardness that interrupts the smooth and easy, the wholeness of front and back. The trickster brings uncertain cycles of forgetting and remembering, displaying and disappearing, sincerity and deception. "There is no deeper dissembler than the sincerest man," Emerson wrote in 1840. Why? Because of the nature of the mind? Reality, as seen by human minds, is layered: "Veil after veil will lift, there must be veil upon veil behind."[305] Because of human nature—even the façade we would least suspect of dissembling may consist of an odd simplicity masking complications, hypocrisy, or lack of self-knowledge. Ignorance lurks beneath veneers of smartness. Also, we often hide our feelings, exchanging pleasantries no matter how we feel. In sadness we smile, distraught we keep a stiff upper lip. There is always a part of the picture of which we are unconscious; education does not enlighten all our depths. Jung observed that the more bright and savvy a person is, the more subtly he or she can humbug (deceive) himself.[306]

Being smart and yet dumb, rich and powerful yet weak and vulnerable to blind spots and Achilles heels, acting in control when we're prone to lose control—the faces of our ironic recognitions, should we personify them, would have trickster smiles and eyes. Very basic plots and predicaments, bodily needs, crises, intrusions, and escapes—these bristle with trickster possibilities. The trickster winks, knowing each thing depends on the other. With the dire needs and humorous surprises of ingesting and expelling, with ravenous appetites splurging and enjoying pleasures, the trickster spirit thrives. With gorging and regurgitating, engaged in exploitation and seeking liberation, passing through a series of deaths and resuscitations, life's indomitable trickster spirit just keeps on going ahead, crazy with life's pulse, teaching us all persistence.

We learn from the trickster to appreciate simple bodily functions. For example, consider the pulse of our vulnerable, hard-working heart, and the ebb and flow of our ever-pumping lungs. The stomach has a mind of its own, grumbling like a malcontent when it resents going hungry. There are simple and necessary pleasures in evacuating waste. If we neglect these matters because of "more important" concerns, postponing urination while on duty for example, we may one day regret it. Every stress has its release. Each function must be given its due. Shakespeare's bawdy tricksters express bodily life, its instincts and flaws. There are necessities and drives not governed by polite social convention with its careful logic: the rude belch bursts forth proclaiming its own necessity. The baby's blasted fart laughs uncontrollably in the face of demure objections. The rough eructation and projectile vomiting of a sick man, the uncontrollable obscenities of an enraged soldier in battle, all are as natural as volcanoes and earthquakes. Rape, murder, theft and vandalism—all disturbances of propriety's order are signs of out-of-control tricksters at work. Disorder is often full of vitality, like impulsive imps running wild, ruining careful plans and civic provisions, improvising outside the margins, for good or ill. Chaos happens. An endless loop of organic possibilities and inevitabilities seems to constitute the trickster repertoire.

We feel the revenge of the flesh when its imperatives are denied. If we mistreat our bodies with foolish extremes, severe insults, shocks, stresses, bad diets, excessive alcohol, and unhealthy pills, our organs rebel. Healthy youths in their twenties die of cardiac arrest from drugs like cocaine. You can't force your body to do whatever you please; it has limits and a homeostatic mind of its own. Eating disorders illustrate this: binge and purge can have disastrous effects. When scandals bring their uncontrollable sexual hijinks out of the closet, repressive evangelicals have to eject themselves from their own pulpits like pilots from crashing planes. Jung observed that people who have not gone through "the inferno" of their passions have never really overcome them. That means passions lurk out of sight, able to pop up when least expected.

Our own unconscious wisdom laughs at our illusions. Love's illusions are notoriously "many splendored," as the song says. We are pulled, enticed into the unknown and its open spaces, our tightrope walking is an act of trust. William James said that most of the things we feel so certain about turn out to be illusions. Life is tricky, sometimes appearing to be a fateful maze choreographed by a supreme trickster. The unconscious trickster is seen in every Freudian slip, revealed in every embarrassing gaff in which a deeper truth betrays a superficial front. The hypocrite thinks she can get away with tricks, but then when least expected irony prevails, and everyone can see—her slip is showing.

Physical body parts can be uncooperative tricksters, surprising us with disabilities that undermine us. We say "I have a trick knee" or "a trick ankle," when we find we don't have a leg to stand on because of an old ailment. Our involuntary bodily functions are tricksters. ("What did one belch say to the other? Let's be stinkers and go out the other end.") Sometimes in the dusk our eyes play tricks on us. Our memory plays tricks too. Our own prejudices, lurking out of sight and then lurching into the projection of stereotypes, can trick us into blindness and deafness to reality. Feeling "scared of your own shadow" is a trick you play on yourself. "Don't kid yourself, it's rough out there," is a caution meaning "Don't delude yourself into a false sense of security, don't trick yourself into unrealistic assessments of the world, or you'll lull yourself into vulnerability," as if there's a gremlin trickster inside us, apt to lead us astray. But the continual rolling forward in time and embracing fate without reductionist one-sidedness involves more than a grim realism; it is a trickster art. Zen masters call it "thusness," not resisting life as it is, but outfoxing your habits and bad attitudes by acknowledging them, to live in a fresh state of being with fullness and depth, embracing life and working with what is.

We all have wounds, and we can't control our physical fates—part of our life is not determined by us, but is sprung on us like a practical joke. The unconscious play of the trickster is about the complexities of body and soul, emotions and mind, altogether—the oneness of body-mind-psyche. Implications of body-mind-psyche complexities are significant. For instance, all feminine traits and associations of the psyche are not simplistic in terms of gender orientation. Each person has the genes of both mother and father as a physical inheritance in every cell, and each personality is a balancing act and dynamic dance of polarities. This needs to be understood as a psyche reality, otherwise one might jump to the wrong conclusion, that all male artistry, tenderness, and nurturance fall in some "unmasculine" category. But on the other hand, what trickster put some souls in the bodies of another gender, as so many transgender people report? However we get dealt whatever hand we have, it's up to us to play it well, or at least somehow deal with it. A wise trickster awareness can help us do just that.

"In God We Trust—all others pay cash!" So goes the logic of the gag placard seen on cash registers all over America in greasy-spoon diners and country gas stations. Only God is trusted—why? Because men are tricksters. But what if we conceive of God—the mystery behind the drama of life around us—to be a trickster? After all, the Old Testament God tested Job, joining forces with the devil to play tricks on the poor man. If we conceive of God as hidden, playful, quirky, given to unknown surprises, we have a wariness and awe at unknowable mystery and not a naive simple trust that we always get what we want. "We trust in the Lord, but we don't expect much," as I heard a humorous southerner say one day. He also said, "The Lord will provide; I just hope he provides until he finally gets around to providing." People sometimes sense that the Supreme Being is the ultimate mystery, a being who plays tricks, causes and relieves troubles, circles like seasons, and meanders like a creek. Some say it's karma, or "the fickle finger of fate," others pray to endure what they can't control or understand.

Relating to Trickster—But How?

This meditation on the trickster in America and in our imaginations suggests that we would do well to be aware of and honor the meanings of the trickster archetype, so that we understand and appreciate its functions, such as fluid resilience, freedom of adaptability to circumstances, connectivity of parts of the whole, and healing. Typically we don't want to be bothered with new tasks and may say, "You can't teach an old dog new tricks" when we need an excuse. "We want convenience. Anything but a trickster," seems to be our wish. We often prefer no surprises, no upsets, no collapses or disturbances. We enjoy resting on our laurels. We like a predictable semblance of well-being; routine is reassuring and comforting. Our great American philosopher Emerson wrote: "People wish to be settled. Only as far as they are unsettled is there any hope for them."[307] To be unsettled puts us out of sorts; it re-sorts us, getting us to work when we would rather relax.

Our chance to know reality requires that we face the embodied energy of life, chaotic order, which is possible to symbolize as a certain kind of trickster dynamic. Cosmic savior figures of world religion literatures often seem to be tricksters, rescuing skillfully, saving mankind any which way they can. It is an amazing trick of wise perspective to assert that spirit, though invisible, is real and eternal, while matter, because it is not eternal or unchanging, is unreal. Jesus can be seen as a trickster who out-tricks death and the devil.[308] Buddha out-tricks Mara and suffering. Moses the trickster out-tricks the Egyptians. A remnant of Native Americans with trickster traditions survived the onslaught of Europeans. Skillful leaders are tricksters inside/outside, above/below their societies. Bluesmen are tricksters, putting on a show, artfully getting sympathy, finding what they need. (I am indebted to Albert Murray for this idea.) Legendary twentieth-century avant garde artists and writers of Greenwich Village, and painters and musicians of Topanga Canyon, were Bohemian tricksters of creativity. Clearly, trickster power is not a flash in the pan, but represents an enduring depth dynamic in life on earth.

The examples discussed in this book are presented to show the positive and negative aspects of the trickster archetype. Our lives involve a delicate balance. We can't live without our refreshing trickster principle, an aspect of life which helps us stay grounded and in touch, forcing us to avoid one-sidedness. Yet we can't allow our pathological, antisocial tricksters to destroy the fabric of our way of life, no matter how charming or polarizing they are in their smoothly persuasive con man personas. Some tricksters, especially powerful ones accompanied by enablers and enforcers, put on a wonderful show of being "just folks," "down home reg'lar guys," one of the pack. When really, whether consciously or unconsciously, it's an act of wishful thinking, and/or useful camouflage. Someone who comes to believe in his own lies lives in his own fantasy bubble where intruders are not welcome. ("It's all about sincerity; once you can fake or pretend to be extremely earnest, the rest is easy," as some people say. Or, "The best cons come from a place of truth."[309] Repeating something until you lull yourself into thinking it is true, you are ready to undertake a con with confidence and panache.)

Tricksters form an integral part of the fabric of America, and the trickster is an integral part of our fiber, as it were, making up our psyches. The coyote howls in the distance, but also shows up nearer—here in the rearview mirror. Visionary America is a long way off, too—the founders died two centuries ago. And yet the beauty of liberty, so inspiring to them, is still attractive to Americans today. Poet Robert Penn Warren once observed that in the third quarter of the eighteenth century Americans had to define themselves and the things they stood for all of a sudden. It was an unprecedented task, and the founding generation, including Thomas Jefferson, was charged with voicing our venture: striving for freedom, equality, pursuit of happiness.[310] These are beguiling ideals that can inspire and befuddle. Freedom not only inspires heroic endeavors; coupled with a myopic pursuit of personal happiness at the expense of others, it can inspire dirty tricks as well.

"Sometimes we're the statue, and sometimes we're the pigeons," as the philosophical joke goes. "Sometimes we eat the bear, and sometimes the bear eats us." Sometimes we play the tricks, and sometimes the tricks play us, reminding us we are integrally interconnected, playing our parts in a dramatic system of attractive forces and dynamic patterns. Reality has a sliding floor, as Emerson observed, and our destiny can activate it to surprise us anytime, causing us to slip around in the cycles until we regain composure.

It is good to respect and come to terms with the trickster in our souls and in our society. Those who imagine that they have rid their psyches of the trickster once and for all have a lot to learn; they will get a laugh. Readers of the Psalms will be familiar with this idea. "He that sitteth in the heavens shall laugh . . . [because] the people imagine a vain thing."[311] We don't need distracting carnival clown entertainments as much as we need something subtler—a true psyche trickster awareness for our own sanity and security. We need that to be more in touch with the way things are—it is valuable for our grasp of reality and our idealism too. It is best to be savvy enough to be on guard, and suave and nimble enough to liaise. We need a balance in our relations to the trickster. If we deny or ignore the trickster, pretending he doesn't exist, or that he is a great distance from us, we are left in the dark, and we may lose our sense of life's surprises. That is a malaise. As a stranger to the unconscious, we are at the mercy of the unconscious. We may also forget how to play the devil's advocate, and how to envision worse case scenarios, possible mishaps due to quirks of fate. Forewarned by knowledge of trickster depths is forearmed. On the other hand, if the trickster runs away with us, we may lose our bearings, forgetting ethics in an anything-goes attitude, becoming antisocial tricksters out for ourselves alone, trying to get ahead by any means necessary. Or we may panic and lose perspective, becoming paranoid.

We need to take the trickster with a grain of salt, since he's marvelous but not the only fish in the sea. At their best, religion, philosophy, and stories that expand our sense of connectedness and remind us of the repercussions of our actions can help people avoid becoming merely cynical, selfish tricksters. Though every day the news shows it isn't, it should be obvious that healthy community values are learned from family, neighbors, leaders, and members of the groups to which we belong. It is a truism that playing responsible parts in society takes practice and care. The trickster in the psyche is always at play in the shadows.

Dream Power and Outlaw Trickster Saints

If what I have been arguing here is true, that useful trickster wisdom is integral to knowing well our bodies, ourselves, and our nation, then why haven't we heard more about it? Is it because any trickster worth his salt remains hidden, laughing up his sleeve at his sly secrets and our befuddlement? Why don't we value and consciously learn more from the trickster archetype?

Why aren't we initiated into it more constructively? Why is it such a hidden, shadowy, potentially quite dangerous aspect of our lives? There is suspicion in us, but often it is aimed at the wrong targets, or it scatters shot everywhere like a blunderbuss. It takes subtle self-knowledge to see precisely one's own subtle tricks, and not everyone is willing or able to look within.[312] Many rules and regulations exist because societies thereby safeguard members from harm that random trickster impulses can inflict.

Some aspects of the trickster resident in our psyches are immensely beneficial. Every night, a trickster process dreams in us, finds the perfect ways to tell dream stories, making suggestive equivalents for topics of concern, experiences, fears, and anxieties, which we don't know how to deal with—that is significant. The trickster impulse in the unconscious both acts in and creates the psyche's dramas; now he seems to know more than you; now less, a complete bumbler—without dreams there is no trickster to mend our souls. He's a funny guy or gal—like the class clown, or a psychic Patch Adams (or Grizzly Adams, or Don Adams of *Get Smart* fame) on steroids. Sometimes he's primal, basic as just plain Adam. The trickster can help coax recalcitrant tasks into completion. For example, when we trick ourselves into practicing a task or exercise when not in the mood, by offering ourselves rewards, perks, or in other ways promoting conducive pathways to "git 'er done," we can make greater strides than we do when we slack off.

While the trickster has qualities like the unconscious art of the dream, Jung points out that this does not mean that the dream weaver in us is a con man. "The dream is a natural event and there is no reason under the sun why we should assume that it is a crafty device to lead us astray."[313] The trickster spirit at its most profound is not an evil con man but a mysterious helper. True, the trickster is unpredictable and easily misunderstood, but at root he is beneficial, not malicious. "Nature is often dark and impenetrable, but not crafty like a human being."[314] Dreams bespeak a deep surreal wisdom, Hermes-like, helpfully revealing what Main Street, Hallmark cards, and seductive billboards never will. Jung wrote about dreams as experiences of another being living within us and showing us different angles on our existence. "When we find ourselves in an insolubly difficult situation, this stranger in us can sometimes show us a light which is more suited than anything else to change our attitude fundamentally, namely just that attitude which had led us to the difficult situation."[315] The trickster dives deep and comes up with inspiration. "I have a dream" may be America's greatest utterance, suggesting a vision of an alternative future.

Normally a traditional religion functions as the teacher initiating people into archetypal mysteries of the psyche. Education and professional training are programs that teach people the ways of the world. Perhaps being "worldly-wise" means being wise to the ways the worldly in all its forms tries to trick us. World religions offer ways to experience the "ever more" to which we belong. Thus we are drawn to sacred forms and values, and structure ourselves with disciplines. Rituals mark our induction into membership and participation in communities. The secular age has often spread oversimplified views widely to tame and homogenize the masses. Instead of experiencing spiritual faith in God, people develop belief in religion. Our Western religions sometimes equated Satan with the trickster, labeling the old shaman stories of Raven, Coyote, and Kokopelli as pure "evil." Christian missionaries in Africa made trickster stories there seem shamefully archaic and sinful, but in the Gospels there is sober awareness of tricks: "I send you forth as sheep in the midst of wolves: be ye therefore wise as serpents and harmless as doves."[316] To be serpent-wise is to have uncanny abilities, to move with a two-sided movement, to be all the better able to out-trick harmful tricksters. From ancient times, serpents have represented mysterious hidden riches and deep wisdom; doves represent clarity's simplicity and airy gracefulness. Together they connote a healthy balance—not a one-sided approach, but a dynamic wholeness.

Without awareness of con jobs out there the naive get bilked; without a childlikeness, one becomes the soul-deadened cynic. Jaded cynicism comes from a loss of awe, forgetting the need for a healthy respect for the trickster. To be too cynical, or too naive—both are off-kilter extremes. To find the right balance in the turbulent flow of life is the tricky skill we need for our own health—to become mature, wise, responsibly aware. America teaches her citizens, "Don't be too dull and simple, don't be a one-trick pony; be a multi-talented, wily, and adaptable improviser to survive and thrive among the landscapes of Turtle Island."

In many Western cultures "The image of a pleasure-seeking body, dwelling place of the Trickster Archetype, came to be more associated with Satan's realm than with Christ."[317] This oversimplification can be problematic in grasping the meaning of the trickster archetype. Puritan America and her descendants are not the only examples of this reductionism. Some cultures try to *include* the trickster in the pantheon. In Guatemala in small Christian churches where Mayans worship there are images of Jesus, but often statues of Maximon as well. Maximon is also called San Simon, and is a trickster and fertility figure who links the underworld and this world, and who is given ritual offerings of alcohol and cigarettes. At these St. Judas-Simon

("Champion of the hopeless") shrines, people pray for help with interpersonal matters—their money and love problems. In local lore Judas-Simon took the thirty pieces of silver for betraying Jesus, and then generously gave them away to the poverty-stricken. People devise the tricksters they need from the old stories and images.[318] Without them they may grow poor in flexibility, less crafty, less hopeful. Naturally, the psyche seeks out what it lacks and finds a way in the shadows to visualize it.

Other examples of folk saints in America may also help us understand the ever-inventive psyche. Jesus Malverde was a kind of Robin Hood figure in northwestern Mexico, killed by police in 1909. Today among some immigrants in California Jesus Malverde is a kind of patron saint of outlaws—including drug pushers and hustlers. His image is seen in home shrines, on t-shirts, and fashioned onto patches for jackets. Malverde is a handsome rebel figure with a mustache; people's psyches know what they need. If an official deity does not offer protection, the folk seize upon a friendly figure and deify him. The Catholic Church does not recognize Jesus Malverde; official authorities did not make him a saint, but in the folk mind a yearning did.[319] I do not represent a church, so I am not saying this is good or bad, I am simply reporting that it is a human activity, a contemporary example of a way a popular trickster figure plays a part in lives.

Flagrant tricksters need trickster heroes, and so there are outlaw guardian angels for outcasts, folk saints who ask no questions but wink at infractions of the law. The disadvantaged in society may seek a God who will turn a blind eye, or even may cheer on their amoral shenanigans, illegal charades, and extracurricular masquerades. The risk-prone psyche needs a protector to help with survival.[320] It doesn't want to feel all alone and needs to feel buttressed by forces bringing good luck.

Folklore offers many more examples of tricky heroes—Speedy Gonzales, for example, is a fast-running rodent in a big sombrero who "goes steady with everybody's sister." In Indianapolis or Detroit you might hear someone tell other urban legends, like, "On my street if you ask about the tennis shoes dangling from the telephone wire, they'll tell the tale of Pascal the pusher from down New Orleans way, who took the tires off his bicycle so he could ride on the rims up there alongtop the telephone wires. I guess he found his tennis shoes just got in the way, so he left them up there, danglin' away, a mysterious calling card."

There is a big difference between the conniving evil figure of Satan in the Bible, and traditional trickster figures such as Raven and Coyote. Consider the typical Judeo-Christian interpretation of Satan as pure evil forever at odds with God, in contrast with typical tribal and folk traditions. McNeely puts it like this: "In contrast to Trickster, Satan represents a singular one-sidedness, and would never distance himself from his evil to admit regrets, whereas Trickster would never be caught in so unilateral a position."[321] There are other views found in world religions that make the unalloyed evil of the fundamentalist view of Satan seem overly narrow regarding the trickster. The trickster in traditional tribal cultures (Raven, Coyote, etc.) is mercurial, ever-adventuring, escaping, changing himself and others. He is an agent of change rather than a merely destructive devil. McNeely sees similarities with Jesus: "The Trickster, like Christ, spans and mediates the lower and higher worlds. From the bestial to the mystical, from the base, contemptible *prima materia*, to the pearl of great price, divine life moves with the swiftness of death."[322] Jesus was a trickster when he was being questioned, and he asked to see a coin, and said, "Give unto Caesar . . ." He was wise to the two-sidedness of life. In southern post-Civil War states, for some black converts to Christianity, Christ became more of a trickster figure. He was pictured as short, and very white, and was a challenger of the white power structure.[323]

If we look closely at the old stories, McNeely reminds us, we see that in traditional stories of tricksters, their acts take place in the context of "a divine plan which orients their continual state of flux and gives meaning to their actions."[324] What happens is not random. "When we identify with Hero, if we do not also relate well to the Trickster, chances are these two archetypes will meet in us in a troublesome way."[325] This is to say we need the trickster so we don't take ourselves or our foes too seriously or rigidly. This requires free play, enough leeway to exercise freedom—wiggle room for following impulses of exploration and improvising creativity. Christian teachings about "resist not evil" and "turn the other cheek" are not always obeyed, but suggest a trickster wisdom instead of brute force, promoting a process of turning enemies into friends. The trickster way implies a gift for finding the means to escape from boxed-in tight spots, and to find whatever is needed to survive. We will always be surprised because of unconscious life's undertow (often appearing to the conscious mind as an unexpected trick).

Our defenses involve the generation of tricks, which consciously or unconsciously emerge as means to protect us by deflecting harm. Soft power is another way to win, and force can be a way that wins battles but loses wars.

One type of fool is depicted in the ancient Taoist classic of China, *I Ching*, in which hexagram four is the situation of "youthful folly." This phrase suggests the heedless youth who does foolish things with a devil-may-care attitude because he has not yet learned from experience. The childlike playful trickster differs from the vengeful angry trickster and the hardened cynical trickster. We could say that in human nature there is a lively capricious trickster impulse, and that one branch of it extends in activities characterized by the idea that lucky "youthful folly has success"—skillful energetic play and trying things out can hit the spot with "beginner's luck." Native intelligence and the healthy impulse of youthful play can grow great in abilities, and learn the tricks of the trade. The trickster in human nature can also point to the other branch—the antisocial old meanie whose tricks are cynical, calculating, systematic and cold-blooded, stale and rigid, requiring a scheme to follow, a plot to use against the unsuspecting to get the advantage, a deceptive design to take the money and run.

McNeely makes an important point, observing that "The Trickster Archetype can have a chaotic effect on the personality if it functions only randomly and not grounded by a positive relationship to the Self (high god) or the Feminine principle (Anima) . . . [I]n mythologies which have persisted in human history, Trickster gods are always related to the center which defines their functions, even as they challenge the central principle."[326] One would not want to become a deliberate trickster con man who ends up unable to look in the mirror or to live with himself. Youthful folly has success because foolishness, not cleverness, is what ultimately grows to find wisdom, as Jung observed. God is the spiritual principle of unity—omnipresence, omniscience, etc.; knowing the duplicity, God cannot be tricked. The trickster is answerable to that principle, after all the tricks, pranks, hidden agendas, and twists of fate are said and done. The trick is on the impish part, because the whole in the end says, "I took you by trick."[327]

"The rogue may be shallow, but the con man is essentially without a self,"[328] John G. Blair wrote in *The Confidence Man in Modern Fiction*, noting how the con artist moves from town to town and alias to alias, feeling life is just a crapshoot anyway. It is interesting that for more than 2,000 years Buddhism has analyzed the self as non-enduring, transitory, changing, composite, and always a part of a larger network. And instead of using this knowledge about the human ego to make irresponsible mischief (which often results in suffering), the Buddhist view seeks for the ultimate reality beyond the illusory self. The acceptance of living with a changing, impermanent self is often too contrary for Westerners with a strong sense of individualism and ego to embrace; they angrily reject it. This leads to confusion. Even if one eschews humbuggery vehemently, or fights it like a trooper, if one's own mind is restless like a monkey, and one's own ego is fickle as a trickster (as Buddhism has diagnosed the situation), one still ends up involved in humbuggery or hypocrisy.

George W. Bush: Tortured Trickster or Simpleton Tricked by Others?

Obviously there is a limit as to how much one person can ever know or understand another person. I was not a direct witness to the personal life of George W. Bush. His public life as we know it—through the records of his actions, his words, and the memories of those who knew him—suggests the following thoughts to me concerning trickster dynamics. I admit that the eight years he acted in the name of Americans, taking the nation to war using misleading evidence of WMD, etc., stimulated my need to study this topic.

The trickster archetype can help us consider some aspects of President George W. Bush's leadership. Because Bush was a prominent and controversial "decider" for eight years, and has often been controversial on issues of duplicity and secrecy, it is natural to consider him in relation to the trickster dynamic. A google search using the words "George W. Bush lies" brings up a list of 9,860,000 items. This shows that many people in America and elsewhere debate Bush's veracity. If I were to omit a discussion of someone making such an impact on America in a book about American tricksters, I would feel I had neglected an important though difficult example. It could be argued that the quirks of the forty-third president's personality affected more lives than any other individual on earth during the years of his presidency. With all due respect, I will make every effort to be fair and to cite sources.

We are all tricksters to some degree or other, so it is no surprise that a prominent person's life and impactful actions would be implicated with this theme. Obviously it would take an entire book to discuss the questions of duplicity and secrecy in the loss of many important White House emails, secret "signing statements," Justice Department irregularities, uses of fear to win elections, torture policy tangles, extraordinary rendition, and administration dealings with science and environment reports. "Smoking gun" red herrings, threats from weapons of mass destruction that did not exist, sending Colin Powell to the UN to get support by presenting fraudulent evidence, are other areas of seeming duplicity. Eight years of presidential activities leave many such shady issues that no single brief study could thoroughly examine. Therefore, this discussion is of necessity a brief look at George W. Bush's personality dynamics in relation to trickster themes of duplicity and secrecy and polarization. It only suggests some basic examples and reflections on a large and complicated subject. Tony Blair and other leaders were involved in some of these maneuvers, and a study could be made of those tricky relations, but this exploration focuses largely on the dynamics of trickster themes in George W. Bush's life. I document my sources in the endnotes, to show my discussion is grounded in specifics.

George W. Bush himself wrote in a book, "I live in the moment, seize opportunities and try to make the most of them."[329] He is not known for reflecting on his actions or being concerned with the consequences of his acts, or for valuing psychology. Some of his childhood experiences are part of the public record. It would seem he was extroverted and craved attention even as a baby. In his mother's memoirs we are told that his grandmother said she hated to be in the same room with him when he was a baby, because whenever she took her eyes off him he always looked hurt.[330] A watershed psychological event is his youth was the death of his younger sister Robin. She died of leukemia when he was seven, in 1953. He was shielded from her illness and death, and was only told about it after she had died, and this gave him no opportunity for closure, no way to learn about mourning. "Children grieve. . . . He felt cheated," his mother Barbara Bush said.[331] The family was self-admittedly not able to adjust well, with his father away on business and his mother occupied with caring for an infant. In his mother's memoir she writes, "I was too much of a burden for a seven year old to carry."[332]

Justin A. Frank, a respected psychoanalyst, described this incident of losing a sister as leaving young George W. Bush feeling psychologically abandoned. Frank suggests it laid a foundation for the development of a powerful, lifelong coping mechanism, grounded in a self-protective indifference to the pain of others.³³³ Those around him remember that young George acted clownishly to cheer up his parents after Robin's death. A cousin of his who had a similar experience, losing a sibling then trying to be lighthearted to buoy up patents, said "we're both clowns."³³⁴ Frank writes that in his assessment of the biographical data, Bush's "antic personality" blossomed in these times of early stress.

"One of the local rituals for children [in Midland, Texas, when George W. Bush was a boy,] were meetings with cookies and milk at the home of a nice old lady who represented the SPCA. The cookies were digested more thoroughly than the teachings. . . . 'We were terrible to animals,' recalled [Bush's childhood friend Terry] Throckmorton, laughing. A dip behind the Bush borne [*sic*—barn?] turned into a small lake after a good rain, and thousands of frogs would come out. 'Everybody would get BB guns and shoot them,' Throckmorton said. 'Or we'd put firecrackers in the frogs and throw them and blow them up.'"³³⁵ Young George W. Bush was a leader of the group composed of Throckmorton and the other boys in these activities. To torture a frog can be fascinating to the torturer, giving the illusion of power, the ability to control the life and death of a living creature. "The child is father to the man," as a great poet once observed, and numbness regarding the pain experienced by other living creatures, and the self-centered lack of curiosity and denial that goes with it, are traits which can last a lifetime.

During his childhood years as an energetic youth playing baseball in the small town of Midland, Texas, because of his hyperactive energy, Bush was known as "Bushtail."³³⁶ He was a C student at Andover prep school (1960–1964), which he said was "cold, distant, and difficult" in comparison with his life in Texas. He had the typical racist and class attitudes of the time, and used nicknames to put people in their place.³³⁷ He was a C student as an undergraduate at Yale (1964–1968), where his father had also studied. As a fraternity president at Yale he is said to have delighted in using the red-hot tip of a coat-hanger to brand the skin of pledges above and between the buttocks.³³⁸

He was in the bottom 10 percent of his class at Harvard Business School (1973–1975), where he made an impression of privileged arrogance on at least one of his professors, Yoshihiro Tsurumi. Bush equated the New Deal with socialism and spoke of the Securities and Exchange Commission as "an enemy of capitalism," and said that poor people are poor because they're lazy.³³⁹ Bush is remembered by many who knew him mostly for being a partier and a budding alcoholic from the 1970s until 1986. He was arrested for DUI during this time. He was accepted into the Texas Air Force Reserves through family connections, after doing poorly on the Air Force

Officers Qualification test, getting 25 percent in pilot aptitude. By most accounts he was AWOL for much of his time in the Reserves, after doing basic training and avoiding the twenty-three months of officer candidate training—"one of the most rapid rank ascensions in American history."[340] Bush borrowed money to go into the oil business, and in that endeavor he failed. He was involved in questionable business practices (he sold 212,140 shares of Harken Energy stock a week before the end of the quarter when Harken announced a loss of 23.2 million dollars, for example, and did not file the sale with the SEC until eight months later). As his self-description ("I live in the moment, seize opportunities . . .") emphasizes, he lived with a restless energy, and had no appetite for looking within, reflecting on his actions, or taking responsibility for his acts.[341]

Some would say Bush fits well into the description of a kind of American—the characterization of "sanctimonious hustler." Some would describe him as a failed businessman (oil company owner and baseball team owner), who went into the politics racket, and, helped by tricky enablers like Karl Rove, became "the decider" who wielded power under the influence of others while wearing a mask of sanctimony. Others see him as the prodigal son, a prodigious wastral, leaving messes for others to clean up.

Bush was named the Safari Club International "Governor of the Year" in 1999 for his support of trophy hunting, and as presidential candidate found allegiance and support from the National Rifle Association. NRA vice president Kayne Robinson famously boasted in a speech during a members-only meeting in early 2000 that Bush, if elected, would be "a president where we work out of their office." As governor of Texas (1995–2000) Bush authorized the executions of 135 convicts during his five-and-a-half years in power. He used a falsetto voice to mock the repentant killer Karla Fae Tucker, which caused some of his Christian supporters to lose faith in him. He also reportedly giggled when answering a journalist's question about how he could execute Gary Graham, when Graham's court-appointed attorney was judicially admonished for sleeping through much of his trial. Self-righteousness can become a blinding illusion of goodness, fostering a religious patriotism that blurs activities of the individual soul's conscience. It numbs what the psyche might feel if cruelty was not wearing the mask of respectable piety and public uprightness. Strange Christian, who finds forgiveness so ridiculous and laughable.

Many observers have remarked that Bush often sported a sadistic smirk when talking about matters involving punishment. In his psychological analysis Justin Frank writes, "The Bush smirk conveys both the pleasure he derives from inflicting pain, and the defense he mounts against that pleasure—a disclosure of the sadistic impulse, and an attempt to deny the destructive self he cannot bear to acknowledge."[342] The trickster impulse finds ways to hide, to disguise what it does, to deflect disapproval. Under a mask of innocence grotesque features grow. Signs of sadism show up just when a trickster thinks he's hidden them.

Generally speaking, some tricksters are able to cultivate fastidious habits, and to project all dirt onto guilty enemies. The trickster can make grandiose promises when he has no intention of following through; he can voice vague concerns for others when he is indifferent to their plight. He can smear others to distract from his own guilt. The trickster, as the instinctive hider, is a master of masks.

The self-serving public personality is a trickster who remains focused on himself a good deal of the time. His words and actions show constant self-absorption. Put on the spot, as a leader in a democracy, a self-serving official will use ploys to distract and dissemble, using "misrepresentations of the historical record which so often read as attempts to deny his own shame."[343] He may use evasive answers to prevent actual dialogue. In a high office, such self-centeredness and indifference to others spell trouble for society, even with checks and balances wisely built into the system of governing. Self-important public officials may be skilled at charming others to get their way, and then may surprise the charmed people with displays of an uncaring attitude. Such psyches would seem to have the ability to exhibit well-honed social unawareness about the other. Obfuscating elected officials are out to get what they want, sometimes seeing little beyond that goal. To finagle influence in wide circles and to tap the resources of necessary connections, the political trickster needs dedicated helpers.

Bush's success in politics was tied to figures like Karl Rove, to family connections, financial support from oil businessmen, and to a selective set of religious issues. When winning is the most important thing in a competitive mindset, the connected trickster becomes skillful at enlisting all kinds of helpers to accomplish the aim. Oilmen gave money to help get Bush elected. Bush family friend James Baker stepped up to the spotlight to hurry the process along when 2000 election results were truly uncertain. With a power-play trick the Supreme Court justices ended Florida recounts and declared Bush the winner. Harriet Meyers and John Yu were other legalistic enablers giving a semblance and pretense of legality, providing cover and respectability, an aura of legitimacy to Bush's whims. For days, weeks, years, it is possible to pretend that tricks have no consequences, but after a while one's shadow is casting one's person.

Some of the people involved in the Bush administration—staff and enablers—broke their silence during the second term and after Bush left office. White House Press Secretary Scott McClellan, for example, in his book,

Washington's Culture of Deception, discusses Bush's claim that he didn't remember using cocaine during the party years.[344] It would seem that some public officials claim they can't remember some things to maintain a veneer of innocence. To someone familiar with the trickster archetype this might seem like a mask to evade responsibility, a two-faced hypocrisy lacking credibility. Pretending to be innocent is not the same as having childlike innocence. It is a refusal of the whole truth in order to hide from inconvenient consequences, and it polarizes others into loyal followers and hostile critics. Pretense and denial raise all sorts of questions,[345] and give few satisfying answers. Tricksters both mythological and historical are expert obfuscators. They cover their tracks, for example, using brush to smooth the dust.

Political trickster Roger Stone, who (among other things) was involved in tricks such as the "Brooks Brothers Riot," in which he led pro-Bush protestors, disarmingly dressed in suits and ties, loudly declaiming the Miami-Dade County election board, which stopped the recount, when the 2000 Bush vs. Gore election outcome was uncertain. Stone has a number of rules: "Lay low, play dumb, keep moving. . . . Nothing is on the level. . . . Hate is a stronger motivator than love. . . . Use a cut-out [a front man stand-in so the prominent candidate doesn't have to do the dirty work]."[346] The results of dirty tricks based on these kinds of principles are toxic to the democratic process. Exploiting fears and stirring prejudices are tricks used by those whose ideas lack intrinsic strength to prevail. (Aristotle reflected that it's a sick or feeble argument that relies on the medicine of trickery to make its effect. Some lawyers today say "Those who don't have facts to rely on resort to smoke and jokes.") Even Roger Stone in 2008, when considering the body count in Iraq, said he regretted his acts during the Miami-Dade county recount in 2000.[347] Sometimes the conscience of the trickster-for-hire (Stone and Lee Atwater, for example) kicks in when the stakes he was playing for finally become clear. Winning a hand of poker is not on the same scale as winning an election by acts that destroy people's faith in their nation's entire political system's integrity. The trick of putting a man lacking depth perception in the driver's seat of a great nation is bound to have serious consequences.

There are other issues, such as feeling above the law in torturing suspects, which also relate to the trickster archetype. Philip Zelikow, the former director of the 9/11 Commission and former adviser to Condoleezza Rice, has said that in time he thinks people will come to see the torture employed in the war against terror as something that resulted when "fear and anxiety were exploited by zealots and fools."[348] As Maureen Dowd put it, after ignoring specific warnings that Al Qaeda planned attacks on America by plane, Bush and Cheney "proliferated a mind-set that there was no step too far to protect us from that happening again"[349]—including invasion of Iraq, torture, wiretapping without a warrant, eavesdropping on allies, and holding prisoners without trial, as is done at the Guantanamo Bay facility. Both zealots and fools may sincerely believe that the ideas they hold are the only truths that exist. One way people get tricked—whether they are the president of the United States or the man on the street—is when an idea is presented and received as a reality, when really it is a verbal idea that is ungrounded, a guess, or an interpretation, and not reality. To assume a cakewalk or a slam-dunk will be the only result of going to war and putting people in perilous circumstances is not just bad judgment. It is self-centeredness, narcissistic love of self, and sadism or indifference toward others. "Planning for the future consequences of present actions is simply not in Bush's psychic vocabulary; his delusions of omnipotence appear to prevent him from thinking about the future as anything but victorious," Justin Frank wrote. "Like the explosives Bush unleashed on Iraq, the time bombs he has planted in our future were inspired by the perverse combination of destructiveness and denial, righteousness and recklessness, that marks the sadist mind-set." Frank predicted that "Our nation will be dealing with the devastation left in Bush's wake for years to come."[350] The Great Gatsby (in F. Scott Fitzgerald's novel with that title) left messes for others to clean up, and the self-deluded trickster leaves chaos in his wake, pretending everything is in order. A sucker for his own spin, fast forgetful of the flimsy source of his spiel, "he didn't know he believed, he believed he knew," as an old phrase goes.

Bush was surrounded by men who were used to feeling very certain of themselves, and did not like questions that doubted any of their certainties. Donald Rumsfeld, who served as Secretary of Defense for the George W. Bush administration, when asked questions about evidence for WMD before the Iraq war, evaded questions with "exit ramp" tricks—such as quibbling with reporters' wording, or educating the questioner with discourses on vague matters such as "unknown unknowns." He was always extremely certain of himself and his decisions, and never showed signs of introspection. He never had second thoughts about his decisions that led to catastrophes. Perhaps the road to hell is paved with "no regrets, I did my best." Rumsfeld seems to have stuck to his wishful thinking about how the war would go, even when nothing turned out as he had expected after the invasion. He seemed blind to signs of policy blunders for which he was responsible in the aftermath of invasion.

When, after extensively interviewing Rumsfeld for a documentary, Errol Morris considered the question: "Was Rumsfeld lying about WMD in Iraq?" he concluded that Rumsfeld convinced himself he was not lying, or "that he lacked the ability to discriminate between truth and fantasy.... [H]e had developed a gobbledygook philosophy that . . . devalued evidence and made a mockery of logic." Rumsfeld developed a defensive style of certainty that created an atmosphere in which there was no way to learn from or correct mistakes. Instead of evidence for WMD in Iraq it sufficed to employ equivocations and philosophical-sounding obfuscations. His answers stonewalled with an "infinite regress to nowhere. What do I know I know? What do I know I know I know? What do I know I don't know I don't know? Ad infinitum."[351] Rumsfeld was not alone; bureaucracies commit unconscionable actions in a lengthy series of linked segments, so that no one person is responsible. Feith, Rice, Rumsfeld, Wolfowitz, et al., have much blame to share for the tricks they were party to, and for never learning from mistakes they made in the name of America.[352]

Living in an age of comforts and ease, it is easy to fall prey to the promise that one can "have it all" and for a fairly cheap price. A tribal person often had to lose a tooth or the digit of a finger to be initiated. A chief might suffer humiliation and other experiences of leveling in preparation for leadership. In the modern world, an immigrant might work fourteen-hour days. In those scenarios some sacrifice of one's comforts is accepted as a part of the cost of advancement. But with slick helpers a modern powerful man can avoid the painful sides, take lots of vacations, get his friends put into high places and promote his partisan agenda with shortcuts and tricks that seem easy. Life doesn't work like that for very long, but the trickster's brain does. The con man's promise of something for nothing should not be confused with the ethos of the American Dream, in which hard work enables one to raise a family in a picket-fenced home. Privilege without self-sacrifice, power without accountability, wealth without concern or effort, waging a war of choice and not showing its high cost in the budget, using irresponsible contractors so no one ever has to answer for all the mistakes made—these are of a piece with reaping rewards without any cost, enjoying pleasures with no thought of repercussions. The power to have pleasure, like the power to cause pain, may be fraught with illusions. We may feel independent and beyond impunity, but eventually repercussions break that illusion. Into each life some reality rain must fall.

On the issue of the Bush administration's policy on torture, Andrew Sullivan has written a particularly strong statement. Addressing the former president with directness, Sullivan, who voted for Bush in 2000, tries to reason with him. Sullivan imputes an innocence to Bush's mindset, a willingness to consider his own wrongdoing that I do not see signs of, because it seems to me that Bush has made himself unaccountable by denial and refusal to reflect honestly on his own acts. But in hopes of getting Bush to understand the problems caused by the tricky business of torture, Sullivan explains to him that he needs to recognize his own denial, which made it possible for him to ignore the policies that he authorized and set in motion, actions including the use of dogs to terrorize suspects, the stripping of prisoners and hooding of them, the isolation of suspects in cells with no windows for months on end, using freezing temperatures to induce near-death states in prisoners, using stress positions to inflict muscle and joint pain beyond human endurance, placing prisoners in coffinlike spaces, and repeated waterboarding. "Those Abu Ghraib prisoners standing on boxes, bent over with their cuffed hands tied behind them to prison bars? You authorized that. The prisoner being led around by Lynndie England on a leash, like a dog? You authorized that too."[353] Extreme sleep deprivation, and other forms of torture could also be added to the list of tricks to make suspects "cave," but for our purposes Sullivan's enumeration of types of torture inflicted by those who carried out Bush's orders will suffice.

Sullivan goes on to explain poignantly to former President Bush why torture is wrong: "When a human being is tortured, his mind and body are used as weapons to destroy his agency and will. The point of torture is to render a suspect helpless in the face of government power, to make him a vessel for whatever the government wants from him." Sullivan points out that this is actually the opposite of the ideal of freedom in Western culture. He has to point it out because Bush showed he was unaware of that. Governments that torture do not govern free societies, and the world now knows that America uses torture, Sullivan points out, and "by condoning torture, by allowing it to take place, and by your vice president's continuing defense and championing of torture as compatible with American traditions, you have done enormous damage to America's role as a beacon of freedom and to the rule of laws."[354] In these insistent assertions, Sullivan is appealing to the former president for the sake of America's future.

Sullivan looks to the future, and explains that "After the next attack, America will need unity—not a poisonous division over the issue of torture. You had that unity after 9/11. Your successors deserve the same support."[355] This is a request based on the need of the American people, not a partisan salvo. But if I am correct in my assessment, the former president is too small—too small-hearted (unmagnanimous), too feeble-minded, too self-centered, and too amoral ever to be able to acknowledge the issues explained in this appeal. Bush would find it too inconvenient and incompatible to the overly simplistic heroic cowboy image he has of himself. He is too weasely of a trickster to mature in humility and humanity. In his 2010 memoir, *Decision Points*, Bush bragged about giving orders to waterboard prisoners suspected of terrorism, but when asked about the fate of American servicemen receiving the same treatment when caught by the enemy, he refused to acknowledge any tit for tat consequences that might occur. When normal conscience is suppressed and a public image of nobility is cultivated, one becomes a soulless shell incapable of humility or acting for the welfare of a higher ideal, such as the well-being of the nation as a whole—and then the trick is on oneself—one fools the world and fools oneself beyond any genuine self-knowledge or understanding of life. Presiding over a policy of torture while denying it, repeating, "The United States does not torture," what kind of forceful yet feeble trick is that? Whom does it fool? Infantile urges demand to do what they please then trickily hide behind excuses. Cherry pickers become expert pretenders. A grown man expecting to get away with such behavior is pathetic.

I think former President George W. Bush and former Vice-President Dick Cheney could be seen as a *puer* and *senex* duo, if we use the language of depth psychology. The *puer* archetypal figure of youthfulness in myth and history often exhibits the behavior of having bright dreams, hopeful self-heroic plans, which turn out to be shabby and pathetic in their execution. We see trickster as "bad boy" character, tomfoolery leader, and mischief-maker; a tipsy mess-up, cutup and muck-up, a crackerjack joker who gets turned around and becomes the cocky comeback kid, often enough. The screw-up who is "born again" as a redeemed *puer* may come to feel in touch with a heavenly Father high above a corrupt and shoddy world. The *senex* archetype is seen in the old man behaviors of reacting with anger and paranoia when one's system is crossed, being rigid, fearful, and hateful. A cynical, mean, calculative cold-blooded outlook, self-centered bitterness, and many other characteristics of the negative *senex* archetype seem applicable to some of Cheney's secretive activities and favored policies.[356] Cheney thought using waterboarding and other abuses that are clearly contrary to the Geneva Conventions to be obvious "no brainer" methods, no questions needed. George W. Bush, like a younger brother of Cheney, was never troubled by uncertainty.

Certainty, as Oliver Wendell Holmes said, is the greatest cause of violence. Ideologues, fundamentalists, brainwashed followers of cults are driven by such certainty. The cruelty of torture is anti-American, making America as bad as the outlaws she stands against. Self-exoneration is a natural reaction when a trickster finds himself out on a limb. Despite all evidence that tortured suspects will say anything to stop pain and do not give useful information, and testimony by experts that subtler methods work best to extract information, Cheney has refused to change his self-justification of torture. Such stubborn rigidity and attraction to using tricks of pain-infliction seem to express the negative *senex* personality, just as the saying "You can't teach an old dog new tricks" does. (Though in late life new behaviors may emerge in a dog—snapping at children.) The very term "no brainer" is callous, offensive, arrogant, and unconsciously senile. The "one-percent solution" promulgated by Cheney was overkill, a brainchild of senile anxiety.[357]

With his heart troubles[358] it is understandable that Cheney might be a "nervous Nellie," as LBJ called worriers, or unconsciously anxious and paranoid people. But to have someone in that condition making decisions in the name of over 311,800,000 people of America was a shame. The Bush-Cheney administration's idea of security came in two phases: "What, me worry?" and then panic overkill.

The defensive tricks of both *puer* and *senex* to shield their actions from criticism and rebuke can seem to devour all their psychic energies that otherwise might be used in more constructive, creative ways; their well-connected situations allow them to employ various enablers, apologists, and defenders to spin protective coloring for their stories, diversions, and eloquent excuses. Meanwhile, popular characterizations and humorous nicknames cast Cheney as Darth Vader and "the power behind the throne." They cast Bush as "bubble boy," "empty suit," "Bush the lesser," "Shrub," and "What me worry?" Another fitting slogan or mantra for the Bush years is a phrase that became popular at that time: "It's all good." This slogan or mantra is an attempt to throw a blanket affirmation over what is by ordinary logic ruinous, immoral, inauspicious, and devastating. It lets the trickster off the hook, even if the phone is ringing off the hook with news of crises. There is a lot more truth in Maureen Dowd's observation that "When [Bush] jumped in pre-emptively, as in Iraq, it was because he and Cheney had conjured up fake disasters out of their own paranoia and obsession with proving their toughness."[359] It takes big bluffs to prove one is a big man.

On September 2, 2012, Nobel laureate and retired Bishop Desmond Tutu wrote in in an op-ed piece for *The Observer* that George W. Bush and Tony Blair should face prosecution at the Hague, in the International

Criminal Court, because the War in Iraq that they initiated "has destabilized and polarized the world to a greater extent than any other conflict in history" and their responsibility for death and suffering should be legally examined, just as in the case of prosecution of African war criminals.[360]

There sometimes seems to be a great deal of denial about deception in various fields by many Americans. On issues of steroid use, torture, lies by politicians, the Iraq War, economic problems, and bad news of several kinds, it seems that many people are distracted, asleep at the wheel, too self-centered in new electronic devices to let serious matters register. With all the sources of information we have, why are we like the three monkeys holding hands over eyes, ears, and mouth? Why do we Americans refuse to face facts, absorb information, vote, and pay the dues necessary to play our parts in America? Is it a psychic numbness, failure of imagination, a feeling of being totally unprepared, or deliberate choice of escapism? In any case the denial postpones dealing with deceptions. The awareness of the trickster sensibility is an aliveness to realities.[361]

Many Americans can't quite bring themselves to believe that there could be a significant number of self-serving con men in high places. This is understandable, because it would seem to undermine the assumptions about human nature at the basis of democracy. But a realistic assessment of the human ability to betray the trust of others in favor of one's own self-interest was part of the wisdom of founders like James Monroe, John Adams, and Thomas Jefferson. Monroe, Adams, and Jefferson shrewdly analyzed human weaknesses and built safeguards against them into the structure of the government put forth in the Constitution. Turning a blind eye to acts of corruption and malfeasance, self-excuse, self-exoneration, self-aggrandizement and acquisition of personal gain at any cost, is a temptation when knowing more might complicate an already busy and difficult life. But looking without flinching into the human propensity to be self-serving and to play tricks, as Monroe and Adams did, is a precondition to actually facing reality and setting things right. Believing in a man's unrealistic pretense of innocence out of a sense of loyalty is a deceptive collusion. Our naiveté about the trickster is shown, for example, in our lack of sufficient inspectors in the food industry, recent scandals regarding peanut products, meat preparations, and products from China.

America began with high-flown Puritan dreams of innocence. The Pilgrims and early settlers envisioned founding an innocent enclave beyond the corrupt realm of kings and Old World excesses. They dreamed of a New World where purity would be possible. The hope for innocence was an important early part of the story of America. A part of the idealistic New World wish for innocence includes convenient amnesia, and a loss of the sense of the inauspicious. It includes a naive sense of a blank slate where there is none and a lack of self-awareness that sometimes leads to a lack of accountability.

James Baldwin wrote that a sense of being innocent can be very dangerous. Self-delusion, unawareness of one's own hidden motives, assuming one is all good because one vocally denies and condemns all badness is a simple-minded hiding from life's depths. James Hillman suggests that "Innocence is America's mystical cloud of unknowing. We are forgiven simply by virtue of not knowing what we do. To wrap ourselves round in the Good—that is the American dream, leaving place for the evil nightmare only in the 'other,' where it can be diagnosed, treated, prevented, and sermonized about."[362] As the other, an alien object out there, evil can be demonized, hated, feared, threatened, shocked, and awed with bombs. Hillman notes that there is "a disastrous, perhaps 'evil' essential, an inherent bad seed, in Western religious denominations, making obligatory as countermeasure their relentless insistence on 'love.'"[363] By dwelling on the professed ideal of love—love as a catchword for fuzzy optimism in a yellow smiley face—while avoiding awareness of the actual policies we live by, we create gaping discrepancies. Embarrassing words on picket signs and bumper stickers sometimes point to this gap, such as "Who would Jesus torture?" Putting on a veneer of perfect innocence is a defensive act that inhibits self-reflective soul-searching and prohibits learning from one's mistakes. America's repeated loss of innocence includes experiences of slavery, mistreatment of Native Americans, coalitions with dictators, alcoholism, drug addiction, and being conned by political leaders.

George W. Bush's world-polarizing inability to look inward, his lack of curiosity and his certainty, and his self-satisfied swagger and self-centeredness, made many public issues related to this self-proclaimed "war-president" appear to be all about him. He reacted to criticisms of his decision to go to war as if they were personal attacks. He was not interested in ideas, or reasoning, or the depth issues, but acted out of gut-feelings and personal inclinations. This made the self-proclaimed "decider" seem brazen and stubbornly inflexible, never able to admit any mistake. His public image was odd—a very religious man who joked about executing a repentant born-again Christian woman, and used military attempts to solve problems, to bomb first and democratize later. His changing reasons for going to war depended on the short attention span of Americans, and a hope that no one would compare speeches in which Bush gave his shape-shifting rationales for going to war in Iraq.

We have to admit that George W. Bush is something of a mystery, though various attempts to understand and explain him, some ingenuous and some oversimplified have been offered. Some think of him as unintelligent. This 2006 painting by artist Rhea Ormond of Bush as the Scarecrow from *The Wizard of Oz*, entitled "If I only had a brain."

Others would see him as the little man behind the curtain in Oz. Editorial cartoonists have often drawn Bush as Alfred E. Neuman-like ("What, me worry?"). Cartoonists Tom Tomorrow and Mike Luckovich present him as stupid, and the likeness pictured on the cover of *The Nation* magazine, and on t-shirts and web-art, present that view. Others say Bush is very intelligent and able to maneuver and manipulate others, to get his way with expertise. Some say he is sinister. He himself likes to lampoon the idea of being Dr. Evil of Austin Powers fame by imitating Dr. Evil to get laughs.[364] Others see him as very religious. His support of corporate powers seems to show indifference to the environment, but he wants to be known as protector of areas of remote oceans. His pastime of clearing brush on his ranch during his presidency seemed to present an image of rural Texan outdoors activity as important in his life. Many have seen the influence of Bush's vice president Dick Cheney as determining many of Bush's policies, especially during the first six or seven years of the administration. Cheney said it was necessary to go to the "dark side" to fight the war on terror. He considered some deep issues, such as the use of torture, to be "no brainers" when they really required much more consideration and multiple perspectives, because the identity and values of America are at stake when they are employed. Karl Rove, Bush's right-hand man for a long time in matters of political advice, campaigning, and public relations, seems to have used "dirty tricks" of controversial wedge issues to polarize parties and mobilize support. And no doubt a collection of tricky personalities played parts in fiascoes like the invasion of Iraq. For example, many see Ahmed Chalabi as a con man who swayed ideologue neocons when evidence of weapons of mass destruction was not forthcoming. Was Bush manipulated, or did he do just what he wanted? This question requires a careful consideration of a variety of factors, especially if the answer is to offer a deepening of understanding, not just a venting of anger.

For one thing, the acts of the Bush administration give the impression of being faith-based—that is, based on faith in public relations, spin, and subterfuge. One Bush speechwriter, Matt Latimer, in his book *Speechless*, describes how the Bush administration's political office was planning an event intended to highlight how much Bush was a kind of modern-day Jefferson. They sought to orchestrate a Bush speech at Monticello to emphasize how Bush and Jefferson had parallel legacies in several ways. They hoped to get across the similarities: Jefferson founded a university; Bush was responsible for "No child left behind." Jefferson composed the Declaration of Independence; Bush initiated and pushed for the freedom agenda in Iraq and Afghanistan. Jefferson wrote Virginia's freedom of religion statute, proclaiming people of all faiths were welcome; Bush promoted faith-based initiatives. Sharing so much, why shouldn't the man on the nickel and the brush-clearer of Crawford shine together? Such a cynical attitude reveals a hope that promotional tricks of public relations can fix all problems, that public opinion is merely a matter of feeding plausible stories and patriotic spectacles to a gullible public.[365]

Psychoanalyst Justin Frank thinks Bush as president had a "bunker mentality" covered over by surface charm and affability. Bush was known for making strangers feel they might like to have a beer with him, instead of with Al Gore or John Kerry. (That too, seems like an odd illusion or deception, since during the years of being a presidential candidate and then being president, Bush did not drink.) Saying that Bush is "desperately devoted to protecting himself," Frank gives the example of the way Bush reshaped "a mandate to get out of Iraq into a message supporting his own needs."[366] This would seem to be a pattern in the Bush presidency: whatever happens, engage in self-serving spin. Bush often seemed extremely self-centered, taking every criticism as an attack, saying that even if only Laura and his dog remained in agreement with him he would never change. This aversion to absorbing new information and rejection of differing views is inappropriate in a democracy, as Frank has observed.[367]

Bush used his charm, his quick, superficial affability, including making up nicknames, to stay in control and continue doing what he wanted without concern for consequences for the nation and for future generations. He insisted he had the privilege of being "the decider" but he did not seriously face the large number of deaths he was ultimately responsible for, as well as the effects of torture, and showed a "self-protective indifference to the pain of others."[368] By denying the value of psychologically reflecting on oneself, self-awareness cannot be developed; because one is ashamed of parts of oneself, one oversimplifies. Insisting on a simple, changeless heroic persona that never makes a mistake, one is blind to one's own complexity and one's alter ego, and hides at all cost one's duplicity. Greek mythical heroes are accompanied by shadowy sidekicks; this is deeply symbolic. James Hillman writes insightfully about the trickster archetype:

> The shadowy doppelganger [image of twin-self or alter-ego] brings a sense of ourselves as opportunists, cheats, weasels. At the same time, this duplicity in our consciousness—between what is felt and what is shown, what is seen and what is said to have been seen—brings awareness that at least two lives are being led at the same time. We are here and yet also not here at all, hidden. To focus on the opposites is to miss the opportunities, the Hermes [the Greek god archetypally symbolic of the trickster, crossing borders, making transactions] whose presence is precisely in the *between*. . . . For Hermes, whose territory is in the borderlands where many currents live side by side, there is no compartment mentality. He can commit "perjury with the most guileless face," the baby-faced little brother is also a barefaced liar. Borders always have two sides and Hermes thrives in this between-world.[369]

If one denies one's own tricky side, it may become all the more active unconsciously; it will be out of control, because one is dangerously out of touch with one's own inner currents, one's motives, and one's desires. One projects all one's faults onto others. A conscious awareness of this trickster dynamic familiarizes and guides psyches by "bringing consciousness to experience the ego-structures of opposites as messages of divine multiplicity."[370] There is a great difference between feeling on the one hand like a great conscious manipulator at the center of things, powerfully creating reality while others merely comment on it from the sidelines, and on the other hand consciously knowing what's going on in one's own psyche, with self-awareness and the freedom it brings. Being in a bubble of advice and maximum security encourages a restricted range of understanding as to what is going on. Ancient wisdom taught an essential value: "Know thyself." Christian wisdom also taught a mirror-like view: "Do unto others as you would have them do unto you." In other words, who would Jesus torture? Perhaps the eight years of George W. Bush's presidency can reveal to Americans something about their own psyches' challenges during the era we all live in. This is the view of Paul Levy, elaborated on in his book *The Madness of George W. Bush*.[371]

Bush displays an aspect of the archetypal trickster: seeming simple but being devious. What made him so devious may never be fully known. Jung wrote: "Nothing has such a convincing effect as a lie one invents and believes oneself." Bush shows an affect of sincerity and persuasive charm on the surface, together with an ego disorder Levy describes as having the hallmark of "diabolic polarization." Levy says this condition expands itself through projections onto aspects of the outside world. If one does not reflect on oneself, or acknowledge what exists within, one's inner characteristics are seen out there as traits in others. The inner and the outer can become confused, as when the wind blows a man's bad breath back into his own face, or a dog barks at the dog in the mirror. (The trickster, conscious or unconscious, never takes boundaries too seriously, but can breach them in play, in trade, and in aggressive actions.) For example, Bush's well-known hatred of South Korean dictator Kim Jong Il, in part, he said, was because he tortured prisoners. A person suffering from this condition denies his own darker side and always projects his shadow "out there" on evil in the world, and sometimes tries to destroy the person or persons who embody it. Bush's hatred of Saddam Hussein, Kim Jong Il, Ahmadinijad, and other powerful dictators is well known. All mistakes and shame and evil are projected out there on others, and the person pointing his finger at them may feel divinely inspired and personally above the law. Bush spoke of feeling he was on a divine mission enforcing God's will. He said, "God is not neutral," unaware that bin Laden believed he also was submitting to God's will.[372] When a pair of enemies project onto each other their own faults they both feel justified in righteous superiority because the enemy is the evil one. They are bound together like two people pointing at each other through a two-way mirror. When engrossed in projecting evil one need not work on one's own faults—especially if one's religion has pronounced one forgiven, redeemed, and divinely guided. This is the danger of the psychological two-way mirror that exists when a George W. Bush and an Osama bin Laden tangle with each other, each issuing orders from his own bubble. In a protective bubble separating him even from himself, such a person cannot recognize his own repressed fear with compassionate self-understanding. And one cannot evince what Jefferson called a "decent respect" for world opinion.[373] With approval ratings in the twenty percentages at the end of the Bush administration, only diehards who bought into Bush's spin so deeply that they could never give it up remained his fans. Bush seems to fear that if he ever changes his story and admits mistakes, then all he has done will be meaningless and worthless. In his view the world is plain and simple, against him or for him; it's all about him.

In reality, the effects of his actions, including duplicity, for supposedly higher causes, are about America, and clarity after an era of so much obfuscation is essential for Americans to find their way forward. If "a lawyer who defends himself has a fool for a client," then maybe a trickster who's so tricky that he hides from himself and tricks himself thoroughly has a simpleton tied up in knots for his victim. That is not an enviable fate. When a Rip Van Winkle wakes up from his partying phase, and fearfully and frantically tries to grasp the world he is now involved in, and forcefully acts out his own delusions, he is likely to botch his official actions, and leave the nation with a terrible hangover.[374] When the government of a great nation small-mindedly distorts, bends, and breaks the agreed-upon laws of modern international civilization, it distorts and breaks apart the fabric of the nation. But the daredevil trickster always makes himself scarce when the time for assigning blame comes—he seeks only credit and praise. And there are always some who give him a standing ovation, allowing his bubble to endure.

In my view Bush's abiding unpopularity ultimately rests on the idea expressed well in a line in a Kurosawa film: "Sometimes one must take a life, but to take a life when it isn't necessary—I'll have nothing to do with such lunacy." Multiply "a life" by the large number of lives lost and wrecked in Iraq. Forgiveness is wonderful, but irresponsibility, unaccountability, self-serving deceit are not, especially when they are used to avoid blame for massive bloodshed and maiming. After eight years of certainty without curiosity (curiosity leads to understanding that life has complexity, which leads to ambiguity and loss of simple-minded certainty), Bush left Washington.

After years of bullying, strutting, stirring fear, and smirking in a bubble of self-importance, the trickster finds himself whittled down to a smaller size than his delusions of grandeur had assumed. Could it be that the trickster is a mere mortal? What a surprise!

Bush, if seen in a life-cycle context, was a trickster as a youth who in later life sobered up to become the impaired stooge of much bigger tricksters. (These include vested interests in the oil industry, handlers, and promoters like Karl Rove, as well as powerful manipulators like Dick Cheney.) It is difficult, because of speechwriters, PR workers like Karen Hughes, etc., to know what was unconscious on Bush's part, and what was deliberate. Often we do not acknowledge our own selfish motives except in retrospect, but Bush took this to an extreme. He often seemed absurdly unironical in his speeches, for example making derogatory statements about Iraqi terrorists harming innocent people when his own policies were also responsible for the same thing. To his fans he will always be a hero, and to his critics, a cowardly weasel. His presidency had devastating consequences for the nation. It will be interesting to see what tricks life has in store for these players who have touched so many lives.

Surely it was an outrageous trick to take official writings by climate scientists reporting about their findings, and give them to a political appointee to delete all mention of the serious problems of climate change. The Environmental Protection Agency reports were edited by Philip A. Cooney, who was then chief of staff of the White House Council on Environmental Quality. Cooney had previously worked for the American Petroleum Institute. A lawyer without scientific training, Cooney led the oil industry's attempt to prevent government restrictions on greenhouse gas emissions.[375]

But for what trick will the fastidious Mr. Bush be most remembered? That would be the way he and his enablers—Condoleeza Rice, Dick Cheney, Karl Rove, and others—used fear of WMD to have a pretext for invading Iraq, using lies about aluminum tubes and yellow cake, and getting Colin Powell to go through a charade at the UN, and Rice to concoct a sound bite about not wanting a mushroom cloud to be the smoking gun. It was a big, long war fought in the name of the American people, because Bush wanted to go to war, to be a "war president." He was a failure at many things, but his biggest failure was as a "decider." To decide well takes qualities he never developed. Relying on "gut instincts" and not a thoughtful examination of many complex factors can make for shortsighted delusional decisions, disappointment, and bewilderment. Someone who insists on pointing out that he is *the decider* should not resist the correlate that he is *the accountable one.* He will be remembered by many as a shabby trickster who wasted America's wealth, reputation for justice, and the blood of American servicemen and women. He may have done something for others without a self-serving motive during his term—I don't know—but his legacy, and his picture in history books, should show him as a charlatan in leader's clothes. On rare occasions when there was no written speech in front of him, and no Rove or other writer on the payroll to feed him phrases of defense, when the occasion made emotional honesty the only response that would not seem insane, Bush could tell the truth somewhat. For example, when the black mother of a Jamaican soldier blamed him for her son's broken body, Bush said he agreed with her.[376]

Bush said he would let history would judge him in the future. I think in history's rearview mirror he is getting smaller and smaller. As Joe Nocera wrote, "Has any president in American history left behind as much lasting damage as George W. Bush? In addition to two unfinished wars, he also set us on the path to the financial meltdown of 2008 and the problems it brought."[377] The cost of waging wars off the budget will be with America for a long time.

Priding himself on being the sole "decider," which is a trickster's way of claiming the right to make unilateral decisions, even though as president he was supposed to represent the whole country, not just his own personal wishes or hunches, George W. Bush proved himself to be a very bad guesser. Maureen Dowd sums up the situation well: "The spectacular error" Bush and his administration made was in assuming America should launch "a post-9/11 demonstration of war to prove our toughness. If they had merely pushed along the Arab Spring, they could have saved a trillion dollars and the lives of 4,500 American troops." The capture of bin Laden and the accomplishment of the Afghanistan war would have been better for America than "nation-building in Iraq when our own nation was falling apart. . . . Before W. tried to outdo his daddy, we were a country that usually had to take a punch before we went to war. We didn't unilaterally start wars . . ."[378] George W. Bush is the poster boy for the principle that when we deceive, we first lie to ourselves, the better to deceive others. For a useful discussion of this see Robert Trivers's excellent book, *The Folly of Fools: The Logic of Deceit and Self-Deception in Human Life*.[379] The difference between a very conscious conniving con man and an unconscious "true-believer" sincere con man is considerable. The former is a con man with a secret he keeps to himself, who knows he's a con artist. The latter is a con man with enablers who believes the lie he's telling, and makes himself think he's not a puppet. It is something like the stage magician or mentalist who comes to believe in his own abilities as a fortune-teller, "a shut eye," in the lingo of that trade.

When there is a situation of Apollonic ideals—publicly displaying one's righteousness and pride commanding an ideal order of light forces opposing evil darkness, as Bush's speeches painted his own motives—Hermes is always nearby like an accompanying shadow, as archetypal psychology thinker James Hillman reminds us: "Together they make a fine pair: the golden gleam of noble ends achieved by sly means."[380] The vaunted noble ideals of George W. Bush making self-righteous speeches in the spotlight were trailed with the shadows of Karl Rove and other offstage trickster-helpers behind him.

We live in a comparatively hip, educated, and psychologically savvy age. Jung put it this way: "We like to think that, on the basis of a widespread knowledge of the unconscious and its ways, no one could be deceived by a statesman who was unaware of his own bad motives; the very newspapers would pull him up: 'please have yourself analyzed; you are suffering from a repressed father-complex.'"[381] But no, deception and self-delusion can thrive, and wage war, and polarize millions on the world stage even today. Psychologically blind tricksters can cause the greatest havoc. Their denials seem so sincere because of their willful ignorance. The banality of the inner life of someone mediocre who has unwittingly done terrible things with horrible consequences is underwhelming. I'm sure the Iraq invasion-urgers like Wolfowitz and William Kristol, stopped reading the daily news about events in Iraq after a while. But as the years went on, the suffering there continued. It wasn't only the many deaths caused by Improvised Explosive Devices. After a while there were constant reports of many deaths by torture—amidst factions of Iraqis, Sunnis and Shiites. Bodies were dumped in the streets after the victims had been tortured with electric drills boring into their skulls. Bush may be happily painting pictures of his dog or cat now, with the help of a teacher whose job is to "find the inner Rembrandt" in Bush, and this may amuse Jay Leno. But many can't forget the suffering and destruction Bush caused. America spent pallets of cash for years, and truckloads of tortured bodies kept appearing every morning because of an unnecessary war. Many feel Bush is a war criminal, and the albratross of his huge mistake should accompany him all his days. The pretenses of a trickster bolstering his ego with delusions of grandeur in the end are unbearable; they seek their own deflation, wishing to dissolve in a grounding of "regular guy" humanity, after riding roughshod over ordinary people with the boots of privilege.[382] A friend who has lived in Washington for decades questioned my exploration of Bush as trickster. "Why? The only trick in Bush's bag of tricks was a 'get out of jail free' card—the 'born again' sense of privilege, feeling already forgiven for anything one might do, favored, chosen, despite any failings. He didn't know what he was trifling with in seeking the presidency—he 'misunderestimated' the abilities needed and the repercussions of his blunders. But 'God is not mocked,' and neither is a nation with millions of intelligent people."

The riddle—was George W. Bush a shapeshifting trickster or a blank-slate fool used by others?—may not be impossible so solve. Perhaps these two are the same. As Bush himself said, "I live in the moment, seize opportunities and try to make the most of them."

What Sort of People are We Americans?

Sometimes in history there are concerted efforts in society to reduce trickery, when it seems too dangerous and too offensive to live with.[383] The challenges facing America in recent years have become especially daunting, but the terrorist tricksters of 9/11 should not be allowed to define American identity. America is much more than the victim of an attack. It's a tricky thing to know and be who you are, to continue on in the face of tricksters seeking to make you live in fear. It is very doubtful that clever daredevil tricksters of security, vengeful political leaders who can only fight fire with fire, could ever achieve security in a complex nation existing in a complicated world. Daredevil tricksters who govern over-rely on hard power, and underestimate the need for soft power.[384]

It is human nature to crave safety and security, as examples from around the world attest. The Chinese traditionally prize stability. Muslims speak of Islam as meaning "safety." American "life, liberty, and the pursuit of happiness" assumes a background of safety and security. So, where does the daredevil exponent originate? Some Americans have an especially long adolescence. Then they may feel shame at their old selves and strive to compensate. They feel the need to prove they are not failures. Having spent a long adolescence in party mode they have limited knowledge, shallow understanding, and a great need for respectability. They acquire power with the tricks of enablers. Then, awakened like Rip Van Winkle to the shock of a world they have neglected, suddenly in a position where they need to protect others, they act like reckless cowboys riding roughshod over the law, seeking to give a semblance of safety, driven by daredevil ideas of security. They need easy answers. They undertake bold actions that rile up large segments of the world's population: belligerence, bombing, "Shock and awe," Guantanamo, Abu Ghraib, extraordinary rendition, disregard of the Geneva Conventions, torture, unilateral acts to prove toughness. Actions such as these, perceived or real, perpetrated by American leaders lose the sympathy of the world. The daredevil security trickster deals in fear and the damaged goods of an ill-informed worldview, increasingly hard to sell in the market of public opinion. The leader using a daredevil trickster mode of security policy refuses to think consciously of his own limitations and faults. A trickster such as Ahmed Chalabi can play loose and fast with the truth, telling various agencies what they want to hear, playing into their plans, and wreaking havoc with gullible people obsessed with their own agendas. The tricks of powerful people's egos planning war can be very self-deluding. Attempts at heroism involve duplicity, risk, and opportunism, inevitably, even for leaders of great character. What then of lesser souls?[385]

It is also human nature to crave ease even when we might be in a precarious position. Technology is the biggest trick of all in our age. Technology offers us the tempting illusion of ease. It seems to give us superpowers. It augments our reach, enhances our abilities, it gives us ways to communicate instantly and interfere with others easily from a great distance. It can give those in power a false sense of security. It is an often-heard truism that our ability to invent clever devices has far outstripped our understanding of their effects. Humanity is still trying to find the wisdom to use sophisticated technology well. Marketing has outstripped reflective thinking about how the devices we use change human character and society. To multiply large numbers of products from an original prototype, to impact others greatly with as little personal energy as the pressing of a button, to broadcast information widely—these kinds of abilities mark a new scale of change and impact in modern life. Technology gives us the power to carve up the earth and exploit resources, making a great impact on geological levels and atmospheric systems; to use power to enact one's whims, to rely on high-tech force when other kinds of tools are needed—and in these and many other technology gives us tempting abilities that may lead to playing with fire. It can be alluring to use a slick simple trick to solve a problem that in reality requires other means. A remote control drone may seem like a cure for one's ills.

In an article by Roger Cohen, Lieutenant General Peter Chiarelli of the US Army is quoted: "Much of our government and interagency seem to be in a state of denial about requirements needed to adapt to modern warfare." Cohen summarizes Chiarelli on the need to master methods of "instantaneous communication to win hearts and minds, adapting rapidly, flattening ponderous military hierarchies, understanding nation-building, and bringing to bear US abilities in fields as diverse as engineering and agronomy." In other words, America needs to become better than her foes at influencing the world's perception by being of service, and to become more ready to make instantaneous responses while living on an interconnected globe, where one person with a video camera can sway hordes of Internet users. Chiarelli notes that there has also been a failure in the new army and America to internalize values, "the moral and ethical codes that define who we are" in the armed services and as a nation, and a reluctance to admit mistakes. Inability to admit mistakes is a serious failure, a slighting of reality. Daredevil security operations ignore these things, assuming overwhelming force will do the job.[386] That one-sidedness is an inadequate response. Thomas E. Ricks, in his book *The Gamble*, about the Iraq war during the last two years of the Bush administration, writes that one of the elements that led to fewer deaths was a new policy of paying off disaffected Sunnis who would otherwise kill our soldiers. This part of the "surge" phase was not presented to the president for approval. It sounds like "negotiating with terrorists," so presumably it would not have been approved. Not much publicized, it was an important factor in the surge. The trick might have been used earlier in the period of massive suffering and Improvised Explosive Devicess, but it was not in Bush's sparse bag of tricks.

Some of the character traits described above may be part of an older American trait. The controversial English writer D. H. Lawrence (1885–1930) long ago discerned patterns of disjointedness in the Puritan strand of the American psyche in the American classic, *The Scarlet Letter*, and noted the hypocrisy in *The Deerslayer*. The hero of *The Deerslayer* says he does not want to hurt, yet he kills. It's de riguer to speak nobly, and to be sensitive, and then to go ahead and shoot the gun and kill. There's a kind of duplicity or trick involved in saying one thing and then doing another. The split-personality trickster talks out of two sides of his mouth at once (as Native Americans said, "he speaks with a forked tongue"); he plays with the crazily rebounding American ball of contradictions.[387]

A false "peacemaker" may use a smokescreen of words about agreements and accords, while actually planning and waging war. This hypocrisy is a kind of trickiness requiring a large supply of euphemisms and expressions of doublespeak. An arms dealer may sell weapons to both sides of a conflict, and also supply goods to the peace brokers, and claim to be a humanitarian.[388] The self-deluded trickster lives in his own amoral world, wearing a mask of lovable humility while planning unilateral actions; he lives in a bubble, paranoid and spreading his own ills, is clever in manipulating others, and only in retrospect are convolutions of his underhanded trickery understandable.

Of course, heroic grandness and wiliness are not separable. "The golden gleam of noble ends achieved by sly means" is a realistic description of two features—hero and trickster together. In the David and Goliath story, David is a hero with a good and tricky slingshot; only a trick would even the odds in that contest. Sometimes a Mahatma wins by political jujitsu, or like a thief in the night, uses stealth and silence to slice through a difficult impasse. George Washington's guerilla warfare in the fight for independence, and Lincoln's suspension of *habeas corpus* to get the advantage in the Civil War, are trickster ploys.[389] The hero-trickster is necessarily an opportunist. Heroic impulses involve trickiness; bravery's realism includes slyness and sneakiness. But a true hero's story involves great skill and wisdom, personal self-sacrifice, and renunciation of selfish rewards. If a would-be hero like Walter Mitty tries to play the hero by ear, flying by the seat of his pants, ill-informed, uncurious, making gut-feeling decisions on national matters, he ends up looking shabby, dumb, pretentious, fly-by-night. But even true heroes cast a shadow with their lives.[390]

To see more of the whole patterns, the paradoxes and nonlinear loops of chaotic reality, it is useful to consider further the trickster nature of life. Thus the trickster story in its varied forms is a constant part of imagination and symbol systems. It grounds us warily in the dynamics of reality. Life is quirky, full of twists and turns, unexpected changes, ironies, and challenges. It's telling and ironic that we banish and deny our fears, only to see them turn up in our nightmares. Nightmares, like exposure to the unpredictable ways of tricksters, can ground us with more careful attention to neglected necessities and bring us to humble clarity, as Jung suggested. Trickster loops are about discovering who we are, what we stand for, and what we will not stand for—the cowardly lion sometimes finds he can strengthen his heart and become more courageous.

An Army Man's Honest Views

To hear a stranger's insights and experiences can sometimes awaken courage in one's own views. I met a staff sergeant in the US Army while writing this in 2008, and his insightful ideas about the trickiness of American troops dealing with people in Muslim cultures intrigued me. He was about sixty years old and he had served in a variety of countries, including Afghanistan and Bosnia. I reconstructed some of his ideas when I got home, writing them up in the following monologue:

> We're not smart enough about extremists, not tricky enough to cope, not wise enough. We betray ourselves with our weaknesses and myopia, so we fail to know what works, what to do to succeed. We don't know the language and culture of enemies or those we want to help. I think it's interesting that many of our translators are Mormons, because they have a background in learning languages, from their missionary work. It's a war that needs wise old guys, not just callow kids rarin' to go. We need

to use our brains and hearts, not just muscle. Kids today don't really mature until thirty or so. In the World War II era a kid of fourteen was more mature and grown up. Life taught kids more hard lessons they knew in their bones by fourteen. American kids today don't learn to be cruel in the Army. They learn that in high school. To get respect they act mean to each other. They see tough guy stuff on TV and in movies. You show you're an alpha male by hard-hearted cruelty. We've even got mean girls, who beat each other up to show their stuff on YouTube. Kids think cruelty is proof of toughness, but no, toughness is the ability to endure adversity, to suffer and persevere. Many Muslims are more skilled at enduring pain and surviving harsh conditions, and more skilled in trickster activities like bargaining (daily practice in the marketplace), and saying one thing while thinking another (from living under a dictator). So, to inflict pain on them is a misguided strategy. No—cruelty doesn't work against Muslims. They're too used to it. It's how they get things done, with harsh treatment, fear, and intimidation. Saddam's regime tortured and killed; the Shah of Iran had SAVAK, the secret police with their dungeons. You should see how they treat their kids sometimes. They're so used to it, it won't help us get what we want. Practically speaking, it's not a good approach. But if you use kindness, it can work. At first Muslims may take kindness as weakness—think you're weak, soft, vulnerable, so they are tempted to take advantage and con you, exploit you. . . . Then they feel guilty, and their conscience kicks in, based on the teachings of compassion in the Qur'an. The ones I worked with, knew I was reaching out to them, that I was going out of my way for them, and in time they said, "Because of your kindness, we would die for you." The extremists are a cult inside of ordinary Islam. OK, Muhammad fought on a horse with a sword in his hand, got wounded in the face, so Islam might be more militant than Christianity. But the extremists have a faith that they should die fighting against oppressors of Muslims, a faith that sacrificing themselves by obliterating enemies of Islam will wipe out their sins, and the sins of their families. To them it's not a sin to fight and kill themselves in the process, but a cleansing of sins. That sacrifice is positive, to them, doing God's will. To them, the presence of American troops in Arabia is an offense against Islam, and Americans seeming to support Israel against Palestinians, and they see invading Iraq as anti-Islam. . . . To understand where the extremists are at, and deal with them, will take all of our patience, endurance, rational skill, good sense, powers of observation, mature wisdom, and long-honed abilities. It takes tough strength and courage to face adversity, not just long-distance shock and awe, not just causing pain to someone in a dungeon. It takes reflective thought, deep understanding. Sometimes a crisis can cause people to reach out, to understand what people who suffer go through, to take a turn for the good.

This US Army staff sergeant had plenty of other insights and thought-provoking ideas but this sampling will have to suffice.[391]

Dealing with serious offenses, violent attacks, anger, and acts of vengeance is a tricky matter. Fighting evil determines what we become, therefore; it requires wisdom, not just "an-eye-for-an-eye" simple-mindedness. Facing and consciously forgiving the fact that something bad occurred makes reconciliation possible. In forgiving we free not only the offender, but ourselves as well. This choice places a higher value on the possible future than on the disappointments of the past. The subtlety of turning the other cheek, going the extra mile, is a tricky dynamic. It is a twist which perhaps one might not expect, "counter-intuitive"—if one's intuition normally tends toward the knee-jerk reflex of revenge. Love, in Christian and other wisdom teachings, involves much more of a trickster dynamic than mechanically brutal dog-eat-dog survival instincts do. Some matters are so simple they elude us because we assume they're very complicated.

Fearless, the trickster breaks taboos, but also the chains of habit, compulsion, common sense: "Love your enemy." Hate plays tricks, whispering, "Strike back! Cause pain! You can get away with it." Love and forgiveness have a larger scope, a more generous spirit, a long-term concern for sustainable well-being.[392] The tricks accomplished by generous, magnanimous love are mysteries. The real trick lies in creatively transforming grim situations, not in brutalizing and destroying.

The deadly serious trickery of suicide bombers or other enemies of democracy must be outmaneuvered by tricks of life. They can be out-tricked by vital intelligence, superior strategies, outside-the-box wits. Increasingly, military strategists and those who study conflict resolution in-depth see reliance on violent reprisals through bombing campaigns as a one-sided response resulting in long-term failure. Winning hearts and minds, and other remedies are necessary too. Brutality is a dumb trick.

Trickster and Morality: The Conscience of Mercury

We've put off the issue of morality long enough. Before we conclude, we must consider some difficult moral issues and gray areas of life, and the trickster's contributions to some answers. Wild laughter—the sound of trickster—when things go terribly wrong, spiraling out of control, is that merely a comic book caricature of the thrill-seeking villain, or does it reflect a deep dynamic in the psyche? Attempts to get away with secret wishes and bad habits—are those not also areas where trickster and addictster are at play? Just as the crafts and professions have "tricks of the trade," so too, don't the passions and drives, as well as disorders and faults, all have their own industrious techniques of survival, including subterfuge and obfuscations? Expertise in getting away with excesses is nothing new—the Romans had their feasts and vomitoria. It is human to fritter away time and make excuses, conduct sexual encounters hidden by night, hide envy and pride with hypocrisy. The trickster brain works overtime to manipulate, finagle and fudge, throw suspicions off the track, and elude detection. Unaware of this mischief, unsuspecting people succumb to manipulative moves disguised as good-hearted, open-handed gestures.

The trickster appears in many forms, from childish teasing ("Cat got your tongue?") and lame excuses ("Dog ate my homework!") to vicious cynical tricks to demean and destroy others and their way of life, like the Janjaweed-mounted militia attacking villages in Darfur, Sudan, or the repeated denials of Assad in Syria that his army was attacking the people. Knowledge of the trickster archetype can begin to give one the needed awareness of trickiness to be free from the worst tricks of the destructive trickster, both within us and out in the world at large.

The soulful kind of trickster talent we need has a lively spirit aware enough of harmful tricksters to deal with them accordingly. We need to know about life's tricks without becoming lost in our own deceptions, which can become deadly. The American nation was founded on a vision of hopeful wisdom, not only on sly deceptions. The founders resisted monarchy, and accomplished a tricky feat in wording the Constitution to install a democratic government for a free society. True, there were tricks to get the land sometimes. William Henry Harrison's trick challenge to an Indian known as "the Prophet," who rallied followers to try to keep their territory by claiming divine guidance, was meant to eliminate the Indians' claim to the land. Harrison said "If the Prophet is a true one, ask him to control the planets; if he does, you can believe in him." The Prophet prayed, and an eclipse occurred, causing the Indians to believe in him. Sometimes tricks backfire. But despite the show of ability in timing, the Prophet could not stop the loss of his people's lands.

We could go back through the examples discussed in this exploration and label the kinds of motivation involved. We have seen greed-inspired con men, and power-driven tricksters. Mischief, hate, revenge, fun, youthful folly, thrill-seeking—there are many kinds of trickster acts. Going out of bounds in hopes of producing dramatic results by torturing captured suspects is a fear-inspired tricksterism. A wiser, subtler "friendly persuasion" tricksterism is less obvious. It's like the "arts of peace" which Confucius praised—cultural contributions that improve life and reduce desire for violent solutions. In the heyday of the Roman empire, the Romans brought civilization to barbarians, making their lives better, so the barbarians lost the need to attack and pillage. If anyone stands for transcending fear and arriving at something beyond, it is the trickster.

Perhaps our whole pack of varied coyotes can be divvied up into tricksters who give the soul its due and those who don't; tricksters who arrogate to themselves what is not theirs to control, and tricksters with a creative and life-supportive vision; tricksters who turn a living creature who loves life into something as lifeless as a walking stick, because they can, and those who don't.[393]

We need to face facts: everybody is gambling, not everyone cheats. Everyone is a trickster, not everyone's vicious. The trickster is in all psyches; sick trickster rules a few. For a variety of reasons I think we are approaching a time when many will take a person seriously only if he is a humble trickster, not a tyrannical one. Hypocrites seeking respectability and power deny their trickery absolutely; humble worthies laugh maturely at the endless tricks of human nature and say, "I'm no more guileless than the rest of you." The soulful trickster is compassionate, respectful, and a good friend, doing unto others as he would have them do to him.

What else does the trickster spirit at its best look like? A trickster inspired by a high quest might be exemplified by Philippe Petit. Petit came from France to America in his youth and performed a wonder-evoking, death-defying feat at the World Trade Center towers in 1974. With a team of friends he surreptitiously installed a tightrope between the two towers, and walked back and forth across it eight times one ordinary morning, amazing hundreds on the street below. This feat took an amazing amount of dedication and focus, talent and trickster faith. Petit and his team thought of the illegal act as a coup, a heist, a prank of utmost skill, artistry, and rebellion. (As a friend who studies ethical behavior put it, "The artistic prank is a kind of virtuosity that breaks the mold of boring virtue.") Motivated by an inspiring admiration for the new towers, seeing them as an irresistible performance site, Petit dance-walked on the wire for forty-five minutes. Using only a balance bar he walked, knelt, and lay down on the wire, amazing all who witnessed the performance. When asked by reporters "why?" in true trickster spirit he said there was no why. He did not try to explain this magnificent and mysterious death-defying act. This impudent act of physical-grace poetry is an object lesson, Petit said later, which showed that the challenges of life should be lived through with the brave and exultant spirit of 'a tightrope walker. He is a useful reminder of the spirit of courage in the post 9/11 age of fear and insecurity. Spirit-moved tricksterism is like the saying "kill them with kindness," meaning trick them into wonder, awe, love, a sense of possibilities of life, human imagination, and skill. Power is vested in the people, but it incarnates only as much as the consciousness of the people is awake.[394] Wisdom is traditionally associated with age and cautiousness, but in this case Petit, a youth in his twenties at the time of the feat, showed that with inspiration, dogged practice, and skill, incredible feats are possible. He performed a unique wonder and lived to accomplish other feats as well. There are many more examples of creative tricksters. Each field has its innovators, imaginative thinkers, free spirits, and sages. They find the passageways through the impassable blockades and win the prize.

Each culture is a great conglomeration of tricks. By this I mean devices that worked and so were self-perpetuating in the flow of time, ranging from the ridiculous to the sublime. If a culture consists largely of those things that are merely meant to satisfy demands of pleasure-seeking and are determined by market demand and supply, power politics, and lack of self-reflection, then the conscience-less, unwise ego trickster has won a monopoly. The wise trickster spirit of true democracy turns cartwheels of change regularly, through elections, opportunities for new ideas and talent to thrive. It's good for America when poor children can become successful and fulfilled instead of wasting their lives—for example the 10,000 children given an equal chance in the organization Harlem Children's Zone. If economics is the "dismal science," then good-natured soulful trickster spirit is the tender strength of freedom's gentle might, the laughing sport, and the exhilarating art. It is the mirror showing what is versatile and resilient and skillful in America, and also showing the potential to go astray, a warning.

    Tricks we play on others affect us. If we act as if we are outside all laws of life we may do high fives and gloat for a while, but eventually we find we are unable to control haunting repercussions. Torture is deceptive—even on the occasions when it extracts information, it can win the battle but lose the war. Some tricks set time bombs destined to go off much later. Even torture can masquerade as a justice system for a time, but there are some cruel and inhuman acts that boomerang, damaging the psyche of the perpetrator.[395] It all depends on what we want America to become—our consciousness and reputation are in our own hands. We are the ones who decide our own way of life. Others cannot change us, as Colin Powell suggested, but our fear of others may cause us to change ourselves in a panic. In urging Congress to renew the Patriot Act, President George W. Bush described opponents of America as "people who have no soul." The effect of making this religious statement—a dogmatic theological assertion—about others being soulless is to urge a ruthlessness toward them as creatures less than human, unworthy of being treated decently and according to law.[396] That attitude conveniently forgets that opponents may have the same argument—that they are fighting against a people seeming so unholy that utter ruthlessness is justified. It also assumes the right to judge others as guilty without due legal process,[397] the right to be judge, jury, and executioner.

An exploitative trickster's beguiling smile looks nice to the gullible, but it disgusts those who were suspicious of him all along, and is sickening to those who were fooled, in fact repeatedly tricked. The ego regarding trickery is a curious thing. A half-wit thinks he's cleverly outfoxing people, even as he digs his own grave, deeper and deeper. And wisdom regarding trickery often sounds blunt because someone who's seen it all will not suffer fools gladly: "Don't try to bullshit a bullshitter."[398] Meaning "it takes one to know one," so it is futile to try pulling a fast one, since someone aware of trickster sees right through all the tricks. (To be suspicious is to be suspicious—to raise suspicions, just as to delve into the unconscious is to sound crazy. To be aware of trickster is to raise doubts—"Is this person who is so interested in tricksters a trickster himself?" because as we just said, it takes one to know one.)

What do we do with our fascination for trickiness, impulse, instinct, joke, revenge, retort, spur of the moment spontaneity? Bury it, celebrate it, act on it rashly, analyze it, employ it? Exploring the trickster archetype helps one think about this. What amount of duplicity or kind of pretension, or hustle—saying one thing and doing another—is acceptable? Everyone has their little white lies, secrets, feints and fake outs, plays and smiles—duplicitous—deceptions made for a good cause, to avoid embarrassment, to keep things simple when to act otherwise would bring too much complexity. These can be innocent, harmless, light, able to laugh at self while doing it or afterwards—without serious, harmful consequences. But where does deliberate exploitative trickery begin, and where does healthy foolery end? It is a question ethicists and others can explore with more nuance, debating just what crosses the line and when.

So, approaching the topic of the relations of trickster archetype and conscience with realistic honesty and meaningful reflection is no simple matter. The attempt to fathom trickster dynamics and conscience is like trying to capture accurately some essence of your shadow, and often the certainty-seeking process threatens to end up like a crude net filtering only the most gross of wrongdoings, undeniable flotsam on a vast sea of gray areas. Much in life is a mixture of playful impulse and learning, and going to excess, then finding happy mediums. Much in life is a mash-up of thoughtlessness, selfish ideas, and second thoughts that are better considered and more considerate of others. People hide from themselves their worst glimpses of their own shadows, especially in cultural times when an examination of the conscience is out of fashion, and might even be punished. To admit to deviousness is embarrassing, socially punishable in self-righteous circles. It's easier to be a selfish rat or comic curmudgeon, a kind of lifelong self-justifying Scrooge, finally seeing only on one's deathbed the scope of one's bad acts and deceits. It's probably better to admit that one is not very good, an imperfect sinner, all along the way, while sincerely striving and doing all one can to acknowledge one's faults, and improve. The trick of the loophole that makes one God's favorite, redeemed because of acceptance of a savior into one's heart for one moment in a lifetime of devilry, is one that only a tricky type of stunted legalistic mind could fall for, because it lacks the subtlety and depth that is the hallmark of soul. It projects onto the depth of cosmic order a vulnerability to cheap tricks. Of course the avoider of conscience denying deceits rather than the person admitting faults might appear more respectable to the conventional world, which often seems senile, gullible, and easily tricked. I'm just saying trickster and conscience form a difficult dilemma to consider—like oil and water, Cain and Abel, God and Job, or love and lust. It is symbolized in the quicksilver image of Hermes, the god of both giving and stealing.

Because the human heart is fickle and because mood swings happen, and such things as temptations and opportunities, fantasy impulses and shifts of focus, and the realities of ambition and revenge are constantly intruding on systems of ideals and moral trajectories, there is a "Last Judgment" archetype. This image of dividing sheep from goats, assigning souls to heaven or hell, represents serious consequences for straying—in our psyches' and worldviews' stories. There are examinations of consciences, retreats, Yom Kippurs, counselors, Father Confessors; there are spiritual rebirths, new leases on life, chances to clear the deck, to forget, and forgive. Going astray with self-destructive mistakes, divulged secrets, and betrayals, all manner of troubled lives call out for some healing, reconciliation, rescue, and liberation. Being civil, in part, means hiding one's true feelings, angers, impatience, one's smoldering resentments and seething animosities, in favor of politeness. Smiling while biting one's tongue, showing good manners when instinct says, "Strike back!"—civilized life calls for a great drama of masks and gestures, with hypocritical tricks on ourselves and others. In a world where image is all, and products, media, and status help give high self-regard, if one hand does not know what the other hand is doing, it can all seem like one great big charade or a long carnival parade.

For the trickster style of consciousness, which is as mercurial as "flying by the seat of one's pants," the occupational hazard involves excessive fluidity. Ever changing with conditions, one might slip from situation ethics to moral relativism to amoral predatory practices all too easily. One may slip from acting like one believes in one thing while in a particular set of circumstances, to then also acting like one believes in other things in the next hundred sets of circumstances too. Without a stable set of values or core of integrity one might adapt too easily to the values found in a den of thieves, if one lands there. It becomes easy to do the unconscionable if one's compass has no true North, only the three hundred sixty degrees of the radius of "anything goes."

Men are often especially "good" tricksters in hiding their true feelings. They think because they are good at it—being out of touch with how they really feel deep-down—they can fool others easily too. This confidence gets them in trouble and wounds them in the long run. Better to own up with honesty. Good-hearted trickster-awareness looks to fellow humans with reverent regard and sympathy, like lyrics of the song, seeing clowns on the left and jokers on the right and the trickster stuck in the middle "with you." The self-aggrandizing trickster makes power plays without regard to others' rights. The healthy trickster appreciates the play of power, and exercises conscience, always aware of mutuality and a need for balance.

America Learns as She Goes

As America changes, her identity takes new shapes. Who is most American? Without an understanding of the trickster we cannot really say. Is Joe McCarthy or Paul Robeson most American? J. Edgar Hoover or Martin Luther King, Jr.?[399] Today to many Sally Hemmings looks as American as Jefferson. Who *really* believes in the American dream, the great corporations known for their polluting and tax shelters, or Pete Seeger, who helped clean up the Hudson River? Does flag waving equate with genuine acts of love of country? The American dream has changed in the last century, and today we find decency where we might not have guessed, and shortsighted anything-for-a-buck heedlessness where soon ruin may arrive. The trickster plays in areas full of shades of gray. Has Old Glory been frayed, worn threadbare by ravenous tricksters? Well then, young idealists have work to do. Have cover-ups and lies sucked the oxygen from the astounding landscapes seen by Lewis and Clark? No doubt you have to be hip to tricks of "the dark side," but if you've become indistinguishable from unconscionable tricksters, you've gone far too far. Oh, you're going to be a trickster, all right—it's inevitable. Ploys and plays of the trickster are endless, needed every time you wish to accomplish something. Every new electronic device has tricks you have to learn. Your need for cleverness is inevitable. It all depends on what kind of trickster you want to be, and how much you want your descendants to pay for your tricks, because it all loops back around, like long macaroni. Be careful what you stick in your hat, and what you call it.

The soulful trickster embodies freedom, the possibility of change—self-correction, getting feedback, and making recalibrations in the system, solving tricky problems. Public debate, thoughtful discourse, infusing needed information and ideas from experience, critical analysis, and inspiration, getting rid of the unwanted—all are parts of the process. We all need that creative inventiveness, without and within. The life-supportive trickster way is one of versatility—can you befriend a stranger, can you be a sister or brother, can you guard and protect, can you nourish like a mother, can you love the simplest, humblest of the people in the country? If we just project the trickster onto other people, minorities like the Jews or the Gypsies, the Muslims or blacks or hispanics, we are not owning and developing needed skills in ourselves in a healthy way. If we scapegoat others as clever manipulators, swindlers shrewd with money, or con men always doing shady things outside the law, we may not see our own tricks and develop our own quick wit, our own conscious play of wily resilience, our own honesty. We need to look to our own trickster hearts. Ultimately conscience's question is usually "Whom did you cheat or mistreat?" What good does it do to recognize yourself in the trickster mirror? It allows you to "know thyself," including your shadow.[400] That's a tall order, but a great necessity.

Americans are coming to realize that not only do we all need joy in our lives ("pursuit of happiness"), but also that America no longer has unlimited resources for con men to shuck and victimize her caretakers, or for honest men to squander in a careless, lazy way. There are mega-troubles to resolve. Fortunately Americans have a can-do attitude, and tools of industriousness and creativity to employ. Perhaps America's creativity validates Jung's observation: "To become foolish is certainly not an art; but to draw wisdom out of foolishness is the whole of art." Jung suggested that the mother of the wise is foolishness from which we learn, while mere cleverness can never give birth to wisdom.[401] Our foolishness and ignorance can be a ground for growing spiritually and wising up. We can salvage from foolish life a sober effort for good. That which is left unsaid in every soft-pedaled attempt at persuasion is the trickster's secret realm; by becoming more conscious of that unconscious area, we grow.

America as arena for selfish ambitions is the scene of endless tricks. America in hucksters' hands (e.g., Enron, Madoff, and other scandals) is not a pretty sight. There are sarcastic terms in American slang—"upright man" has winkingly meant "chief of a crew of rogues." "Knight of the road" has meant "chief highwayman." It is a truism that destructive tricksters who gain power try with all their might to stay in power. To go up against a powerful system requires a great deal of trickiness. The legendary John Henry, who valiantly pitted his muscles and stamina against a steam-driven engine, used no tricks; he somehow won his race with the machine by mechanically competing against it with honesty and endurance. Nevertheless, stubbornly swinging his hammer again and again, lacking tricks, options, or flexible approaches to the challenge, he lost his life.

America is a vast land that in many ways embodies tricky conundrums to work on, and to spend generations working out. The core issue of what America means is about realizing ideals. If Old Glory has faded and grown tattered, how to restore vibrant intensity and wholeness; if liberty is wounded, how to clean and bind the wounds and help the system heal? If it was always a trick of the self-serving privileged few, none of these questions matter. If it was about higher ideals for human life, that is a call to work beyond the mere hustle and scam. To be wise to the trickster side is not the end of the story, it is an education in survival, protective and wary knowledge in one's striving for a more just and equitable union.

Monkey Shines in the Dark

The wordless trickster wiggles his ears, crosses his eyes, thumbs his nose at us; he sticks out his tongue, he gives us a "raspberry" (or "Bronx cheer"); he wolf-whistles, flips the bird to us and winks; as Coyote he urinates to leave his mark, and ululates, and the shrill trill keeps sending shivers up our spines. The trickster archetype in the world and in our psyches reveals only as much as it wants. The trickster thanks us for our attention and packs everything back into his big bag of tricks. He's busy—all those tricks aren't going to play themselves, you know. All who consider the trickster attentively will find much more about his ways from their own personal observations. Even then, the trickster, who specializes in foxy surprise, always keeps some of his ways hidden, like secret compartments in a travel bag or hidden pockets in a garment—the better to challenge us with—and keeps a step ahead of our questions, making us scramble in pursuit. We are left in his wake picking up the pieces and trying to fathom his tricks.

    The poet Gary Snyder observed, "Coyote doesn't belong to anybody. Coyote is the trickster. The trickster is an archetype inside all of us. There's no cultural monopoly on any of this." It goes without saying that the trickster is universal. Humanity is the playground where the trickster does his thing.[402]

    Whoever you are, you're going to have to face the great trickster realm of dynamic reality in yourself and in the squirrelly world—so roll with it. The trickster resonates in the joy of laughter, life's crazy fox maneuvers, the quicksilver interweaving of realms. Human beings have intelligence and free will—it's our choice. We can be wise as serpents and simple as doves, or we can be crooked as lightning and ravenous as wolves. May we be cunning enough to live artfully, and not foolishly outsmart ourselves; may we never become so clever that we con ourselves into using our power in ways that result in self-destruction. The ultimate trick is to stay alive and help life thrive, gracefully. The trickster awareness brings necessary gifts and a measure of spontaneous gusto to that process.

How do we acknowledge the ape and the tricky I in the human condition, the inner trickster busy forever? For isn't there an ancient, chthonic force in the psyche—a shadow force, a dynamic that shows up in the endless play of the joker, clown, harlequin, buffoon, baboon? Aren't humans called the "sapient apes," aren't we pretentious primates, with tricky antics, inevitable cycles of mischief and seriousness, maturation and loss, hide and seek, tempted and valiant, innocent and guilty? Our trickster dramas are deep and long like the memories in our blood, the history in our bones, for we are the ache and the arched-ape, the arched-up ape, the archetype of divine animal, angel creature, Grampa Bonzo with the wisdom of nature—hairless apes of crazy jokes, madness and brilliance, self-destructive losers and graceful dancers, big-brained royalty acting like idiots. We are the host and the tricky fungus among us. The trickster's names are legion: rascal, wiseguy, hood, hellraiser, class clown, dumbass, village idiot, total fool, goofball, chucklehead, knucklehead, cut-up, screw-up, joker, bozo, jester, jackass, ne'er-do-well, gadfly, social critic, talk show host, commentator, comic, bloviator, reveller revelling in acting up, smart aleck, wild man, smartass, funny girl, practical joker, life of the party, laugh-a-minute nut, silly bastard, rat from the word go, happy-go-lucky dream peddler, the old grinch and the little imp, the old goat and the little kid.[403] We are, to sum the picture up in a haiku—

> The organ grinder
> And his old dancing monkey
> Make fooling shadows

In nineteenth-century England a critic named Bishop Wilberforce sought to ridicule Darwin, asking: "Was it through your grandmother or your grandfather that you are descended from apes?"

Having his wits about him, Darwin answered something rather humbling and sobering: "I wouldn't be ashamed to have an ape for an ancestor, but I would be ashamed to be connected with a man who used great gifts to obscure the truth." The curl of the tail, the snarl of lip, the gleam of the teeth, the art of elegant feigning all go back a long way and persist well into this day. All depends on what our trickery is in service of: the welfare of our family/community/living world, or the deathly glamour of self-aggrandizement. Some of our antics stoop lower than any ape would deign to go; some play Kokopelli music and entrance everyone in the vicinity. What potentials lurk in the hearts of humankind? The shadow knows.

Nelson Algren wrote wisely and musically of small-time hustlers, carnival workers, minor con men: "Born on the hooks and looking for prey, they were all fly-by-nighters and hustling rogues, hip to the lay and the hold out box: accomplices in putting the bends or playing the humps." Algren's use of hustler lingo is poetry, but it is more than sounds—it is knowing. "They'd caught early-on to the Gypsy switch. Yet when hit with the swag when the hooks were out, they could take a drop without hollering cop. They were no whit less honest for all that."[404] As poetic as the word music of Dylan Thomas and Seamus Heaney, Algren's American argot is full of savvy. In it you feel the sentiment Tennessee Williams evoked when he wrote "God bless all con men and hustlers and pitchmen who hawk their hearts on the street, all the two-time losers who're likely to lose once more."[405]

What is the meaning of Algren's lines? The two-bit carny games were rigged, sure. That's obvious to anyone with a pulse. But the dealers still had a basic decency. They didn't have the phoniness and pretenses of those who are strangers to themselves, lacking soul, but putting up a good front. The lovable hustlers keep alive some depths of soulful life, not investing everything in the masks, wardrobes, and props of their public personas. There is "honor among thieves," and respect among parasites ("name me someone who's not a parasite and I'll go out and say a prayer for him"[406]); and so self-respecting carnies can look themselves in the face in the mirror. And it is popular demand that stimulates their come-ons and hype, their front-man routines and displays. As Algren wrote, "[T]hough they pitched their tents on the very same lots where, but a year before, they'd sheared the rubes and flapped the jays, flimflammed them at the jam auctions and suckered them at three-card monte . . . their tents were hardly pitched before the rubes were jostling each other to try again: crawling under the flaps for the chance of being sheared, suckered, conned, hooked, fleeced and flimflammed one more time."[407] In that single sentence, Algren expresses the perennial allure, America's romance with con artists. We could translate it this way: "You gotta love the decent trickster living by his wits because he's charming as life itself and he is us. He gives an illusion of a chance, enjoyable in itself." We like stories of con artists; they're fascinating, entertaining, and they make life interesting. They attract us and teach us things. They reflect the playful twists of our own vitality, the play of conscious/unconscious intelligence in our souls. Just as the word "cunning" is from the Norse *kunna*, to know, the original meaning of cunning was "possessing knowledge and skill." The sense of deceitfulness came into the meaning of cunning in late Middle English usage. Our deeper intelligence is a shrewdness, a quiet cunning we are not always aware of.

A reward of considering tricksters, as we have been doing here, is that we are not caught unawares when trickster bullies, tyrants, and regimes do not play by the rules. Forewarned is forearmed. Disillusioned, one's own integrity is not destroyed; purified or at least tribulated by experiences, it can be reborn in childlike caring and love. Wary, it is more realistic, wizened by depth, fortified by the life-spirit's soulful necessities. It knows the dangers that lurk and can be more forearmed than wide-eyed innocence ever is. It trusts a deeper truth than the fickle ego and shifting desires. Aware of all the ways a craft can capsize, it values balance and alert vigilance. It is not caught off-guard, surprised by an inevitable shadow, or shattered by an alter ego.

I suppose that no serious attempt to examine tricksters these days would fail to note that in recent years the American ethos has changed. Some will say it was ever thus, but as someone who grew up in the decades after World War II the changes seem dramatic. Lee Siegel noted one aspect of the changes: "In our time of banker hustlers and Internet hustlers, of suckers and 'muppets,' it is unlikely that anyone associates happiness and dignity with working hard for a comfortable existence purchased with a modest income. Even what's left of the middle class disdains the middle-class life. Everyone wants infinite pleasure and fabulous riches."[408] It is a time of greater complexity and cynicism, of more temptations and seductions to self-centeredness.

There are tricksters in every psyche, and in every field of endeavor—some we can't do without. They allow amazing saves when we have painted ourselves into a corner. But some would ruin everything, and give no apology, if allowed. The trickster is as the trickster does, because because because. There will always be plenty of tricksters in America. Damon Runyan's warning is wide: don't bet against a con man, especially when his angle seems far-fetched. Kokopelli is never far away; Coyote's out there in the dusky distance with the wildcat, the joker and the thief, and he's in every psyche where a shadow plays games. And as Coyote says, "We all are foolish and wise. Embrace your inner fool. It is your inner fool who will believe you can do things you couldn't possibly do."[409] Don't confine yourself to a one-sided view of yourself; you are always part of deeper processes, soul is always more and more.

The thief of complacency and partiality, the gifter of realizations and fulfillment, the mystery of cunning,[410] and the emblem of survivance, the trickster is as the trickster does and undoes. The trickster flourishes, he ties himself in knots and then escapes. The trickster vanishes, leaving few clues in his wake, like the after-image of jagged lightning, or Kokopelli's silent song. Then he returns to see if he can find himself. Then he remembers himself and poof! "Yo! How'd he do that?" Where will the howling loon pop up next? Will he surface next at Lake Pontchartrain, Mount St. Helens, the Green Mountains, or the Black Hills? Palm Beach, Times Square, Golden Gate Bridge, in Congress or at the White House? He's coming out of the woodwork, fooling around all over the place, tickling funny bones, getting laughs, making headlines, disappearing into the shadows. You can't live with the trickster and you can't live without him either, you rascal you.

NOTES

1. Edgar Allan Poe, "Diddling Considered as One of the Exact Sciences," *The Works of the Late Edgar Allan Poe*, volume 4 (New York: J. S. Redfield, 1856), 267. Also available at http://www.eapoe.org/WORKS/tales/diddlngc.htm.

2. Ralph Ellison called America "a land of masking jokers." Cited by Gary Lindberg, *The Confidence Man in American Literature* (New York: Oxford University Press), 250. Gore Vidal called America "a sanctimonious society of hustlers." See "The Education of Gore Vidal," *American Masters* series, season 17, episode 8, 2003.

3. The word "trick" comes from Middle English *trik*, from Old Northern French *trique*, cognate with *trikier*, meaning "to deceive, to cheat." It means, among other things, a crafty procedure or practice meant to deceive or defraud, a mischievous act, a prank, an indiscretion, or childish action; an ingenious feat meant to puzzle or amuse, and a ploy to present a delusive appearance; a freakish act or frolic. It means both a stupid act, and a clever or adroit exploit (as in "tricks of the trade"); it means dexterous artifice, toy, or knick-knack.

4. Robert Bly, "Male Naivete and Giving the Gold Away," audio cassette of a talk given by Robert Bly, published in 1990. In the talk he says that when someone acts naive the universe has to trick him. The too-trustful youth doesn't hide his gold and so it gets stolen. A fool and his money are soon parted by the nearest trickster.

5. Felipe Fernandez-Armesto, *Amerigo: The Man Who Gave His Name to America* (New York: Random House, 2007). Fernandez-Armesto describes Vespucci as not studious enough to succeed as a diplomat, not prudent enough to be a great merchant, not competent enough to be an expert navigator, and not knowledgeable enough to be a reliable cosmographer—such a jack of no trades can nevertheless learn to make do with his wits.

6. B. A. Botkin, ed., *A Treasury of Mississippi River Folklore* (New York: Crown, 1955), 255–57.

7. Everett Dick, *The Lure of the Land: A Social History of the Public Lands from the Articles of Confederation to the New Deal* (Lincoln, NE: University of Nebraska Press, 1970).

8. J. Sterling Morton and Albert Watkins, *History of Nebraska from the Earliest Explorations of the Trans-Mississippi Region* (Lincoln, NE: Western Publishing and Engraving Company, 1918), 188. Available online at https://archive.org/details/historyofnebraskoomort. See also C. C. Rister, *Western America: The Exploration, Settlement,*

and Development of the Region Beyond the Mississippi (New York: Prentice-Hall, 1947), 307.

9. Oklahoma Historical Society's Encyclopedia of Oklahoma History and Culture website, http://digital.library.okstate.edu/encyclopedia/entries/B/BO005.html.

10. T. D. Allman, *Finding Florida: The True History of the Sunshine State* (New York: Atlantic Monthly, 2013).

11. Gary Lindberg, *The Confidence Man in American Literature* (New York: Oxford University Press, 1982), 5.

12. Ibid., 7. Mark Twain's *Huckleberry Finn* features "the Duke" and "the King" as characters who pretend they are rulers temporarily away from their rightful thrones. They are tarred and feathered when caught by angry townsfolk they've cheated. H. L. Mencken, an insightful thinker about American swindles, saw Twain's great novel as a tale showing America's wildly funny shadow world, where democracy is "the worship of jackals by jackasses." H. L. Mencken, *A Little Book in C Major (Opus 11)* (New York: John Lane, 1916), 43.

13. Lindberg, *The Confidence Man*, 294.

14. For the text of the story access http://www.readbookonline.net/readOnLine/1827/.

15. See also John G. Blair, *The Confidence Man in Modern Fiction* (New York: Harper & Row, 1979). Blair includes a discussion of Herman Melville's landmark novel *The Confidence-Man* ("... life in Melville's mature view, is an elaborate masquerade in which any unmasking only reveals a further mask" [50]). Blair also discusses Kurt Vonnegut's novel *Cat's Cradle* (New York: Dell, 1988).

16. Perhaps out of a sense of realism, Benjamin Franklin saw commerce as cheating; if the merchant is a thief it is only natural to justify and idealize theft. Norman O. Brown, *Hermes the Thief: The Evolution of a Myth* (Great Barrington, MA: Lindisfarne, 1990), 82.

17. *Ocean's Twelve* is a sophisticated heist film in which a number of con jobs identified by odd nicknames are mentioned: the "Smuggler's Paradise," "Hell in a Handbasket," "Swinging Priest," "Soft Shoulder," "Crazy Larry," "Baker's Dozen," and "Lookie-Loo with a Bundle of Joy."

18. See "Confidence trick" at http://en.wikipedia.org/wiki/Confidence_trick. Some colonists were con artists; already in the 1600s some counterfeited wampum. See Ernest Ingersoll, "Wampum and Its History," *The American Naturalist*, 17:5 (May 1883) 467–79. There is sometimes an assumption that the urge to deceive and cheat is greatest in rootless people, such as gypsies. It is assumed that the craftsman chiseling wood or stone all day in his own workshop has less of an urge to chisel money from his neighbors, but this may be a romanticized view. There are honest vagabonds, and stay-at-home deceivers.

19. John Locke, *Two Treatises of Government, The Second Treatise*, published in 1690. Sec. 49. "Thus in the beginning all the World was America, and more so than that is now; for no such thing as Money was any where known. Find out something that hath the Use and Value of Money amongst his Neighbours, you shall see the same Man will begin presently to enlarge his Possessions." Available at "Discover John Locke," http://www.discoverjohnlocke.com/secondchapter05.html.

20. In myth, Anansi was a chieftain in what is today Ghana. He had spider qualities—could climb high in trees and swing from tree to tree. Once he climbed higher than ever before, arriving at the sky. There he climbed on a cosmic web into heaven, meeting High God Nyame, his father. He asked for wisdom. Nyame asked Anansi to make an offering to him in exchange for wisdom. Anansi offered his service to Nyame for as long as he lived. Anansi taught wisdom to his people, and this gave them culture and knowledge. Anansi, as son of the sky god, brings rains to stop forest fires, and determines the new borders of rivers and oceans after flood waters subside.

21. The Jackal in Dogon myth is called "God's mistake." In some ways he is like the rebel troublemaker Lucifer in Milton's poem, *Paradise Lost*. He is a trickster figure whose story describes how he went astray at the beginning of time. In some stories in prophetic religions, Satan is not eternally lost, but returns to the fold, forgiven, e.g., in the Qur'an. See Deldon Anne McNeely, *Mercury Rising: Women, Evil and the Trickster Gods* (Woodstock, CT: Spring, 1996), 25. It seems undeniable that "Suppression of pagan gods entailed a suppression of a particular kind of spiritual complexity." See Lewis Hyde, *Trickster Makes the World: Mischief, Myth and Art* (San Francisco: North Point, 1999), 183. When native peoples are Christianized by evangelicals, and Islamicized by fundamentalists, they are likely to forget how to appreciate the trickster of tribal traditions, losing some nuances, humor, and other humanizing qualities taught by the trickster stories.

22. Books on such trickster myths include William J. Hynes and William G. Doty, eds., *Mythical Trickster Figures: Contours, Contexts, and Criticisms* (Tuscaloosa, AL: University of Alabama Press, 1993); Richard Erdoes, ed., *American Indian Trickster Tales* (New York: Penguin/Putnam, 1999); and Robert D. Pelton, *Trickster in West Africa* (Berkeley, CA: University of California Press, 1980). In formative Western stories, David out-tricked Goliath, Ulysses tricked Cyclops, and the Greeks in the wooden horse out-tricked the Trojans.

23. Besides Hermes, there are other great tricksters in Western literature. Homer's Ulysses is wily and survives by defensive tricks, including protecting himself from the Sirens' songs and blinding Cyclops, who captured him. Merlin is a problem-solving mysterious wizard-trickster in Arthurian tales.

24. In stories, "magic happens on the threshold of the forbidden." Maria Tatar, *Secrets Beyond the Door: The Story of Bluebeard and His Wives* (Princeton, NJ: Princeton University Press, 2004), 11. The taboo stirs excitement, and the taboo breaker fascinates.

25. The term "archetype" may require some explanation. See appendix 1.

26. Carl G. Jung, *Psychological Reflections*, ed. Jolande Jacobi (New York: Harper & Row, 1961), 17.

27. For some basic ideas about archetypes in fiction, see Christopher Vogler, *The Writer's Journey: Mythic Structure for Writers* (Studio City, CA: Michael Wiese Productions, 1998).

28. Carl Jung explored the elusive subject of archetypes insightfully. "Archetypes resemble the beds of rivers: dried up because the water has deserted them, though it may return at any time. An archetype is something like an old watercourse along which the water of life flowed for a time, digging a deep channel for itself. The longer it flowed the deeper the channel, and the more likely it is that sooner or later the water will return." Jung, *Psychological Reflections*, 36. In Freudian terms, the id is a kind of trickster—impulsive, childish, goofy, playing around in youthful folly. But the child is not skilled in

looking from another's view; the practiced trickster can do this, playing around beyond himself. Many people have a limiting quality of the autistic child—they go blank when trying to imagine the subjective views of others. The trickster often artfully tunes in to others' thoughts to get a manipulative advantage.

29. James Hillman's work characterizing qualities of archetypes is also helpful: archetypes are "the deepest patterns of psychic functioning, the roots of the soul governing the perspectives we have of ourselves and the world . . . Like invisible crystals in solution or form in plants that suddenly show forth under certain conditions, patterns of instinctual behavior." "Essential to the notion of archetypes [is] their emotional possessive effect, their bedazzlement of consciousness so that it becomes blind to its own stance . . . The archetypal perspective offers the advantage of organizing into clusters or constellations a host of events from different areas of life." Unless we are intrigued by the trickster, the charm and complex power of the image eludes us. Hillman, *A Blue Fire* (New York: Harper Perennial, 1991), 23–25.

30. Ibid., 26.

31. Natalie Angier describes these kinds of ploys and other scams of nature in "The Art of Deception," *National Geographic*, August 2009, 70–87. The praying mantis is another example of trickiness. It is as green as any leaf, and can stand still and ambush other creatures that come close. It can hold them tight in its forelegs, and slash them. It can seem to be big by opening its wings. It can move like a leaf in the wind. The female is a cannibal who bites off the male's head while they are joined together. It can move its head around almost 360 degrees. See also Robert Trivers, *The Folly of Fools: The Logic of Deceit and Self-Deception in Human Life* (New York: Basic, 2011), esp. Chapter 2, "Deception in Nature," 29–51. Trivers includes such examples as tiny blister beetles who group together in the form of a female bee to attract a male bee, and plants that develop their own egg-shaped growths to discourage insects from depositing eggs on them.

32. Sometimes the Rock Island Line song is sung with an anecdote about a toll taker being tricked by the train man saying he was carrying livestock, when he was actually carrying pig iron. Lead Belly singing the song can be heard at https://www.youtube.com/watch?v=7iJEVOUqepo.

33. Some suggest that Paul Radin, who reported this strictness, may have been fooled by Winnebago trickster informers with this information. That would be a funny irony, if true. David McAllester and Mary Wheelwright, *The Myth and Prayers of the Great Star Chant and the Myth of the Coyote Chant* (Santa Fe, NM: Museum of Navajo Ceremonial Art, 1956).

34. Based on a telling of the story in Katherine Berry Judson, *Myths and Legends of the Pacific Northwest* (Lincoln, NE: University of Nebraska Press, 1997), 85.

35. Ibid., 40–41.

36. Ibid.

37. Thanks to my deceased colleague Professor Johnny Flynn, a Pottawattami spokesman and scholar of Native American studies at IUPUI, great storyteller, and wise man on all things Coyote.

38. Bill Reid and Robert Bringhurst, *The Raven Steals the Light* (Vancouver, BC: University of Washington Press, 1996), 17–24.

39. It is interesting to think about what kind of psyche and imaginal activity America's famous animals reveal. E.g., the eagle (which Benjamin Franklin argued should not

be chosen as America's emblem because it is a scavenger bird of prey); the elusive whale Moby Dick, pursued by the obsessive Captain Ahab; the haunting Raven of Poe's poem; the buffalo that was nearly made extinct by white men in the 1800s; the bear, a creature in many Indian stories, in a famous Faulkner novella, and now a favorite in children's literature, and in cuddly teddy bears. And Br'er Rabbit, Donald Duck, Mickey Mouse, Bambi the deer, Wily Coyote, Archie the cockroach, loyal Lassie, companionable Old Yeller, trustworthy Rin Tin Tin, cute Jiminy Cricket ("Let your conscience be your guide"), Daffy Duck, Road Runner, Tweety Bird, Woody Woodpecker, Snoopy, Yogi Bear, Jonathan Livingston Seagull, etc. Their animal intelligence, humor and energies, and their trickster traits, are considerable.

40. Paul Radin, *The Trickster: A Study in American Indian Mythology* (New York: Schocken, 1971), 120–21. For other Winnebago trickster stories see David Lee Smith, *Folklore of the Winnebago Tribe* (Norman, OK: University of Oklahoma Press, 1997), 33–101.

41. My novel, *Diving for Carlos* (Indianapolis: Sliding Floor, 2011), explores the theme of brothers in America on a few levels. Also, in modern lingo, male friendships are now called "bromances."

42. *The Tall Tales of Davy Crockett: The Second Nashville Series of Crockett Almanacs 1839-1841* (Knoxville, TN: The University of Tennessee Press, 1987).

43. John V. Young, *Kokopelli: Casanova of the Cliff Dwellers: The Hunchbacked Flute Player* (Palmer Lake, CO: Filter, 1990), 18.

44. Tony Guay writes, "The true origins of Kokopelli as the fluteplayer most likely come from the loud buzzing and whistling sounds the male cicada uses to attract females," which is like the use of the Hopi flute. Hopi legend tells of cicadas who played enchanting music on their flutes to heal their arrow-wounds. The fortuitous Maahu or cicada helped helping Hopis thrive in this world. See Guay, "Profile of a God: Kokopelli," *Catalyst Magazine*, May 2007, http://www.catalystmagazine.net/regulars/profile-of-a-god/profile-of-a-god-kokopelli.html. "The name 'Kokopelli' is probably derived from combining 'Koko,' a Hopi and Zuni deity, and the word 'pelli,' a Hopi word for the desert robber fly, which sports a large proboscis and curved back, and is known for zealous sexual proclivities." Thus the humpback musician figure is a visual pun. "Kokopelli," http://en.wikipedia.org/wiki/Kokopelli.

45. On the ironic transmutation of physical matter, consider this: in 1776 revolutionary forces in New York melted a statue of King George III, because they needed the metal to make bullets to shoot at the king's soldiers. Transmutable matters can be used against the forces that control them, if the need is great and the trickster spirit of ingenuity and skill is alive and well. In Indianapolis there is a sculpture of Martin Luther King, Jr., and Robert Kennedy, made from melted-down guns, symbolic of King's message of nonviolence.

46. Constance Rourke, *The Roots of American Culture* (New York: Harcourt Brace and World, 1942), 117.

47. Ibid., 118.

48. "The Contrast" is accessible online at http://www.gutenberg.org/etext/554. Jonathan calls himself a "son of liberty" more than once.

49. Rourke, *The Roots of American Culture*, 19.

50. In England in the mid-eighteenth century, fops who mixed French and Italian styles with English fashions were called "macaronis." ("Macaroni poetry" combined English and Latin words to make a cleverly comic effect. Exaggerated hairstyles, effeminate clothing, eccentric tastes in food, wine, and sexuality were associated with the macaronis.) In the "Yankee Doodle" song the idea was that the American was such a provincial rube that he thought the mere sporting of a feather in a hat would be a sign of a macaroni's modish attire, his refinement and European sophistication. Visually, "macaroni" a suggests a fancy dish of quirky curlicues, unruly rigamarole twists.

51. Another Jonathan—Johnny Appleseed—outsmarted Indians on the warpath; submerged in a pond, he breathed through his exposed nose, and none could detect his presence. In folk memories he had remarkable abilities to endure pain, understand animals, heal the sick, etc.

52. Rourke, *The Roots of American Culture*, 116–117.

53. Ibid., 120.

54. Ibid., 129. In "The Contrast," Jonathan has a satirical take on the theater.

55. Marjorie Tallman, *Dictionary of American Folklore* (New York: Philosophical Library, 1959), 322.

56. Ralph Waldo Emerson, "Self-Reliance," *The Selected Writings of Ralph Waldo Emerson* (New York: The Modern Library, 1968), 162. The ambidextrous, multi-talented New England lad is of course not the only regional origin for this personality type of versatility. Various southerners, westerners, and Canadians like John Kenneth Gailbraith, who became an American, qualify too.

57. Ferdinand Lundberg, in *America's Sixty Families* (New York: Vanguard, 1938), researched the American economy in the 1930s and concluded that a group of trickster magnates and crooked financiers had formed a "plunderbund" to exploit the public. Using underhanded schemes they amassed fortunes, while the poor felt lucky to get by on a shoestring.

58. To hear "The Ballad of Davy Crockett" sung by Fess Parker go to https://www.youtube.com/watch?v=txcRQedoEyY.

59. *The Tall Tales of Davy Crockett*, xxvi.

60. Another "big man" is the flat-boat river-man Mike Fink, whom Crockett described as "half horse and half alligator." The legendary Fink was a big bully and braggart who performed tricks with his rifle; he and daredevil friends gambled, shooting bottles balanced on each other's heads.

61. *The Tall Tales of Davy Crockett*, xviii-xix.

62. Ibid., 4.

63. Bob Thompson, *Born On A Mountaintop: On The Road with Davy Crockett and the Ghosts of the Wild Frontier* (New York: Crown, 2013), explores reasons the legend of Davy Crockett has endured.

64. Will Ferguson, "Canada's Black Heart," *New York Times*, July 18, 2007.

65. Moses Coit Tyler, *History of American Literature* (New York: G. P. Putnam's Sons, 1879), 164.

66. William Babcock Weeden, *Creating Indian Money as a Factor in New England Civilization* (Baltimore: Johns Hopkins University, 1884), 15.

67. The author's pen name was "Philanthropist" and his book was titled *An Account of... Ransford Rogers...* (Newark, NJ: Printed by John Woods, 1792), 15.

68. Ibid.

69. Anonymous, "Salem, May 5. An Impostor," *Massachusetts Spy, or Worcester Gazette*, vol. XXX, issue 1466, May 13, 1801, 3.

70. "From a New York Paper, A New Velocipede," *Farmer's Repository*, vol. XII, issue 585, June 6, 1819, 2.

71. Nelson Algren, *Chicago: City on the Make*, 50th anniversary edition (Chicago: University of Chicago Press, 2001), 11–12. Long before Algren used the term "on the make," Chicago social worker Jane Addams said Chicago was a city "on the make" in chapter two of her book *Democracy and Social Ethics* (New York: MacMillan, 1902).

72. Tallman, *Dictionary of American Folklore*, 21–22.

73. One punishment sometimes used was the "water cure," which involved pouring water into the nose and lungs, like modern waterboarding. See Douglas A. Blackmon, *Slavery by Another Name* (New York: Doubleday, 2008), 347.

74. Ibid., 348.

75. "Parker eventually found the world he was most comfortable in as a carny, working hustles along the midway on the Southern circuit and reveling in the knowledge that he was part of an elite brotherhood put on earth to fleece the rubes." Despite Parker's humble beginnings as Bible salesman, and concocter of odd schemes, he was a survivor. He ran into difficulties with the police in Tampa when he buried a pony's forelegs in the earth and charged a dime for people to see the smallest pony in the world. He ran a pet cemetery, and then became an advance man promoting performers' concerts. Eventually he became "the engineer on the Elvis Presley gravy train." Fred Goodman, "Without You I'm Nothing," review of *The Colonel*, by Alanna Nash, *New York Times*, August 24, 2003. Parker became legit promoting Elvis, but according to some he always retained the aura of a successful con man gaming the system.

76. Leslie Katz, *The Bitch-Goddess Success: Variations on an American Theme* (New York: Eakins, 1968).

77. Acts of warfare can also use misdirection, such as unexpected noises or visual tricks, to confuse or distract from what is actually going on.

78. The character Hardeen in the TV series *Boardwalk Empire*, season 1, episode 11.

79. The Greek trickster god Hermes is associated with commercial culture, which, taken to extremes, can become acquisitive individualism run riot. Unscrupulous American capitalism of a century ago was largely concerned with making as much money as possible, something like some corner-cutting, unscrupulous Chinese and Russian capitalist ventures today.

80. Karen Halttunen, *Confidence Men and Painted Women* (New Haven, CT: Yale University Press, 1986), 6ff.

81. Pope Brock, *Charlatan: America's Most Dangerous Huckster* (New York: Crown, 2008).

82. For further information see Halttunen, *Confidence Men and Painted Women*.

83. In this scheme, investments are gathered for a nominal project, then further investments taken in are used to repay the original investors, and many more investors

are gulled into investing more funds, with which the con man absconds. E.g., Bernie Cornfeld (1927–1995) ran a Ponzi scheme garnering investments of 2.5 billion dollars.

84. "Swindling" denotes "a transaction where the guilty party procures the delivery to him, under a pretended contract, of the personal property of another, with the felonious design of appropriating it to his own use." See *The 'Lectric Law Library's Lexicon*, http://www.lectlaw.com/def2/s214.htm.

85. For a list of some con men of American literature, films and TV, see appendix 2.

86. Will Ferguson, "Canada's Black Heart," *New York Times*, July 18, 2007.

87. For stories about thimble-rigging, card-sharp tricks like bottom-dealing, false shuffling, and card-marking, see Botkin, ed., *A Treasury of Mississippi River Folklore*, 226–44.

88. The "mark" is so-called because a con artist would tap him on the shoulder after fleecing him, leaving a chalk mark identifying him for the next con man. This was something like the hobos' trick of leaving signs marked in chalk at doors and other places to show where a generous handout could be received.

89. To get "punked" means to be pranked, have a practical joke pulled on you, to be fooled by a funny trickster. In a more serious sense, to be punked means being harmed by a hustle, robbed, mistreated, harassed, etc. "Punked" derives from prison slang; in that argot, a "punk" is a vulnerable prison inmate who is victimized, forced to submit to homosexual sex.

90. The blessing scam targets elderly Chinese women, and it plays on fears and superstitions in Chinese culture. It is operated in Chinatowns, such as the one in San Francisco.

91. In this multi-state fraud a scammer calls on the telephone, claiming to be a jury coordinator, saying the person being called is under arrest for dereliction of duty. If the person called insists he did not receive a summons in the mail calling him to jury duty, he is asked for his Social Security number and date of birth, to verify that information so that the arrest warrant can be cancelled. The scammer than uses the information to steal the person's identity. See http://www.FBI.gov/page2/june06/jury_scams060206.htm.

92. Affinity group frauds are perpetrated upon ethnic, religious, and social groups. For example, a scamster may target members of predominantly African American churches, or immigrants from Korea, Latin America, or the Philippines, or members of a profession. After gaining the trust and friendship of people in the group, the confidence man betrays them, taking their savings and leaving them feeling horribly used and personally betrayed.

93. I have compiled these words describing tricks of con men from many sources. For a list describing some common scams see Wikipedia, "List of Confidence Tricks," http://en.wikipedia.org/wiki/List_of_confidence_tricks. Notable scams and confidence tricks included in the list are: the 2G spectrum scam; the art student scam; the badger game; bogus escrow; coin rolling scams; drop swindles; the embarrassing cheque scam; the fiddle game; the fodder scam; the foreclosure rescue scheme; the forex scam; the green goods scam; the Indian mining scam; intellectual property scams; the Kansas City shuffle; the long firm scam; the miracle cars scam; mock auction; patent safe; pump and dump; the reloading scam; the sick baby hoax; the strip search prank call scam; telemarketing fraud; the Thai gem scam; the Thai tailor scam; the Thai zig zag scam; the

Trojan horse; and the work-at-home scheme. See also Jason Kirsten, *The Art of Making Money: The Story of a Master Counterfeiter* (New York: Penguin/Gotham, 2009); Daniel Heller-Roazen, *Dark Tongues: The Art of Rogues and Riddlers* (New York: Zone, 2013); Daniel Heller-Roazen, "Learn to Talk in Beggars' Cant," *New York Times*, August 19, 2013.

94. To hear Tim Hardin sing this song go to https://www.youtube.com/watch?v=-bW6VZi0ICs. Humans may learn to prefer a fancy dance of sneaky fake outs over the plain and simple truth. "A man who calls a spade a spade is only fit to use one." The behaviors of dissembling are found in large-brained creatures—monkeys, chimpanzees, apes, and dolphins. See Natalie Angier, "A Highly Evolved Propensity for Deceit," *New York Times*, December 23, 2008.

95. For more see Sean P. Steele, *Heists, Swindles, Stickups, and Robberies that Shocked the World* (New York: Metro, 1995). Paul Gregory Kooistra, *American Robin Hoods: The Criminal as Social Hero* (Charlottesville, VA: University of Virginia Press, 1982). See also the bibliography at "Non-fiction Books about Outlaws," http://www.wright.edu/~martin.kich/Murder/OutNon.htm.

96. Tom Folsom, *The Mad Ones: Joe Gallo and the Revolution at the Edge of the Underworld* (New York: Weinstein, 2009).

97. Osama bin Laden was portrayed as a Robin Hood figure, a sympathetic "little guy" who was "sticking it to the man" in Calcutta street operas in 2003, expressing some Indians' anger at America, aroused in part because bin Laden championed Palestine and Kashmir, and because he spoke about sovereignty and dignity for oppressed people. NPR broadcast "The World," reported by Arun Rath, September 11, 2012.

98. Also playing on the theme of "it takes a trickster to know a trickster" is the TV series *White Collar*, in which a slick forger and scam artist who is out on parole helps the FBI solve cases.

99. See Dary Matera, *John Dillinger: The Life and Death of America's First Celebrity Criminal* (Cambridge, MA: Da Capo, 2005).

100. See the Walt Disney telling of the Johnny Appleseed story at https://www.youtube.com/watch?v=484AJlOnOnc.

101. Algren, *Chicago*, 20–21.

102. See David Lewis, *The Life and Adventures of David Lewis, the Robber and Counterfeiter* (Newville: C.D. Rishel, 1890). Online at http://www.archive.org/details/lifeadventuresofoolewi. And see Ben Tarnoff, *The Wicked Lives and Surprising Adventures of Three Notorious Counterfeiters* (New York: Penguin, 2011).

103. The ancient Taoist ideal of bending down the high and lifting up the low is like stringing Robin Hood's bow, in which the lower part of the bow bends up and the upper part bends down.

104. The Robin Hood Foundation, http://www.robinhood.org/.

105. Eric Hobsawm, *Bandits* (New York: The New Press, 2000). There are Robin Hood figures outside America too. The Taliban leader Mullah Omar became known as a kind of Afghan Robin Hood, gaining legendary status as the leader of a band of religious scholars who were intent on cleansing Kandahar, protecting the poor from powerful and brutal commanders riding roughshod over the region.

106. "Tricking (martial arts tricking) is the informal name of a relatively new underground alternative sport movement, combining martial arts, gymnastics, breakdancing, and other activities to create an 'aesthetic blend of flips, kicks, and twists.' It incorporates moves from different arts: the backflip from gymnastics, 540 kick from Taekwondo, butterfly twist from Wushu and double leg from Capoeira . . . [It] is recognizable by its flashy kicks, complex flips and twists, and its highly stylized movements which separate it from other arts. An individual who practices tricking is typically referred to as a 'trickster' or 'tricker.'" See http://en.wikipedia.org/wiki/Tricking. Consider also the art of Parkour.

107. "The superficiality of the American is the result of his hustling. It needs leisure to think things out; it needs leisure to mature. People in a hurry cannot think, cannot grow, nor can they decay. They are preserved in a state of perpetual puerility." Eric Hoffer, *The Passionate State of Mind* (New York: Harper & Row, 1954), 97. Hustling—hurrying, jostling, scamming, diddling—keeps life shallow, moving on to the next thing, never fathoming meanings.

108. The documentary *"Little Melvin" Williams and the Baltimore Hustle* (BET American Gangster series, October 17, 2007) shows the gambling activity of a real hustler who pulled himself up from poverty gambling on pool, dice, cards, and went on to selling heroin.

109. L. Jon Wertheim, "Jump the Shark," *New York Times*, November 24, 2007. "Pool hustlers are—or were—the kind of outlaws we root for, 'honorable swindlers' who usually dripped with charisma and eccentricity." Hollywood films such as *The Hustler* (1961) and *The Color of Money* (1986) portrayed them.

110. Horatio Alger's nineteenth-century novel heroes had names like Ragged Dick, Andy Grant, Frank Fowler the Cash Boy, Dan the Detective, Jerry the Backwoods Boy, Nelson the Newsboy, Young Captain Jack, Randy of the River, and Joe the Hotel Boy. Alger's biography suggests he had to reinvent himself by writing about self-made men after resigning from the ministry because of inappropriate relations with youths.

111. This is the argument McNeely makes in the book *Mercury Rising*. See also James Hillman, "Hermetic Intoxication" in *Mythic Figures* (New York: Spring, 2007), 259–75 for more recent examples of the archetypal signs of the trickster as Hermes active in the world today.

112. For more reflections on this see Appendix 3.

113. To paraphrase Terence McKenna, a society based on hierarchy, male dominance, accumulation of physical goods, suppression of the weak is problematic. McKenna suggests that ego-inflated people need a deconditioning from culture. "Culture is a scam, a shell game run by weasels for the amusement of rubes. If you don't want to be a weasel or a rube, you have to see how the shell game works, and what lies beyond the carnival midway of civilization." McKenna, "Language About the Unspeakable," part 1/6, February 1994, http://www.youtube.com/watch?v=6hv_TPlmjkQ.

114. Zeese Papanikolas, *Trickster in the Land of Dreams* (Omaha, NE: University of Nebraska Press, 1995), 3.

115. Washington residents and tourists cast more votes for Berry to be represented in wax than they did for Denzel Washington, Oprah Winfrey, Halle Berry, Marilyn Monroe, Cal Ripken, Al Gore, Carl Bernstein, Martin Sheen, and Nancy Reagan. Ariel Sabar, "A Vote to Immortalize a Former Mayor for Life," *New York Times*, August 9, 2007.

116. See Susan Wise Bauer, *The Art of the Public Grovel: Sexual Sin and Public Confession in America* (Princeton, NJ: Princeton University Press, 2008).

117. Thomas Powers, *The Man Who Kept the Secrets* (New York: Knopf, 1979).

118. FUBAR means "Fucked Up Beyond All Recognition." NOYFB means "None of Your Fucking Business."

119. G. Gordon Liddy is still seen today, bald, with a dyed mustache, pitching spiels for gold. He looks like a skinhead in a large Brooks Brothers suit, as famous as Bon Ami or Mr. Clean, an American icon with something to hustle.

120. See for example, Joe Cummins, *Anything for a Vote: Dirty Tricks, Cheap Shots and October Surprises in Presidential Campaigns* (Philadelphia: Quirk, 2007).

121. See http://www.boogiemanfilm.com/.

122. "Lee Atwater," Wikipedia, http://en.wikipedia.org/wiki/Lee_Atwater. See also John Joseph Brady, *Bad Boy: The Life and Politics of Lee Atwater* (New York: Da Capo, 1996).

123. Perhaps this led to people in the George W. Bush administration saying they were the ones who would "create reality." A senior aide from the administration told journalist Ron Suskind, "We're an empire now, and when we act, we create our own reality. And while you're studying that reality . . . we'll act again, creating other new realities, which you can study too, and that's how things will sort out. We're history's actors . . . and you, all of you, will be left to study what we do." Suskind, "Without a Doubt," *The New York Times Magazine*, October 17, 2004. http://www.nytimes.com/2004/10/17/magazine/17BUSH.

124. For the sources of the various quotes and facts cited in this paragraph, see *Boogie Man: The Lee Atwater Story*, aired on PBS on *Frontline* in November 2008, and available as a DVD.

125. Lenin is often credited with the saying, "A lie told often enough becomes the truth." William James is credited with, "There's nothing so absurd that if you repeat it often enough, people will believe it." I have not found written sources for the origins of the sayings.

126. See George Packer, *The Unwinding: An Inner History of the New America* (New York: Macmillan, 2013). See the chapter "Total War: Newt Gingrich" in Part One.

127. Cover-ups are a type of tricky suppressive activity deserving a category all its own. The Watergate cover-up, the cover-up by Army brass of Pat Tillman's death by friendly fire, the silencing of whistleblowers, CIA destruction of tapes of interrogations, the deleting of emails, the shredding of memos, the disappearance of documentary evidence, the vanishing of witnesses, loss of memories in legal cases, are examples of cover-up trickery.

128. Thomas Jefferson, letter to William S. Smith dated November 13, 1787, *The Papers of Thomas Jefferson*, vol. 12 (Princeton, NJ: Princeton University Press, 1955), 356.

129. For a useful list of federal political scandals in America see "List of political scandals in the United States," Wikipedia, http://en.wikipedia.org/wiki/List_of_federal_political_scandals_in_the_United_States.

130. Peter H. Stone, *Heist: Superlobbyist Jack Abramoff, His Republican Allies, and the Buying of Washington* (New York: Farrar, Straus and Giroux, 2006). Senator John McCain's Senate Indian Affairs Committee stated in a report that in exchange for a

small cut, Norquist's group "Americans for Tax Reform" served as a conduit channeling money from Abramoff's clients, enabling secret finance of lobbying campaigns without public scrutiny.

131. See Bill Moyers's *Capitol Crimes*, http://www.pbs.org/moyers/moyersonamerica/capitol/index.html. Transcript at http://www.pbs.org/moyers/moyersonamerica/print/capitolcrimes_transcript_print.html.

132. Jacques Barzun, *Lincoln's Philosophic Vision* (Gettysburg, PA: Gettysburg College Press, 1982), 19–20.

133. This line is in dispute. Lincoln gave a speech in Clinton, Illinois, September 1858, and these lines were not printed in a local newspaper text of the speech. But in 1919, two who said they'd been present at the speech nearly sixty years before, recalled hearing Lincoln say it.

134. Charles White, *The Life and Times of Little Richard: The Authorized Biography* (New York: Omnibus, 2003).

135. Tony Norman, "Bob Dylan, stuck inside of New Jersey," *Pittsburgh Post-Gazette*, August 18, 2009.

136. See the VH1 TV series *Behind the Music* and bio-pics of musicians for many examples.

137. For example, James Parish,*The Hollywood Book of Scandals* (New York: McGraw-Hill, 2004); Kenneth Anger, *Hollywood Babylon* (San Francisco: Straight Arrow, 1981); Laurie Jacobson, *Dishing Hollywood* (Nashville: Cumberland House, 2003); Graydon Carter, *Vanity Fair's Tales of Hollywood* (New York: Penguin, 2008); and Scott Siegal, Barbara Siegal et al., *The Encyclopedia of Hollywood* (New York: Facts on File, 2004).

138. Hoffer, *The Passionate State of Mind*, 99.

139. For example, McNeely in *Mercury Rising*. The trickster Eros in a man is more like a cupid than a Euclid: impulsive, playful, rough and tumble, improvising with what turns up, not perfectly rational, orderly or set in his ways.

140. See, for example, Robert D. San Souci, *Sister Tricksters: Rollicking Tales of Clever Females* (Little Rock, AR: August House, 2006). This children's book consists of eight stories from Southern folklore, retold from Anne Virginia Culbertson's out-of-print *At the Big House* published by Bobbs-Merrill in 1904.

141. Kathleen DeGrave, *Swindler, Spy, Rebel: The Confidence Woman in Nineteenth Century America* (Columbia, MO: University of Missouri Press, 1995).

142. A "fast trick" was a slang term meaning a sexually permissive woman.

143. See Wendy Doniger, *The Bedtrick: Tales of Sex and Masquerade* (Chicago: University of Chicago Press, 2000), for a variety of examples.

144. Joyce Carol Oates, *The Gravedigger's Daughter* (New York: Ecco, 2007).

145. Ibid., 446.

146. James Baldwin, *Another Country* (New York: Dial Press, 1962), 409.

147. Francois duc de La Rochefoucauld, *Maxims and moral reflections* (Calais, Lepoittevin-Lacroix, 1797). Online at https://openlibrary.org/books/OL23317999M/Maxims_and_moral_reflections. Maxims numbers 68, 69, 67, 73.

148. Famous examples of men whose infidelities made the news in recent years include Tiger Woods and Arnold Schwarzenegger. See Trivers, "Deceit, Self-Deception and Sex," in *The Folly of Fools*, 95–113.

149. S. L. Clemens (Mark Twain), letter to President Timothy Dwight, Yale University, June 26, 1888. Reprinted in the *Hartford Daily Courant*, June 29, 1888, 5.

150. *30 Rock*, season 4, episode 21. Written by Tina Fey, perhaps in collaboration with Tracy Morgan.

151. The comic Jerry Seinfeld says the best feeling in life is "not cheating" but doing stand-up comedy honestly, getting laughs with sheer wittiness, not manipulating audiences with technology, etc. Getting away with something with tricks often makes one feel precarious.

152. Lenny Bruce, for example, was harassed by the FBI, as was John Lennon; the Smothers Brothers were taken off the air. The Nixon administration was fearful of Lennon, an anti-establishment, anti-Vietnam war voice. Lennon's "Give Peace a Chance" became the anthem of the anti-war movement. The FBI saw Lennon as a dangerous trickster, too capable of using his music and his wits to stir sympathy for the cause of peace.

153. See Appendix 4 for more on the clown in America.

154. Henry Miller, *The Smile at the Foot of the Ladder* (New York: New Directions, 1975), 125. There are also clown jokes, such as, "They say penis size is related to shoe size. Which makes the fear of being raped by a clown that much scarier." Monkeys are also said to be afraid of clowns' bizarre appearances, their mystifying otherness.

155. Documents from Booth's life can be accessed at "FBI Files: John Wilkes Booth," http://www.theblackvault.com/article7887.html.

156. Todd Haynes believes Bob Dylan is all about "changing, transforming, killing off one Dylan and moving to the next, shedding his artistic skin to stay alive." Haynes wrote of "America obsessed with authenticity/authenticity the perfect costume/America the land of masks, costumes, self-transformation, creativity is artificial, America's about false authenticity and creativity." Quoted in Robert Sullivan, "This is Not a Bob Dylan Movie," *The New York Times Magazine*, October 7, 2007, 60, 65. A. O. Scott wrote, "[Dylan's] persona has been as inclusive as Walt Whitman's and as unsettlingly splintered as that of Herman Melville's Confidence Man." Scott, "Another Side of Bob Dylan, and Another, and Another . . .," *New York Times*, November 21, 2007.

157. For playing roles which seem to embody the Anima archetype, I would suggest the elegant shapeshifter Meryl Streep and the mischievous gamine Julia Roberts, as well as the smoldering beauty Angelina Jolie. *The Muse* (1999), with Sharon Stone, is also one of American cinema's great Anima portrayals. The soulful expressiveness of Giulietta Masina is an example of Anima, too.

158. David Denby, "Past Shock," *New York Times*, July 21, 2008. See also Jonathan Lethem, "Art of Darkness," *New York Times*, September 21, 2008. Lethem's insightful piece concludes, "I have no theory who Batman is—but the Joker is us."

159. A documentary about Wavy Gravy (Hugh Romney), peace activist and advocate for personal empowerment, and official clown of the Grateful Dead, is entitled *Saint Misbehavin'* (2006). The Bread and Puppet Theater's base and museum is in Glover, Vermont.

160. Brando's statement is found widely on the Internet, and was quoted in the 2014 Academy Awards show by Harrison Ford.

161. Juliet Macur, *Cycle of Lies: The Fall of Lance Armstrong* (New York: Harper, 2014).

162. Mark Bowden, "Sacks, Lies and Videotapes," *New York Times*, May 18, 2008.

163. Ibid.

164. Ibid.

165. Jonathan Abrams, "All-Star Acting Is Part of Game," *New York Times*, November 11, 2008.

166. See "Key & Peele: Futbol Flop," https://www.youtube.com/watch?v=o7mBfR8erMY.

167. In Norse mythology, the trickster Loki becomes a fiercely stinging fly, and harasses an elf blacksmith, preventing him from making a magic hammer.

168. *Philadelphia Inquirer*, February 20, 2009, http://www.philly.com/inquirer/world_us/39898667.html.

169. Jarrett Murphy, "Rush Limbaugh Arrested on Drug Charges," *CBS News*, April 28, 2006, http://www.cbsnews.com/news/rush-limbaugh-arrested-on-drug-charges/. Howard Kurtz, "Bill O'Reilly, Producer Settle Harrassmen Suit," *Washington Post*, October 29, 2004, http://www.washingtonpost.com/wp-dyn/articles/A7578-2004Oct28.html.

170. See Meghan Kennealy, "Glenn Beck regrets playing 'a role in helping tear the country apart' with his Fox New show," http://www.dailymail.co.uk/news/article-2544005/Glenn-Beck-regrets-playing-role-helping-tear-country-apart-Fox-News-show.html#ixzz2w3ku9xlY.

171. Lew Welch, "The Basic Con," in David Lehman, ed., *The Oxford Book of American Poetry* (New York: Oxford University Press, 2007), 803.

172. Pema Chodron, "Troublemakers," YouTube http://www.youtube.com/watch?v=m7qFi52FX1Q. One author writes: "I'll put Pema Chodron up as the greatest Buddhist teacher today . . . including the admittedly wonderful Thich Nhat Hanh and the . . . charismatic Dalai Lama . . . She does not show any interest in converting anyone to Buddhism, just in teaching us how to be gentler and to suffer less." See http://www.squidoo.com/pemachodron.

173. For interesting observations regarding ideas and language concerning excrement and genitals, see Steven Pinker, *The Stuff of Thought* (New York: Viking, 2007).

174. McNeely, *Mercury Rising*, 104.

175. David Sedaris spoke about this on Ira Glass's PBS radio program, *This American Life*, December 30, 2007.

176. See Daniel McGinn, "Don't Forget the Purell," *Newsweek*, October 20, 2008, E18.

177. Wikipedia, "Winchester Mystery House," http://en.wikipedia.org/wiki/Winchester_Mystery_House.

178. Hampton Sides, *Hellhound on His Trail* (New York: Doubleday, 2010). Lynette Mong wrote: "Sides traces the alter egos Ray created after escaping from prison and

beginning his haphazard journey toward Memphis," where Martin Luther King, Jr. was murdered. Sides describes Ray as "a nondescript loner with a spurious and violent history, whose identity was as fluid as his motives." From the Amazon.com review by Lynette Mong.

179. Quoted in Janet Semple, *Bentham's Prison: A Study of the Panopticon Penitentiary* (Oxford: Clarendon, 1993), 152.

180. Gerald Howard, "I know why Bret Easton Ellis hates David Wallace Foster," http://www.salon.com/2012/09/07/i_know_why_bret_easton_ellis_hates_david_foster_wallace//.

181. See Jeanne Rosier Smith, *Writing Tricksters: Mythic Gambols in American Ethnic Literature* (Berkeley, CA: University of California, 1997).

182. "Like the esthetic act, moral systems are wasteful in that they acquire to spend. Moral systems are . . . destructive . . ., they are liable to change and, in order to certify themselves, are forced to travel to their limit, expending energy value on the way. Upon arriving at their limit, moral systems decay . . . Therefore, history is not continuous, but a discrete system in that there must be a rejection of the past in order to invent the validity of the different present." Summary from a 1951 Bard College student newspaper quoted in David Lehman, "Paul de Man: The Plot Thickens," *The New York Times*, May 24, 1992.

183. See James Atlas, "The Case of Paul de Man," *New York Times*, August 28, 1988.

184. Many say he was guilty of chicanery. E.g., Christine Smallwood in a *Harper's* magazine review of Evelyn Barish's *The Double Life of Paul de Man* called de Man "a slippery Mr. Ripley, a confidence man, and a hustler who embezzled, lied, forged, and arreared his way to intellectual acclaim." *Harper's*, March 2014, 77–78. Joyce Carol Oates in a March 2014 tweet wrote that "Paul de Man and Yale literary theorists erected a barrier of language/jargon to establish a priestly elite." De Man's friend Jacques Derrida defended him, and his former student Peter Brook called attention to the poor scholarship in Barish's biography. See Louis Menand's excellent article "The De Man Case," *The New Yorker*, March 24, 2014, 87–93.

185. Julie Bosman, "Parodist of Goldman Finds a New Publisher," *New York Times*, March 20, 2014.

186. Edgar Allan Poe wrote that the ambitious man's "road to immortal renown lies straight, open, unencumbered before him. All that he has to do is write and publish a very little book. Its title should be simple—a few plain words—'My Heart Laid Bare.' But—this little book must be true to its title. No man dare write it. No man could write it, even if he dared. The paper would shrivel and blaze at every touch of the fiery pen." The truth of this insight about human nature is as valid today as when Poe wrote it. See J. Gerald Kennedy, ed., *The Portable Edgar Allan Poe* (New York: Penguin, 2006), 601.

187. For information and quotes in this paragraph, See "Barefoot Bandit gets 7 years for crime spree," http://www.msnbc.msn.com/id/45696590/ns/us_news-crime_and_courts/t/barefoot-bandit-gets-years-crime-spree/#.TwTXlUrlXqo.

188. See for example http://thecomplexchrist.typepad.com/thecomplex_christ/index.html.

189. John Leland, "Psychedelia's Middle-Aged Head Trip," *New York Times*, November 18, 2001.

190. See the Wikipedia entry for "Poster Boy," http://wiki/Poster_Boy_(street_artist), and Randy Kennedy, "Poster Boy Is Caught, Or Is It A Stand In?," *New York Times*, February 4, 2009.

191. To discern the real wolves in sheep's clothing requires investigation. Some say that when Jerry Falwell took over Jim and Tammy Bakker's PTL empire it was a case of cunning trumping scheming. Belief is partly wanting to believe, and sincerely fooling oneself is possible.

192. The "Travelers" constitute a small clan of itinerant Irish gypsies. They travel America in R.V.s, and are said to rely on cons like house repair schemes, etc., to support themselves.

193. James Baldwin, *Collected Essays* (New York: The Library of America, 1998), 269, 300.

194. The teachings of the Nation of Islam put an end to that sensibility of Malcolm Little: "Every instinct of the ghetto jungle streets, every hustling fox and criminal wolf instinct in me, which would have scoffed at and rejected anything else, was struck dumb." *The Autobiography of Malcolm X*, Malcolm X with Alex Haley (New York: Ballantine, 1973), 387, 163. Of course being associated with the mean streets and tough life has a valuable panache, and may be cultivated by those in the public eye to convey a charismatic image and street cred.

195. Albert Murray, *From the Briarpatch File: On Context, Procedure, and American Identity* (New York: Pantheon, 2001), 4.

196. "Introduction to the Imposter syndrome," http://www.counseling.caltech.edu/articles/The%20Imposter%20Syndrome.htm. There are also examples of other kinds of complex double lives. Clarence King, born in a distinguished Rhode Island family, was white and lived a bachelor's life as an accomplished nineteenth-century explorer and scientist, but simultaneously passed for a black man, married to a black woman. Martha Sandweiss, *Passing Strange: A Gilded Age Tale of Love and Deception Across the Color Line* (New York: Penguin, 2009).

197. Some names in themselves have a trickster resonance, such as "Hell's Angels" and "Merry Pranksters." "Bankster" is a portmanteau word combining "gangster" and "banker," used to describe those involved in crooked banking practices.

198. Nate Blakeslee, *Tulia: Race, Cocaine, and Corruption in a Small Texas Town* (New York: Public Affairs, 2005).

199. Jennifer Steinhauer, "Arizona: Sex Offender Plea Deal," *The New York Times*, September 11, 2008.

200. Malcolm Gladwell, "In Plain View," *The New Yorker*, September 16, 2012, http://www.newyorker.com/arts/critics/atlarge/2012/09/24/120924crat_atlarge_gladwell#ixzz26kGMmzvs.

201. There have been numerous anthrax scares in America since 9/11. For example, in February, 2009, a man upset that he had lost over $60,000 because of a bank failure, was arrested in New Mexico for sending sixty-four threatening letters containing a white powder to financial institutions and federal regulatory offices in eleven states. Stephanie Simon, "New Mexico Man Charged in White-Powder Mailings," *Wall Street Journal*, February 4, 2009.

202. Eric Lichtblau, "Attacks on Homeless Are Rising, Many Simply Motivated by Thrill," *New York Times*, August, 2009.

203. Bernard Mandeville, *The Fable of the Bees: or, Private Vices, Public Benefits* (New York: Capricorn, 1963), 28.

204. See Paul Babiak and Robert D. Hare, *Snakes in Suits: When Psychopaths Go to Work* (New York: Regan/HarperCollins, 2007).

205. Algren, *Chicago*, 13–14. "Emotionally hollowed" conveys a sense of soullessness, lack of compassion, and numbness.

206. Devra Davis, *When Smoke Ran like Water: Tales of Environmental Deception and the Battle Against Pollution* (New York: Basic, 2002).

207. Peter Van Buren, *We Meant Well* (New York: Metropolitan, 2011).

208. Robert Booth and Meirion Jones, "UK Businessman Found Guilty. . .," http://www.guardian.co.uk/uk/2013/apr/23/somerset-business-guilty-fake-bombs. Jonathan Franzen, *Freedom* (New York: Farrar, Straus and Giroux, 2010).

209. James Risen and Mark Mazzetti, "30 False Fronts Won Contracts for Blackwater," *New York Times*, September 4, 2010.

210. For example, Ken Silverstein wrote an article demonstrating how Washington lobbyists work. Silverstein, undercover, pretended to be an intermediary hired by Turkmenistan authorities to improve the country's bad reputation. He met with various lobbyists and they promised to help accomplish his aims via leaders of both parties, fixing up meetings and photo-ops between those figures and leaders of Turkmenistan. They confided in him that they would use think tank personnel to distribute public relations spin favorable to Turkmenistan. Silverstein, "Their Men in Washington: Undercover with D.C.'s Lobbyists for Hire," *Harper's*, July 2007, 53–61.

211. Janet Malcolm, *The Journalist and the Murderer* (New York: Vintage, 1990).

212. McNeely, *Mercury Rising*, 20.

213. For example, financier Samuel Israel III. See Abha Bhattarai and Nelson Schwartz, "Ex-financier who faked death gives up after weeks on the run," *New York Times*, July 3, 2008. For the *Slate* article, see "Know Your Fugitive Financiers," http://www.slate.com/articles/news_and_politics/chatterbox/2001/02/know_your_fugitive_financiers.html.

214. Wikipedia, "Howe and Hummel," http://en.wikipedia.org/wiki/Howe_and_Hummel. For a book-length study see Richard H. Rovere, *Howe and Hummel* (New York: Farrar, Straus and Giroux, 1985).

215. "When Patents Attack," NPR's *This American Life*, July 23, 2011.

216. David Callahan, *The Cheating Culture: Why More Americans are Doing Wrong to Get Ahead* (New York: Houghton Mifflin Harcourt, 2004). Diane Ackerman lists a few market tricks used to attract our senses to products: "Panels help design just the right 'mouth feel' for new yogurts, the right crunch for potato chips, the right degree of pucker for lemon sorbet. Used-car dealers spray 'new car scent' in their vehicles. Malls waft 'eau de pizza' around the heads of hungry shoppers . . . Realtors bake bread or spray 'cake bake' around the kitchen before showing a house to a potential buyer." Ackerman, "Evolution's Gold Standard," *New York Times*, August 9, 2011.

217. Stephanie Strom, "Report Sketches Crime Costing Billions: Theft from Charities," *New York Times*, March 29, 2008.

218. See Bee Wilson, *Swindled: The Dark History of Food Fraud* (Princeton, NJ: Princeton University Press, 2008).

219. Janet Cappiello Blake and Bruce Schreiner, "Face is real; everything else is fake," Associated Press, February 28, 2011.

220. McAfee, a security vendor, estimated that 12 million computers were taken over during the first four months of 2009. Eighteen percent of these hijacked computers are in America, and 13 percent are in China. The security costs rise as the threat environment expands by about 40 percent each year. See "Security Considerations for Retail Systems OEMs," http://www.cmcafee.com/us/resources/solution-briefs/sb-intel-retail-system-oems.pdf. For constantly updated statistics about malware, see http://home.mcafee.com/virusinfo/regional.

221. See John Markoff, "Beware the Digital Zombies," *New York Times*, October 21, 2008. Internet scams and countermeasures include advance-fee fraud, Avalanche (phishing group), click fraud, CyberThrill, DarkMarket, domain slamming, email authentication, email fraud, El Gordo de la Primitiva Lottery International Promotions Programmes, employment scams, Internet vigilantism, lottery scam, phishing, referer spoofing, ripoff report, Rock Phish, romance scam, Russian Business Network, Safernet, scam baiting, ShadowCrew, spoofed URL, spoofing attack, stock generation, cramming (fraud), website reputation ratings, and whitemail.

222. Marc Santora, "In Hours, Thieves Took 45 Million in ATM Scheme," *New York Times*, May 10, 2013, http://www.nytimes.com/2013/05/10/nyregion/eight-charged-in-45-million-global-cyber-bank-thefts.html.

223. Quoted in Nina Burleigh, "Sexting, Shame and Suicide," *Rolling Stone*, September 26, 2013, 55.

224. Maureen Dowd, "Spying Run Amok," *New York Times*, December 18, 2013.

225. Hemingway famously said a writer needed "a built-in shit detector," noting that "This is the writer's radar and all great writers have had it." Hemingway interview by George Plimpton, *Paris Review*, http://www.theparisreview.org/interviews/4825/the-art-of-fiction-no-21-ernest-hemingway.

226. For example, the Bank of England released 100 billion dollars into the banking system in mid April 2008, in response to the credit crisis, to relieve the mortgage squeeze. The US Fed had already pumped 350 billion dollars into the banking system as of mid-April 2008.

227. NPR, *All Things Considered*, "Criminal Records No Bar in Florida Loan Business," July 22, 2008, http://www.npr.org/templates/story/story.php?storyId=92793930&ft=1&f=1006

228. See Appendix 5 for more on mortgage fraud and related swindles.

229. See the *Economist*'s "Crash Course" on this topic, "The Origins of the Financial Crisis," http://www.economist.com/news/schoolsbrief/21584534-effects-financial-crisis-are-still-being-felt-five-years-article.

230. Michael Lewis, *The Big Short: Inside the Doomsday Machine* (New York: W. W. Norton, 2010). See also James Kwak, "Causes: Subprime Lending," *Dateline*, http://www.nbcnews.co/id/29827248/ns/dateline_nbc-the_hansen_files_with_chris_hansen/t/

if-you-had-pulse-we-gave-you-loan/#.VBIIfS-HfQM. On this piece one expert avers that signs of the subprime lending crisis were "visible early in 2007—it's impossible to say exactly when they were first visible, because some people had been warning of the problem for years, to little effect . . ." Among those who tried to alert financial authorities were Karen Weaver, top analyst at Deutsche, and Elizabeth Warren. For more background, see "Baseline Scenario," http://baselinescenario.com/2008/12/13/causes-subprime-lending/.

231. Stephen Mihm, "Dr. Doom," *The New York Times Magazine*, August 17, 2008, 29.

232. Hayes said this on *Countdown* with Keith Olbermann, MSNBC, September 19, 2008.

233. Farid Zakaria, "There is a silver lining," *Newsweek*, October 20, 2008, 28.

234. See Gillian Tett, *Fool's Gold: How the Bold Dream of a Small Tribe at J. P. Morgan Was Corrupted by Wall Street Greed and Unleashed a Catastrophe* (New York: Free Press, 2009).

235. Securities dealers are bundlers involved in a process of "securitization." They repackage mortgages, and sell them again as a "security" to a bank.

236. Ezra W. Zuckerman, "The Mail," *The New Yorker*, September 7, 2009, 7.

237. Joe Nocera, "Swept Up By Insanity of Markets," *New York Times*, October 11, 2008. The term "credit" derives from the Latin word for belief: *credo*. A system of faith, trust, confidence, an immense confidence network can grow beyond the actuality, then turn to doubt, loss of belief, panic.

238. Ira Glass's NPR episode, "The Giant Pool of Money" on *This American Life*, May 9, 2008, offers a summary of what happened in this American mortgage market fiasco that wreaked financial havoc worldwide.

239. Lincoln is quoted from his speech "The Perpetuation Our Political Institutions," in Roy P. Basler, ed., *The Collected Works of Abraham Lincoln* (New Brunswick, NJ: Rutgers University Press, 1953), 108. Tagore's quote comes from Amiya Chakravarty, ed., *A Tagore Reader* (Boston: Beacon, 1971), 272. Here is another example: ". . . Eisenhower understood that misguided national priorities that place military expansion and unchecked cronyism above other vital aspects of our national life condemn us to 'destroy from within what we are trying to protect from without.' He argued that crises must be met not by spectacular and costly exercises of radical governance but through a consistent commitment to 'balance in and among national programs.' This requires a holistic understanding of what makes a nation strong." Eugene Janeki, "BigGameHunt.net," http://www.biggamehunt.net/forums/viewtopic.php?t=18840.

240. Riva Richmond, "Online Scammers Target the Jobless," *New York Times*, August 6, 2009.

241. Roy Furchgott, "With Software, Till Tampering is Hard to Find," *New York Times*, August 30, 2008.

242. See Misha Glenny, *McMafia: A Journey Through the Global Criminal Underworld* (New York: Alfred A. Knopf, 2008). See also Moises Naim, *Illicit: How Smugglers, Traffickers, and Copycats are Hijacking the Global Economy* (New York: Doubleday, 2005).

243. Stephanie Schlosser, "Burger with a Side of Spies," *New York Times*, May 7, 2008.

244. "Short-selling" or "shorting" occurs when someone sells a financial instrument that he does not actually own, in hopes of buying it later at a lower price. Shorting is betting that a venture will fail. Hedge funds use short-selling like insurance, making payoffs when bad things happen in business ventures. Short-sellers thus profit from an expected decline in the price of a stock or bond. The short-seller usually borrows or temporarily "rents" the securities, which are to be sold, and then after a time, he buys identical securities to return to the lender. If the security price declines as the seller expects, the short-seller makes money later from the sale of the borrowed securities at a higher cost than he paid for them. "Shorting" differs from usual investment deals, in which the investor "goes long," buying a security expecting that in the course of time the price will rise.

245. A company in Phoenix (Mini-Me ModelWorks), in February 2009 began marketing a "Smash me Bernie doll" for angry investors to vent their rage on. The $99.95 doll, in a red devil suit and holding a pitchfork, came with a golden hammer to smash it.

246. Frank Rich, "Some Things Don't Change in Grover's Corners," *New York Times*, March 7, 2009.

247. Zachary Kouwe, "Waiting for Madoff, Angry Crowd is Disappointed," *The New York Times*, June 30, 2009. In March 2014 five of Madoff's employees were convicted also. Others who bilked the public in recent years include Shalom Weiss, who in 2000 was sentenced to 845 years in prison for cheating National Heritage Life Insurance Company of 125 million dollars; Bernard J. Ebbers, who was sentenced to 25 years in 2005 for his 11-billion- dollar fraud in WorldCom accounting records; Jeffrey Skilling, who in 2006 received a 24.3 year sentence for his fraud at Enron; and Dennis Kozlowski, who in 2005 was sentenced from 8 to 25 years for his deceptive practices at Tyco.

248. Ibid. Could it be that all the public personas we grow, devise, borrow, and alter—as singers, actors, politicians, and charismatic wheeler-dealers, etc.—can be seen as tricks we resort to *because we can't be who we want to be in everyday life?* Each individual at play on the social stage has an ego that is capable of self-trickery by constructing a public image that is antisocial. We all have anxieties and the need to prove ourselves. Sometimes we lose our bearings, and will do anything to appear successful, even if it makes for a precarious situation, teetering along smiling for a day at a time, passing ourselves off as what we wish we could be.

249. Michael Zuckoff, *Ponzi's Scheme: The True Story of a Financial Legend* (New York: Random House, 2005). Ponzi's scheme involved fifteen million dollars. Ivar Kreuger worked out a scheme much larger than Ponzi's; Kreuger's crashed in 1929. See Frank Partnoy, *The Match King: Ivar Kreuger, the Financial Genius Behind a Century of Wall Street Scandals* (New York: Public Affairs, 2009). Brooklyn bookkeeper William Miller in 1899 swindled investors out of many thousands of dollars of their life savings, an amount that would be the equivalent of 25 million dollars in 2012.

250. Plato, *The Republic*, translated by Benjamin Jowett (Oxford: Clarendon, 1894) Book III, 413c.

251. Michael Lewis, *Flash Boys* (New York: W. W. Norton, 2014).

252. John Tierney, "A Clash of Polar Frauds and Those Who Believe," *New York Times*, September 8, 2009.

253. I derived these examples from Kenneth Katkin, "Scientific Fraud," *Dictionary of American History,* http://www.encyclopedia.com/doc/1G2-3401803766.html.

254. For more on this topic see David Goodstein, *On Fact and Fraud: Cautionary Tales from the Front Lines of Science* (Princeton, NJ: Princeton University Press, 2010); *P. B. Medawar: The Threat and the Glory* (New York: HarperCollins, 1990); and William Broad and Nicholas Wade, *Betrayers of the Truth* (New York: Simon & Schuster, 1982).

255. Blaise Pascal, *The Miscellaneous Writings of Pascal*, (London: Longman, Brown, Green, and Longman, 1849), "Miscellaneous Thoughts," XC, 221. Rochefoucauld, in *Maxims and moral reflections*, wrote interesting reflections on self-love in maxim numbers 394–403. The trickiness of self-love, which of necessity is often concealed from us by repression or cunning, is a powerful hidden dynamic in humans. Like Pascal, Rochefoucauld was wary about man's fickle self and self-love's fluidity and endless disguises.

256. James Baldwin, *Collected Essays*, 668.

257. Ray Bradbury, "We have our arts so we won't die of truth," in *Zen in the Art of Writing* (Santa Barbara, CA: Capra, 1990), 151.

258. Johnny P. Flynn, "Becoming Coyote: How Indians survive the Columbus lie," *The Bloomington Alternative* newspaper, http://www.bloomingtonalternative.com/subscri bers/newsarc.php?ac.

259. Insights about the ways of Coyote are found in a variety of places. For example, the poet who writes tweets with the account name @coyotesings has a series on his website at the page "Coyote Thoughts," http://coyotesings.weebly.com/tricksterthoughts.html.

260. Katrina Schimmoeller Peiffer, *Coyote at Large: Humor in American Nature Writing* (Salt Lake City: The University of Utah Press, 2000). Discussions of works by writers such as Simon Ortiz, Ursula LeGuin, and Gary Snyder are featured.

261. The points about fake Native Americans in the latter part of this paragraph are distilled from David Treuer, "Going Native: Why do writers pretend to be Indians?," http://www.slate.com/id/2185856. See also Laura Browder, *Slippery Characters: Ethnic Impersonators and American Identities* (Chapel Hill, NC: University of North Carolina, 2003) and Shari M. Huhndorf, *Going Native: Indians in the American Cultural Imagination* (Ithaca, NY: Cornell University Press, 2004).

262. Sir Walter Scott, *Marmion* (Boston: James R. Osgood and Co., 1885), canto 6, line 532.

263. Hoffer, *The Passionate State of Mind*, 80.

264. 1 Thess 5:2–4.

265. Like a geometrician's dream of neat, orderly, logical changes, Transformers, whether in a toy-line, a TV series or a major motion picture (2007), depict the trickster shape-shifting quality brought to efficient mechanical geometry—rectangles becoming whatever is needed, all personality suppressed. Transformers have become extremely popular toys in recent decades, though there is no denying that in the process of proliferation they are being transformed into ever-new shapes and functions.

266. E.g., Rose Hill was an American who showed a really admirable sense of humor even at death's door. With jokes in a letter to friends whom she'd arranged to give some of her ashes in vessels, she remarked that she'd become a know-it-all now that

she was dead, and said it's hard to be "the new kid" in the afterlife. NPR, "One Last Love," People and Places feature of Day to Day, February 14, 2008, http://www.npr.org/templates/story/story.php?storyId=18991484

267. McNeely, *Mercury Rising*, 9.

268. Ibid.

269. Benedict Carely, "Feel Like a Fraud? At Times Maybe You Should," *New York Times*, February 5, 2008.

270. Ibid.

271. *The Free US Law Dictionary* defines "Hazing" as "an often ritualistic test and a task, which may constitute harassment, abuse or humiliation with requirements to perform random, often meaningless tasks, sometimes as a way of initiation into a social group. The definition can refer to either physical (sometimes violent) or mental (possibly degrading) practices; it may also include an 'erotic' element (notably nudity)... Often most or all of the endurance, or at least the more serious ordeal, is concentrated in an orgiastic collective session, which may be called hell night, or prolonged to a hell week and/or retreat or camp, sometimes again at the pledge's birthday (e.g. by birthday spanking), but some traditions keep terrorizing pledges... over a long period... Hazing is often used as a method to promote group loyalty and camaraderie through shared suffering..." See http://www.uslaw.com/us_law_dictionary/h/Hazing.

272. See Botkin, ed., *A Treasury of Mississippi River Folklore*, 226–27.

273. James Hillman, *Senex and Puer* (Putnam, CT: Spring, 2005), 57.

274. PBS, *Frontier House, Frontier Life*, "Homestead History," http://www.pbs.org/wnet/frontierhouse/frontierlife/essay9_3.html.

275. For example, the US Marine game in which a fellow marine points a gun at a man and asks, "Do you trust me?" and sometimes pulls the trigger, was played in barracks all across Iraq and Afghanistan. Emery P. Dalesio, "Deadly Marine trust game leads to 8 years in the brig, demotion," *Indianapolis Star*, September 12, 2009. Scandals regarding hazing in the canine unit on the US Naval base in Bahrain (which led to a suicide), and regarding hazing among the US Embassy guards in Kabul in 2009, involving severe abuse and irrational humiliating actions, are also examples. High school hazings and bully tauntings and violence in New Jersey, Massachusetts (such as the Phoebe Prince case in South Hadley), and elsewhere also highlight the continuing abuse, which can become dehumanizing and lead to suicides and felony charges. Tina Kelley, "A Rite of Hazing, Now Out in the Open," *New York Times*, September 19, 2009.

276. James Hillman, *Senex and Puer*, 229. Sometimes the hurt is severe. Tribal groups may break out an initiate's tooth or cut off a piece of a finger. Gangs today, such as MS13, have violent ceremonies in which a new member is "jumped in," during which a male member may be beaten; a female member may be "sexed in" by rape.

277. David Sedaris, "Loggerheads," *The New Yorker*, December 7, 2009, 48.

278. Akira Kurosawa's film *Scandal* was released by Shochiku Company Limited, Japan, April 1950.

279. Higgins: "Either you're an honest man or a rogue." Doolittle: "A little of both ... like the rest of us, a little of both." George Bernard Shaw, *Pygmalion*, Act 5.

280. Winnebago Trickster Cycle, in Paul Radin, *The Trickster*, 22–24.

281. See http://www.hotcakencyclopedia.com/ho.TricksterGetsPregnant.html. See also "The Trickster Cycle" by Richard L. Dieterle at http://www.hotcakencyclopedia.com/ho.TricksterCycle.html. Variations on the story include this one: Coyote disguised as a good-looking girl seduces a proud youth and then "she" has children. She won't let anyone gaze upon them. After some time she leaves him and people see the offspring left behind—wolf pups—and they laugh, realizing the good-looking girl was none other than Coyote. The humbled youth leaves the village, shamefaced. McNeely, *Mercury Rising*, 43. See also Paul Radin, *The Trickster*, 22–23.

282. As a joke went, Mary's lover watched her take these parts off, and said from the bed, "When you get to the part I'm waiting for toss it here!"

283. Jung, *Psychological Reflections*, 116.

284. Ibid., 118.

285. Ibid., 120.

286. Ibid., 122.

287. Ibid., 125.

288. Ibid., 128.

289. Ibid., 129.

290. Carl G. Jung, "The Stages of Life," in *Modern Man in Search of a Soul*, trans. W. S. Dell and C. F. Baynes (New York: Harcourt, Brace & World, 1933), 96.

291. Ibid., 99.

292. Ibid., 100.

293. Ibid., 103.

294. Ibid., 104.

295. Ibid., 106–7.

296. Ibid., 113–14.

297. Selling the Brooklyn Bridge may be the most notorious con in American scam lore. In everyday parlance this offer ("If you believe that, I have a bridge in Brooklyn to show you") is a common reference to trickery.

298. McNeely, *Mercury Rising*, 13.

299. Ibid., 14.

300. Ibid., 20.

301. When secret tricks are exposed in tabloids or blogs, the kind of trickster one is comes to light, if the reports are true. People are exposed as the income tax evader, secret philanderer, viper, drunk driver, embezzler and absconder, bigoted hypocrite, etc.

302. April Dembosky, "At Clown Class, Reaching Deep Into the Psyche for Something Silly," *New York Times*, September 12, 2008. "You have to strip away lots of clever ideas and socializing impulses to get at something much more simple. Much more naive . . . If we can find a way to shed some of that polite behavior, a different kind of sparkle starts to show up in the eye of the actor." It's the trickster improvising.

303. White House press secretary Mike McCurry played along when questioned, saying the Lincoln Memorial had also been purchased and was now called "the Ford

Lincoln Mercury Memorial." See http://www.museumofhoaxes.com/hoax/aprilfool/comments/859/.

304. Mark Santora, "Naughty or Nice? Not Everyone Is Jolly About SantaCon Coming to Town," *New York Times*, December 13, 2014.

305. *The Light of Asia, or the Great Renunciation*, trans. Sir Edwin Arnold (New York: T. Y. Crowell, 1884), 208. Available online at http://www.theosophy-nw.org/theosnw/books/lightasi/asia-hp.htm. The Emerson quote comes from his *Early Lectures, 1838–1842* (Cambridge, MA: Harvard University Press, 1972), 357.

306. "The so-called civilized man has forgotten the trickster," Jung wrote. "He remembers him only figuratively and metaphorically, when, irritated by his own ineptitude, he speaks of fate playing tricks on him or of things being bewitched." Jung notes that civilized man doesn't suspect his own obscured and seemingly shadow self might have dangerous aspects that are beyond his wildest dreams. "As soon as people get together in masses and submerge the individual, the shadow is mobilized, and, as history shows, may even be personified and incarnated." Carl G. Jung, "On the Psychology of the Trickster Figure," vol. 9.1, *Collected Works*. Online at http://www.the16types.info/vbulletin/content.php/211-On-the-Psychology-of-the-Trickster-Figure-Jung.

307. Ralph Waldo Emerson, *Early Lectures of Ralph Waldo Emerson, 1848–1842* (Cambridge, MA: Harvard University Press, 1964), 357.

308. In the New Testament account, doubting Thomas suspected there was a trick when Christ appeared after the resurrection, and he asked to touch hard evidence: Christ's wounds.

309. As the character Neal says in an episode of the TV series *White Collar* ("Honor Among Thieves," August 14, 2012).

310. Robert Penn Warren, "The *Paris Review* Interviews," 1957, http://www.theparisreview.org/viewinterview.php/prmMID/4868.

311. Ps 2:4 (KJV). This seems to be a teaching of being cautious about our own sense of self-righteous importance, as if to say that heaven's mysterious trickster may just stare at our features and then say, "I never forget a face, but in your case I'll make an exception."

312. Freud and Jung discuss this quality of life, that human nature has also a black side, and that not only individuals have it, but also their beliefs, human works, and human institutions as well. See Carl G. Jung, *Modern Man in Search of a Soul*, 41.

313. Jung, *Psychological Reflections*, 62.

314. Ibid., 62–63.

315. Ibid., 67.

316. Matt 10:16.

317. McNeely, *Mercury Rising*, 167.

318. This is like Claude Levi-Strauss's bricoleur handyman, who composes myths of cultural scraps. In the combining of odds and ends from old sacred names, symbols, and stories we reflect the multiple urges and guises of the soul, and perennial themes.

319. Kate Murphy, "Mexican Robin Hood Figure Gains a Kind of Notoriety in U.S.," *New York Times*, February 8, 2008.

320. Ginger Thompson, "On Mexico's Mean Streets, the Sinners Have a Saint," *New York Times*, March 26, 2004. In Buenos Aires, there are shrines to another saint venerated by the poor—Gauchito Gil, a colorful Robin Hood figure mustachioed like Frank Zappa, a figure given offerings like food and drink.

321. McNeely, *Mercury Rising*, 166.

322. Ibid., 167.

323. See Edward J. Blum and Paul Harvey, *The Color of Christ: The Son of God and the Saga of Race in America* (Chapel Hill, NC: University of North Carolina Press, 2012), 9–10. See also Paul Harvey, *Moses, Jesus, and the Trickster in the Evangelical South* (Athens, GA: University of Georgia Press, 2011).

324. McNeely, *Mercury Rising*, 166.

325. Ibid.

326. Ibid., 105.

327. 2 Cor 12:16.

328. Blair, *The Confidence Man in Modern Fiction*, 24.

329. George W. Bush, *A Charge to Keep* (New York: William Morrow, 1999), 6.

330. Barbara Bush, *A Memoir* (New York: Scribner, 1993), 27.

331. Amy Cunningham, "Good-bye to Robin," *Texas Monthly*, February 1988, http://www.texasmonthly.com/story/good-bye-robin.

332. Ibid., 47. In George W. Bush's book *Decision Points* (New York: Crown, 2010), he said that when he was a teenager his mother showed him a jar containing the results of a miscarriage she experienced.

333. Justin A. Frank, *Bush on the Couch* (New York: HarperCollins, 2004), 16.

334. Bill Minutaglio, *First Son: George W. Bush and the Bush Family Dynasty* (New York: Times Books, 1999), 47.

335. Nicholas D. Kristof, in the George W. Bush's Journey series, "A Boy From Midland: A Philosophy With Roots in Conservative Texas Soil," *New York Times*, May 21, 2000.

336. Ibid.

337. Minutaglio, *First Son*, 66, 68. Bush repeatedly called an Asian-American student "Chief" and when the classmate told him the nickname was hurtful, Bush called him Cochise. Frank, *Bush on the Couch*, 105.

338. Frank, *Bush on the Couch*, 105.

339. Simon W. Vozick-Levinson, "Former Harvard Business School Professor Blasts Bush," *The Harvard Crimson*, July 16, 2004. Also at http://able2know.org/topic/29063-1.

340. J. H. Hatfield, *Fortunate Son: George W. Bush—The Early Years* (London: Vision Paperbacks, 2004). There are many blogs about Bush's indiscretions, e.g. "Counterpunch" edited by Alexander Cockburn and Jeffrey St. Clair, http://www.skeptically.org/curpol/id6.html

341. This information is published in many places. One place is James Hoopes, *Hail to the CEO: The Failure of George W. Bush and the Cult of Moral Leadership* (Westport, CT: 2007), 42.

342. Frank, *Bush on the Couch*, 102.

343. Ibid., 111.

344. This may be similar to Clinton saying he smoked marijuana but did not inhale. Clinton's trickiness is remembered in the way he parsed "what the meaning of 'is' is," etc.

345. For example: What is really going on if any world leader smiles like an angel, playing a saintly figurehead in public, and behind the scenes gives manipulative operatives the go-ahead to engage in whatever illegal and unethical skullduggery he desires, such as killing without judicial process, as Mafia bosses do? Is this just politics as usual, or destructive of the decency and integrity of a democratic nation? What happens to our trust when we are taken into a trickster's scheme? What if you are a deluded trickster thinking your model of reality is accurate, when actually it's far off the mark? In that case, nothing, including waging a war, turns out as you expected. Doesn't claiming innocence (for example, saying, "As a forgiven Christian, I'm innocent") leave the psyche with just as many habits, compulsions, and the need for crutches and excuses, and tricks of obfuscation, ready to inflict more injuries? The effect of learning about the inhumane techniques on suspects in "black sites," as a retired Air Force Major said, "makes one almost physically ill. But much worse than this physically nauseating feeling is the spirit-numbing, immutable image of our president assuring us time and again, 'The United States does not torture.'" Dorian De Wind, *The New York Times*, Letters to the Editor, March 20, 2009.

346. Jeffrey Toobin, "The Dirty Trickster," *The New Yorker*, June 2, 2008, 61–63.

347. "Stone expressed second thoughts about what he did in Florida. 'There have been many times I've regretted it . . . When I look at those double-page *New York Times* spreads of all the individual pictures of people who have been killed [in Iraq], I got to think[ing], 'Maybe there wouldn't have been a war if I hadn't gone to Miami-Dade . . . Maybe there hadn't have been, in my view, an unjustified war if Bush hadn't become president. It's very disturbing to me." Benjamin Sarlin, "A GOP Dirty Trickster Has Second Thoughts," *Daily Beast*, November 20, 2008, http://www.thedailybeast.com/blogs-and-stories/2008-11-20/a-gop-dirty-trickster-has-second-thoughts/.

348. Jane Mayer, *The Dark Side: The Inside Story of How the War on Terror Turned into a War on American Ideals* (New York: Doubleday, 2008).

349. Maureen Dowd, "Spying Run Amok," *The New York Times*, December 18, 2013.

350. Frank, *Bush on the Couch*, 118–19. Other analysts and medical doctors basically agree with Frank's diagnosis. These include psychoanalysts Carolyn Williams (a Republican), Irvin Yalom (professor emeritus at Stanford University Medical School, and James Grotstein (professor at the UCLA Medican Center). See "New Information Shows Bush Indecisive, Paranoid, Delusional," Infowars.com http://www.infowars.com/print/Bush/bush_delusiona.htm.

351. See Errol Morris, "The Certainty of Donald Rumsfeld (Parts 3 and 4)," *New York Times*, April 2, 25, 2014.

352. See Errol Morris, "The Certainty of Donald Rumsfeld (Parts 1 and 2)," *New York Times*, March 25, 2014. Morris observed that almost all of Rumsfeld's answers "are

designed to deflect and manipulate. But I think he's also manipulating himself. Any account of him has to deal with the gobbledygook, the lies, the glibness, the cleverness—but also his emptiness... an absence of thought." Fred Kaplan, "Seeking Truth in a Blizzard of 'Snowflakes,'" *New York Times*, March 30, 2014.

353. Andrew Sullivan, "Dear President Bush...," *Atlantic Monthly*, October, 2009, 82.

354. Ibid., 86.

355. Ibid., 88.

356. Hillman, *Senex and Puer*. See the chapters "Senex and Puer: An Aspect of the Historical and Psychological Present," 30–70; "On Senex Consciousness," 251–70; and "Negative Senex and a Renaissance Solution," 271–307.

357. Cheney said: "If there's a 1% chance that Pakistani scientists are helping al-Qaeda build or develop a nuclear weapon, we have to treat it as a certainty in terms of our response. It's not about our analysis... It's about our response." Ron Suskind, *The One Percent Doctrine* (New York: Simon and Schuster, 2007), 62.

358. See the CBS *60 Minutes* interview with Dick Cheney, October 20, 2013, http://www.cbsnews.com/news/dick-cheneys-heart/. See also *The World According to Dick Cheney*, Showtime documentary, 2013.

359. Maureen Dowd, "'Blindsided': A President's Story," *New York Times*, November 7, 2010.

360. Tony Helm, "Tony Blair Should Face Trial...," http://www.guardian.co.uk/politics/2012/sep/02/tony-blair-iraq-war-desmond-tutu.

361. See the piece on denial by Frank Rich, "What We Don't Know Will Hurt Us," *New York Times*, February 22, 2009. The "honest services law" (18 U.S.C. para. 1346) makes it a criminal offense "to deprive another of the intangible right of honest service" from a public official. No president has been prosecuted for breaking this law, though possible grounds for lawsuits no doubt exist.

362. James Hillman, *The Soul's Code: In Search of Character and Calling* (New York: Random House, 1996), 247. For the Baldwin quote, see his *Collected Essays*, 270.

363. Hillman, *The Soul's Code*, 247.

364. "Bush Shows off Dr. Evil Impersonation," *Huffington Post*, May 14, 2008. The imitations are also discussed in Robert Draper, *Dead Certain* (New York: Free Press, 2007), 350. A seriously wounded soldier from Trinidad, who was not a US citizen, was in critical condition when Bush visited him, and died soon thereafter. The soldier's mother asked Bush, "How could you do this?" Later, Bush said, "That big black woman was angry at me, I don't blame her." It was a rare moment of admitting he deserved blame, or at least when he didn't blame someone for accusing him of causing the destruction of a life.

365. This is discussed further by Maureen Dowd in "The Devil Wears Crocs," *The New York Times*, September 27, 2009.

366. "Justin A. Frank, M.D., Author of 'Bush on the Couch' Gets to the Heart of the Matter: We Have a Sociopath as President," *The Buzzflash Blog*, January 2, 2007, http://www.buzzflash.com/articles/interviews/049.

367. Ibid.

368. Ibid. Frank explains: "A sociopath . . . exhibits external and surface empathy and amiability, but internally cannot actually empathize with the pain and suffering of others. In fact, a sociopath may take hidden pleasure in being able to cause emotional distress, suffering, and even death to others, while—on a day to day basis—appearing as Mr. Affability." In the revised edition of Frank's book *Bush on the Couch*, he discusses Bush's symptoms of Attention Deficit Hyperactivity Disorder. ADHD is characterized by impulsivity, hyperactivity, inattention, and inability to control the temper.

369. Hillman, *Senex and Puer*, 108.

370. Ibid., p. 101.

371. Paul Levy, *The Madness of George W. Bush: A Reflection of Our Collective Psychosis*, in *Alternatives—Resources for Cultural Creativity*, Fall 2004, issue 31, http://www.alternativesmagazine.com/31/levy.html. A longer version is available from Authorhouse, n.p., 2006, on Amazon.com.

372. See "Bush's Messiah Complex," http://www.progressive.org/feb03/comm0203.html for a discussion of Bob Woodward's book, *Bush at War* (New York: Simon and Schuster, 2002) and David Frum's *The Right Man: An Inside Account of the Bush White House* (New York: Random House, 2005).

373. Levy, *The Madness of George W. Bush*. Some of the points in this paragraph are attempts to paraphrase Levy's ideas.

374. See also Martha Stout, *The Sociopath Next Door* (New York: Broadway, 2005). A sociopath displays certain traits, including acting on impulse, using deceit, and showing no remorse. Sociopaths are often charming and manipulative, ruthless, and concerned only about themselves; when possible they get others to do their work for them.

375. "Climate Change Research Distorted and Suppressed," Union of Concerned Scientists, http://www.ucsusa.org/scientific_integrity/abuses_of_science/climate-change.html.

376. Robert Draper, *Dead Certain: The Presidency of George W. Bush* (New York: Free Press, 2007).

377. Joe Nocera, "While the Markets Swoon," *New York Times*, August 9, 2011.

378. Maureen Dowd, "The Pungent Aroma of Paranoia," *New York Times*, December 17, 2011.

379. Trivers, *The Folly of Fools*, 247–75.

380. Hillman, *Senex and Puer*, 105.

381. Jung, *Modern Man in Search of a Soul*, 205.

382. See Appendix 6 for more on the paintings of George W. Bush.

383. Prohibition of alcohol, reform of campaign finances, illegalizing gambling—such drives sometimes seem to force tricky activities underground. The simplifying spirit of the original impulses behind faiths like Zen, Quakerism, and Islam, at their best, involved the reduction of ritual and downplaying of priestly intermediaries. Believers sought pared-down faiths to experience plain truth, avoiding manipulative trickster's complicating shenanigans. But intermediaries can muscle their way back in and disguise themselves as truth, hijacking a religion's reputation. Osama bin Laden and Ayman al-Zawahiri have proved themselves to be cunning antisocial tricksters.

They often won public relations battles in some quarters of Islamdom, despite the fact that they were responsible for so much harm done to fellow Muslims.

384. Roger Cohen, "A U.S. General's Disquiet," *New York Times*, September 10, 2007.

385. For further archetypal examples of this see James Hillman, *Senex and Puer*, 104-9. See also Marjorie Cohn, *Cowboy Republic: Six Ways the Bush Gang Has Defied the Law* (Sausalito: PoliPointPress, 2007). By "cowboy" Cohn means someone who fools around with dangerous enterprises needlessly.

386. Cohen, "A U.S. General's Disquiet."

387. In his 1923 book, *Studies in Classic American Literature* (New York: Penguin, 1990, paperback edition) D.H. Lawrence observed that, as depicted in *The Scarlet Letter*, spirit and sense in the Puritan lifeway are quite divided. We should note that tricksters such as Coyote and Raven unite sense and spirit in the mythic scenarios of Native American traditions, combining life's power and appetite, flesh, and soul. Puritanism often lacks that trick of bothness. Lawrence noted that word and deed are divided and out of sync in James Fennimore Cooper's *The Deerslayer*. Perhaps the attraction to killing is echoed in lines like "You're only happy when you see something die," as voiced by the character played by Marilyn Monroe in the movie *The Misfits* (1961).

388. Russian arms dealer Viktor Bout is an example of such a trickster, transforming himself very adaptively into anything that will make money, selling guns and planes to belligerent people in conflict. It is said, for example, that Bout had Liberian president Charles Taylor start a war, invading Sierra Leone to get diamonds, so that Bout could furnish weapons. The film *Lord of War* (2005), starring Nicolas Cage, is said to be loosely based on Bout's activities.

389. In 1861 Lincoln began suspending *habeas corpus* (the legal writ that safeguarded individual freedoms) and established martial law, giving the state judicial system much more authority in arresting and imprisoning supporters of the rebellion, etc. In 1862 he officially proclaimed the suspension, and in 1863 Congress ratified the proclamation.

390. Hillman, *Senex and Puer*, 104. At Hercules's birth, a weasel hailed his arrival, according to Greek literature.

391. The ideas suggested by this serviceman who spoke to me in a supermarket are confirmed as accurate by Matthew Alexander and John Bruning, *How to Break a Terrorist: The U.S. Interrogators Who Used Brains, Not Brutality, to Take Down the Deadliest Man in Iraq* (New York: Free Press, 2008). See also Susan Sontag, "Regarding the Torture of Others," *New York Times Magazine*, May 23, 2004, http://www.nytimes.com/2004/05/23/magazine/23PRISONS.html?ex=1400644800&en=a2cb6ea6bd297c8f&ei=5007&partner=USERLAND.

392. See N.T. Wright, *Evil and the Justice of God* (Nottingham: InterVarsity, 2006).

393. My friend Amy Frazer suggested that parallels may exist between coyotes and wolves and their packs, and human tricksters and their societies. The bad trickster, like a lone wolf, preys on the society. The good trickster interacts in ways that benefit the group. Perhaps it is like the shaman in tribal cultures, who lives on the outskirts of the village. He is an outsider of sorts, but is welcome, not shunned by the group. Herd dogs also may be loners, but they have a bit of pack drive, and a bit of prey drive, and are

able to balance their duties with restraint, serving as guard and herder. Coyotes travel in packs but hunt in pairs. Coyote packs are smaller than wolf packs.

394. See Philippe Petit, *To Reach the Clouds: My High Wire Walk Between the Twin Towers* (New York: North Point, 2002), and the documentary film *Man on Wire* (2008).

395. See Appendix 7 for more on this.

396. "The attitude toward animals, and their treatment, in twentieth-century American industrial meat production is literally sickening, unethical, an a source of boundless bad luck for this society." Gary Snyder, *The Practice of the Wild* (San Francisco: North Point, 1990), 21. The attitude associated with the belief that animals have no souls and are meant to be used by humans any way they please, so that ill treatment and cruelty mean nothing, is problematic. To make oneself numb to the pain of other living creatures is to become dehumanized. The heartless disregard of animal suffering (beginning with childhood acts like blowing up frogs with firecrackers) led George W. Bush to a numbness regarding other living beings, including Iraqi people living in Saddam Hussein's regime, slaughter of Iraqis as collateral damage, torture of suspects, and the death of American servicemen.

397. A useful book on this topic is Glenn Greenwald, *A Tragic Legacy: How a Good vs. Evil Mentality Destroyed the Bush Presidency* (New York: Crown, 2007).

398. A line from the AMC series *Breaking Bad* in the 2009 season.

399. Maybe John Lennon, by exercising his freedom and by living in New York, became more of an American than J. Edgar Hoover, who encroached illegally on the rights of dissenters.

400. Jung points to the importance of recognizing our own darker sides. "The guilt ... [is] there before our eyes if only we would see. Man has done these things; I am a man, who has his share of human nature; therefore I am guilty with the rest and bear unaltered and indelibly within me the capacity and the inclination to do them again at any time ... we are always, thanks to our own human nature, potential criminals." As Goethe said, nothing human is alien to a human being. Jung continues, "[O]nly the fool can permanently neglect the conditions of his own nature ... [and] this negligence is the best means of making him an instrument of evil." Such a person projects unconsciously all the darkness onto the other, and "the projection carries the fear which we involuntarily and secretly feel for our own evil over to the other side and ... increases the formidableness of his threat ... [W]orse, our lack of insight deprives us of the capacity to deal with evil." C. G. Jung, *The Undiscovered Self* (New York: New American Library, 1964), 95–96, 106.

401. C. G. Jung, *Psychological Reflections*, p. 270.

402. Gary Snyder, *The Real Work* (New York: New Directions, 1980), 156. See also Gary Snyder, "The Incredible Survival of Coyote," in *A Place in Space* (Washington: Counterpoint, 1995), 148–62.

403. This paragraph was partly inspired by some thoughts of James Hillman in his essay "Of Milk and Monkeys," in *Senex and Puer*, esp. 336–37.

404. Nelson Algren, "The Last Carousel," in *The Texas Stories*, ed. Bettina Drew (Austin, TX: University of Texas Press, 1995), 140.

405. Tennessee Williams, Esmeralda's prayer in the play, *Camino Real* (New York: New Directions, 2008), 106.

406. Bob Dylan, "Visions of Johanna." While in a certain sense everyone is a parasite living on the bounty of nature and the work of others, flat-out parasites are cynical. It is as if their actions say: "Why should I work hard for the wherewithal of life, when I can connive a way to let others slave away and I can pocket the pay?" A little clever rigging can deceive gullible victims, and from their loss of resources, the clever parasite can live without expending effort; this seems to be the parasitical logic.

407. Nelson Algren, "The Last Carousel," in *The Texas Stories*, 140.

408. Lee Siegel, "Death of a Salesman's Dreams," *The New York Times*, May 3, 2012.

409. This is a tweet by the poet who writes haiku on Twitter under the name "Coyote Sings."

410. La Rochefoucauld's observations on cunning are insightful. For example: "The greatest of all cunning is, to appear blind to the snares laid for us; men being never so easily deceived as while they are endeavoring to deceive others. Those who have the most cunning always affect to condemn cunning, that they may make use of it on some great occasion, and to some great end. The common practice of cunning is a sign of a small genius; it almost always happens that those who use it to cover themselves in one place, lay themselves open in another. Cunning and treachery proceed from want of capacity. The sure way to be cheated is, to fancy ourselves more cunning than others. The reason we are angry with those who trick us is because they appear to have more wit than ourselves. One man may be more cunning than another, but not more cunning than all the world." *Maxims and moral reflections,* maxim 114.

APPENDIX 1
On Archetypes

Archetypes are inherent in the psyche's subconscious dynamics, as Jung and Hillman have extensively demonstrated. An archetype embodied in an image with a spectrum of associations has both negative and positive potentials. For example, the archetype of the Anima, the attractive feminine image of the soul, and the image of the collective unconscious depths of existence, leads into the unknown, sometimes luring one into deep troubles like a fallen angel temptress, sometimes like a beautiful lover or helper inspiring one to the greatest of achievements. Similarly, the trickster can seem kind or cruel, depending on his acts, and their results—if he helps you win, or if he causes you to lose. If you hoard light and he frees it (as Raven does) you are angry—but the rest of the world is grateful. It is useful to consider the trickster in further relation to the Anima. Anima is the feminine image of the soul, representing the depths of psyche, the life spirit of each and the mystery of all. The trickster is an image of the soul's predicaments of embodiment, undergoing life experiences, solving, unknotting the problems of being. Both the trickster and Anima are aspects representative of our unconscious or depth experiences; both seem to stir things up, keep life alluring, troubled, sparkling with change. Their ambiguous possibilities mean they can bring problems or resolutions, depending on which aspects we bring out in our lives. The trickster, like the Anima, often seems like a symbolic reflection of the collective unconscious, the stripteasing soul, life's elfin spirit of vitality. The trickster acts out spritely impish life's irrepressible vivacity.

APPENDIX 2
Some American Stories about Con Men

Mark Twain portrays confidence men in *Huckleberry Finn*, in which "Duke" and "King" are wandering con artists taking advantage of gullible small town Americans. Harley Granville-Barker's play *The Voysey Inheritance* (1905) features a friendly financial advisor who cheats the unsuspecting. William Burroughs's prose reflects American swindlers' spiels, in his surreal novel *The Naked Lunch* and other writings in the second half of the twentieth century. We see con men in such films as *The Lady Eve* (1941), in which Barbara Stanwyk plays a con artist, and *Elmer Gantry* (1960), in which Burt Lancaster is a fraudulent preacher. There are many films on other trickster figures, including *The Hucksters* (1947); *The Music Man* (1962), in which a con man helps a community by luck rather than intention; *Charade* (1963); *The Con Artists* (1976), starring Anthony Quinn; and *Carny* (1980), directed by Robert Kaylor. In *The Grifters* (1990), John Cusack plays an emotionally vulnerable con man caught in a tug of war between his mother (Anjelica Huston) and his girlfriend, both of whom are also con artists. *Paper Moon* (1973) is about a father and daughter surviving by using their wits during the Depression. *Scam* (1993), directed by John Flynn, is about the relationship between a male and a female thief, played by Christopher Walken and Lorraine Bracco. Johnny Depp starred in *Con Man* (1997). *Dirty Rotten Scoundrels* (1988) is about two men pulling romance scams, while *The Producers* (1967) is about haphazard, accidental scam artists. *The Flim Flam Man* (1967), *The Italian Job* (1969 and again in 2003), *Leap of Faith* (1992), and *Traveller* (1997) are all about con men. In *The Usual Suspects* (1995) Kevin Spacey portrays Verbal Kint, a con man who throughout the story (which is composed of interrogations and flashbacks) throws the police off his tracks by inventing a mysterious villain, Keyser Soze. It gradually dawns on the viewer that instead of being a simpering cripple, Kint is a shapeshifter escape artist. Tony Curtis played the part of Ferdinand Waldo

Demara Jr. (1921–1982), who took on the identities of professor, engineer, doctor, warden, monk, editor, cancer researcher, and other professions, in the 1961 film *The Great Imposter*. Frank Abagnale (b. 1948) posed as pilot, doctor, professor, and was a forger of checks. His biography *Catch Me If You Can* was made into a 2002 film starring Leo DiCaprio and directed by Steven Spielberg. It's the story of a young bluffer who's slippery as an eel, getting away with incredible tricks of imposture until he is caught. In *The Talented Mr. Ripley* (1999) a character kills a wealthy young man and takes his identity. *Matchstick Men* (2003) features Nicolas Cage as a con artist who teaches a girl named Angela the tricks of the trade, including " Make sure the person you're conning isn't conning you." The disingenuous Great Pretender type of trickster lies while saying, "That's my story and I'm sticking to it." Producer/director Jesse Moss made the documentary film *Con Man* (2005), about James Arthur Hogue, an imposter who invented a series of identities to embody, conning his way into an impressive performance at Princeton University as a student. *The Informant* (2009) is about a businessman who is a pathological liar, stringing along the FBI, his associates, and family for years, before ending up in jail. The film's structure is odd, with one series of lies collapsing into the next, and the next, and the next. The phony is despised in J. D. Salinger's *Catcher in the Rye*, and in Ernest Hemingway's stories. He fails to "keep it real," lying even to himself. As the Jack Nicholson character in *A Few Good Men* (1992) says, he "can't handle the truth." The film *Criminal* (2004), was based on *Nueva Reinas* (2000). The TV series *Firefly* (2002–2003) features a confidence woman named Saffron. In the FX cable TV series *Weeds* (2005–2012) a suburban California widow with children learns the ropes of being a drug dealer the hard way, by mistakes, and from a family of African American marijuana distributors, from a Latino gang, etc. In the school of hard knocks this housewife learns what it takes to be a trickster. Uncle Andy, the brother of her dead husband, is also a sort of incompetent outlaw and con artist slacker in the series. The extremely popular HBO series *The Sopranos* (1999–2007) depicts the crude and brutal tricks and outside-the-law antics of sleaze and violence in the lives of Mafia mobsters' families. In the AMC series *Breaking Bad* (2008) a a chemistry teacher in a New Mexico high school leads a double life, making crystal meth to pay for his cancer treatments. In the FX TV series *Nip/Tuck* (2004–2007) two plastic surgeons endlessly surprise themselves with their feelings of desire, greed, depravity, and altruism, conning themselves, catching themselves, trying again to be humane, and then falling for their own temptations and grotesque tricks of vanity and vengeance, malice and generosity, venality and power, skewering the Miami ethos as they go. Naive turns cynic, cynic acts naive, in scenarios of indulgence and repentance;

these clowns never seem to learn. The most tricksterish diagnostician in the history of TV medical series is seen in *House*. Dr. House breaks taboos, crosses boundaries, insults with wit, brilliantly discovers hidden secrets, and helps patients with rare illnesses find healing in unconventional ways. The high-tension Showtime TV series *Dexter* (2006–2013) features a serial killer who is also a Miami police department blood analyst. He must conceal or smooth over his killings while also being a conscientious employee, a father of a young child, and the brother of a woman who is also a police officer in the department in which he works. The Showtime TV series *Shameless* (2011–2014) features a Chicago family on the skids, whose alcoholic patriarch Frank Gallagher, played by William H. Macy, is an inveterate scammer and manipulator. The Gallagher family is a family of hustlers—each family member drags the other ones down, and they all exploit every window of opportunity they see, yet somehow (or consequently?) they are full of recognizable humanity. The Showtime series *House of Lies* (2012–2014) is about a handful of high-living, amoral, and unscrupulous management consultants and their always edgy, seat-of-the-pants conning and conniving. This is just a small list of American con artist and trickster stories, chosen as a suggestive sampling.

APPENDIX 3
On Masks and Head Coverings

In recent years there has been a worldwide proliferation of face coverings, some of which have a trickster-like quality. Newspapers and magazine illustrations show various ski masks, for example. (I recently saw a teenager with a skull-face ski mask, and wearing a skeleton design hoodie.) Others wear scarves wound around faces like bandages, leaving only the eyes visible, or wear burqas and veils. There are medical masks, gas masks, sunglasses, goggles, oxygen masks, and helmets of many kinds, which, whether for safety, combat, or motorcycle riding, are all curious extensions of the head. Yes, many of these have specific functions, but they also become a kind of costume obliterating the features of the face. There is headgear for diving, for looking at eclipses, for virtual reality games, and medical research appurtenances with wires and tubes feeding into and out of the head, hooking the brain up to measuring systems and tests. There are many mask-like devices for covering one's head and face, hiding it from danger and preventing identification, protecting the wearer from threats. There are masks that disguise, and masks that entertain and celebrate. In Thailand, traffic police on motorcycles are required to wear a smiling mask. (Some people use the "happy face" icon sincerely, others cynically—no doubt there has been Pavlovian use of the smile to manipulate reactions for many millennia.) There are sports helmets, vehicle driver helmets, head coverings to add an extra layer to the skull, to out-trick the slings and arrows of misfortune, to add other features to the face. There are full-body masks—hazmat suits and large coverall prophylactics. Stick-up men wear nylon stockings over their heads to distort features. Riot police have strong face shields that bottles and bricks will bounce off. Hangmen and terrorists, and soldiers patrolling hostile areas, wear coverings of cloth or other substances, giving them wall-like faces to present to the belligerent world and its fire and fists, cameras, and recognition technologies. Members of the Russian women's activist group known as Pussy Riot wear stocking caps pulled over their faces with holes cut out by scissors for eyes and mouth—homemade ski masks. There are scary masks, historical iron masks which were put on slaves, masks for cannibals (like Hannibal Lecter), masks associated with horror film monsters. Masks distort the presentation of personality, confuse identity, play around with multiple presentations of self. Masks mock sincerity and show that the trickster will use any trick to save face, hide identity, elude detection. The trickster loves a good masquerade—as long as he is the one whose mask is not pulled away, for that gives away the name of the game.

APPENDIX 4
On the Clown in America

The sad-funny clown type has long been a favorite in American entertainment. W. C. Fields said Bert Williams (1874–1922) was "the funniest man I ever saw and the saddest man I ever knew." America's first nationally known black star, Bert Williams made hit records on the Columbia label, with the hallmark of wistful melancholic wit. Bozo the Clown was the archetypal American clown on TV for a half century. Bozo began as a voice on a series of children's records in 1946. Then Bozo became a TV show with various actors in different cities. Bozo was especially associated with Larry Harmon, who bought rights, portrayed and popularized the Bozo character with red, white, and blue costume, tomato-like nose, greatly exaggerated eyebrows, and smiling mouth. Music's clowns include the Everly Brothers' "Cathy's Clown" (1957), jazz artist Charles Mingus's "The Clown" (1957), James Darren and Gloria Shayne's "Goodbye Cruel World" (1961) (with the lyrics "a mean fickle woman made a cryin' clown outta me"), Gary Lewis and the Playboys' "Everybody Loves a Clown" (1965), and Smokey Robinson's "The Tears of a Clown" (1967). The most famous American clowns include Emmett Kelly, Joe Jackson, and Lou Jacobs the Rodeo Clown. Chameleon-like artist Cindy Sherman's clown photographs are, enigmatically, probably the hardest to recognize as self-portraits. They are so unlike her that some suspect she was playing tricks. Children fear clowns because they present themselves as bizarrely other, fearfully unknowable tricksters, whom social convention demands that you be happily appreciative to see; this causes inner conflict and confusion. Clowns are scary because nobody looks like that—so strange—and no one in his right mind would choose to look like that; therefore the presence seems inherently wrong, off, ajar. Stephen King's novel, *It*, published in 1987 and made into a TV miniseries in 1990, features a horrific clown. In *It* a monster takes the shape of forms most feared by the characters. One form is the sadistic demonic clown "Pennywise," who terrorizes a Maine town in 1967. Some say *It* contributed greatly to a generation of American children's fear of clowns. For a classic study see William Willeford, *The Fool and His Scepter: A Study of Clowns and Jesters and Their Audience* (Evanston, IL: Northwestern University Press, 1969).

APPENDIX 5
On Mortgage Fraud and other Cons

Mortgage fraud was investigated by David Jackson, "Mortgage Fraud is the Thing to Do Now" (*Chicago Tribune*, November 5, 2005, http://www.chicagotribune.com/business/chi-mortgage-1-story,0,3971381.story). Terms used in investigations of the mortgage fraud scene include "air loans," in which a swindler invents borrowers and houses for purchase, and obtains fraudulent loans. Swindlers may use different phone lines with different numbers, posing as the borrower, the borrower's employer, and also the appraiser, and the credit agency, or they have associates answer when the lender calls to verify borrowers' information. "Chunking" is a scam in which some swindlers would hold seminars offering to teach investors how to profit from purchasing property with no money down. Then the swindlers would use the investors' identities and personal information to submit multiple mortgage applications, taking the loan proceeds and disappearing. "Double sales" refers to a scam utilizing the fact that weeks pass between the time of filing a property record and its appearance in computerized registries used by title-search companies. The swindlers recorded deeds, arranged loans, and then quickly filed another deed and loan application for the same property before those transactions would appear in computer records, taking money from multiple loans for one house. The "land flip scam" is a fraud in which property is purchased, falsely appraised at a much higher value than its worth, then quickly resold at a huge profit. Some properties are flipped as many as three or four times between conspiring associates with no money changing hands, only skyrocketing values being changed. "Straw owner" refers to a scam involving a loan application for which the swindler pays an acquaintance or relative to use of his identity and credit rating.

APPENDIX 6
George W. Bush as Painter

Hrag Vartanian wrote "Do Bush's Paintings Tell Us Anything About the Former President?," which concludes, "Maybe it shouldn't surprise us that the man who brought us a vision of compassionate conservatism would turn to art to express the angst of a crappy Presidency that got us into two wars, used homophobia, racism, and sexism as an electoral tool, crashed our economy, and made the world hate America." Vartanian observes that obviously Bush must be feeling his mortality. "He sits in the bathtub alone. Nothing to contemplate. Nothing to see beyond reflections of himself and his body...This is Bush, the old man, with lots of time on his hands..." (*Hyperallergic*, February 8, 2013, http://hyperallergic.com). The paintings seem dull-witted, psychically impoverished. (See also David Hoppe, "The soul of an ex-president: Bush paints," *NUVO*, http://www.nuvo.net/blogs/hoppe.)

In April, 2014, George W. Bush's portraits of world leaders were exhibited at The George Bush Presidential Library and Museum on the campus of Southern Methodist University. The amateur portraits of the thirty leaders look familiar. Some have suggested that the paintings are based on photo images that are the first to appear if the leaders' names are Googled. The paintings, as the *New York Times* critic noted, do not show the faces who enabled and shaped Bush's eight years in office—Rove, Cheney, Rice, Rumsfeld—but rather "a world of smiles and friendship that can rarely be taken as the whole story. The show reflects an attempt to burnish the Bush presidency and distract from his failures." (See Roberta Smith, "Faces of Power, from the Portraitist in Chief," *New York Times*, April 7, 2014.) Thus, it appears to be a trick of misdirection. Bush's art seems to be an attempt to humanize his image, as if to say, "Look at this cavalcade of people I met—don't think about the botched war, ruined economy, crimes of torture, etc. I'm a regular guy, no real feeling for art, but as Reagan chopped wood, so did I, and as Ike painted, so did I. Pay no attention to the horrors I caused, the stains on

America. I'm just a regular guy." *The Daily Telegraph*'s critic, Alistaire Sooke, observed, "These dreary and compositionally identical likenesses couldn't feel more impersonal if they tried." (See Sooke, "George Bush paintings: review: 'all the hallmarks of outsider art,'" *The Daily Telegraph*, April 4, 2014.) All in all, the paintings seem more of a product of political activity than an artistic endeavor, a calculated attempt to manipulate opinion rather than a meaningful product of the psyche.

APPENDIX 7
On Torture

This is a difficult subject, one which human beings bury and hide, but it is necessary to confront. "The C.I.A.'s interrogation program is remarkable for its mechanistic approach. 'It's one of the most sophisticated, refined programs of torture ever,' an outside expert familiar with the protocol said. '. . . It was almost automated. People were utterly dehumanized. People fell apart. It was the intentional and systematic infliction of great suffering masquerading as a legal process . . .'" The former CIA officer who was explaining this spoke of psychic damage to the *interrogators*, surfacing as horrible nightmares: "When you cross over that line of darkness, its hard to come back. You lose your soul. You can do your best to justify it, but it's well outside the norm. You can't go to that dark place without it changing you." (See Jane Mayer, "The Black Sites," *The New Yorker*, August 13, 2007, 57, 56.) In *The Dark Side: The Inside Story of How the War on Terror Turned into a War on American Ideals*, the same author further examines the struggle for the soul of America in the issues of torture and imprisonment of suspects.

Even if leaders are sincere in their fear of terror, if they con themselves and/or the American people so they can do as they please beyond the law, the nation must come to terms with what they have done in the name of America. Senator Dianne Feinstein, chair of the Senate Intelligence Committee, has made fearless efforts to ensure that a report on CIA detention and interrogation practices launched after 9/11 be acknowledged. She called the report, based on six million pages of CIA memos, "shocking," and a record that is "a stain on the nation. Feinstein said the report "exposes brutality that stands in stark contrast to our values as a nation." The report reflects detainee mistreatment and torture techniques used in secret black sites around the world, including in budding democracies. (See Evan Perez, CNN Politics, "Shocking report on CIA interrogation closer to public release," April 3, 2014, http://www.cnn.com/2014/04/03/politics/

senate-cia-report/.) The torture that left this blot on America's record was seen as a "no-brainer" by Vice President Cheney, a mere business-as-usual technique. But for a free nation, it was not just a logical method to keep safe from terror. It was a behavior as grotesque as the line spoken by an evil scientist character in an American horror movie, circa 1950. "I am crazy, but by torturing others I become the sanest man in the world." Images of torture in American history and culture are anguishing and sometimes self-servingly delusional, reflecting being of two minds on the subject.

The torture of battle captives held by Native American tribes (including Iroquois, Apaches, Sioux, Arapahoes, Blackfoot, and many others) was rightly described as savagery. There were some peaceful tribes and also individuals who risked their own lives to protect captives, but most tribal practices across America were brutally cruel. We know that modern bureaucrats wearing neat suits are also capable of tricks that we must describe as savagery. During the war in Iraq, the fictional wily trickster hero Jack Bauer, in the Fox TV series *24*, captured America's imagination. Bauer is a resilient survivor, with a bag of improvisational tricks for tight spots, wearily and warily bouncing back from traumas again and again. Significantly, the actor who played the role, Kiefer Sutherland, was asked to give an anti-torture speech to West Point cadets in 2006, to remind them that the result-getting torture he portrayed was fictional. In season seven (2009) the storyline of *24* seems to advocate torture—the plot pictures refraining from torture as weakness. Torture is an addictive practice for some personalities. Torture makes for suspenseful TV, but experts tell us it does not work.

"Enhanced interrogation" is a term that shows a numbed bureaucrat's attraction to tricks of technique. Poet Robert Bly observed in a 1966 interview: "In America there is an obsession with technique. . . We are determined to win our wars by using superior technique. . . helicopters, napalm . . . Instead of trying to think, to imagine what the people want, we are going to use technique and defeat them no matter what they think . . .[Workshops teaching technique and conformity instead of original experience, humanity and personality] are all part of the same fatal American mistake." (See Robert Bly, *Talking All Morning* [Ann Arbor, MI: University of Michigan Press, 1980], 52–53.) Deference to the attitudes and conclusions drawn by public servants operating with terrified ruthlessness is not compatible with the American identity, which emerged as a way out of tyranny and the assumption that "might makes right."

SELECT BIBLIOGRAPHY

Algren, Nelson. *Chicago: City on the Make.* 50th anniversary edition. Chicago: University of Chicago Press, 2001.
Babiak, Paul, and Robert D. Hare. *Snakes in Suits: When Psychopaths Go to Work.* New York: HarperCollins, 2007.
Baldwin, James. *Collected Essays.* New York: The Library of America, 1998.
Blackmon, Douglas A. *Slavery by Another Name.* New York: Doubleday, 2008.
Blair, John G. *The Confidence Man in Modern Fiction.* New York: Harper & Row, 1979.
Botkin, B. A., ed. *A Treasury of Mississippi River Folklore.* New York: Crown, 1955.
Brock, Pope. *Charlatan: America's Most Dangerous Huckster.* New York: Crown, 2008.
Brown, Norman O. *Hermes the Thief: The Evolution of a Myth.* Great Barrington, MA: Lindisfarne, 1990.
Callahan, David. *The Cheating Culture: Why More American are Doing Wrong to Get Ahead.* New York: Mifflin Harcourt, 2004.
Cummins, Joe. *Anything for a Vote: Dirty Tricks, Cheap Shots and October Surprises in Presidential Campaigns.* Philadelphia: Quirk, 2007.
Davis, Devra. *When Smoke Ran Like Water: Tales of Environmental Deception and the Battle Against Pollution.* New York: Basic, 2002.
Dick, Everett. *The Lure of the Land: A Social History of the Public Lands from the Articles of Confederation to the New Deal.* Lincoln, NE: University of Nebraska Press, 1970.
Draper, Robert. *Dead Certain: The Presidency of George W. Bush.* New York: Free Press, 2007.
Erdoes, Richard, ed. *American Indian Trickster Tales.* New York: Penguin, 1999.
Greenwald, Glenn. *A Tragic Legacy: How a Good vs. Evil Mentality Destroyed the Bush Presidency.* New York: Crown, 2007.
Halttunen, Karen. *Confidence Men and Painted Women.* New Haven, CT: Yale University Press, 1986.
Harvey, Paul. *Moses, Jesus, and the Trickster in the Evangelical South.* Athens, GA: University of Georgia Press, 2011.
Hatfield, J. H. *Fortunate Son: George W. Bush—The Early Years.* London: Vision Paperbacks, 2004.
Heller-Roazen, Daniel. *Dark Tongues: The Art of Rogues and Riddlers.* New York: Zone, 2013.
Hillman, James. *A Blue Fire.* New York: Harper Perennial, 1991.
———. *Mythic Figures.* Putnam: Spring, 2007.

Select Bibliography

———. *The Soul's Code: In Search of Character and Calling.* New York: Random House, 1996.

Hyde, Lewis. *Trickster Makes the World: Mischief, Myth and Art.* San Francisco: North Point, 1999.

Hynes, William J., and William G. Doty, eds. *Mythical Trickster Figures: Contours, Contexts, and Criticisms.* Tuscaloosa, AL: University of Alabama Press, 1993.

Judson, Katherine Berry. *Myths and Legends of the Pacific Northwest.* Lincoln, NE: University of Nebraska Press, 1997.

Jung, Carl G. *Modern Man in Search of a Soul.* Translated by W. S. Dell and C. F. Baynes. New York: Harcourt, 1933.

———. *Psychological Reflections.* New York: Harper & Row, 1961.

———. *The Undiscovered Self.* New York: New American Library, 1964.

Kirsten, Jason. *The Art of Making Money: The Story of a Master Counterfeiter.* New York: Penguin, 2009.

Lewis, Michael. *The Big Short: Inside the Doomsday Machine.* New York: Norton, 2010.

Lindberg, Gary. *The Confidence Man in American Literature.* New York: Oxford University Press, 1982.

Lofaro, Michael A., ed. *The Tall Tales of Davy Crockett: The Second Nashville Series of Crockett Almanacs 1839–1941.* Knoxville, TN: University of Tennessee Press, 1987.

Mayer, Jane. *The Dark Side: The Inside Story of How the War on Terror Turned into a War on American Ideals.* New York: Doubleday, 2008.

McAllester, David, and Mary Wheelwright. *The Myth and Prayers of the Great Star Chant and the Myth of the Coyote Chant.* Santa Fe, NM: Museum of Navajo Ceremonial Art, 1956.

McNeely, Deldon Anne. *Mercury Rising: Women, Evil and the Trickster Gods.* Woodstock, CT: Spring, 1996.

Minutaglio, Bill. *First Son: George W. Bush and the Bush Family Dynasty.* New York: Random House, 1999.

Murray, Albert. *From the Briarpatch File: On Context, Procedure, and American Identity.* New York: Pantheon, 2001.

Papanikolas, Zeese. *Trickster in the Land of Dreams.* Omaha, NE: University of Nebraska Press, 1995.

Pelton, Robert D. *Trickster in West Africa.* Berkeley, CA: University of California Press, 1980.

Petit, Philippe. *To Reach the Clouds: My High Wire Walk Between the Twin Towers.* New York: North Point, 2002.

Pinker, Steven. *The Stuff of Thought.* New York: Viking, 2007.

Radin, Paul. *The Trickster: A Study in American Indian Mythology.* New York: Schocken, 1971.

Rourke, Constance. *The Roots of American Culture.* New York: Harcourt Brace, 1942.

San Souci, Robert D. *Sister Tricksters: Rollicking Tales of Clever Females.* Little Rock, AR: August House, 2006.

Smith, Jeanne Rosier. *Writing Tricksters: Mythic Gambols in American Ethnic Literature.* Berkeley, CA: University of California Press, 1997.

Stone, Peter H. *Heist: Superlobbyist Jack Abramoff, His Republican Allies, and the Buying of Washington.* New York: Farrar, Straus and Giroux, 2006.

Tallman, Marjorie. *Dictionary of American Folklore.* New York: Philosophical Library, 1959.

Tarnoff, Ben. *The Wicked Lives and Surprising Adventures of Three Notorious Counterfeiters*. New York: Penguin, 2011.
Thompson, Bob. *Born On A Mountaintop: On The Road with Davy Crockett and the Ghosts of the Wild Frontier*. New York: Crown, 2013.
Trivers, Robert. *The Folly of Fools: The Logic of Deceit and Self-Deception in Human Life*. New York: Basic, 2011.
Tyler, Moses Coit. *History of American Literature*. New York: Putnam, 1879.
Waddington, Warwick. *The Confidence Game in American Literature*. Princeton, NJ: Princeton University Press, 1975.
Weeden, William Babcock. *Creating Indian Money as a Factor in New England Civilization*. Baltimore: Johns Hopkins University Press, 1884.
Willeford, William. *The Fool and His Scepter: A Study of Clowns and Jesters and Their Audience*. Evanston, IL: Northwestern University Press, 1969.
Wilson, Bee. *Swindled: The Dark History of Food Fraud*. Princeton, NJ: Princeton University Press, 2008.
Young, John V. *Kokopelli: Casanova of the Cliff Dwellers: The Hunchbacked Flute Player*. Palmer Lake, CO: Filter, 1990.
Zuckoff, Michael. *Ponzi's Scheme: The True Story of a Financial Legend*. New York: Random House, 2005.